CLIMBING DAYS

Dorothy Pilley (1894–1986) was a trailblazing writer and mountaineer who led the way for women's climbing and co-founded the Pinnacle Club for women in 1921. She climbed ridges and sheer faces around the world, creating a legacy that is admired to this day. In 1928, together with her husband I. A. Richards and Swiss guides Joseph and Antoine Georges, she pioneered a route up the north-north-west ridge of the Dent Blanche in Switzerland. *Climbing Days*, a celebrated memoir of her early life and climbs, was published in 1935.

Dorothy Pilley, c. 1926.

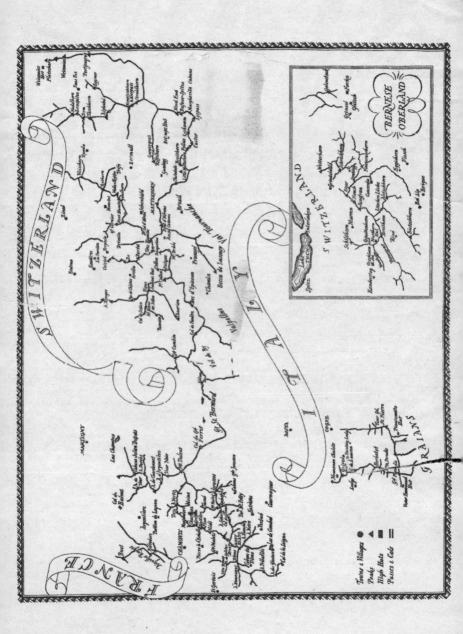

to
I. A. R.
and
JOSEPH GEORGES
and
ALL MY MOUNTAIN FRIENDS

CONTENTS

ILLUSTRATIONS

INTRODUCTION

You hold in your hands a wonderful book, one that I love very much. It's a memoir filled with adventure and triumph over adversity, a coming-of-age story, a record of two extraordinary people bound together by a passion for mountaineering. Between the lines of these pages, a great love story can be traced, a delight in high places and a questing partnership which endured for over fifty years.

As a child, I knew very little about my great-grand aunt, Dorothy Pilley. I was aware of her, as a child knows the names of cities but could not place them on a map, but she seemed always to me mentioned in conjunction with her husband, Ivor Armstrong Richards: I.A.R. – mysterious initialled academic and literary critic, whose books we had in the house but nobody seemed to have read: revered, abstruse relics from another age.

There were stories of their 'royal visits' to my father's boyhood home. Slightly awkward gatherings, the pair impossibly elderly to his young eyes. There were rumours that they were mountaineers but the walking sticks made it all seem so unlikely . . . and there was another enigma, a name, a particular mountain: the Dent Blanche.

In Dr Richard Luckett's succinct preface to I.A.R.'s *Selected Letters*, Dorothy Eleanor Pilley/Richards *(1894–1986)* is described as:

The daughter of a strict father . . . [who] achieved her independence by climbing mountains, writing for newspapers, and working as a secretary for the proto-feminist British Women's Patriotic League. Her looks and vivacity ensured her the many suitors she periodically repulsed as threats to her hard-won liberty. Ivor

Richards (whom she met in Wales in 1917 and married in Honolulu on 31 December, 1926), though a special case, had not only her disinclination to overcome, but her family's as well . . . The marriage was an exceptionally happy one.[1]

Luckett's biographical sketch runs on to say that Dorothy's account of their early mountaineering feats together – *Climbing Days* (London, 1935) – is a classic of its kind, 'and her significance as a pioneer of women's climbing is well recognised.' I was in my mid twenties when I first read *Climbing Days*; it was an experience that changed my life. Not only did it reveal to me the astonishing truth about my relatives – their dynamism, tenacity, bravery, physical strength, positivity and zeal for the peaks – but the extent of Dorothy's trailblazing example and practical support for woman's climbing around the world.

The memoir inspired me to follow in her footsteps (and handholds) in order to tell her story and celebrate her many achievements before and after the autobiography's publication – a daunting task. The *Oxford Dictionary of National Biography* calls Dorothy 'one of the most outstanding mountaineers of the interwar and post-war periods.' But perhaps her most enduring legacy is co-founding *The Pinnacle Club* in Snowdonia, the world's first female climbing club, with the aim of encouraging rock climbing and mountaineering among women (the club celebrated its centenary in 2021). As Dr Ann Kennedy Smith has noted, the fact that Dorothy took on the editorship of the *Pinnacle Club Journal* provided a public platform for female

---

1   *Selected Letters of I. A. Richards*, I. A. Richards, John Constable, and Richard Luckett, Clarendon Press, Oxford, 1990

climbers' voices to be heard without interference from male editors.

> Both the club and its journal helped to normalise climbing as something all women could do, not just a few extraordinary individuals: as a lifelong feminist, Pilley wanted to use her experience and enthusiasm to encourage others.[2]

In terms of Dorothy's own mountaineering, her record of achievement is vast and the exploits detailed in *Climbing Days* are only the tip of the Eiger. Her memoir's chapter titles tell of her passion for the peaks: the Lake District, Skye, the French Alps, the Mont Blanc Chain, Corsica, the Swiss Alps, the Pyrenees, Italy. Not included in the book are adventures and first ascents in China, Japan, Korea and Burma.

The Wander Years chapter details a period Dorothy spent climbing alone in the North American and Canadian Rockies. At the end of that trip (summer 1926) she climbed Mount Baker, the first woman to do so. I.A.R. had travelled over to attempt the mountain with her and ask if she'd reconsider his proposal of marriage (she did).

A film made during that trip shows them leaping crevasses, cutting steps up snow banks and striding purposefully up icy slopes. The whole thing looks fantastically dangerous and glamourous. Berets are worn; zeniths are vanquished; the film ends with the subtitle *Excelsior!*

Climbing Days records the fight for acceptance, access and equality which defined much of Dorothy's life. When she started climbing, women were routinely chaperoned for walks round London parks, ladies in trousers risked derision and violence, and male climbers would disavow climbs that female mountaineers had completed, as

2   https://akennedysmith.com/2021/01/30/manless-climbing-dorothy-pilley-richards-1894-1986/

poet Helen Mort reports so brilliantly in her 2016 collection, *No Map Could Show Them*:

> When we climb alone
> en cordée feminine,
> we are magicians of the Alps –
> we make the routes we follow
> disappear' [3]

It was stories like this, and how such attitudes were confronted, countered, and blown sky high by The Pinnacle Club et al, that spurred me to learn to climb (badly), the better to follow and write about Dorothy's accomplishments. I realized that an attempt to write about such a life could not be vicarious – contact with Alps and Munros were vital to the subject – so I picked my way gingerly up several routes in Snowdonia and the Cairngorms, scrambled in the Lake District and scaled some summits in Spain and Switzerland, beloved of Dorothy and Ivor. And I met many people who'd known and loved them, discovering so much about their relationship with each other and my family – and a great deal about my father, as well as myself. All the time I was closing in on the Dent Blanche: that mysterious, serrate peak in the Alps of Valais, the magnificent apex of Ivor and Dorothy's climbing lives.

That book, also named *Climbing Days* – in light, honour and celebration of Dorothy's memoir – was published by Faber in 2016. I meant it to stand as a companion and commentary to the original but, until now, it has had to carry the flame for Dorothy's memoir since that has been out of print for several decades. I've always found this hard to fathom since, as you'll shortly discover, her autobiography is a superb chronicle of vertiginous exploits and

---

3   'An Easy Day for a Lady', *No Map Could Show Them*, Helen Mort, Chatto & Windus, London, 2016

derring do, together with beautiful, moving descriptions of land-scapes, friendships, triumph and tragedy. In short, a true orographic odyssey, in pursuit of the sublime, aware all the while of the risks involved.

Thanks then to Canongate for republishing Dorothy's alpine opus.

The copy of *Climbing Days* I first read was a Secker & Warburg hardback of 1965 and it is that version upon which this new Canons edition is based, complete with all the wonderful photographs, endpapers and Dorothy's original Preface complemented by her 1960s Retrospection in which the author looks back on her commu-nity's achievements, the state of alpinism to date, the current challenges and her hopes for the future.

One of my great discoveries while writing about Dorothy was a recording made towards the end of her life in which she speaks about Chris Bonington's summiting of Everest in 1985, several years after his previous attempt which ended with the tragic deaths of his companions, Joe Tasker and Pete Boardman.

The tape was made by her nephew, Anthony, and on it you can hear her moving crockery and cutlery around to elucidate the story she's telling. I find the whole thing very moving and illustrative of how connected she remained with the contemporary climbing world. Even in Dorothy's ninth decade, her energy and optimism is audible, just as it radiates from the pages of this memoir — she led by example, blazed a trail – and I'm delighted to be able to help share and celebrate her life and ongoing legacy.

'For me, as well as her mountaineering achievements, it was the way she brought a feminine perspective to mountaineering,' Dr Sarah Lonsdale told me recently. 'The gentians too beautiful to tread on, the hairpin needed 10,000 feet up a mountain . . . the way she worked so hard to find the right words to describe what she saw', as evinced in the diaries she kept as a daily journal of her life for nearly eighty years.

The successful climber must be adaptable and expedient, evolve their thinking in light of challenging territory, seek out and articulate routes through, on and up. As on rock, so on the page.

Dorothy Pilley – pioneer, leading light and inspiration.

I hope you enjoy her *Climbing Days*.
Perhaps it will inspire you to journeys out and up, as it did me.
If so, good luck.
Take care.
Go well.

Dan Richards
October 2023

RETROSPECTION

'In that awful instant the whole of my past life flashed before me.' So runs the caption beneath a beautiful Bateman drawing which used to be one of our favourite references. The climber, who is obviously on his first (and last) ascent, is seen dangling just out of reach of an overhanging cliff. But what steals your attention is his past life: a million bottles and glasses of all kinds and sizes are radiating his nostalgic anguish.

The people whose doings these pages recount are addicts too. Nothing but the mountains –the best climbs they could do— would content them. How much climbing accumulated through those years! Perched, say, on the Gemmi (to which a wire rope nowadays can convey you) a reminiscent search finds only three little stretches of the horizon, each no more than a finger wide, of ridge we had left untrodden. Spread out so, simultaneously before our eyes, the proportion of existence that I have spent in the hills comes home with a bang and this book, which in various ways tries to wonder why, feels almost a case history. But a case suggests a clinic and I am not ready and do not expect ever to be ready to admit that what is described here is a disease.

Doubtless the climber's craving is a compensation, the pursuit of a release from things like telephone calls and rush-hour buses that are unnatural and warping in useful life. Perhaps too, for some climbers, the sport is symbolical: an ascent may enact something that a day's work does not clearly show. Perhaps again, the very inutility of climbing, in an over-all view of it, gives a special relish to the real plain usefulness of a saving hold. It is easy to raise plenty of unanswerable questions about any passion. What would have happened, most climbers have asked themselves, if what was put into mountaineering had gone into something else? But this wondering may be misguided. You could equally ask: Where would you have been without what you believe you have gained from the hills?

Such speculations are at their liveliest on mountain mornings early on in one's holiday. 'Nothing like it!' you feel again, breathing the crystalline air—muscles, tendons and joints as it were champing at the bit. All the delights of who-cares-how-many seasons then come crowding aboard to get themselves lived through once more. Better at such hours to be 'untouched by solemn thought'.

How would it have helped, for example, if something had told me what the future held? In New Hampshire, at rainy dusk on November 9, 1958, a drunken driver was to swing across the traffic and there we were with no choice but to ram into the wreckage in the middle of the road. Result: my head through the windscreen, a broken hip and the joint all chaos within. Afterwards, well, the scale of the Alps, and of much else, is strangely changed.

Even before this horrid accident, the relativeness of mountain efforts had been growing upon me. How arduous the simplest trips may become! 'A great proportion sum', I kept saying to myself all that last good season, 1958. A: B:: C: D, this little peak is to me now as my best adventures were in earlier years. The Blümlisalp! Once upon a time, I seem to remember, could I have talked as if a *traversée intégrale*—a scamper over all its summits—would be the only trip worth planning here? Did the Oeschinen See really have to listen to such airy stuff from me in the year that Sir Austen Chamberlain was saving the world at Locarno? And as to the Fusshorn—call it even the Grosser Fusshorn—keep that (did I rule?) for the doddering days. It would come into its own then! Well, and indeed it did!

On our last long expedition, the year of the accident, we came to the Grosser Fusshorn with our friend Josef Imseng of Brigue. I began the day by falling all the way down the near vertical staircase of the Ober Aletsch Hut. I. A. R. was just warning me of it when down I came in the dark. It hurt. I marvelled to have nothing broken. In order not to come back to this awkwardly placed hut, we took everything with us in our sacks as we picked our way from ledge to ledge by moonlight. Why is it that by moonlight you have so often to walk in your own shadow? Ungrateful remark in view of what was to happen. It might have been—but wasn't—'bad magic'. This was before 4 A.M.; it was September and dawn took her time. We left our sack-loads where we crossed what Imseng told us would be a swift and restful way home: down pleasant snow streaks we gathered: 'Swish! Ah! La-la!' But, up to the col and the nice rocks of the summit mass, there was no snow, only ice and poorly embedded débris. Nuisance all the way.

However, the summit rocks were solid, their flanges poked up boldly between vast dark clouds that occasionally threw hail at us but opened grandly to show us now the Ofenhorn, now the Ebnefluh and Mittaghorn. The day wore on. Back again at the sacks it turned out that a hot year had removed the much anticipated snow. No 'Swish! Ah! La-la!' about it at all! Only the most exasperatingly tiresome rubble. Below that, expert local knowledge is quite necessary if you are to get down on to the glacier. People without it just don't get down; there are too many big overhangs. Imseng had the local knowledge; it led us on little sheep tracks from one shelf to another. At the glacier edge, too, the way is not easy to find or to follow. Dawn had taken its time but dusk seemed to be in a hurry. It came at a gallop and the flashlight had been a bit too useful too early. We were relieved to be off the moraine and on the real path just as black night shut down. But there is a lot of that path between where we were and Bel Alp. We quenched our thirst at a stream and sat down to enjoy the evening Alps and rest.

As fresh energy welled up, what could that gleam be across the

vague Aletsch trough, somewhere in the Rieder Alp direction? After
getting so suddenly dark, very dark indeed, how could it be getting
lighter again—so soon? A cloud shifted, and there it was; we saw
our rescuer. It was the lovely Moon! Having lit us up the ridge, it
was back to light us home. Such a friendly, serviceable luminary!
As I write, I wonder if men will before long be hanging reflector
satellites in the sky to light night wanderers. No more surprising
than what, since my Days, they have been doing on the cliffs.

However, we ancients felt triumphant when we succeeded in
knocking up the patron of the old wind-battered Hotel Bel Alp.
Cognac, cake and bed—fatigues forgotten. And, oh, the over-all
renewal of the morning hours! A: B :: C: D, we thought again,
remembering long-past days.

Dorothy Thompson in *Climbing with Joseph Georges* blissfully
remarks of such moments that there are Alpine hours when 'You
feel you could knock a bus over.' It must have been in such a spirit
that she set off (1933) with J. G. to traverse Mont Blanc—up by
the Bionnassay, down by the Peuterey; the whole trip for the first
time ever, the halves as firsts for a woman; 34 hours going in all.
Of the descent, by night, she writes: 'I have always regarded the
hours spent on that magical, incredible arête, under the light of
the full moon, without fear of foul weather, as the most open-
handed gift the mountains have ever given me.'

Her leader on this great traverse, Joseph Georges, our companion
in so much that follows, died in September 1960. He was a puzzling
figure who grew more puzzling through the years. After his
illness—a lung and heart trouble which precluded further ascents—
his retirement, spiritual as well as physical, became very marked.
He passed his last twenty years or so with his sisters in his own
village, La Forclaz, as carpenter and farmer.

He combined extraordinary mountaineering abilities with a
most appealing nature and the highest ideals, above all for his
profession as Swiss guide. This was exemplified in my third season
(1923) when I. A. R. had planned a second ascent of the N.E. Ridge

of the Jungfrau. On p. 245 below there is mention of 'a reconnaissance, about which we were sworn to secrecy'. What had happened was this. In the course of this exploration J. G. found himself taking the mountain to pieces on a vast rotten *gendarme* that has since fallen *in toto*. The more he picked away the more got ready to fall. Once up it, advance was far wiser than return. So we, resting for the morrow at the Joch, had the mixed pleasure of watching him complete the traverse. Joseph felt so keenly about this that the only way in which we could console him was by solemnly undertaking—for his sake as a guide—to keep it dark.

The mountain verities remain unchanged but much else about climbing has developed in ways that were not even dreamed of in 1928. For example, more new climbs have been discovered in North Wales and the Lakes in the last two decades than in all the years before. And many of these are nowadays thronged not to say overcrowded!

What will happen, we may all wonder, when there really are no new local crags and routes to be found? I doubt whether the inexhaustible resources of still unexplored remote ranges can supply this need. Somehow to climb new routes that no one else will ever follow seems a waste of effort that lacks allure. Even about 1918 plenty of good judges were saying that the barrel was pretty well empty. By 1935 so much more had happened that even more and even better judges saw the end in sight. And since then, of course, the whole standard in the upper brackets has been transformed again and again.

Take Cenotaph Corner: 'Exceptionally severe' in the Guide and 'a ferocious bit of work demanding exceptional strength and skill.' It was first climbed by Joe Brown, in 1952. In the next six years it was only climbed fifteen times. Nowadays it is climbed two or three hundred times a year. And there are now perhaps some two hundred British climbs that are harder. It is not surprising, therefore, that the attitude to the Devil's Kitchen evinced on pp. 44–47 is now out of date. In those days we could not see or conceive such a thing as Advocate's Wall on the opposite side of the cleft. Now it is one of the most popular climbs in the district.

Amid all these, that tall ship, Lliwedd, is out of fashion and near abandoned. A pity! For, as Charles Evans has pointed out, it offers so fine a training ground for route finding on the greatest mountains.

The technique of free climbing: safe use of nylon rope, *piton* (metal peg to be hammered in), snap-link, runner, *étrier* (stirrup ladder), demolitionists' helmets . . . has leaped up incredibly. But novelty has always its penalties; with new materials new hazards can enter. There have been a sad number of unexplained accidents, sometimes to climbers so gifted and experienced that no one can believe that what happened could be their fault. Here is Charles Evans, leader of the model first ascent, Kanchenjunga, in his grand book *On Climbing*, writing of the use of a sling or runner (a loop secured by a belay, by a stone jammed in a crack or by a *piton*):

> Never must the climbing-rope be put direct through a rope sling, particularly a nylon one, but always through a snap-link clipped to the sling. If no snap-link is used, the mechanical stress, together with the heat generated by friction at one point, will cause the climbing-rope, in the event of a fall, to go through a nylon sling like a knife through butter, and may break even a Manila sling. (*On Climbing*, p. 52.)

A snap-link (*karabiner*, or 'biner as the American super-cracksmen call it) is a smooth, light-metal, oval ring, a small hands-width long and as thick as a thin little finger. It has a secure spring-to segment which will open to admit a rope. This little device by itself has worked a revolution in climbing technique.

But skill has more than kept up with the improvements in equipment. The improvements themselves are prodigious, so great that mid-winter scalers of the greater North Faces (unthinkable, almost, even as mid-summer madnesses, in 1928) can quite tranquilly weather out a two-day blizzard in their *duvets*, hammock-hung on *pitons* half-way up the wall. And yet, along with all the aids there has been an at least equal lift in the competence and enterprise of climbers as well as in their numbers. When *Climbing Days* was written one could expect to know, and know the record of, any British mountaineer who did notable climbs. Nowadays hundreds lead up pitches that would have been classed then as 'utterly impossible'.

With the multiplication of climbers, accidents must increase and so do the gallant and efficient activities of mountain rescue teams. Few who have not themselves been out on a search or rescue operation can realize what an exacting and self-sacrificing commitment these can be. Or how much organization, preparation and training these devoted volunteers impose on themselves. In comparison with the 'twenties the response now available in case of need is something to make the misanthropist blush.

Climbing formerly was a decidedly shy sport, gaining for its devotees some added flavour from being, parentally and generally, under disapproval as dangerous and unbecoming. It is quite a twist to reconcile this approach with the spectator-appeal of the Eiger Nordwand, not to mention roadside cliffs nearer home: three splendid ones in the Llanberis Pass and—for Wordsworthians to ponder—the Castle Rock of Triermain at Thirlmere. This cliff has been described as 'holding a greater number of top grade Very Severes than any other crag in the Lake District'. Clearly enough, the sport I grew up through was embryonic—as a sport. To me and kindred spirits it was more than a sport and the sport aspect did not interfere with the other interests. This may become true of the pure roadside gymnasts. But one's hopes are climbers too, and there are impossibles and unascendables in their world also.

It would be invidious, odious and so on, to mention by name the famous men and women who have been stretching the limits of the feasible in mountain accomplishment through this last lustre. There are so many stars among them. I would not dare even to sketch the development of men's mountain performance; Joe Brown's and Don Whillans' achievements and such just surpass the bonds of my imagination. I will confine myself to a few notes on the progress of women's climbing—a progress exemplified by the existence, in Gwen Moffat, of a brilliant professional woman guide. In 1920, what a joke the idea would have been. Her comment: 'I knew I must make no mistakes. One accident, and everyone would say: "that's what comes of having a woman as a guide!" The men could afford to have the occasional slip, but not I. *They* would watch me like hawks.'

A decade hence—who knows?—another leap forward in unforeseen human ability will be in the record. But underneath all these records there is the live enjoyment. As Evelyn Leech, one of those to whom the Pinnacle Club—that once outlandish freak—owes so much as a leader and in every way, has written of the Cwm Dyli hut in Gwynant:

'The standard of climbing done from the Hut (we were the first Women's Club to have our own Hut) has changed indeed, yet I imagine that the feeling of today's tigers leading Cenotaph Corner, Spectre or Ivy Sepulchre are much the same in quality as those of yesterday's tigers leading Great Gully, Terrace Wall, Longland's or Javelin. So, after all, and thirty years on *plus c'est la même chose*.'

Names of climbs, these, many of which we looked at and gave up as beyond reasonable human ability in the 'twenties. Craig Lloer, Dinas Mot, Clogwyn Du, how often we scanned you in those days, concluding that your so tempting routes were impossible. Our Lethargica (p. 43) was one of several such in the Llanberis Pass. Good to think now that they are the happy playground of our successors, with multiple routes criss-crossing them at every angle.

Within this general technical and achievement rise the development of the Pinnacle Club and the British Women's Mountaineering Clubs takes an honourable place. About 1928, as Editor of the *Pinnacle Journal*, I was surprised one morning by a peremptory communication from Authority: Why had I not sent copies, as the law requires, to the British Museum and the other statutory recipient libraries? The fact was that I had forgotten the Law. Remedying my fault made me realize that the implied feminist claims to equal opportunities, responsibilities and obligations for women, built into the Pinnacle Club Charter, amounted to a conspicuous symptom of a Revolution. A good deal later I was at a Pinnacle Club Meet in the Avon Gorge. I knew of those steep, rather rotten and quite spectacular cliffs through I. A. R., who had had, as an undergraduate, some fine routes and adventures upon them. In his days what you had to look out for were the police. That meant dawn climbing. But here at midday, for the Pinnaclers as they clung, crawled or floated up, fly-like, upon the precipices— the police were gaily and gallantly at hand controlling the beholding crowds and guarding them from the motor traffic. How Pat Kelly would have marvelled at what was to be seen. Incidentally there is now a Handbook on the routes.

Both in the Alps and in the greater ranges the advances in women's climbing have fulfilled all expectations. The Ladies' Alpine Club celebrated its Jubilee in 1957, the Ladies' Scottish Climbing Club in 1958 and the Alpine Club its Centenary the same year; fine occasions for retrospective survey. Some interesting achievements came to light: Miss Richardson, the first woman up the Meije (1888) went straight through from La Bérarde starting at 9 P.M.; Mrs Nettleton led the traverse of the Grépon in 1903 with her husband and a porter. She had however led Owen Glynne Jones up Kern Knotts Crack a few years earlier. Such doings, for their dates, can be compared with those, say, of Mlle Loulou Boulaz: Mont Blanc, Pear Route; Punta Gugliermina, South Face; Grand Capucin du Tacul, South Face; Grandes Jorasses, North Face— Pointe Croux (2nd ascent); Pointe Walker; Aiguille Verte, Couloir Couturier, North Face; Petit Dru, North Face (2nd ascent); Matterhorn, Furggen ridge; Zinal Rothorn, North Face (1st ascent); Mont Durand, North Face; Studerhorn, North Face (1st ascent); Cima Grande di Laveredo, North Face. Naturally, conditions and party have to be considered in all comparisons. Mlle Boulaz' descent in bad weather from the Ramp on the Eiger Nordwand may well be a greater mountaineering performance than Fräulein Voog's successful ascent in good conditions.

A contrast, all this, to the days when Geoffrey Howard's aunt wore a white linen mask against the sun and an *opéra bouffe* crinoline, and when members of the Alpine Club thought the ladies should climb in uncrowded July and leave an unmolested Alps to them in August. It is worth recalling that one of the great pioneers of those days, Miss Lucy Walker, second President of the Ladies' Alpine Club, always wore a red petticoat when climbing so that she could be easily found if she had a fall. An orange anorak would be today's equivalent.

Every Alpine season now finds a number of *cordées féminines* taking, as a matter of course, routes that call for highest standards of skill, knowledge and *résistance*. Among the continuing leaders in this startling progress is Nea Morin, Oread of Harrison Rocks, floating up them and X. S. climbs in Wales with arabesque elegant ease. She had traversed the Meije as far back as 1933, with Micheline Morin and Alice Damesme. And she repeated this twenty-five years later, leading Janet Roberts. Perhaps even more notable— among her many extraordinary achievements—is her Mer de Glace face of the Grépon with her daughter, Denise Evans, leading alternately. The contemporary lists of young tigresses include nowadays any of the great classical Alpine routes.

In 1957 Denise Shortall and Rie Leggett did the Rotengrat of the Alphubel (in bad conditions), the Kanzelgrat of the Rothorn, the Matterhorn and the Wellenkuppe-Arbengrat. In their spectacular 1962 season, Faye Kerr and Dorothée Borys had the North Ridge of the Weisshorn, the Monte Rosa-Lyskamm traverse, the Zmutt Ridge of the Matterhorn and the Mitteleggi of the Eiger, as all-feminine firsts among a score of other big climbs.

These are what Bernard Biner of Zermatt describes as 'manless, guideless, women's climbings'. Impossible to do all the girls justice: anything resembling a list would take pages and leave out probably the most brilliant. How am I not to offend my friends by some memory blackout?

Here are Mare's mouth notes (1963) from Nancy Smith climbing with Denise (Shortall) Wilson: 'Denise and I set off up the Nantillons Glacier for the Blaitière thinking of doing the normal route, the Rocher de la Corde, but I had a hankering after the North-West Ridge—*Une des belles escalades, la plus élégante, fort longue*, strenuous and serious . . . So we turned to the right and had a magnificent climb. It's a Ryan-Lochmatter route and has everything—eighty-foot *dièdre*, a blind *rappel*, a rising hand-traverse (the crux), with incredible exposure. At first we thought we had the mountain to ourselves, but as we climbed higher saw two little crash helmets ahead . . . Two tough lads from Liverpool who had bivouacked at the foot. They thought we must be with two big Frenchmen whom we later found behind us and the two Frenchmen thought we must be with the two English ahead. Neither could believe it was our own climb. The Spencer Couloir was a sheet of green ice, not climbed this year. So we descended by the Arête Brégeault, another route . . . Snow on loose rock and a *rappel* over the *rimaye*. We just got down off the dangerous part of the glacier by dark, and stumbled down the moraines until 10 P.M., 17 hours since we left the tent. This was our best climb and one I've dreamed of for years.'

Other good climbs were done by her including a traverse of the Courtes in a *cordée féminine* of five. Two days later the Charmoz-Grépon traverse was foiled by rain. 'Cleared later so we did the N.N.E. ridge of the Aiguille de l'M—Hard but short and swarming with frivolous Frenchmen. One pushed past me and followed Denise up the crux (grade 5) pinching her calves. Another pinched mine as I followed. Oh là là! Vive la France!' (Vite, vite! les Alpes! *L.A.C. Journal*, 1964). And the two concluded with the East Ridge of the Weisshorn with snow in poor condition. That is where women's independent Alpinism has got to.

But these latest triumphs of parties *sans guide et sans garçon*—to quote the title of Jo Scarr's account of how she and Muriel Baldwin in 1959 took in the Forbes Arête of the Chardonnet and a super-complete traverse of the Aiguilles Dorées *en route* to the Dolomites—should not make us forget great climbs of earlier days in more mixed parties. Freya Stark's 1924 ascent of the Marinelli Couloir with Tofi, the Macugnagna guide, has now been described as only she could: 'For women, who were chivalrously exonerated from the fatigue of cutting ice-steps, the long slope with every step a pause; the chance to turn—cautiously, with the point of the axe well jammed into the ice above—to see the outlines of the sleeping world below our pale sub-lunar spaces; the sound of the whispering ice-crumbs as they slid into their chasms from the head of the rope where the new step was being cut; the *leisure* of the ice-slope in fact—was an almost purely receptive pleasure.' (*L.A.C. Journal*, 1964). In the same category belong the classic ascents on the South Face of Mont Blanc by Una Cameron and Dora de Beer in the mid-thirties. An outstanding event of the same period was Wren (Corry) Robinson's rescue of her guide, Mark Lysons, when he broke his leg on the descent from Goldsmith (9532 ft), New Zealand, after their first ascent. In memory of this the glacier has now been named Corry Glacier.

Further afield than the Alps, the promise is as lively, as might be expected in a period which has seen the ascent of Everest, K.2, Kanchenjunga and all the Himalaya 8000 m. peaks except one. All-women ascents in the Andes and in the Himalayas are now no longer unheard of. As early as 1951 Claude Kogan with Nicole Leininger climbed Quitaraju (6100 m.) in the Cordillera Blanc in the Andes. A year later she led her party to the summit of Salcantay (6200 m.). In 1955 came the Ladies' Scottish Climbing Club's Expedition to the Langtang Himal, and the ascent by Monica Jackson and Betty Stark of an unclimbed 22,000-footer. Next year came the Abinger Expedition to Kulu. In this expedition, organized by Joyce Dunsheath, Eileen Healey not only led unclimbed peaks up to 21,000 feet but made, with two porters, the second ascent of Deo Tibba (19,687 ft) a notorious toughie which had defeated many assaults. Deo Tibba is almost a woman's preserve. Later, two of a Japanese women's expedition climbed it with two Ladakhis and in the first ascent (1952) were Clare Graaf and her husband. Eileen also casually flits up home climbs commenting: "The easiest V.S. I have led.' She writes of her Kulu triumphs: 'I realized that the climbs were only of an Alpine scale, the summits were 5000 feet higher than the Alps, but so also were the valleys.' That is the way it is done!

The most ambitious all-woman assault yet has been the 1959 international attempt on Cho Oyu (8150 m.) by a party that included Eileen Healey, Dorothea Gravina and Margaret Darvall as British members and Tensing's two daughters and niece. Alas, that through no one's fault it cost the lives of its leader, Claude Kogan, and of young Claudine van der Stratton and of Chewang and Da Norbu, Sherpa porters. A sudden unforeseeable thaw set the slopes running with avalanches and the highest camp was swept away. Claude Kogan was probably the most distinguished woman mountaineer of her day, as experienced in high altitude snow conditions as anyone. So there is no ground here for adverse comment, only for deep regret. What might have been a great triumph was by sheer accident turned to disaster.

The splendid doings in Kulu (1961) of Jo Scarr and Barbara Spark and the Jagdula (Pinnacle Club) Expedition (1962) in wildest Nepal (the same two with Dorothea Gravina, Denise Evans, Nancy Smith and Pat Wood) have continued the advance. All the memsahibs ascended Kanjiroba (21,500 ft) except those laid up with influenza (temperature 105°). The expedition climbed six new peaks in all, each the tallest in its region.

Such have been some of the changes in the quarter century since *Climbing Days* first went to the printer. There are hundreds of changes. Where to start and to stop? Huts are higher and better placed; there are more of them, wonderfully outfitted: running water, washing nooks, inside lavatories. Oh, that totter to the sentry box at the edge during a blizzard! On bigger expeditions in Alaska, etc., there are frozen foods, pressure cookers, radio communications, plane drops . . . all of which simplify operations enormously. There have been other and more fundamental transformations: the shrinking of the glaciers and the breaking up of major rock walls newly denuded of their ancient ice covering. Some climbs that used to be delightful have become tottering ice-falls and stone-swept grimy messes. The *bergschrund* obstacles grow more formidable. It is rare for the dessication to improve a route. The North Face of the Grivola (p. 295), in 1924 a shining curve of ice, can nowadays be not much more than steep, loose rubble. Against these we may set the awakening of the Alpine Valley populations to the joys their mountains can offer. The high picnic ramble was not a pleasure conceived of or indulged in by peasants of a generation ago. Nowadays, jolly local parties, cheese and wine in hand, are a common sight at the huts. All this part of what some call a decline from tradition and others a release. It is shown in countless ways: the scything woman; that lovely motion used to be man's privilege; she kept to the rake, but did not toil any the less for that.

I should perhaps say something about my own high-level life since 1928, for my climbing days did not end then. They took me, with I. A. R., into many ranges—into the Western Hills that encircle Peking and into the Chinese Himalaya of upper Yunnan, up high unclimbed peaks there and in the Selkirks and the Bugaboo; and all over the Canadian Rockies; up Adam's Peak, Ceylon; Mont Herman, Lebanon; Ulga Dag, Turkey and Parnassus, Kylléné and Olympus in Greece. By myself, in 1938, I had the adventure of following on foot the 200-mile Old Jade Trail from Tali in Yunnan to Bhamo on the Irrawaddy in Burma, crossing by bamboo suspension bridges the Mekong and Salwyn in their stupendous gorges, coming down from the 10,000 foot camellia-covered ridges to the monkey howlings of the tropical forest festooned with orchids.

Soon after this we were introduced, through the Appalachian

Mountain Club, to the resources of snow-shoeing. Snow shoes are the key to safe travel for small parties in deep unvisited snows. They will take you, without risk, through soft, tree-tangled drifts where skis are only too likely to break your leg. With crampon spikes under the ball of your foot they let you hop up hard steep slopes like a bird. Sometimes, of course, you have to take them off and use your ice axe. But they have let us, mostly *à deux*, go up all but three of the winter 4000-foot mountains of New Hampshire.

In large jolly Club outings snowshoers proceed in long caravans, with a group of leaders taking turns to break the trail, the others coming along on the smooth firm track so formed. It can become monotonous for those in the rear. I remember a weary voice from far back which kept calling, 'How much further? How much further?' The leader gave what we felt was a perfect answer, so satisfying and so truthful. He turned and bellowed: 'It's only a matter of minutes!' Actually, as he well knew, we had just about three-quarters of an hour more to go.

For a party of two snowshoeing is the way to savour mountain isolation, to get away when you want to from others and have your route all to yourselves. Oh, those arrivals at dusk, by storm or by starlight, at the bare ice-lined shelters that the winter White Mountains provide. Winds up to any figure and temperatures below consideration, real challenge to the fire-lighter's art; how strange that these should be what the heart pines for in recollection. Snowshoeing was the invaluable technique we lacked in Corsica and the Pyrenees. With it, and the *igloo*, what an enlarged world of adventure would have opened up! Winter climbing lets you imagine that no one has been that way before, but there is a certain sameness to it, however lovely. Snow is snow and only snow, as you feel with rapture when spring comes and you see a sunny bank of earth and grass, bilberry or heather, pushing up through it. The full variety of the hills shows best in summer.

Between these world ranges, as between the more delicately contrasting sub-systems of the Alps, what inexhaustible differences!

How strangely individual most mountains are to the mountaineer. There may be plainsmen to whom they are all alike, as there may be those to whom flowers are 'just flowers' or people 'just people'. I have often thought that if I were suddenly carried by an Angel to some high place in any range I have ever walked in, I would know within a few minutes which it was. Tall talk! The vanity perhaps that goes along with elevated spirits? Harmless at least, and it was good to feel like that. 'High places' in Petra have an ominous ring. They link up with spiritual pride. But if there is one thing which long enough frequentation with mountains can teach it is awe-filled humility. Exaltation? Yes. But the feel of littleness still more. May these pages serve as reminders of mountain hours.

I am indebted for information and suggestions used in this Retrospection to Roger Chorley, Robin Collomb, Margaret Darvall, Nea Morin and I. A. R.

CAMBRIDGE, MASS.   D.E.P.
CAMBRIDGE, ENGLAND. 1965.

PREFACE

I began to write this book in China, being homesick for European hills. It was a substitute for climbs in Britain and the Alps. In the final stages it was only too truly a substitute; stealing away days that might have been spent high, for a low struggle with commas. May some other temporary exile from the mountains find in it a moment of solace!

The novice in snowcraft sometimes, on a steep crevassed slope, finds himself with divided fears. Will he fall down the slope or through it? There is even some comfort in the conflict of alternatives. So here for me. Do I run more risk by explaining too much or too little? The mountaineer will find too little climbing, pure and simple, here; but the hill-lover, pure and simple, may find too much. I can hear a climber's disappointed voice exclaiming, 'What! Only 14 pips in 21 days! What were they doing the other days?' or 'No *bivies* this year? Can't have been very enterprising!' or 'Monks again! I want to hear what she *did*; not what she thought about or saw!' Against these breezes, a quieter, steadier gale seems to beat. It sighs, 'Oh dear, more footholds and handholds, more *passe-montagnes*, more eyelashes tinkling with ice, more stones falling, more steps to be cut! I think I may as well do some cutting myself.'

But, if there is safety in a multitude of counsels, this humble confession of faith should escape. I owe heartfelt thanks to Miss Gwyneth Lloyd Thomas for a hundred and one corrections of my grammar, as well as for much more; to Mr Sydney Spencer for modernizing and revising my shocking Alpine spelling; to Mrs R.

S. T. Chorley and Mr W. P. Haskett-Smith for reading the original draft; to Miss Dorothy Thompson, Mr Herbert Carr, and Mr C. F. Holland for allowing me to quote from their articles; to Colonel E. L. Strutt, Editor of the *Alpine Journal*, to Mr G. R. Speaker, Editor of the *Journal of the Fell and Rock Climbing Club*, to the Committees of the Ladies' Alpine Club and Pinnacle Club, to Professor J. H. Clapham and Messrs Culling Carr, J. H. Doughty, Darwin Leighton, N. E. Odell, and many others who helped me to find my illustrations, and to all the photographers whose names appear under their work—which so much relieves my text. I also owe my acknowledgements to the Editor of *Blackwood's Magazine*.

Those of my fellow climbers who share a need to analyze our common passion will understand that this long attempt to explain a love of mountains yet ends with—Why?

PEKING, 1929   D. E. P.
CAMBRIDGE, 1934

CHAPTER I

INITIATION

Welsh walks—The first climb—Solitary efforts—A broken leg on Lliwedd—Ropes, leaders, pitches and belays—Gwern-y-Gof Uchaf—Cautious-controlled and hopeful-hazardous—Falling off the Direct on Glyder Fach—All kinds of leaders—Silence while the leader is advancing—Fluctuations of form.

Long ago a young soldier gave a school-girl a novel with a vivid description of the Brenva Route of Mont Blanc—modelled on Moore's account in his Diary. The knife-edge ice ridge, the desperate night on the slope, the earlier pictures from *Running Water* of the Pavillon de Lognan and the Aiguille d'Argentière mingled in her mind with fairy-tale Glass Mountains, Mountains of the Moon, K'un Lun Western Paradises—abodes of ice-princesses from which ordinary mortals are dragged back by the hair. A strange, now unrecapturable farrago of fantasies, remaining perhaps a vague haunting background to all my mountain experiences.

—

The first entry of these dreams into actuality came with a visit to Beddgelert. In place of the pleasant family holidays by the sea— the esplanades, the sands, the young 'nuts' with their ties and canes, the warblings of the fair young tenor at the Pierrots, in his beautifully creased white flannels and 'Varsity blazer—came the grey village street, the tawny blotches of the bracken, the reeds swaying in the breeze round the shores of Llyn Dinas, the smell of the moss and the peat. What did it matter that we went up Craig-y-Llan in long skirts and in what the boot-sellers regard as feminine walking boots? We found our way down by the mine-shafts in the dark. It was like waking up from a half sleep with the senses cleared, the self released. It was as if I had never seen anything before to strike me as beautiful. The Aberglaslyn Pass seemed the limiting possibility of awful grandeur. Sheer rock walls were edged with sentinel trees in dark silhouette against the sky. Wordsworth does not exaggerate at all; the hills, the cliffs, the cataracts haunt the mind that first gives itself to them 'like a passion'. I was distraught by the feelings that arose. They came with a shock of utter newness upon me, and a mossy rock would stare at me like a stranger until nothing in the world seemed to matter except my desperate attempts to discover what its signifi-cance could be. Hours passed trying to describe, in a note-book, the flowing water, clear, softly lipping over stones with a chase of fleecy foam-mice running out from under them over amber and cat's-eye depths. They were both a joy and a pain, an endless excitement and an endless disappointment. I was helpless before these feelings and knew my helplessness.

The visit culminated in a stupendous ascent of Snowdon. It was all due to a grandfatherly schoolmaster, bearded and Ruskinesque, with a flock of thirty little boys. To us all, the ascent of the highest mountain in England and Wales was a terrifying feat. Our bearded senior fortunately had Alpine experience to comfort us, but when, on reaching the narrow saddle just below the Llechog ridge (as Baedeker might say 'fit only for adepts with strong heads'), he developed vertigo and could go no further, our sense of adventure was redoubled. Breathlessly we scampered up to the summit. Idle to pretend I remember the view. All that comes to the mind is a memory of effort and achievement, intoxicating ginger-beer at four-pence a bottle, a picture of our old friend sitting on the slope by the saddle, and the exact forms of the grey spiky rocks about him with the moss between them.

Next year in the spring the mountains had their chance to lay hold of me for good. Work with the Soldiers' and Sailors' Families Association and an attempt to become an Egyptologist led to a two-months rest. Hieroglyphics had been too much for the eyes. With a small cottage in Beddgelert as our base, my school friend, Winifred Ellerman, a tireless and imaginative walker, and I ranged the surrounding mountains. On Moel Hebog, when we reached the last shale slope, we halted—not knowing whether it was not the safest plan to crawl over the slippery surface on all fours. It seemed to us we should slide down with the whole mountain. What moments of terror we enjoyed! After trying it gingerly we walked up boldly, to be welcomed as courageous mountaineers by hotel acquaintances on the summit. A fateful meeting, for we were invited to make with them the circuit of the Moel Wynns over to Ffestiniog and back—which we counted thirty miles. After this we were singled out as 'indefatigables'. Herbert Carr, then beginning his very active and enterprising climbing career, asked us to come with him up a *real* climb—the Y Gully and Notch Arête of Tryfan. Tryfan, the grim guardian of the upper Nant Ffrancon, the rockiest peak south of the Tweed and the only Welsh mountain that cannot be climbed without using the hands; what a chance! I knew then that I should be for ever grateful to him. Never shall I forget my breathless anticipations. All night I lay sleepless with excitement.

—

As we rounded the bend of the road above Capel Curig and first caught sight of it, I remember trembling with delight and fear. The two summit rocks (ten feet high) were to me, as to so many others before and after me, two humans spell-bound in eternal conversation. I was told that they were called Adam and Eve and that a climber's duty was to spring lightly from one to the other. I asked naïvely (I have since blushed to recall) why one should not be content with ascending the mountain by the easiest route. The question to the non-climber or 'mere walker' seems natural and proper enough; but I was soon to learn the climber's answer. In fact, from that day on, 'climbing' was to become a word with a specialized meaning not to be used just for walking up steep slopes. The climber speaks generally of 'going up Snowdon' when he follows the zigzags of the path, and 'climbs' only when he uses his hands as well as his feet.

When I got out of the car by the tenth milestone from Bangor on the Ogwen lakeside—for the first of how many times?—the mountain seemed to hang over our heads. We wound up the boulder-strewn slope to the foot of the climb and then I made my first acquaintance with scree. Harmless substance enough but singularly terrifying to the uninitiated. The mountaineer knows that if he jumps on to that rock scrap-heap it will slide with him about a foot and then settle down till he jumps again. But the beginner feels sure that he will start sliding and never stop till he lies a mangled body at the bottom. So the heroes of Crockett or Rider Haggard novels have their most ghastly escapes on scree-slopes. And years later I recall that an American friend, after coming gallantly and recklessly up an east-face climb on Tryfan, halted at this very scree funnel, to declare that it 'sure was a mighty mean slope to fall down'.

This danger past, the climb that followed showed no terrors. It was a journey full of discoveries as to how well the body fits the rocks, how perfectly hand- and foot-hold are apportioned to the climber's needs. I was later to find out that this was a peculiarity of Tryfan rather than of climbing as practised by modern experts. In the exhilaration of these discoveries the climb seemed over before it had properly started. I felt like a child when the curtain goes down at the pantomime. Why hadn't I enjoyed it ten times more while it was on? Every moment was glorious and as quickly gone. The cold wind was whistling round Adam and Eve by the time we reached the summit. It persuaded half the party to walk down to the car. Herbert Carr and I descended the South Gully and, undamped, rushed off in the dusk to scramble up the windswept Bristly Ridge, that comes down Glyder Fach to Bwlch Tryfan, and make our way over to Pen-y-Gwryd. If we had conquered the hardest climb in the district we could not have rejoiced more. 'Mountain madness' had me now for ever in its grasp.

Thereafter followed four days of ecstatic climbing in perfect weather. Bluebells were in the woods and ranunculus in the swamps as we passed on our way up to the cliffs. They were lovely beyond belief; but my thoughts were mainly on *footholds* and *handholds*. Each *pitch* or passage of the climb seemed as important as the Battle of Waterloo. The Horseshoe of Snowdon for the first time, the Parson's Nose, the Crazy Pinnacle Gully on Crib Goch, and a day on the Nantle Y Garn, were each, as a member of the party was fond of repeating, 'a day which will live'. Y Garn gave a lesson which was to prove useful. It is a mountain with a bad reputation for large, loose, treacherous blocks. In 1910, Anton Stoop, the brilliant young Swiss climber, was killed there. He was lowering himself over a huge block that two heavier men had first descended without its showing signs of danger. It heeled out with him and carried him down helpless. Knowing this story, we treated everything with our utmost care. Nevertheless, just as the party left a terrace of poised blocks, one of them, like a slice out of a cheese, slid away without warning. The crash and the sulphurous smell shook us violently and re-affirmed the need for caution.

After this I was alone in the hills for some weeks. It was now impossible for me to keep away from the high ridges. I wandered round the Horseshoe of Snowdon alone and with any party that would follow me. Greatly venturing, I went up 'Lockwood's Chimney', a dark chasm under Pen-y-Gwryd, alone. With what wild glory in my heart did I wriggle out of the hole and find myself in the sunlight on the giddy upper wall. I induced a large, not too willing party of novices to come up the Great Gully of Clogwyn-y-Garnedd after me. By this time I had become the proud possessor

of an Alpine rope (from Beale's, with a red strand through it!).
How I had studied all the particulars about its strength in George
Abraham's *The Complete Mountaineer*. How ashamed I was of its
brilliant newness; it had to be muddied at all costs. A first pair of
climbing boots shine like twin stars in memory, too. They were
large, much too heavy and too high in the leg, but the whole village
used to come to see them. I still did not dare to go about Beddgelert
without a skirt, and was rather balloony in a thick, full pair of
tweed knickerbockers under a billowy tweed skirt which I put in
the sack at the foot of the climb. I was particularly careful never
to hide it under a rock, having read of Mrs Aubrey Le Blond's
adventure on the Rothorn. How I admired that great woman climber's exploit. To traverse the Rothorn from Zermatt nearly down to
Zinal and then—discovering that her skirt had been left on the
summit—to go all the way back again and down to Zermatt to
round the day off! What an exemplar to contemplate when the
ridge of Crib-y-Ddysgl seemed long and narrow in the windy
morning.

June came and a week's leave for Herbert Carr. We were both
more full of enthusiasm and energy than ever. Our joint ambition,
we hardly dared to whisper it, was the conquest of Lliwedd. It is
impossible, now that Lliwedd climbs have become such well-known
ground, to recapture all the awe and fascination which hung about
them then. Though from the shores by Llydaw on any cloudy day
the gloom of those black precipices can still daunt the heart. The
water laps against the boulders in an inhuman, endless song. The
wind streaks the surface with thin lines of foam. Across Llydaw, a
loose strip of rusty corrugated-iron roof bangs drearily in the gusts
and a sheep baas as though in anguish. There in the hollow of the
Cwm the dark smooth walls of Lliwedd tower up. The men who
made those steeps their playground seemed to me a race of giants—
mysterious beings hardly of this world, undauntable, diamond-nerved
and steel-sinewed. Many a time I had peered down from the sharp
crest, to shudder at the curve of its terrific slabs. To the lay eye

there seems no room for a human foot upon it. That men could have worked their way up by scores of routes was incredible. Most of all when clouds swept down from Y Wyddfa and the gulf under the crags seemed bottomless. The precipice of Lliwedd then might be ten instead of merely one thousand feet high.

But there were no clouds about when we set out. It was hot walking in my thick tweeds across the green slopes above the lake. The long swamp grass rustled dry underfoot; the sunlight cut out the ribs of the cliff above the Horned Crag, showing the Terminal Arête in sharp definition against the blackness of the shadowed gullies. We came into the shade on the litter of scree at the foot as though into a cave of secluded mysteries. Lliwedd from here heels over—like a *Titanic* just about to take its plunge. The immense parallel sweeping lines of its buttresses, echoed by every one of their scores of minor ridges, tilt over together. This heel does not disguise the steepness of the cliff; it gives it indeed an extra touch of loftiness (as of a ship's spars) from the scree and is one of the secrets of the mountain's hold on the imagination. Climbing on it you can never for a moment forget where you are. We put on the rope and set to work somewhere on the West Peak. I doubt if I could find the exact point to-day.

It was the first time we had been on ground which felt really *steep*. Or rather, it altered our conception of steepness for us. On Tryfan you halt on ample ledges—places where you can walk about and sit down with a choice of comfortable positions. On Lliwedd, for long stretches at a time, when you halt you have to stand where your feet are, for there is nowhere else to put them. Or this at least is the novice's impression—on the harder routes of the East Peak an exact one. As we mounted, the sense of the scale of Lliwedd gained on us. We felt like tiny insects creeping from ledge to ledge, from scoop to scoop, insects lost among the vertical immensities about us. All went well, the excitement of achievement blended with the radiance of the day. Crib Goch across Llydaw swam in a haze of sunlight; and when we came, after hours that had seemed like minutes, to a pleasant grassy nook that invited us to pause for rest and lunch, there could have been few happier beings in the world than we. The main difficulties were overcome. Above was easier climbing at a gentle angle. We seemed to have done what we had set out to do.

When we had eaten and smoked we went on. I had become an avid reader of the famous Climbers' Club Pocket Guide-books to the Welsh Crags, and phrases from that master of terse description, Archer Thompson, were always echoing in my memory. One of them about 'belaying the rope around a stook of bollards' wandered from nowhere into my mind just then. It was well that it did so. Herbert was cautiously mounting a steep rib built of massive blocks. A tempting bollard adorned my ledge and acting more in the spirit of Thompson's phrase than from any particular apprehension I had cast a turn of the rope around it. Herbert was to my right and about fifteen feet above me.

Just as he clasped the crest of a block with both arms—somewhat in the monkey-up-a-stick position—the block yielded and heaved out with him clinging to it. How he managed to disengage himself from it I hardly saw. The physical sensation of horror, a quick but heavy pulse of sickness, flashes through one almost before one sees what is happening. Then, as though all feeling had been plucked away, a clear mental calmness follows. I had time to cry 'My God! Look out!' before the block thundered down the cliff with Herbert after it. He hit my ledge and rebounded outwards, disappearing backwards from my view over the edge. Though I held him, the rope ran a little through my hands, leaving a white burn-scar that lingered on my palms for weeks. Quickly though these things happen, they seem in passing to be almost leisurely. One has time to take in the rope, time to think whether there is anything more one should do, time to decide that there is nothing, time to reflect that if the *belay* holds all will be well, and that if not . . . time to perceive with complete and vivid particularity the whole scene—the greenness of the grass ledge, the shape of the lurching boulder and the movement of the falling man, the play and course of the rope cutting into the turfy edge. Time for all this and for a pause of anguished expectancy in which to wonder just how bad what has happened will turn out to be. The pause was broken by a small voice that seemed to come from very far away saying, 'I'm all right!'

He was not all right by any means. Somehow with some pulling he managed to get up to my ledge, white and shaking but composed and self-possessed. Then we could see what the damage was. One leg was broken, the shin-bone being exposed for five inches. Fortunately the bleeding was slight. What proved worse was a bad sprain to the ankle. For a while he rested on the ledge. We had no brandy flask and an orange was the best I could provide as a restorative. The sleeves of the white blouse I used to sport in those early days came in usefully as bandages.

But the time came when our further movements had to be planned and undertaken. With great courage and resolution, Herbert insisted on leading up the remaining four hundred feet. He thought my climbing-experience still too little to deal with such loose terrain. We were more than half-way up the cliff, no one within sight or hearing. Fortunately the day was long. The leg was less painful on the way up the cliff where it could be dragged than on the way down the endless slopes into Cwm-y-Llan. I can recall all the struggle, the coming out into the sunlight at the summit— Snowdon in a dreamy distance above us—the agonizing progress down into the Cwm, Herbert using me as a crutch. After a long while we reached a stream where we bathed the leg and I went on to telephone to a doctor and fetch a car. I recall all this and going up again at dusk to fetch him in, and then a blank of oblivion falls.

In the eyes of those not infected with mountain madness this episode should have put a proper and summary end to my climbing aspirations. And, in fact, strong parental and other influences were marshalled to prohibit them. I was forbidden to climb again. Beddgelert shook its head. The lack of all proper perspective shown in such climbing enthusiasm was pointed out to me. But in vain!

After his six weeks in splints my climbing partner and I, with keenness unabated, were at it again. Even before Herbert was on his crutches, I was out on the rocks with his father. And each evening I would look in to cheer the invalid with stories of the day's doings and he, in imagination, would be sharing the climbs. The instant he was well enough, such was his ardour, he would come out to shout ribald comments to us from the Ogwen Road, as we struggled with the Milestone Buttress.

—

The transition now followed that is almost as palpable and decisive as the larval-imago change. Before, I had been a tourist and a walker; afterwards I at least *felt* a mountaineer. I suspect all climbers have a secret, cherished history of this phase of their development. With the change came a youthful intolerance of parties that set off to picnic with hampers, plates, knives and forks, heavy bottles of ginger-beer, tea-kettles, knitting and magazines—all the impedimenta that root us to one spot. They seemed to bring with them all the commonplaces of everyday life and spread a blight of sacrilege on the scene. Such comforts seemed to anaesthetize one. To go up to Idwal on high-heels in mackintoshes seemed an outrage. Rocks from above should have been hurled by an infuriated mountain spirit on those so out of place. I broke away with two other girls and we went up the Devil's Kitchen track to look down into its horrific recesses. My eye of a budding mountaineer, be it noted, had spotted a walking-route down the true left of the Kitchen, on a grassy ledge somewhere near the Hanging Garden Gully! But I had mistaken the scale; what looked like a step was a fifty-foot drop; and, when we got to its edge, panic broke out in our party. Once we had looked over the drop, the moral effort required to get us up the grass we had cheerfully slid down was no slight one. This was quite a good lesson in itself and I was chastened by the episode.

Little by little better judgment came and with it the collective opposition lost its power. Solitary wanderings with map and compass across the hills gave confidence—in more than merely technical matters. To lie on the summit of Moel Hebog alone with aneroid, compass and map and successfully identify all the mountains in sight, was better than being given the freedom of any city. Before, it had been possible to spend months in Beddgelert without dreaming of going up any of the mountains. They were unreal distant places, too far, too tiring, pathless and dangerous in mist. Now space seemed to unfold itself in great waves before me. To find the top of the Bristly Ridge of Glyder Fach in mist, at dusk, alone, and come down it, was an adventure that nothing in later mountaineering could surpass. The curlews wailing over the swamps, sheep coughing invisibly out of the greyness on the chilly flats, the pinnacles of the ridge looming enormous and the wind whistling through the broken wall on Bwlch Tryfan were impressions that stamped themselves deeper than the memory. They were patents to the faculties, licences to the imagination and the will.

Only on a wave of memory that ebbs and flows capriciously can I recapture—not the mere facts, those are tabulated repetitiously in endless diaries—but the impulses and emotions of those first years of Welsh and Lakeland climbing. The passion that made even a month's incessant rain an almost continuous delight expressed itself plentifully in the above-mentioned diaries. Rhapsodies, in a turgid exclamatory style, relieve the descriptions of scores and scores of climbs, minute accounts of the positions of footholds and handholds, talk of useful rugosities, exiguous traverses, delicate balances, strenuous chimneys, fearsome cracks, exquisite slabs, exposed arêtes, holdless walls, A.P. (Absolutely Perpendicular) overhangs, chockstones, corridors, gangways, belays, bollards, hitches, spillikins and stances, hand-traverses and toe-scrapes, lay-backs and back-ups. The climber's jargon is really a terrifying affair, magic words full of rapture for the chosen. In those days I could read unlimited pages of technical descriptions with never a threat of weariness. The books of W. P. Haskett-Smith, George Abraham and J. M. A. Thompson (especially the latter) were gospels. Who could fail to thrill to this account of the North Gully on Tryfan?—

'Moderately difficult. The best known climb in Wales. Between high walls are set five pitches: the first a cave, the second a stairway, the third a cavern, the fourth a hybrid and the fifth a crux. The leader needs thirty feet of rope. Suitable for any number of climbers, provided close order is kept between the obstacles.'

Or to this detail in the account of the Great Gully of Craig yr Ysfa?—

'Exceedingly difficult and delectable . . . The cave is spanned by two huge boulders, forming bridges. The further is the easier of access. By utilizing a small foothold on the right wall the climber effects a lodgement upon it, and then reaches its sharp upper ledge by a struggle, in which he comes near to defying all the laws of anatomy. A novel expedient is to lay the palm of the right hand on the block, and using the arm as a pivot, perform a pirouette to the south; the climber thus lands in a sitting posture, with one leg thrust upwards to the roof of the cave to maintain the equilibrium. To describe a movement of the body many words are required; but this device, seemingly complicated, is in execution simple and innocent. Any Gallio, however, will complacently demand a shoulder.'

One lay awake before these climbs, trying to imagine just what each step would feel like. 'The gully contracts gradually to the dimensions of a chimney; herein a sense of glorious isolation may be experienced by the solitary climber, who finds himself close cribbed in the narrow fissure.' The imagination shivered and thrilled at the prospect. Everywhere we went we quoted our masters; the modern climber now murmurs maxims from Geoffrey Winthrop Young.

From Archer Thompson and Abraham I gathered also more than I can say of the technique of the sport. Technique unfortunately implies technicalities and the mountain-lover who has not actually handled a rope on a cliff will be puzzled perhaps in what follows unless I give here a brief explanation. I can tick it off possibly under four heads, *Rope, Leader, Pitch, Belay.*

Every climber has been asked how he gets the *rope* up first before he climbs it! It is hard to be confounded with Indian conjurers who toss their rope into the air and then swarm up it. All we do is tie ourselves on, with intervals according to the climb. Then the *leader,* who on an ordinary climb takes all the risk and responsibility, climbs the rocks to a point at which he can pause in security and hold the rope for the second man. Intervals between such pausing points are called *pitches.* Usually, for his security, he will find a *belay,* that is, a spike or knob of rock round which the rope can be passed. The second, when he reaches him, will use the belay both to safeguard the leader's further advance and to bring up the next man. The proper use of belays is rather more intricate than is here shown, but this is the principle. So managed, the rope reduces the leader's risk to a minimum, and the others, clearly, if they slip, will at worst slide or swing a few feet only. But, of course, there are climbs where belays are lacking, where the leader must take out as much as 150 feet of rope to reach any anchorage, and these come into the class of super-severe climbs on which only the great masters disport themselves.

A chronicle of my Welsh adventures would be a toil for me and a hardship for you. I can give only some account of the feelings of those days and of the characters of the peaks and cliffs which, for me, took something of the place that a university may hold for others. I learnt in the Welsh hills to test myself against some external standard, when to trust myself, with caution, and when not, and to meditate upon matters not merely personal. Companionship with men and women of all types, often under conditions of hardship and strain, gave useful lessons in human nature. And friendships formed which have a solidity that other contacts do not often give.

The emergence from the larval state—from the degree of walker to that of climber—coincided with a change of centre from Beddgelert to Gwern-y-gof Uchaf, the farm right under Tryfan in the Ogwen Valley. It stands at the darkest point of perhaps the grandest and gloomiest pass in Great Britain. Broken moorlands, flecked with grey boulders, stretch before it up to the crest of the Carnedds. After rain, white threads show in every hollow of their slopes. The Cwm Tryfan stream rushes by behind it, and over the lilac slate of an outhouse roof the gleam of Lake Ogwen is just visible. A solitary ancient ash, now cut down, used to roar in the winds in the little stone-walled enclosure in front. Above, and overwhelming one whenever one went out, was Tryfan. From the upper ledges of Tryfan, through rain or sunshine, its roofs are visible two thousand feet below.

The extraordinary generosity of climbers in adding me to their parties and leading me up difficult climbs was a wonder to me even then. It was no doubt a tribute to my desperate enthusiasm. The fact is I had almost exhausted the climbs I could do safely by myself—from Lockwood's Chimney to the Parson's Nose. In those days I would run after any pair of climbing-boots. I followed a pair once all the way to Idwal to suggest with horrible shamelessness to its wearer that he should second me up the Idwal Slabs. At which he looked most alarmed and said that he wouldn't go up such a dangerous place for worlds, but wouldn't I like to go for a walk! On the whole I was miraculously lucky in finding kind leaders. At least I can say, for the opposite reasons to those in the case of Queen Mary and Calais, that 'their names are graven on my heart'. In this way I found myself attached to all kinds of ropes and able to observe the methods of most types of climbers. Would that I could have profited more from their good examples.

The examples were of every kind, positive and negative. It might be argued that it is useful to know how to fall off, but it is still better to learn how not to have to! Leaders soon sorted themselves out into the hopeful-hazardous and the cautious-controlled; or rather, these were the extreme cases between which there were puzzling variations according to the climb and the party. The difference was that the cautious-controlled knew, in the ideal case, just what was happening all the time, whereas the others didn't. The cautious-controlled, if a movement felt uncomfortable, simply stopped making it and tried another. There were, it is true, some very cautious-controlled leaders who never got up anything for these reasons. On the other hand, there were hopeful-hazardous who fell off in most undesirable places, on an average, weekly.

One of these (I will call him Fortunatus), who at the time vastly enlarged my mountaineering experience, belonged to the old school. He might, in fact, have been my grandfather, but his manœuvres on the cliffs had a care-free irresponsibility which made me feel like his grandmother. To hear him with two of his contemporaries forcing a hard chimney on the Milestone Buttress was like being at a Cup Final. We were girdling—cautious and silent—and round each rib the storm of jolly shouting burst upon us like a spring gale. 'Higher up! You've nearly got it! Hang on a minute! *And* again!' Do the young, we wondered, take their climbing pleasures too seriously? Fortunatus, with his spectacular climbing, impressed me and the party I was climbing with (I. A. Richards and R. A. Frazer) enormously. Frazer bore a charming resemblance to Don Quixote—both physically (if we picture the Don in early youth) and in his whimsies. When I told him so, he said he was a descendant of Cervantes. He it was who on a bitter winter day carried a wooden pyramid up the crags to *Belle Vue Terrace* on the North Buttress of Tryfan and planted it in the cairn. After remaining there for some ten years it was doubtless thrown down by purists. This aerial platform overlooks Cwm Tryfan from the top of some of the best climbs in the district. He had a passion for mountain animals, from I. A. R.'s faithful nondescript spaniel who, in a little harness, would come gallantly at the tail of the rope up the Idwal Slabs, to crag-bound goats. As to the sheep which often get stuck on the Corner Chimney ledge of the Milestone Buttress, Frazer would ever be the first of those

> Who upward ragged precipices flit
> To save poor lambkins from the eagle's maw.

He was longer, much, in the limbs than ordinary mortals and could often begin a pitch where others finished it. I suspect he believed in both ghosts and fairies and he had adamantine streaks of determination in his generally obliging and chivalrous disposition. One of these streaks served us well in the adventure I am about to relate.

Fortunatus was one morning at a loss for a party. We had watched him performing marvels on the crags and admired the dash which we ourselves did not possess. So when he asked us if we would care to come with him for an attempt on the Direct Route on Glyder Fach, we jumped at the suggestion. This climb has a distinct *cachet*. In the books it is classed as 'exceptionally severe'. It goes up the middle of the steepest crag in the Ogwen district. We had looked at it often from neighbouring climbs with longing eyes; so we were overjoyed and most grateful for the offer.

We set off gaily by the track that leads up to Llyn Bochlwyd. It was a fair summer morning and the pale grey crags of Glyder Fach were in their most inviting condition when we reached them. From their foot they tower up vertiginously into the sky and come much nearer than most cliffs to realizing the non-climber's picture of the cragsman's 'dreadful trade'. Soon we were well on our way up them, Fortunatus clambering with all a monkey's agility from flange to flange of the massive grey shafts of which they are composed. We, sixty feet apart, followed either in more sedate or more laborious fashion. At intervals, ledges and niches occur, charming little halting-places, where two, or, at a crush, three can gather. Here Nature has provided a good supply of belays, strong pins of rock, very comforting to the party. The pitches between the ledges are solid and sheer. As you tiptoe up them you do really feel suspended over the valley with nothing but air below. 'Exposure', in other words, to use the climbing technicality, is continuous. When all is going well the experience is singularly exhilarating. As you look upwards from a ledge the soles of the leader's boots are what you chiefly see of him, and he is often stepping up on wrinkles no larger than the edge-nails of his boots.

We were rather more than half-way up and had taken the delicate little sideways movement known as the 'toe-and-finger traverse'. Above this the 'hand traverse' faced us. A crack slants diagonally up across a steep, smooth slab. It offers sloping and not very good hold to the hands, and the hold gets worse as it rises. The slab gives a little friction to the knees but not very much. Just below the leader's dangling feet in this passage the cliff drops to a small, turf-covered, but sloping, ledge. Thence it plunges down to the screes at the foot of the cliff. At the top of the 'hand traverse' the leader is about eighteen feet above this ledge and so out of reach.

Our party had been repulsed by this traverse some days before and we were ready to take it with great respect. So I. A. R. placed himself on the ledge with his heels dug in as deeply as the shallow, sloping turf would allow and Frazer and I held both his rope and our leader's from the best belays available some twenty-five feet over to the left. Fortunatus now threw himself on to the traverse. He arrived half-way quickly but stayed there rather a long time. His boots began to scrape about blindly. He exclaimed, 'Find me a rugosity! Find me a rugosity!' with some insistence. Slowly he concertina'd out until he was dangling at full arm-stretch by his finger-tips. He made no attempt to return. Suddenly with a grating screech (I have never heard a sound quite like it before or since) his hands slipped off and he dropped clear through the air on to the ledge below, where I. A. R. pounced on him with a Rugby collar. If they had rolled off they would have had a horrid sideways swing across the sheer face of the cliff and we could not have been certain that their ropes would have held them.

By this our ardour was a good deal dampened. Not so with Fortunatus. Before we could discuss the matter he hopped up to the beginning of the crack and sprang at it like a cat again. This time his impetus carried him further—right to the upper end, in fact, and correspondingly further from us and higher up over I. A. R.'s head, who was clearly preparing himself for the worst. We were just hoping that he would win the good holds that lead up from the top of the crack when the same process began again. Knees and toes searched hopelessly over the smooth rock. Obviously his strength was going fast. Horrible moments, which seemed to pass very slowly. Little by little his arms stretched out, his fingers could not last much longer. We were ready, there was nothing further to be done except to stand taut and expectant. Again came the shrill, 'Ar-r-r!' and, twisting in the air, down he bounced on to I. A. R.'s ledge. This time he landed squatting on its very verge and was in the act of diving off into the void, head-first, when he was clutched by the collar of his jacket and held for a second time. There he sat wringing his hands and ejaculating 'Curse me for a tailor! Curse me for a tailor!' again and again.

We should have laughed if the moment had not been still so full of suspense. For, entirely unshaken by these flights, he was all for reorganizing the party for a fresh attempt. I was to work the belay while Frazer joined I. A. R. on the ledge. A long argument between him and Frazer followed. 'We won't ask you to do anything, Frazer, that you don't want to, *but*, if you were to stand here underneath me you could take forty pounds off my weight or find me a rugosity for my feet, and then—' This was the moment when Frazer's adamantine streak came to our aid. With good sound sense he pointed out the weakness of the party's position if the ledge were still further crowded. Someone would be certain to be bowled off it. There was no hold there except a thin layer of soft grassy mud that was already much scored and cut up by our antics. The belay was too far to the side; whoever fell must swing through a whole quadrant of a circle. The probabilities were altogether too clear after these experiments. The vote went solidly three to one against a disappointed Fortunatus and we went off by an easier climb to the summit of the crags.

Not many days of Welsh climbing are as adventurous as this— happily. Excitement, for a moderate climber like myself, centres on the question 'Can I lead this pitch?' or, if following, 'Will I need any help from the rope?' Performance on the pitch soon settled this question definitely enough. There are polite leaders who, when the eager aspiring novice asks, 'Did you help me at all?' reply 'Why, of course not!' Later on one knows only too well how often the rope gives more than a 'merely moral' support. Leaders differ enormously in their conceptions of a properly managed rope. There are the gallant, who feel that climbing of any kind is 'hardly suitable for a lady' and translate their feelings into a strong pull and a long pull, whether one is within sight of wanting any or not. There are the *insouciant*, who take the rope in only as loops of it embarrass you in following up. There are the impatient, who think that a gentle tension always hastens matters. This theory has a good deal in it. Alpinists of slight experience who have done all their climbing behind a guide are sometimes surprised to discover something lacking when they join a guideless party.

There is no end to the ways in which leaders differ. There are those who curse when you lose your *savoir faire* and gasp helplessly that you 'can't' do it. There are those who are tenderly sympathetic or cajoling. There are the scientific who explain just how the balance must be distributed and which pressures must be applied. There are leaders who only climb on a limited range of superior routes. They like sound, spectacular, severe rocks and keep, without wearying, to the same repertory. There are those who can hardly bear to revisit a climb, they have such a craving for novelty and the unexpected. There are the historically minded, who like to puzzle out any route that has been described by the pioneers but are not known to have discovered any new ones for themselves. There are those who are so enamoured of 'virgin climbs' that they will grovel in any grass-cleft rather than touch rocks that have been desecrated by nail-marks. There are the jolly who keep to easy moderates and think a holiday should be a holiday, free from nerve strain and filled with cheerful chatter and, if possible, with song. The larger 'the crowd' for them, the better. And there is the grave and dignified leader who turns on his party if anyone ventures a remark to observe, solemnly, 'Silence while the leader is advancing!'

This wise remark is attributed to G. A. Solly, ex-President of the Fell and Rock Climbing Club and first conqueror, in the boot epoch, of the Eagle's Nest Arête Direct on Gable. A photograph of this in Abraham's *The Complete Mountaineer* used alternately to thrill me with desperate resolves or give me a sick sense that I should never become a *real* climber, in spite of all my desire and will. These fluctuations corresponded roughly with the beginnings and ends of holidays. In those days one hoped naïvely to take up the sport after each interval more or less where one left it, prowess unimpaired, strength unabated—as though climbing were a language one could learn progressively, so many new sentences and constructions mastered for good in every lesson. But it proved not so at all! To my bitter chagrin I seemed to go back to the beginning with each holiday—or to a point before the beginning, if such a thing is possible. For on my very first climbs I seemed to remember showing distinct aptitudes for the sport! It was infuriating to find myself, after some months of London life, sprawling helplessly on the rocks—as though one had never seen a mountain before. This was especially annoying when it happened under the eyes of companions who did not suffer such violent fluctuations, and who, as they knew one better, tended to become franker in expressing their opinions. So that sandwiched between days when heaven could not have been better—in such perfect equilibrium seemed body and spirit—were days of humiliated rage at one's ineptitude.

It was all a good preparation for later Alpine experience. The new guide who, on the first expedition compares you to a chamois because he finds that you do not need your hand held on a moraine, as so many of his clients do, later may hurt your feelings by allusions to mythical beings he describes as *de très bons Alpinists* and by classing you apparently as a *tourist d'une force moyenne*. These were shocks for a later period; they maliciously occur on the day you are most fatigued and out of form, when your buoyancy is least able to cope with them. It is all very well to suspect these things oneself but how they rankle when they appear as public truths.

However, the reply, the soothing restorative, comes probably a few days later, when suddenly the rocks, however smooth, seem to offer themselves as staircases, and everything is easy. On such days the Eagle's Nest Arête Direct seems just what one is looking for instead of a place to be avoided at all costs. One longs to oust the gentleman of 1905 from those holds and show him how it really ought to be tackled! These fluctuations are the penalty one pays for being what is called a 'temperamental climber'.

After a while I discovered that these fluctuations were not my own particular curse. To some degree nearly all my companions suffered from them, often for inexplicable reasons. There are a few happy mortals who can come straight from months of city life and lead, say, Route II on Lliwedd in a rain-storm without turning a hair. But one seemed to notice that these men of equable nerves rarely attempted to lead anything new or severe and exacting. They would put themselves for these behind a leader of another type who quite possibly might have been found a fortnight before stuck at the slab of the Milestone Buttress or paralysed by the exposure of the Idwal Slabs. Not that all 'temperamental' climbers become on occasion 'super-experts'. Far from it. How happy would I have been, if this were so!

CHAPTER II

EXPLORATIONS

New climbs for old—Gardening—The Devil's Kitchen—A treacherous block—The Holly-Tree Wall—An early glider—The great hour—Amphibian.

New climbs, by my second year, had become somewhat an obsession. This was largely the fault of I. A. R. who would at any time give up a perfect day, when any number of standard climbs, as yet unvisited by us, would have 'gone', to poke about round neglected corners of the crags in search of something new. In fact our association opened with a new climb, the Spiral Variant on Glyder Fach, as our third expedition. With Philip S. Minor I had been strolling up and down the road outside Ogwen Cottage, wondering what we should attempt together, when I. A. R., in a green corduroy suit and a blue 'onion-seller's' tam-o'-shanter, turned up to suggest the Oblique Gully. At the time this was a fearsome-seeming cleft to me, with great overhanging walls concealing pitches of I knew not what difficulty. I had never been on the Glyder Fach climbs before, with their peculiar balance and finger-tip grips, so different from the comforting horizontal-bar handholds of Tryfan. When we came out of the narrow exit chimney I felt that my mountain education had taken another step forward. A June day had turned as cold as December, dark grey clouds wrapped the mountain and finely divided water was blowing in gusts every way. P. S. Minor wisely decided that the Chasm Route was no place for a man of his scale. Once, according to him, in the Manchester Special Constabulary the Sergeant ordered all those with size No. 6 boots to take one pace forward, and so on up to size No. 11,

P. S. Minor had not yet had occasion to move. 'Size 12?' tried the Sergeant. In vain. 'Size 13!' No result. Then the Sergeant came to look at the boots himself and gave the problem up.

The Chasm is a curious place where the main mass of the Buttress near its top is split with an extraordinary deep cleft. It seems as you slide down it, or force yourself up, to give just enough room for the tip of your nose if you press the back of your head hard against the opposing wall. About the darkest point in the heart of the mountain the cleft turns at right angles and it is possible to get very firmly fixed here in what is known appropriately as 'the vertical vice'. Even when the rest of you is through, your boots are apt to stay obstinately behind, and double-jointed legs are useful. We two wriggled our way down and out and went out to join Minor who had walked round. I have rarely known a colder half-hour than our sandwich pause at the foot of the cliff. The wind lashed with whips of rain at the crags and made it very hard for me to see what I. A. R. was talking about when he tried to point out to me the lines of the main climbs above and sketched his idea of a new one.

Next day, as is the way with Welsh weather, all was changed. The cliffs were positively steaming in the sunshine as we roped up. Even I. A. R.'s usually melancholy black spaniel, Sancho Panza, was full of *joie de vivre*. In fact he became a positive nuisance to us through his eagerness to join in the climb. The Glyder Fach cliff was no place for him, however. Most new climbs in Wales involve a large amount of 'gardening'. This means cleaning away from the route anything which is not permanent—grass, earth, loose stones, wherever they may embarrass the climber. Panza, whining and bobbing about far down below at the foot of the climb, was always in the direct line of fire of anything we had to throw down. Whenever we disinterred some particularly large stone out of the recesses of a crack, and threw it sideways away from him, off he would charge to chase it, usually following it in a series of somersaults down the scree.

The most persistent and successful pioneers of this epoch in Wales, E. W. Steeple and Guy Barlow—the inventors of the

Grooved Arête Route on Tryfan—used to carry what they called a 'pioneer pick' for gardening purposes. White gashes, where mats of turf had been cut away, would appear mysteriously on the cliffs and the discerning would recognize their handiwork and speculate as to what they were 'up to'. Later, on some new climb of their creation, one could detect, in the character of the climbing, the special marks of their excellent taste in pitches, for many climbers have a distinctive style which is recognizably their own.

I. A. R.'s speciality in those days was high steps. Being loose in the limbs he seemed to like using footholds near his chin. Analytic and scientific by disposition he would sit at the top of a pitch and give me the most extraordinarily detailed instructions as to the precise movements which would bring me up with the least stress and strain. He was in fact of the cautious-controlled type *in excelsis*, tentative in his movements and always seemed able to come back without difficulty from any position, however experimental—a sign of conscious, deliberate planning of the balance. Perhaps through being not particularly strong, he seemed to me to be more reflectively aware of how his holds were supporting him than any other leader I had ever followed. I felt, as I reached the top of the first 'new climb' I had ever been on, like Christopher Columbus sighting a new world.

I have heard those who are not interested in new routes maintain that a taste for pioneering is governed, chiefly, by a desire for fame. If so, the fame is slight, ephemeral and worthless enough. But certainly the impulse to find new climbs is obscure. It is a part of that general passion for the unseen and the unvisited which is behind so much travel and exploration. A passion not less strong because it is not easy to justify rationally. After all, most deserts are deserts because they are not worth much in themselves. Central Asia is under-populated for very good reasons. But to come up some steep and, at a distance, impossible-looking wall of rock into a grassy corner of the cliff that you know has never been visited before by a human being, to sit there speculating upon whether you can force a way onwards up the wall above, to try half a dozen lines before you hit on the secret of the escape, is to go through a range of elemental feelings—not less enjoyable because it is so surprising that one should be able to enjoy them within sight of motor-cars on a main road.

The quest for new routes can become a mania, of course, leading one, since the possible lines on attractive cliffs are limited, to unfruitful haunts on disintegrating, or vegetation smothered, or overhanging or waterlogged masses of rock that the sagacious have long ago decided are not worth investigation. One such near Gorphwysfa, too small and too broken up to yield anything really interesting, occupied us all one wet Easter. It became known to us as Lethargica, either because it was suitable for wet and lazy weather or because we were too sluggish to think of anything better or because we happened to be suffering at the time from a mild attack of an influenza that was being written up in the newspapers as a cousin of *encephalitis lethargica*. Wrapped up to the limit of our resources and repelling the proffered local remedy for the disease (a stocking full of hot bacon and potatoes to be wound tightly round the throat), we tramped out daily in the rain to go through the series of hopeful surmises and final disappointments that are the normal fate of the hunter of new climbs.

But at times there was better game on foot. There were four days one Whitsuntide, sandwiched between two night-journeys from and back to London, which will always be for me an epitome of all that Welsh climbing has to offer of its best. The car from Bangor Station rushed up between the stone walls in the early morning through an air filled with hawthorn scent over the moist freshness of the young uncrumpling fern. The great barrier of the Glyders ahead was in sunshine as we swept up the last winding mile, but Tryfan was still shadowy above the lake as we breakfasted at the slate table that stands like an altar in Ogwen Cottage Garden above the water. We used to pass the tea-pot and the porridge out of the window and carry them across on sunny and windless mornings.

C. F. Holland and I. A. R. were waiting for me. Holland had been a white-faced invalid fresh from hospital when I last saw him, with one arm in a plaster-cast from shoulder to elbow. A piece of shell had taken away much of the bone between and the surgeons were building up a bridge out of slivers bent over from the sound sections. His prospects of climbing much again seemed poor and I remember feeling sad for him as he told us of his days on the Central Buttress of Scafell with Herford before the War. Short, tough, virile, and, as far as I could see, not knowing what fear meant, he was not the man, however, to let a mere smashed-up arm interfere for long with his wishes. He had been in the mountains all through the spring and news had come from time to time of most improper ventures for a plaster-cast to attempt on the crags. When we met, I found that he had recently developed one of his characteristic enthusiasms—for the Devil's Kitchen of all places.

The Devil's Kitchen is one of the most notorious climbs in North Wales and deserves its ill-fame. It is the great cleft up in the decaying limestone wall above Llyn Idwal, a dark, dank, noisome ravine with slimy, rotting cliffs echoing at all seasons with the splash of its waterfall, an ill-omened place associated with fatal accidents and daunting escapes from disaster. To this grim spot Holland had suddenly taken a liking, after tiring of daily ascents of the Black Cleft—a somewhat similar affair on a smaller scale over in the Llanberis Pass. When we arrived we found he had been making a series of solitary ascents and descents of the climb. Nothing would satisfy him but that we should begin by coming with him to be convinced that it was not nearly so difficult or dangerous as people supposed. It was quite a sound climb, he insisted, and if it were in the Lake District people would be going up it every day! Cleverly he asked me whether I wouldn't rather like to be the only woman to have been up the thing.

On the wave of his unquenchable ardour we set off, stopping at Idwal shore for a swim. At the door of the Kitchen one goes into shadow and the huge, bulging, 400-foot walls seem to hang over one threateningly. Daylight comes down through the scimitar-shaped gap above and you make a watery way over a large jammed boulder and up by a semi-detached pinnacle from which the inner recesses and the climb itself are revealed. It is easy climbing so far, and sometimes a tourist who has penetrated to this point believes himself to have 'been up the Kitchen' and tells you so with emphasis. But the real climb up to the plateau above is quite another matter. Perhaps these pitches up the South Wall would not be really difficult elsewhere. But the water falling noisily down, the gloom, the splashed ooze everywhere, the peculiar texture of the rocks, rather like slippery and brittle toffee, combine to make the scene far from cheerful to a would-be climber. Holland's spirits, however, rose as we approached. He had lately become a devotee of 'rubbers' (gym-shoes), even on wet ground, where most climbers—bar the latest 'tigers'—find that they slip as treacherously as on ice. The rubber shoe had just come in and divided the climbing world as sharply as later the question of oxygen or no oxygen for Everest was to do. 'Dangerous and dishonest, and quite out of the true tradition of the sport', said one party. To which the other replied, 'What about the nails in your boots, the rope and your carefully chosen ice-axe? Equally they make climbs much easier.' The same dispute arises with every technical innovation which in any way changes the standard of difficulty. I am not sure that the Devil's Kitchen was much easier in rubbers, but Holland insisted that we should only enjoy the climb if we joined him in this footgear. So, with for my part a feeling that it would be good to get the thing over, we took off our boots, left them to be fetched later, and got ready.

The first pitch was a winding discontinuous sort of crack in the steep wall with a number of wobbly holds and a few small spikes that seemed so likely to crack away in the hand that one hardly liked to pull on them. It leads to a little sloping shelf, the size of a small door-mat, and another rather similar crack goes on upwards to a fairly roomy sort of bulge or bracket. Roomy here means that you can stand on it and turn round if you want to. From this bracket a line of small bosses leads sideways over one or two flanges, where semi-secure black rocks stick out, to a point just above the lip of the waterfall, whence you can step on to solid level ground and the climb is over. Holland, with the ease of a bird hopping from twig to twig, flipped up the first crack in a moment. Remarking that it was hardly worth while stopping, he went on up the second, and began to shout down praises of the holds and especially of the belay he had on his airy perch. I was glad to hear of this, for as soon as I was launched up the crack the holds all seemed to me of the sort that really will not bear inspecting, much less using! Spray from the waterfall was splashing all round. Its racket made communication with the others difficult, and I was very glad to reach the half-way ledge, and still happier to join Holland, rather breathlessly, on his bracket. His belay proved to be surprisingly reassuring and I held his rope while he went off along the traverse. One or two of the blocks he passed seemed to be not far off giving way and I made a mental note of them before turning to bring I. A. R. up out of the pit towards me. He too seemed glad enough to be up nearer the sunlight and further from the nerve-racking din of the cascade. We changed ropes round the belay, and, calling to Holland that I was coming, I made my way as warily as I could across the giddy gangway of the traverse. I was almost on terra-firma, when with a snap like a mouse-trap one of the chief holds of the passage, a jutting block that I had finished stepping on for more than a minute, broke away, seemingly of its own accord, and toppled down into the chasm. It was startling confirmation of one's suspicions about the whole place, and I. A. R. came across even more gingerly than I had. On the whole, I suppose I was glad to have done it, but I have never felt anxious to do it again. This was in 1918 after a long spell of, I think, deserved neglect. From time to time the climb comes into a brief vogue among the 'tigers' of the moment. It is being much climbed just now. Perhaps, if frequented enough, it will become sounder. But that is not enough for me; they will have to divert the waterfall before I fancy going up it again.

Collecting the boots, we dashed off to the Western Gully of Glyder Fach, a climb of a different class, far more difficult but infinitely safer. It is a strenuous as well as a delicate affair, and after my night journey I was tired enough before we got up it. My arms felt as weak as lambs' tails as I waggled them over the rocks looking for non-existent holds. The main long scoop-pitch is climbed by jamming the knees: you screw them into a corner and they stick. I have never been able to see exactly why, and I watched Holland's progress upwards as though he were a magician.

Our great dream was a climb above the Idwal Slabs, since known as the Holly-Tree Wall. It had been I. A. R.'s pet project for years, ever since he had been second to Mrs Daniell in her climb, Hope (first christened Minerva to mark the fact that it came from feminine skill and prudence). Hope—the name looked forward to the projected completion of the climb by a continuation up the steeper cliffs above—is an extraordinarily elegant route. It goes up for 400 feet over solid, smooth, perfectly clean and sound slabs. A line of holds—pockets and wrinkles in the surface of the unbroken rock—just large enough and near enough together for comfort, leads from one ledge to another by stretches of about eighty feet. Where they are needed, neat little belaying-pins appear as though set there on purpose. The slabs are steep enough to give you, if you have not been climbing for a while, a sense of high exposure as you tiptoe up them. They are just half an hour from Ogwen, tucked away in a sheltered corner of Cwm Idwal. How many an evening have I spent upon them, working out with I. A. R, new variations across them, crawling down in rainstorms (recommendable, as wet clothes cling to the surface of the slabs and assist descent), or going up to look into new notions about continuations upwards. Always our eyes came back to the same point. Right in the middle of the upper wall, flanked on all sides by smooth, apparently holdless faces of rock, was a holly-tree. It was self-evident that, if only one could reach it and then go on upwards from it, the Proper Route must pass by this holly-tree. But, as we had often proved, reaching it would be no easy matter, nor, to an eye looking from above, would an escape upwards from the recess in which it grew be easy. Our explorations had led to this result, that a party in form would be needed and a perfect day for the attempt. If it was successful, we should have on the cliff nearest to Ogwen a continuous climb of 700 feet in length, counting Hope, as our reward. A climb on the soundest, most interesting kind of rock and with fine possibilities of natural continuations still higher. This was the project; it was familiar enough to us all—in fact all through the winter I had been receiving drawings of the cliffs from I. A. R. with new suggestions for attempts.

I. A. R. had to take a rest day, and Holland's idea of a 'day off' for me before the big effort, was to take me up the Bochlwyd Buttress and the Hawk's Nest Climb on Glyder Fach. As I lay in bed that night, wondering if my stiffness would ever let me get up again, I went over in my mind all our many previous attempts. They had been at times very discouraging, but we had never been there in really good weather and feeling strong. Perhaps this time the fates would be kind at last!

The perfection of the weather was arresting as we walked up past the shores of Llyn Idwal next morning. Hot though the morning was, one of us was carrying an ice-axe—of which more anon. By the boathouse was Cochram, the painter, at work upon a large water-colour, with an enthusiastic amateur at his elbow exclaiming at each stroke of his brush. He told us a wonderful story of a brother painter who was up there one windy day doing the enormous charcoal sketch of the Devil's Kitchen that now adorns Ogwen Cottage Coffee-Room. Whether the devil did not approve of his art, or for whatever other reason, there came suddenly a most astonishing roar of wind in the Kitchen and the Llyn waters rose in water-spouts and came charging across towards him. The unlucky artist seized his work with both hands—it is as large as a sail—and then the blast struck him. Off they went, sketch and sketcher together, clear up into the sky, right over the wire fence and souse into the pool among the peat-hags

below the path on the other side. After this the artist finished his
sketch of the Kitchen inside Ogwen Cottage—which is supposed
by some to account for the results.

We were soon up Hope and gathered, in carefully controlled
excitement, at the foot of the problem. We became very business-
like. I was stationed up to the right, round a corner by a belay, while
I. A. R., with Holland to give him a shoulder and an axe, if he
needed them, went to the attack. They chose a corner well to the
right of the now usual start. (The corner that later became the start
of Other Kingdom or, as it has recently been called, the Piton
Climb.) Unfortunately for me this took them out of sight and I
could only judge progress from the voices and the movement of
the rope. Presently a kind of crisis seemed to develop. I was told
to flick the rope up, if I could, over the crest of the flange of rock
that was hiding them from me. To my joy it went at once where
we wanted, and a moment later a call to me to come round showed
that a first success had been gained. There was I. A. R. comfortably
standing on a ledge that had several times resisted our former
attempts to reach it. Now it was Holland's turn, and, when his legs
had finished waving in the air and he had declared the place quite
impossible without assistance from the rope, it was mine. I looked
at the pitch aghast. So far as I could see, there were no holds
anywhere. I looked up at Holland, grinning down diabolically to
me with rope over his shoulder ready to lift a mountain if necessary.
'Do you suppose you can pull me up bodily?' I asked, feeling like
a piece of macaroni.

As everyone knows, pulling a person up bodily is not at all like
giving them some help. Holland's cheerful 'Come along!' was
encouraging and as best I could I addressed myself to the pitch.
There was a kind of sloping scoop for an elbow but it was covered
with compressed slime, and there were some wrinkles like those on
a walnut on the other side of the corner but I couldn't find any
way of keeping my feet on them. 'Pull!' I said, 'pull!' and the rope
grew tighter and tighter: 'Pull!' and I could hear Holland breathing

deeper and deeper. But nothing further happened. I didn't soar aloft at all. I merely hung there with my toes just off the ledge I had started from and my head jammed in a recess under the ledge Holland was standing on. He declared that he was 'endeavouring to pull up half the mountain as well' and that the turf ledge he was standing on was starting to come away! Plainly this would never do. And besides, a start to a climb that invited the assistance of an axe seemed unsatisfactory. So the two above renewed their explorations. Soon I was watching enthralled a series of climbing manœuvres that led them across and down to the left to a belay at the head of what is now the First Pitch. And then it was my turn again. Somehow I struggled up it, I seem to recall, largely by fingernail holds in a thin mud that came away as I scratched.

After this initial pitch every movement of the climb was a delight. Small recessed holds led across and up a clean steep rounded slab of rock, pockmarked as though some biting acid had been splashed upon it. How firmly those rough hollows took the toes of one's rubbers! In a very few minutes I. A. R. was writhing among the prickles of the holly-tree. It was a very robust growth, leaving little or no room to squeeze oneself past between its trunk and the walls of the deep little cleft it grows in. Deep enough for us all three to gather there, though I was left perched amid the worst of the prickles wishing I had on the leather coat I sometimes wear in winter.

It is impossible to be happier than we were in this strange lofty little eyrie. The wall is so steep that the lower reaches of the slabs, though tilted themselves at a fair angle, flatten out beneath. You look out to the dark opposite wall of Y Garn and the grim line of the Devil's Kitchen cliffs on one side, and on the other, across the opening of the Ogwen Valley with its glimpse of raft-like Anglesey, the summit slopes of the Carnedds look infinitely remote and high in a dim haze of sunshine. Ordinarily all this, and especially the far-awayness of the Carnedd summits, is more than half a pain. Its beauty is full of aches and queer qualms very like hunger. Hunger for what, though? But now, in our Holly-Tree Niche, I found I could face up to all those half-intolerable quickenings from the scene. One need not either smother the yearnings or submit to their ache. There were ways of changing them into something quite different, and in this discovery one seemed to grasp, fleetingly, both the reason for our ecstasy of the moment and, ultimately, the best reason why we climb. In this illumination a new person was really looking out on the world.

Down below we could see Cochram still at work by the lake-side, a tiny active figure, with his amateur now sitting on a boulder beside him. The buff rocks were warm to the hand, a light breeze tempered the sunshine and we were alone in a world of our own, in a place that had hitherto only existed, so we felt, in our imaginations. If one could land suddenly in Robinson Crusoe's island itself (not Juan Fernandez or any other island that a ship has ever sailed to) one would know, I fancy, something of the same exultation.

Now began a determined struggle with the narrow crack above the tree. As Holland later wrote: 'We inspected the fierce-looking crack that now confronted us and which is invisible from below. First one tried to climb it, then the other. We stood on the tree in turn and sweated in vain attempts to ascend; in turn we fell exhausted into the safe but painful embrace of the tree. It was no use; the victory was with the enemy; we could do no more.' Why it beat us I do not quite know, since a few days later, I. A. R. hit on a method which took him up it easily. But this time first I. A. R. and then Holland wrestled arduously and pertinaciously with it, but in vain. Down went our spirits like a barometer before a thunder-storm. Had we triumphed so far to be beaten in the end, and was this prickly recess to be the delusive end, the grave of our over-mounted hopes? In a grim disconsolate mood Holland went down to traverse out to the left, without much expectation in any of us that any possible route lay that way. Soon he was far out on the bare, almost vertical wall at about our level. He felt, as he said afterwards, 'like a sparrow on the housetops, though without a sparrow's advantages as to the methods at his disposal of removing himself therefrom'. But to us he looked like a little eagle with his aquiline nose and intent fierce air as he stood poised on a narrow ledge scanning the rocks above him. Twice he levered himself up and twice his boot-nail slipped from an almost imperceptible toe-scrape and he 'dangled on handholds that were none too satisfying'. Then quickly his hands went up to what were evidently mere finger-tip holds, up went one boot—it seemed to nothing—and, with a swift springy movement, he was rising. A moment later his knee was on the crest of the wall and he was over the difficulty.

Soon we were beside him, back in a rapture again. To have just the holds you need on a first ascent of such a wall, no more and no less, gives every step the flavour of a victory. At the hard step there is almost one hold too few, or rather the holds are small enough and distant enough to make you really enjoy the large round handholds and the comfortable bay in the crags at which you arrive by these means. In the bay we sat down to relish the moment. Everyone who has enjoyed a first ascent will understand our sublime content.

Reverie can still follow the remainder of the climb step by step. I like to recall most the turn and turn about mood in which Holland and I. A. R. divided the pitches above. They worked out very evenly, giving two more minor climaxes. At the top, on one of the wider quartz-floored terraces that make this part of the Glyder Fawr such a regal lounging ground, we sat down to review again what had happened. We were all feeling a little surprised at our good fortune. It struck us all, however, that another start to the climb, if we could find one, would be preferable. Suddenly the happy notion came— Why not go down the climb at once, and look at the possibilities again from above? Also, why not take the opportunity to clean away one or two bulges of turf that had proved awkward? We regretted this last after-thought a little later. The turf as we threw it down disgorged showers of moist earth that spread out over the reaches below and filled the holds with a sprinkling of greasy mud, horribly troublesome to feet in rubbers. We were cursing ourselves heartily by the time we reached the holly-tree to find the stretch below only manageable with a rope doubled round its trunk—so desperately slippery had the holds become through our gardening. The alternative line for the first pitch (now the standard route) proved to need much cleaning. However, in the end we disinterred a sufficiency of holds and got down it, only to begin at once to go up it again. We had to test its adequacy as the opening pitch of the climb. By this time, we were beginning to feel a little like a complicated human pendulum doomed to swing up and down on our climb forever.

A year or so later more cleaning revealed another finger-hold just where it was most needed on this first pitch. Recently again this has disappeared, to the regret of many and the joy of some. The pitch is now approximately of the same difficulty as on the first ascent. So climbs change.

With this route—since Hope gives some 400 feet and the Holly-Tree Wall about 230—a very long climb is available on Glyder Fawr. Above, by way of Abraham's Chimney and a stretch known as 'the lava slab', it is possible to continue over perfect rock, interesting throughout, right on to the main upper cliff of the mountain; and with the Central Arête for a finish, you have something like 1400 feet of good climbing.

Our fourth day took us up the Great Ridge of Criegiau Gleision—aerial climbing on rock that made one uneasy by its appearance of fragility. And so to finish off with a struggle up the Gribin Angular Chimney and a slide down the Monolith Crack before the night journey back to London. How the contrast shook one! To go back to gloves and high-heeled shoes, pavements and taxicabs. Walking with an umbrella in Piccadilly one felt as though with a little more strain one would become a case of divided personality. This time yesterday! One lay munching a dry sandwich on a rocky ledge, plucking at a patch of lichen and listening to the distant roar of the white Ogwen Falls. It wavered, faded, and grew again louder and louder as the breeze caught it. What had such moments

to do with to-day, and what reckoning could compare the personality now moving through the noisy street on her way to meet
people who knew her in one guise only, with that other personality
that came to life only among such a different order of existence
and was known only to such other minds and assessed by them for
such other qualities. The strangeness of the dual life made, in those
days, a cleft, a division in my mind that I struggled in vain to build
some bridge across. Kind, firm friends would say, 'All good things
come to an end', or 'You can't expect all life to be a holiday'. But
to me, and to climbers before and after me, this was no question
of holidays. It went down into the very form and fabric of myself.

Oh these spring days!
A nameless little moutain
In the morning haze.

MATSUO BASHO (1644–94)
Translated by H. G. Henderson

CHAPTER III

VARIATIONS

A fall on the Far East Cracks—How not to patch a knee and how to catch a climber—An avalanche in Shallow Gully—Winter climbing—Rescue—A night out with the Waits—Snowdon Summit—The Birch-Tree Terrace Climb—A nap on a slab—W. E. Durham—Other Kingdom—The open secret.

A few days later came news from Holland and I. A. R. that made me jump. There had been great doings after I left. More ascents of the Holly-Tree Wall, a new and apparently hair-raising climb—the Oblique Buttress—on Glyder Fach and a series of climbs on Lliwedd. It was the final episode on Lliwedd that gave me the shock. Holland, always very adroit with knee-jam methods in climbing, had been destroying the knees of his breeches at an alarming rate. Blodwen, the chambermaid at Pen-y-Gwyrd, used to get half a crown from him for each repairing job she did. This was becoming, since he tore them through every second day, a serious drain upon his pocket, so he gave her instructions to find something to patch with that would be guaranteed not to wear through again. What she found was a piece of excellent Axminster carpet, and for a while Holland was very proud of a red and green decoration that distinguished him from all other visitors in the region. It had its disadvantages, however, and from these derives my story.

He and I. A. R. had been climbing without a pause through a long spell of fine weather. Perhaps they grew stale. Whatever the reason, they were suddenly attacked by a fit of 'out of form' mistakes that nearly put an end to them both. One evening after a long day on the East Peak—up and down the Shallow Gully, the Great

Chimney and Route II—they had gone up the Central Chimney as far as the Summer House. Puzzled, as others have been, by the route ahead, they came down with the intention of working it out thoroughly on another day. And next morning they were back early at the foot of the climb. The Central Chimney Route starts with a steep fifty-foot groove, then comes a traverse to the right with a tricky step up over a very steep exposed corner. Now the evening before they had been twice across the passage, up and down, without trouble or hesitation. This morning, however, I. A. R. when leading found himself suddenly and without warning at a loss in the very middle of the tricky movement. As he wrote to me, the experience was utterly unexpected, something he had never known when leading before. It was like forgetting a familiar name. In a flash he forgot everything about the pitch, he didn't know where any of the holds were, or what he had done, or what he should do, and this in a position half-way between one balance and another, a position in which it was impossible to stop and wait. He was just beginning to fall off when his hand, wandering over the rock behind him and out of his sight, happened on a hold and saved him. Now unexpected holds are not common on such pitches on Lliwedd. He lost no time in rejoining Holland in the Chimney and explaining that he was 'off' leading for the day, and they agreed that they had better go to something easier.

They chose the Far East Cracks on Lliwedd's eastern-most peak, partly because Holland had lately been frequenting it with Odell and others, and it was new to I. A. R. Holland had invented a special direct finish of his own that he was anxious to demonstrate. So down they went; I. A. R., still rather shaken, going first so as to have the rope above him. He had hardly come to the first halting-place when, with an exclamation, down came Holland sailing through the air on top of him! What had happened was this. He had begun his descent by curling his carpet-clad knee into the recesses of the groove in his favourite fashion, quite forgetting that it was not as his knees usually were. It slipped out, and, as at that instant he had no other holds, off he came. He landed luckily astride I. A. R.'s neck and the two of them managed to stay where they were. Though the distance they had to fall is not very great, it might have been quite enough!

It has often been remarked that mischances tend to come in threes. They agreed that they had better be very careful indeed about the third as they walked over to the Far East Peak. All went well up the climb, Holland leading, until they reached the beginning of his new direct finish. The whole thing is a long V-shaped groove, of the type so characteristic of Lliwedd, like a slightly opened book and very steep. It is punctuated by little patches of grass in the back of the V, which make ledges on which the leader can rest and the second man join him. At the top, the groove is closed by a wall, but there are ways of escaping to easier ground on the right and left which are usually taken. Holland's direct finish went up quite straight for sixty feet or so, very exposed and even steeper than the groove below. The crags underneath plunge down for 400 feet and the steep screes at their foot make the height seem much greater.

I. A. R. was placed in the last reach of the groove, standing on an earth patch which is about the size of a dinner plate, playing the rope round a belay as big as his thumb. Holland went on to attack the wall above. He had climbed up about fifty-five feet when I. A. R. was alarmed to notice that the method required for finishing the pitch was that very identical knee-jamming that had led to the mischance in the Central Chimney. The rope meanwhile was finding the belay most unaccommodating and kept slipping off as it was paid out. The leader's progress now came to a halt and I. A. R. became more and more uneasy. Holland was stretched out, his hands high up on what were evidently none too good holds. The carpet-clad knee was writhing and writhing in a shallow furrow; the other toe at full stretch was on a small hold below. Then it was brought slowly up to a sloping nick to the side; it slipped off; and I. A. R. could see Holland's whole body shake with the extra tension.

His own position was then described by Archer Thompson, a

connoisseur in exposed situations, as follows: 'The spot thus reached is, hardly a landing-place—it accommodates one foot only, but the desired rest can be obtained by leaning well back against a projection; in this half-recumbent attitude above and athwart the crack we are in a good position to enjoy the circumambient air, a wide view of the face, and an unobstructed outlook over Cwm Dyli'.[4]

He was beginning to expect bad trouble and fortunately just then caught sight of a flange of rock on the right of his groove at about the level of his shoulders. Quickly he levered himself across the groove until he was lying braced with both feet on one wall and a shoulder on the other. Then he looked again to see how the leader was getting on. Holland was still in the same position wrestling with the same problem. Up again came the toe to the sloping nick, wavered on it, then the whole body lifted and the toe slipped off! Out came the carpet knee that should have taken the weight and the jolt plucked his straining finger-tips from their holds. Without a word Holland slipped down a little, then fell out backwards and came like a loose sack, head-over-heels, down the wall. At this instant I. A. R. noticed that the rope had again worked off the belay.

A body is travelling fast by the time it has fallen fifty feet down cliffs of the angle of these. I. A. R. avers that Holland was making quite a loud whizzing noise in his fall before he caught him, and that he swerved a good deal in his flight. There was no use now in worrying about the rope; the thing to do was to catch the climber. Actually he landed head down, face out, between the cliff and I. A. R., who clutched him wildly round the thighs. Then a moment passed during which, rather slowly, they realized that they had not gone; they were still on the crags and alive; and then Holland began to climb up round the outside of I. A. R.'s bridged body and re-establish himself right-side up on the little grass ledge.

The first thing now was a solemn lighting of Holland's pipe.

---

4   *The Climbs on Lliwedd*, p. 19.

I. A. R. says that Holland's hands were absolutely steady as he sheltered the match. Then the vitally important question of the plaster-cast round Holland's arm had to be looked into. It proved to be a good deal chipped, but the arm inside was all right.

Holland now was for having 'another shot' at the pitch. He always seemed to me not to know what fear is, and this was an example of his indomitability. But I. A. R. had been watching and had had enough. So he vetoed the motion. They went down instead, as quickly as they knew how, to easy ground. This evidently was right, for in ten minutes' time the effect of the shock showed. Though Holland remained as cheerful and composed as ever, puffing his pipe tranquilly as he worked his way down, every muscle soon began to shake and shiver. They were glad to get off the climb, coil up the rope and go off to Gorphwysfa for a soothing drink.

Later I came to know the scenes of these adventures better. Easter days, when there were snow-banks at the foot of the gullies; Whitsuntide days, when hawthorn whitened Cwm Dyli and overhung the bathing-pool. Odd week-ends whenever I could fit them in, framed between night journeys in which the endless serried lights of Crewe shunting-yards seemed the great gateway to the hills. Through a week of cloudless June weather, with Holland, with H. M. and Pat Kelly, I almost lived on Lliwedd's East Peak. We would get to the foot of the Avalanche Route or Paradise while it was still early, go up and down all the summer day, and would be lingering by the summit cairn late into the dusk. The sea-gleams turned from gold to silver, Siabod and the Glyders grew smooth and blue with haze before we ran down back to Pen-y-Gwryd for a specially arranged cold ten-o'clock supper. It seemed impossible to go down while the shadow of Crib Goch was still creeping up and the crest of Lliwedd glowing in the last sunshine. How could one sit at a dinner-table through the most beautiful hour of the day? We went up most of the well-known Lliwedd climbs, though not the Far East Cracks! I remember once the string of Holland's sack breaking, while I was struggling to move quickly down the

Shallow Gully, and thinking my last hour had come as a shower of missiles began to bound and whizz past me. There is not much room to share with an avalanche in the Shallow Gully. But they were nothing more than oranges and we picked them up 'good and juicy' on the scree.

Halcyon days, sunny, windless, the rocks dry and clean under our rubbers and Holland climbing tirelessly and magnificently, up the most hopeless-looking reaches of the slabs. His air of a Roman legionary fitted well with his iron confidence and grim cheerfulness. I shall never visit Lliwedd without thinking of him. I owe him some of my very best climbing days.

To each group of climbers who are exploring Lliwedd extensively for themselves for the first time, its climbs—with their own variations—come to seem in a sense their possession. No mountain seizes hold of its devotees more strongly, and the bond is capable of appearing reciprocal. The very difficulty of identifying many of the routes, exactly, makes a climb seem more one's own, and it may reasonably be wished that detailed descriptions of them did not exist. Then every fresh visitor would taste more fully the savour of exploration. Mallory once remarked as much to I. A. R. Coming from one who had put so many splendid new climbs on the crags, and in the Climbers' Club Book at Gorphwysfa, he had to admit that it was perhaps Satan rebuking sin. This was just before he left for that last time for Everest in 1924—to reach, as Odell, who saw him last, still thinks possible, the supreme point of any climber's ambition.

—

It is one of the advantages of winter snow-climbing that all one's routes are new—at least they are not quite as they are on other occasions. A scree-filled gully in Snowdon's upper cliff, or a shoulder of Crib-y-Ddysgl which you could walk up in summer, is a mountaineering problem when muffled in snow and perhaps streaked with ice. For some reason, in Wales, the delicious habit prevails of combining strenuous climbing with late rising, and the short days—so shortened—turn most serious winter climbs into dramatic races against the dusk, with often a doubt, against which to measure one's judgment, whether what is ahead will take too long or not. From near its foot an average snow-lined gully can look very deceptive indeed. The lower pitch or two are buried in drifts, and you begin by tramping out a staircase with surprising ease in the floury snow. It compacts itself under the boot-sole if you press it gently twice. Your hopes rise; all you see ahead is one not too bad-looking portal in the crags, with the side-walls draped in white, and a cap of snow on the boulder that spans its cleft. Above, the angle of the cliff always seems to ease off and, unless you know the place well, you will be tricked into thinking that your main difficulties will soon be over. On closer approach, the white drapery shows itself to be ice and the floor of the gully under the chockstone may be growing a crop of ice-stalagmites to meet the gleaming fringe of icicles that gets in your way as you come to grips with the obstacle. Time passes quickly for the leader, as he tries to uncover holds from beneath this mantle or to fashion adequate nicks in the ice itself. It passes less rapidly for the others whose toes and fingers are not being kept warm by such vigorous exercises. But these wintry waiting-rooms, if not comfortable, are surpassingly decorated. The enclosing walls of the gully fall majestically on either side and are a giant frame for the snow-clad opposite slopes and the dark fretted waters of the Llyn below. And upon this vast complex symmetry of structure a multitude of microscopic patterns is mounted. Frost crystals in thousands of feather-whirls and star-diapers crust each flange, altering with every angle at which the winds have brushed them. Where the rock is bare it glows in the frost with colours unknown to the summer, as though each morsel were of a semi-precious substance, and every blade of grass, wisp of heather or sprig of bilberry is charged with filaments finer than the eye can follow.

At last the leader—elbow-deep in bosses of snow, or clinging to his implanted axe—struggles up over the bulge above. You follow, only to find that the general slope is rather steeper, if anything, and that a similar but larger obstacle is frowning down upon you. On the best of these days, you are still digging and kicking a staircase up the snows as the last daylight fails and the moon silvers your way to the summit. Such rare unearthly climaxes explain why some climbers—in spite of the normal Welsh winter weather—are almost as devoted to winter climbing as to summer.

Unhappily, rain and cloud are more often the climber's lot than snow. Only a mere white sprinkle falls on the upper 600 feet of the peaks, making the rocks chill and slippery. Too little to give snow-climbing, too much to allow good rock-climbing. It was on such a day that six of us set off for Lliwedd's West Peak. At the foot I joined the Kellys' rope on the usual Central Gully and West Peak climb, leaving my sister, Will McNaught and Herbert Carr to take the near-by parallel route from the foot of the West Peak. The rocks were wet and cold, the well-known slab seemed very hard to numbed fingers and above it we went briskly to warm ourselves up again. Thinking we were the last party off the mountain, we ran down care-free to a hot bath and dry clothes at P.-y-G. It was dark on the road and a thin rain was falling. Not till we took our places at the dinner-table did anyone realize that a party was missing. They were neither in the billiard-room, nor in the lounge, nor in the bar, nor in the bath. In a few moments their absence ceased to be a joke and became worrying. Perhaps, however, as parties have been known to do, they had preferred, in the darkness, to go down by the grassy slopes by Cwm-y-Llan into Cwm Gwynant rather than take the more complicated way down over Lliwedd Bach. If so, they would arrive, wet and weary and a subject for chaff, about 9.30 P.M. Dinner over, I went out to look at the weather. It was getting worse and steady rain was falling. Everyone was keeping up an ostentatious cheerfulness. By ten o'clock, beneath this, there was a general conviction that an accident had probably occurred. It became impossible to remain inactive any longer. Taking a lantern

I walked with Frazer the mile up the road to Gorphwysfa. The wind came in roaring gusts round the corners of the road and the sound of the streams in the grey opaque gulfs about us was a gloomy accompaniment to our imaginings. Just below Gorphwysfa, a gap came for a moment in the clouds and through it there showed an unmistakable flicker of light from the direction of Lliwedd. Then instantly the clouds closed down again and it was gone. It was hard to be certain that we had seen anything, but we ran back to Pen-y-Gwryd, with some of our apprehensions lifted. I, at least, was convinced that they were perched somewhere on that vast wall of darkness.

Inside, a rather incredulous rescue party was putting on boots, collecting hot drinks, packing up blankets and brandy. We set out, twelve of us, at 11 P.M. Everyone had had a long day's climbing already, but that seemed to make no difference to the pace. Ghostly luminous figures appeared and disappeared about the lanterns as we tramped up the track and across the marshes. Holland, with shoulders hunched under a vast sack, seeming to walk through rather than round the boulders. Frazer, his immense height caricatured by the candle's gleam. The gnome-like figure of O'Malley, philosophically puffing at his pipe. I. A. R. agitatedly endeavouring to prevent the three men with lanterns from getting together and outstripping the rest. The rain beat down upon us and there came no second opening in the clouds.

Just beyond the outlet from Llyn Llydaw is a short steep slope. As we topped it, out of the darkness ahead came a sudden hail. It was Herbert's halloo. In a moment we realized that all was still well. Dread of what we might find on the screes vanished and I was brought back to the happy reality by a violent smack on the back. Relief flowed in like an intoxication, and from midnight till dawn a spirit of freakish conviviality animated the rescuers. The hail had sounded so near and clear that for a while we were all persuaded that the missing party must have got down the cliff somehow and be shouting to us from only a little way up the grass-slopes ahead.

But Lliwedd's acoustic trickery is famous. Instead of being within a few minutes' distance, they were perched high on a tiny shelf two-thirds of the way up Lliwedd's West Peak. It took more than a little shouting, however, to establish this. After a few experiments, Frazer seemed to have by far the most piercing voice. So he was made spokesman. But the other eleven seemed to be brimming over with messages for above. Gusty shouts from Herbert were wafted down only to be lost in the animated babble round the lantern. We fell into silence to hear him, and he, in the clouds, would choose that moment to strain an attentive ear. We moved up nearer Lliwedd to improve communications. The nearer we went the less we could hear! The cliff wall for some reason throws sounds outwards from its base and from its foot Herbert was as inaudible to us as we were to him.

I stood a little apart watching all this—as bewildered as though I had strayed out of the first act of a tragedy into a farce. At last Frazer's yells seemed to be reaching them and faint return hails built themselves up into sentences. Just where the climbers were was our problem. The West Peak is an enormous expanse of precipice and to climb either down or up to a party in the dark without exact information would be a hopeless venture. The question was complicated too by the looseness of some of the upper reaches. To sweep them from their ledge with an avalanche of dislodged *débris* would be a poor way of coming to their assistance!

A highly interesting debate developed. One group held that two strong climbers could and should climb up to them carrying lanterns, presumably, in their teeth. Others argued that the marooned party was unhurt and could be rescued by the very earliest of the daylight without risk to them or to anyone else. This side won in the end, and the rescuers, since it was now the small hours, decided to stay where they were till daylight singing all the songs they knew. So, like a party of Waits, the ground being too wet to sit down, they stood first on one foot then on the other, roaring up into the darkness Grand Opera, Gilbert and Sullivan,

Comic Songs from 1890 to 1920, Hymns and Folk Songs, while the shivering three, crouched on their tiny sloping gallery, listened— sole occupants of a theatre vast as the night. From above, they said next morning, only the pin-point gleam of the lantern held the stage; the actors and chorus were invisible. But the entertainment, they felt, halved the rigours of their ordeal. Their ledge was only about four feet by four feet and they had tied themselves to a spike of rock for safety. A single squashed sandwich, a few raisins and a stick of chocolate was all they had to see them through their fifteen hours' vigil. Wet snow sifted down all night over them—the same unexpected snow, beginning just before dusk, which had trapped them only a little below the easier upper reaches of the cliff. Luckily the wind, though wet, was warm, and they were none of them, after hot baths and breakfast, much the worse for the experience. But their 30,000 shivers, at a moderate estimate, were a sufficient reminder of the stakes implied in the climber's winter race with time.

—

One Christmas the whim seized us to spend a week on Snowdon Summit in one of those rather dilapidated shacks which were a familiar eyesore to many. I went to Selfridge's and bought all the food that looked to me good. It was a great deal! What it totalled in weight we never discovered. By the time we had carried it all up Snowdon and most of it down again, its quantity was represented by quite fantastic figures in our minds. In a moment influenced by winter-sport posters I invested in a number of pink jellies which the others would never let me forget. We had saucepans, frying-pans, soup-ladles, a complete kitchen, and a Ham fit to win a prize at any Exhibition. Alas! If the weather had been kinder how we should have relished all these delicacies!

In our imaginations the sun bathed the peak by day and shone brightly upon the sheet of cloud that covered the lower lands of

England and Wales with a gloomy drizzle. By night a full moon rode in the starry vault of heaven, as we came in up the crisp, final snow-slope from great climbs on Lliwedd or Llechog. In actuality it rained, it was misty, it snowed and chiefly it *blew*. We knew all the elements in their fury and never saw beyond a heavy, grey sea of cloud that tore and beat at our draughty door and windows. We were too busy battling with the elements at home to think of climbing and the only expeditions we made were down to Gorphwysfa—at first hopefully, to bring up more provisions for the glorious days to follow; later economically, to carry down the said provisions for use in more habitable zones.

It was a shock to discover that our plans were already known as far away from Snowdon as Caernarfon, by porters and others. We were treated somewhat like fools or lunatics or cinema performers, since everybody knew 'that the place was uninhabitable'. Even the hotel at Llanberis, from whom we rented the shack for a modest ten shillings a week, paid in advance, did not conceal their belief that they were getting something for nothing and that we should be down again after one night at most. As it was, we stayed up five, more to prove to our friends that we were sensible than for any other reason. It was not a very successful demonstration.

I. A. R. and I were deputed to get the provisions up from Llanberis to the Half-Way Hut, while the other two (Dorothy Thompson and C. F. Holland) came up to Gorphwysfa, where we met to make final plans. On our preliminary inspection we were lucky enough to find a small donkey who took the heavy plum-cake, among other things, for us. With his aid, the quantity of stuff we left in the Half-Way Hut was enough to give our friends a great respect for our carrying powers next day when we all four came down to fetch them up—until unfortunately they somehow discovered about the donkey.

The first night in our quarters was not encouraging. The floor was like a skating-rink—covered with a thick sheet of ice extremely hard to walk on steadily in climbing-boots. An old rickety table and a rusty stove were the only furniture. Where were the fine dry boards on which we were to curl up in our sleeping-bags beside the fire or read comfortably on off days? A pitch-dark coal-cellar-like pantry had a slightly drier floor. The early winter dusk gave the empty barn-like place a drear appearance as we busied ourselves settling in as best we could. Down in the station we had been told was a little coal and some kindling. Both were damp and it was long before we had triumphed over the obstinacies of the rusty stove. Hardly had we got it going when we almost wished we had failed, so dense was the smoke that filled the Hut and, worse still, so copious the floods of water that began to flow down the walls as the crusted hoar frost upon them melted. It never dried out, but made straight for our spare clothes and sleeping sacks, where it lurked through the rest of our sojourn.

All evening the wind rose. We knew Snowdon Summit of old as a windy spot. But it seemed resolved to give us a lively welcome that night. When at last we had eaten and wriggled into our sacks and put the wavering, guttering candle out, it leapt suddenly into a commotion that astonished us singly and collectively. It fluted on the crags around, whistled on our chimney-pot, sang dismally on the stay-ropes that (we hoped) held the shack securely on its basis. It sucked greedily at our foundations and swirled under-neath the floor-boards. A strip of linoleum across one end rose in waves to its upward thrust and flapped, maddeningly out of time with the shrieks and wails without. At moments there would come a lull. Then, in the distance, the uproar would begin to sound again. Up the slope it came, nearer and nearer; with a preliminary rattle of stones and pebbles dashed against the outer corrugated iron, the whole shack would heave and strain in the grasp of the gale. The singing of the stays would change to a crazy shouting, and an unearthly hullaballoo would burst out—under-neath which could be heard the whole top of the mountain vibrating like a diapason. I. A. R. was moved to recant a passage in a book he was then writing, which reads: 'Consider the mountain-top, it hums not neither does it spin'. Snowdon Summit seemed to be doing both!

According to Tommy's account: 'Next morning the enthusiast, slowly awakening to the racket, enquired whether the wind had been blowing much during the night. He had heard nothing. One could only look at him with dumb admiration.

'Some snow had fallen, and had drifted in underneath the outer door—to be hailed with joy. It was splendid to have a supply so handy. However, facing the fiends outside was still the coalheaver's lot, and anyone sufficiently ill-advised as to describe the hut as chilly was given the coal bucket and the opportunity of learning something of the first principles of relativity at the same time; it certainly did change one's point of view.

'The Summit Railway Station was our coal-cellar, and the journey there and back, as long as the gale lasted, seemed to me very exciting. One felt much as an atom of thistledown must feel when careering along before the wind, wondering where in the world it is going to stop. Having successfully hit the door, you clung breathlessly to the handle as to your last hope, the gale joining in the game with spirit, until somebody inside heard you and unlocked the door.'

All next morning the gale grew fiercer. In darkness for some reason wind always sounds louder, but there came gusts about breakfast-time that made us all look at one another with questioning eyes. The shack is perched on the extreme verge of the precipice that falls to Glaslyn and the direction of the wind pressure was all in favour of sending it off like a bit of torn paper into the gulf. From time to time blasts went by that made us feel as though we were sitting inside a golf-ball that some gigantic but incompetent golfer was just missing with his driver. We were beginning to discuss moving our stuff across into the other building, which seemed rather more solidly fixed and more sheltered, when suddenly there came an onslaught from the wind that made its former attacks seem mere antics. The linoleum strip leapt into the air and, with a bang and a clatter, the whole wooden lining of one side of the hut, which had been bulging most ominously, sprang inwards and fell with a crash on to the floor.

That settled it. In transporting our baggage the dozen yards or so round the base of the cairn to the other shack, we found the safest plan was to go on all-fours! Even so, it was a relief to see anyone arrive safely in the opposite doorway. We thought seriously of putting the rope on for the passage!

As Tommy wrote at the time: 'The gale, now on its mettle, continued to blow *fortissimo*. The narrow passages between the cairn and each of the Summit buildings formed funnels down which the wind raced at many miles an hour. To elude the strong probability of being whisked down either of those funnels into eternity, the furniture remover had the hut door held open for him, so that he could rush out with his gear into the gale—to be driven back against the cairn, whence, cannoning off again into the wind, he found himself abruptly planted against the door of the opposite shack. The remainder of the afternoon went speedily, and great was our pride when all our belongings, including live coals, a bucketful of snow and a saucepanful of Bovril, were safely conveyed across.'

This time we were housed in a smaller, darker hole than before, for the windows were boarded up and we were quite glad to have the extra protection from the colossal blows. By this time evening was approaching. And, mockingly, no sooner had we changed houses than the gale subsided.

Next day, in mist and rain now, we went down to Gorphwysfa, where a large party made many sly enquiries as to our comforts. We were not surprised to hear that our gale had made its mark all over England, blowing down trees and telegraph posts and walls and knocking people about widely. We felt we had not been exaggerating.

The next two days we sat by candlelight in our little dark hole no larger than a bathroom. Tommy and I slept (or tried to) on shelves and stacks of biscuit-tins to get up out of the damp of the floor, which we callously left to Holland and I. A. R. Each day was

varied by carrying something either up from or down to Gorphwysfa.
With the third day arrived my brother John, looking magnificent
in a Teddy Bear Jaeger flying-suit and burdened with a vast acetylene searchlight signalling lamp. On New Year's Eve the clouds
thinned a little and he had the pleasure of behaving like an immortal.
People of the villages for miles around swore to each other that
they had seen a heavenly light. But heavy snow put an end to his
lofty sport and brought a new complication. We had retired to our
black hole. The stove had never done much else than smoke. Now
it became nothing less than devilish and belched incredible quan-
tities of gritty smoke into the room. We could see nothing for tears
and could not speak for coughing. It was pure good luck that
someone discovered in time that somebody else had brought up a
bucketful of coke instead of coal for the fire. Otherwise we should
probably have provided a macabre item for the newspapers and an
opportunity for a sermon by the coroner. The coke was promptly
put where it came from, but the smoke grew even worse than before.
It was as though we had no chimney at all! With that the right
idea dawned, and John, our physicist, went up on to the roof with
an ice-axe and found that the chimney was constantly being snowed
up. A few probes cleared it and we slept the better, but a general
impression was growing that our game was hardly worth the candles
we were burning day and night. On the morrow a queer procession
of figures hung about with sacks fore and aft, with frying-pans and
saucepans festooned about them and clanking in the wind, helmeted
with *passe-montagnes* and wound in sleeping-bags and other wodgy
wrappings, could have been seen winding down the zigzags through
the muffling snow and trailing across the causeway of Llyn Llydaw
in the rain. If Tweedledee and Tweedledum had joined us they
would have passed unnoticed. But that night, in the comfort of
Gorphwysfa, I suppressed a sigh that was not only my own for our
late station. If only the weather had played fair! I am not yet satisfied that Snowdon Summit—with a well-designed stone Hut high
on its flank, and the giant precipice of Clogwyn Du'r-arddu so

near—ought not to become the best of all the climbing centres of Wales. One day I shall try again.

—

Twice, on our return from the Alps, I. A. R. and I went up to Wales in early October to taste, as it were, a liqueur of rock-climbing after the feast of the Alpine season. October is often a dreamy Elysian month in Wales. Large dry masses of cloud float about in a thin misty autumn sunshine, the orange of the bracken and the scarlet and purple of the bilberries clothe the slopes, and the cliffs gain in mystery from the emptiness of the hills. For us there was the added joy of being in that fine-drawn training that only the Alps can give. It is no slight witness to the forms of the Welsh mountains and the majesty of their cliffs that eyes fresh from the Alps do not find them in the least diminished by comparison.

We were sufficiently emboldened by this extra fitness to look for new routes on Lliwedd's East Peak and were rewarded by what we called the Birch-Tree Terrace Climb. It went up the ridge that supports the Birch-Tree Terrace and then up lovely sound slabs between the Central Chimney Route and the Roof Route. We entered it painstakingly in the Gorphwysfa Book and then discovered that the first section had been climbed already by Mallory. The new upper part made a fine direct continuation.

One of Lliwedd's chief defences is the special sense of exposure it produces. On its best slabs you feel more up in the sky on nothing with nothing beneath you than in most other places. It shows how much an Alpine season can immunize a climber from such feelings that on a traverse near the 'Summer House' of the Central Chimney Route, which was part of our explorations for the Birch-Tree Terrace Climb, I actually for a moment went to sleep! We had come up on a night train from London, the day was warm, and my excuse is that I had been drowsily waiting a very long time for I. A. R. to discover some method of crossing the next rib. When my turn came and the responsibility of belaying him was over, he caught me nodding in the middle of the manœuvre.

On one Whitsuntide visit our goal was a companion climb to the Holly-Tree Wall, using, but with no ice-axe this time, the first corner pitch we had taken with Holland as a beginning, and then going on as near to the Holly-Tree Wall Route, on its right, as we could. As a visionary climb it was in our minds for years under the name of 'Other Kingdom'.

When we reached Pen-y-Gwryd there was bad news. W. E. Durham, an old climbing friend, the author of a book of Alpine reminiscences I used to re-read each time I stayed at Ogwen Cottage, where a presentation copy lives in the drawer of the table, had, we heard, been killed on Tryfan. Details came later. He had been leading the difficult top chimney on the Central Buttress—a favourite climb of his which he first visited with I. A. R. some years before. For a man of over sixty, he was an extraordinarily strong and agile climber. High up in the chimney he had left its close-fitting angle to go out on the slab to the right. Here he reached handholds but could find no way of finishing or of regaining the holds he had left. His companions below rushed round as quickly as possible to lower him a rescuing rope from above. But just as they reached the top his strength failed. He fell and was killed instantly. All this we learned the next day. For the moment we knew only the bare fact of the accident.

He had begun his climbing after the age of forty, and when the War put an end to a long series of well-filled Alpine seasons he turned to North Wales as a substitute. Like others who begin late in life, he brought an extra zest to his climbs, as though the new sport had given him a second youth. As we went round to Ogwen next day, the memory of my first day with him was strong and clear. A spring day, very like the present, with the same bog-myrtle scenting the marshes as we went up to Idwal. That day we had gone, he and I. A. R. and I, up Hope, quickly across to the Central Arête of Glyder Fawr's upper cliff—a ridge new to him and to me and hard to surpass in the lofty splendour of its situation and its sound climbing. How we had revelled as we balanced up and over its narrow pinnacles! Then, insatiable of such delights, down and round to the Twisting Gully and home along the ridge of the Gribin. To think of him lying dead at Ogwen gave a tragic aspect to the cliffs he had so enjoyed; but his end was one that most mountaineers would envy—to pass, after a full life, in a flash, from a moment of physical triumph, without lingering illness, or pain or distress.

We went up to our cliff sadly. All went well. At the foot of the climb an uncanny thing happened. Tucked in a cranny an iron *piton* just showed. What mysterious person had left it there and for what purpose? It seemed, on that haunted morning, a hint too clear to be ignored. Up above, where belays are lacking, and the climbing is delicate, I. A. R. sought out a crack for this iron Finger of Fate and hammered it in securely with a stone carried up for the purpose. So placed, it was of no assistance to the leader on the pitch, but with my rope belayed about it I could guarantee that, whatever occurred, no serious harm could come. As it happened, he went up without noticing any difficulties. But the whole climb, including the first pitch, which had formerly caused us so much anguish, had gone as though it were the rocks which were inspired. We were triumphant, but as we lay ecstatically happy on the warm rocks above the critical final pitch, rather absurdly, in the melancholy of the hills mingled a faint streak of the queer paradoxical disappointment that comes when a wish is fulfilled.

To write about Wales is to describe a series of particular climbs, of plans, explorations, disappointments, renunciations, renewed hopes, changes of 'form' and weather, and sometimes eventual triumph. Actually, when one is there, the dramatic fabric of these schemes is overlaid by the massed impression. The cliffs, the oblique rain across the slopes of the Carnedds, the purple chaos of rocks heaped out into a gusty Ogwen, the spongy masses of sphagnum in the swamps, the clean, sheep-bitten turf, the drier shelves above, the endless crying of the streams and dark gulf at evening of the lower valley. Mornings when Y Garn and Foel Goch soar up out of the shrouds of lifting cloud and the Lake glitters through the curtain of the rowans with their dark coral berries. The springiness of the bilberry clumps as you lie in the sunshine on the Heather Terrace, the squeak of the lambs as you wind down between the long-snouted rocks. Out of all these is composed a bodily feeling, nameless and definite and irreplaceable, like a scent or a taste or an ache. When one is away, some accident—a sheep's baa, a lichen patch on a stone wall—awaken it; but it is none of these things. It is the reverberation of one's life among them, known completely only to those who have lived the same life among the mountains. For others, other scenes will take their place. Such evocations as I can attempt are at best a hieroglyph to be read in other terms as you please. But in each case the sense of an uncapturable significance will arise, and its secret—for the mountaineer as for any other pilgrim of a passion—is almost an open one. Therein, reflected, is the experience of being ardently alive.

'How much of the glory of the imperishable or continually renewed creation is reflected from things more precious in their memories than it in its renewing.'

CHAPTER IV

THE LAKE DISTRICT

The Napes Needle—Cairns or no cairns—Handholds of the Great—
Club climbing—A fatal delay—Coleridge on Borrowdale—My room
or yours?—Rain-charm—Lost in the mist—A Niagara of scree on
Gable—Foodless for twenty days—Owen Glynne Jones—Fell
walking—Natural hazards—Scafell Pinnacle Face—The Pinnacle
Club—Peace Night.

Nobody could have been luckier than I on my first visit to
Wasdale. The late afternoon sunlight was on Great Gable as I
arrived. Yewbarrow and Kirkfell stood about the head of the valley
in a sweet serenity that I shall never forget. Ever afterwards I somehow
connected this with the perfect flowing smoothness of their green
slopes. A warm and gentle peace flooded the scene as I stood with
Holland—who had met us—puzzling over the problem of an
old-fashioned tin trunk that, for now unrecoverable reasons, had
come with me. Perhaps, having heard about the rainfall at Seathwaite,
I thought it would keep my clothes from damp! But Holland's
resources were inexhaustible. He wandered off to return, jubilant,
with a tiny wheelbarrow. Somehow we poised my trunk upon it and
trundled off towards Burnthwaite. Deafeningly we bumped along
the stone-walled narrow lane past the church, destroying the slum-
brous afternoon, while sheep lifted their busy noses from the grass
in all the neighbouring fields to wonder at us.

Burnthwaite has changed since those days. Baths and moder-
nity have come to it. Then, one sat in a dark, cosy little room and
ate in a narrow whitewashed cell, which I believe had once been
the dairy. If you were much favoured, old Mrs Wilson would let

you sit and gossip in the kitchen. There one spent delicious long evenings by the open fire. The other day an old friend said to me: 'The first time I saw you was in Burnthwaite kitchen and you were showing them how high you could kick with climbing boots on. You kicked and you kicked and it was superb; till suddenly your other foot slipped on the stone floor—and then how we laughed!'

On that first evening, Holland, with energy as unfailing as a mountain torrent, dragged us off—my brother Will and I—to climb all the Napes Ridges then and there. The rose-red of a perfect July sunset was creeping up the rocks as we tore, at Holland's 'slow pace', up the long green grind of Gavel Neese. After a train journey from London we panted for mercy in vain. Round the slopes we contoured on the tiny path; then, suddenly, the Needle was there! In that breathless moment it surpassed I don't know how many dreams. I must have read of it and gazed at its picture since my earliest mountain ambitions awakened—and there I was, in a wild flutter, actually on it. What a struggle the mantel-shelf was, and how smooth seemed the slab polished by how many famous boots! Down my parched throat flowed a long imaginary toast in nectar to Mr Haskett-Smith—the first solitary conqueror—as I stepped up on to the summit, feeling there could never possibly be room for three—but there was.

Wondering, as all do, whether the top block would topple as we sat on it and go crashing into the valley with us, we watched the edge of the shadow now leaping up the Napes Ridges above us. Over our heads the 'towering foolscap of eternal shade' was very visibly being fitted. I was on an emotional pinnacle quite as much as a real one. Our perch still held the warmth of the sun; the soft evening air flowed past; sheep out of a distance called; London and the Midlands seemed centuries away. The solitude of the Fells absorbed and refreshed us. Feeling like beings of a different race, we set our hands again to the still warm rocks and slid down, to run quickly back to the farm and dinner.

Next day felt rather like a piece of the Grand Tour. With Herbert and Mr and Mrs Carr we all walked over Sty Head. In its lonely roadless splendour, as the node of so many historic valleys, it keeps a spirit of other days and makes one feel more of a foot-traveller than any other place in England. By Sprinkling Tarn and Angle Tarn we passed. I saw them first under a cloudless sky, calm, unruffled, reflecting the boulders and grass of their margins. I was to see them later scores of times, dim in mist, or lashed into whirls of white fury by the wind, or choked with snow; but on this day every stone on the slopes, every curve of the near hillsides, was crisp and clear under the sunlight. The distances spread away in a dreaming distinctness and the valleys dropped into unconcealing haze. The signpost at the turn, holding up its little arms, looked pathetically human, long-suffering and constant in its duty.

How often I have heard modern mountain purists abuse signposts, cairns, paths, paint-marks on the rocks and 'anything that makes the mountains safe for people who ought not to be on them!' The competent do not need them, so the argument runs, and as for the incompetent, the more *they* stay away the better. Nature and the lure of 'the untrodden places' are also appealed to. How jolly to feel that one is perhaps the first to go over the ground! How fine to escape 'the hiker-beaten paths with their myriad cairns and destruction-inviting signposts'.

It *is* exciting to be dependent upon one's mountainsense, one's map and compass, in an unknown or mist-shrouded stretch of country. To feel that unless one pays strict and unintermittent attention, only good luck will prevent a night out. Cairns and tracks and signposts are safety and labour-saving devices, and a nuisance where the labour and the slight risk are part of the pleasure. It is easy to agree with this much of the purist's case. Again, where stacks of stones on all sides of one encumber the clear crest of some unmistakable ridge, the picture of the eager, triumphant trippers who have built them may get in the way of one's contemplation of Nature. I have several friends who take a joy in scattering such cairns. Though of kindly disposition, they would be happy to throw them at the offenders. One of these biters, however, was once bit. He spent so much time plucking up and distributing a magnificent arrow, picked out in white quartz, to show the way down from Castell-y-Gwynt to Pen-y-Gwryd, that, when he got up from his hands and knees, dusk had fallen and he himself went down to Llyn Bochlwyd on the other side of the range—instead of to Pen-y-Gwryd.

But cairns, after all, like tracks, can have much more than mere utility in their favour, and can offer finer visions than that of a mere unvisited Nature. She does sometimes need Man as her complement to appear at her best. I wept when I found the great summit cairn of Lliwedd demolished. It served no guiding function, but there are places where Man has a right to assert his presence. After coming up the Terminal Arête from Lliwedd's East Peak one could shelter behind that cairn with a sense that pioneering humanity deserved such a memorial to its triumphs.

And, down again at the utility level, a line of cairns will often generate a track, which—over a moraine, for example—may save fresh and weary feet alike hours of stumbling. Who would suppress the High Level Track to the Pillar? Perhaps one may venture a principle. Where utility strictly rules, cairns become not merely useful but 'romantic'. Where the sporting interest alone enters, they are—like the nail scratches on the cliffs—regrettable. The principle seems to me to apply to other things too. A lighthouse, a harbour, a jetty are no blots on even the wildest sea-coast. But an esplanade, a pier and a bandstand may be?

A test case perhaps is the memorial to some 'lover of the mountains' at a place in which he would be the last to wish it. Conspicuous on a grassy hillock one such used to distract the attention of passers-by in the upper reaches of Borrowdale. However, the disintegrating forces of Nature, working in part through human agencies, removed it! Equally, to me there seems no case for marble crosses at the foot of cliffs on which accidents have occurred. No climber

would wish to be commemorated so. Better far the yew-shadowed
churchyard at Wasdale where Frankland, that superlative climber,
is buried:

> Here he lies where he loved to be,

and the 1903 pioneers of the Pinnacle Face of Scafell:

> One moment stood they
> High in the stainless imminence of air,
> The next they were not.

There the passage of innumerable lives, the sense of the ages through
which these hills have been subdued to human uses, of the travellers of other times who have gone by to other fates, gives a juster
perspective.

It is a peculiar quality of the Lakeland hills and valleys that
working humanity seems so closely knit into the landscape. The
passes that lead from dale to dale, the tracks that go back to
pre-Roman times, seem here to link the modern traveller with an
intelligible past in a way which for me somehow seems to be lacking
in North Wales. So, up on the Sty Head I could not wish the
signpost or the track away. But how mixed one's feelings are!
Travellers of other days, excellent! Contemporary tourists, not so
good. It is the same with camping. One little tent, romantic! Fifty,
spread everywhere, beastly!

Leslie Stephen's *Playground of Europe* opens with this anecdote:
'A highly intelligent Swiss guide once gazed with me upon the dreary
expanse of chimney-pots through which the South Western Railway
escapes from this dingy metropolis. Fancying that I rightly interpreted
his looks as sympathetic of the proverbial homesickness of mountaineers, I remarked with an appropriate sigh, "That is not so fine a
view as we have seen together from the top of Mont Blanc". "Ah, Sir,"
was his pathetic reply, "it is far finer!" This frank avowal set me

thinking. Were my most cherished prejudices folly, or was my favourite guide a fool?'

Dr G. G. Coulton's comment on this is: 'To the amateur mountaineer, Mont Blanc is magnificent, partly as teaching us the littleness of man, and partly in its violent contrast with, and therefore relief from, the routine of our workaday life. To the mountain peasant, on the other hand, that wilderness of chimney-pots was impressive in its suggestion of warm firesides literally innumerable, and in its contrast with the difficulties and tragedies of his own bread-work. I am told by a man who was born and bred in a North Welsh village that, when a farmer from those parts finds his way for the first time to Shrewsbury or Oswestry fair, he comes home saying, "England is a beautiful land; it is as flat as a penny!"'

This somehow helps me to understand the paradox that in the crowded British Hills you crave solitude and empty spaces, but in the unexplored ranges of Canada or Sikkim, it is for some human touch that the heart hungers.

But to return to Esk Hause. The Grand Tour feeling was much increased at Dungeon Ghyll when we mounted into a waggonette after a copious early dinner. Evening saw me surveying with mingled feelings Mrs Harris' celebrated Table at Parkgate, Coniston. To one accustomed to Welsh frugalities—small-scale mutton and mere rice pudding—all Lakeland catering seems fabulous. But Mrs Harris was famous even among these northern trenchermen. Joints of all kinds, birds, pasties, turnovers, vats of potatoes and bowls of cabbages, puddings, pies, jellies, jam rolls, cakes, biscuits, cheeses, quart jugs of cream . . . made the board creak as at all hours of the day and night she loaded it for the 'Barrow boys' to lighten. And she was not content to put it before you and sit by while you ate. She plied you continually with good food and good cheer. The Gargantuan scale of this truly medieval banquet was something I had never imagined. I was seeing life! Parkgate, as was only to be expected, was always full. Opposite, however, were some primitive cottages, the week-end haunts of some of the 'Barrow boys'. To them Mrs Harris conducted us and left us to settle ourselves into what rather obviously looked like other people's bedrooms—of which more anon. However, all was so strange to me here that I thought at the time very little about it.

My mind was full, instead, of Dow Crag, our destination on the morrow. Little did I realize, as the full fair sunlit hours sped by, how rarely I was to see those rocks in such perfect conditions again. This was chiefly because most of my visits have been at the times of the Annual Meetings of the Fell and Rock Climbing Club, which used to be held in November. But even the coldest day holds its rewards. One winter evening when the summit bristled with hoar frost and an utterly still, moonless sky overspread the snow wastes, suddenly like luminous fingers of the night the Northern Lights rose over the North-western horizon. They spread, grew brighter, became a fan of quivering rays that waved and flapped above us, shot in vast shafts across Heaven and dropped soft radiance into the Duddon Valley. As we watched, the suffusion faded, its pulse waned; no flicker returned when we had glissaded down the dim slopes to the old pack-horse road on Walna Scar.

Dow seemed then and seems still a strangely secluded crag—as though, when the gentle curving walk across Little Arrow Moor lifts you up to the entrance of the Goats' Water hollow and there the crags hang, dark and clear-cut above the tarn, you were entering some sort of private world sacred to climbers. The definiteness of the nail-ground track up the screes to the Cave struck me then, as it does now, as asserting a peculiarly established usage. Halting at that sheltering boulder to scan the cliff and choose a climb felt like a ritual. A shyness as of a provincial contemplating Westminster Abbey was part of my feeling. I was to feel it again with Scafell and with Pillar. Here the Great had passed, this was classic ground; mingling with the awe which all fine crags inspire was pious hope, not unmixed with modest resolve, that I might find myself worthy of hand- and foot-holds so sanctified.

It was in a solemn mood, then, rapidly developing into an

entrancement of exultation, that I followed Herbert up 'Gordon and Craig'. The splendid friendly quality of the rock, the airy height of the situations, the boldness of the moves, these were the physical background—like the trappings and trumpets of an initiation or an investiture—to emotions like those associated with a coming out or a presentation. Here I was now, I thought, as we swung down the Great Gully, *climbing in the Lakes*, finding it all I had ever dreamed it could be. We scampered up 'C' Buttress and over into Easter Gully and I felt as though I had been given another degree by my Mountain University.

The name 'Gordon and Craig' has a silly connection in my mind with posters of Gordon's Gin and Haig's Whisky. I used to think it odd that so many Lakeland climbs carried the names of individuals— whereas Welsh climbs were named descriptively or picturesquely: North Buttress, Hanging Garden Gully, Hawk's Nest, the Celestial Omnibus. The uninitiated reader when he meets a stray possessive name in these pages, as 'Collier's', must know that a climb is spoken of. It would be interesting to speculate on the reasons for this differ- ence. The delicate refrainment shown in Wales is possibly a very novel and sophisticated product. The early Lakeland climbers may have followed a more ancient and established tradition. But I must not let myself be tempted too far out on such insecure ground.

These first days mingle in memory indistinguishably with later hours; with the thrills of leading 'the awkward step' on 'D' for the first time; or days when Pat and H. M. Kelly and I sat in the Cave consuming damp sandwiches and discussing Samuel Butler, Bernard Shaw and the reform of the world, before going out in the rain to Woodhouse's; or watching Denis Murray working out the beautiful climb which now goes by his name. Once he fell off it as I watched, and rose unhurt from the scree, before my horrified eyes, with the buoyancy that was part of his charm. Sometimes we would have the cliff to ourselves. More often, when the sociable meets of the Fell and Rock were being held, every buttress would be festooned with hilarious parties and the slopes below be dotted with lunching and lazing groups: scenes that the climber can see well enough in his mind's eye, that no description can conjure up for the non-climber. I find in my Diary scores of notes; how on one occasion, with Holland and I. A. R. and Will McNaught, Jones' route seemed easy; how on another the descent of Intermediate felt like the end of all things. It was bizarre that a *severe* should sometimes seem simple, when a *moderate* caused nerve storms of impotent despair. How preoccupied one was with the day's form! How vast the difference in secret inner satisfaction between floating up a climb and just somehow managing it! This was no difference merely between soothed and chafed self-esteem, though this no doubt came in; it was more a question of 'belonging' or not to something that for me had by this time become the object as much even of a cult as of a passion.

But the ups and downs, the ins and outs of form are not communicable. If I can suggest only how much they meant, how completely success or frustration seemed to change the look of Coniston Water in the evening light as one hurried back to supper, or the gloom of the gullies or gleam of wet slabs under the rain-storm, I may give the non-climber an inkling of the explanation of this mysterious sport. A single step on a climb, in its 'feel' as one makes it, can renew or break the peculiar mountaineering bond between the climber and the scene. The climber knows it in feeling, if not necessarily explicitly. I do not believe I was then at all aware of any reasons why how one climbed should seem to matter so desperately. I can see indeed from my Diary that I was almost perpetually mystified by the problem. But it was clear early that it was less what was done than how one did it that counted.

And this applied as much to the routine of technique as to the more variable matter of confidence and skill. Not to see and use a proper belay seemed as black a dereliction as a stupid movement on a pitch. On the day mentioned when we did Jones' Route, for example, there came an illuminating moment. The climb goes, after gaining a considerable height, across the cliff to a roomy jutting flange of rock known as the Band Stand. Here several can sit in comfort, looking down an extremely steep wall to the screes in the bed of the gully 100 feet below. Holland had gone on across Hopkinson's Crack and was finishing the climb when we became aware of a disturbing situation just behind us. Three girls were coming up the climb and, with fine intrepidity, the leader was grappling with the distinctly difficult fifteen-foot crack which leads to the Band Stand. She seemed far from happy, but what made us anxious was that her rope was not being managed in a model fashion! There is a stance and belay at the foot of the crack, and she should have been safeguarded from it. In fact, had she fallen, it seemed very clear that the rest of her party would have gone with her. Nor did it seem likely that she would be able to climb down if she had difficulty in finishing; for she was gradually being forced into a more and more spread-eagled position, plastered against the rock on smaller and smaller holds. Luckily our party was able to reach down to give a hand and a rope at the critical moment. Unluckily a large audience on the opposite 'D' Buttress was watching the performance, some of whom later lost few opportunities of commenting on feminine rashness.

This was in very early days of women's parties, and the lesson of rope-management has been well learned since then. Every young climber, man or woman, has to master this, and it is one of the functions of Climbing Clubs to speed the process. There is the delicious story of Charley and Syd, for example, two young lads from Kendal who romped up all the 'super-severes' in Lakeland without 'fussing about belays'. One afternoon A. B. Hargreaves and A. W. Bridge ventured to point out an admirable belay to them on one of the hardest passages of Gimmer, only to overhear them later wondering who those doddering old buffers were. To those who know of their feats, the notion that there are minds to whom *these* two climbers appear in this light is refreshing. Charley and Syd are now, however, much commended for their safety tactics.

This last pitch of Jones' Route was the scene in 1931 of a bad accident. The leader had finished the climb and was standing on the grass ledge above the last pitch. There is a belay here but he may not have allowed himself enough rope to reach and use it. The second, having finished the traverse, was standing at the foot of the final scoop using a small hitch. The novice was last on the rope, and fell off in crossing from the Band Stand into Hopkinson's Crack. The second was dragged away, and the shock of the whole weight of their two bodies found the leader without anchorage. After a few seconds, he was torn from his ledge. The other two were severely injured, but he was killed. The second managed heroically to get down to Coniston, and the fetching down of the novice by J. C. Appleyard and some quarrymen in darkness is counted one of the finest bits of rescue work on record.

But these are grim descents. Let us leave them and run down to Parkgate—now, with the Dow Crag Climbing Hut, picking up the old tradition of hospitality, good-fellowship and abundance of superlative food, and let me continue with my first days of wandering.

I left Coniston with my brother, parting from him on Sty Head with an agreement to meet next day—oh these appointments in the mountains!—in Langdale, and went down alone into Borrowdale to meet a climbing friend. I had tea and slept at Thornythwaite, later to be hung with so many memories of Whitsuntide Fell and Rock gatherings. Of this first visit, the roses, the moss on the walls, the deep peace and the buzzing of the summer bees stay with me most. What a contrast to the stern bare life of the high Welsh farms I knew best!

In fine weather and in rain alike, Thornythwaite, under its solitary, towering sycamore, with its vast barn and sheltered court, spoke another language to the eye. Here man has triumphed, his life has won in its struggle with the hills; there, in the Ogwen trench, he is, if not defeated, engaged in what looks like a losing battle. But even in an autumn downpour, Borrowdale warms the heart. I cannot describe it; Coleridge could.

October 21st, 1803, Friday morning.

A drizzling rain. Heavy masses of shapeless vapour upon the mountains (O the perpetual forms of Borrowdale!) yet it is no unbroken
tale of dull sadness. Slanting pillars travel across the lake at long
intervals, the vaporous mass whitens in large stains of light—on
the lakeward ridge of that huge arm-chair of Lodore fell a gleam
of softest light, that brought out the rich hues of the late autumn.
The woody Castle Crag between me and Lodore is a rich flower-
garden of colours—the brightest yellows with the deepest crimsons
and the infinite shades of brown and green, the *infinite* diversity of
which blends the whole, so that the brighter colours seem to be
colours upon a ground, not coloured things. Little woolpacks of
white bright vapour rest on different summits and declivities. The
vale is narrowed by the mist and cloud, yet through the wall of mist
you can see into a bower of sunny light, in Borrowdale; the birds
are singing in the tender rain, as if it were the rain of April, and
the decaying foliage were flowers and blossoms. The pillar of smoke
from the chimney rises up in the mist, and is just distinguishable
from it, and the mountain forms in the gorge of Borrowdale consub-
stantiate with the mist and cloud, even as the pillar'd smoke—a
shade deeper and a determinate form.

Coleridge took to the hills in an astonishingly modern spirit—
so I. A. R., who is just finishing a book about him, tells me. He
was a strong walker, going over Helvellyn or Fairfield on his tramps
from Keswick to Grasmere and even getting his fingers frost-bitten
crossing the Kirkstone Pass in a storm. There is some case for his
being the first tourist (1802) to ascend Scafell Pike. He was caught
up there in a thunder-storm, and wrote a letter to the Wordsworths,
the first from 'the central mountain of our Giants'. The view he
found 'the most heart exciting of all earthly things I have beheld'.
After rousing the echoes by calling out the names of his children,
hunger drove him down—sad at being unable to linger for the
sunrise!

His equipment is worth noting: 'On Sunday, August 1, ½ after 12, I had a shirt, cravat, 2 pairs of stockings, a little paper, and half dozen pens, a German book (Voss's Poems), and a little tea and sugar, with my night cap, packed up in my natty green oil-skin, neatly squared, and put into my net knapsack, and the knapsack on my back and the besom stick in my hand, which for want of a better, and in spite of Mrs C. and Mary, who both raised their voices against it, especially as I left the besom scattered on the kitchen floor, off I sallied over the bridge, through the hop-field, through the Prospect Bridge, at Portinscale, so on by the tall birch that grows out of the centre of the huge oak, along into Newlands'. (MS. Journal of tour in the Lake District, August 1–9, 1802.)

Even twenty years later the usual attitude is represented by Dr Robinson who, in 1819, got as near Scafell as Sty Head Tarn, to find 'the scenery calculated to inspire emotions of the most awful kind—however charming and extensive the prospect may be, the idea of its beauty is lost in the overpowering sensation of danger'. All the same Dorothy Wordsworth, in 1818, reached the summit, to record, 'Mountains of Wastdale in tumult; to our right, Great Gavel, the loftiest, a distant and *huge* form . . . the Den of Wastdale at our feet—a gulf immeasurable . . . round the top of Scawfell-Pike not a blade of grass is to be seen. Cushions or tufts of moss, parched and brown, appear between the huge blocks and stones that lie in heaps on all sides to a great distance, like skeletons or bones of the earth not needed at the creation, and there left to be covered with never-dying lichens, which the clouds and dews nourish; and adorn with colours of vivid and exquisite beauty. Flowers, the most brilliant feathers, and even gems, scarcely surpass in colouring some of those masses of stone, which no human eye beholds, except the shepherd or traveller be led there by curiosity, and how seldom must this happen!'

Next day began with Raven Crag Gully and Sergeant Crag Gully—both wet and full of the most luscious grass I had ever seen or tasted—thence over High Raise and the Langdales to Middlefell

Farm where I met Will. It was Bank Holiday and he welcomed me
with the news that there was no bed to be had in the valley. At
this, our bedrooms waiting for us over at Coniston and scattered
with our things, began, though far off, to exert a glamorous lure.
As dusk fell we shouldered our packs again and set off up the little
steep hill to Blae Tarn. The rising moon saw us slogging along amid
the eerie slate pyramids of Tilberthwaite; it was one o'clock when
we arrived in the cobbled yard of Parkgate cottages, ready to sink
into bed with no further ado. To our horror, as we turned in at the
door, we heard deep breathing. We both paused in mute consternation.

'You go and see,' I said. 'It sounds like men asleep in our rooms!'

'You go!' said Will. 'You probably know them.'

The more I listened, the less likely somehow this seemed. In the
end Will, with great resolution, set off up the creaky stairs. At the
bend he was arrested by a violent voice.

'What are you doing there?'

'Looking for my bedroom.'

'Who are you?'

'It's me!'

'Who's me?'

'Pilley.'

'Who the hell is Pilley?'

Will seemed to have no answer to that; but the party upstairs
had decided to come down to have a look at us. They were astonishingly quick to take in the situation. They offered a varied and
sumptuous midnight feast, and some of them went as far as to give
up their (or was it our?) beds to us. There was an elaborate reshuf-
fling of rooms, but before long deep breathings had begun again
and the slab of Sergeant Crag Gully faded into a dream that I had
to hurry back to London by a boat whose captain was Owen Glynne
Jones. The decks were crowded and I sought seclusion up a ridge
I found in the rigging.

Those were the youthful, rapturous days when the very rain

could be enjoyed for weeks on end. I find an account in my Diary of a walk up Moses Trod and round home by Aaron's Slack, an encircling of Great Gable. Moses seems to have been a moonshiner, who kept his still on the Ennerdale face of Gable, but others maintain that this skilfully traced path, which connects Honister with Wasdale and is also known as Moses Sledgate, was originally, like other sledge tracks on the fells, made for drawing peat from the upper mosses and takes its name, like the various Mosedales, from them. I have lately heard it called, by a perversion, the Whisky Path. Whatever it is, I walked round it and described the experience as follows:

'I went up into the obliterating mists, those drifting veils which thickening hide all distance, close in the sodden turf to a dim travelling region of the unexpected. The wind blew a fine rain into my face from the mysterious wall, wind brushing past, damp earth under my feet. What is that sensation that excites me so unaccountably?'

Walking so, in a circle of vision as restricted as the light of a glacier lantern, was a pleasure quite independent of route-finding. It was the privacy of this shifting mist-world, and the unreality of the things that appeared to and vanished from it as one moved, that gave the chief fascination. These and something else, perhaps, harder to be sure about—an allegoric quality of the experience, as though what could be seen was knowledge. How much there was that could be known if one changed the view-point. And yet from one view-point how completely all that was could be surveyed. Stepping so alone across a moorland it was as though one possessed all knowledge and all power.

Route-finding, however, though quite a different and a much more humdrum interest, was great fun too. The odd conventional terror of the mist that haunts so many novelists' and tourists' minds gave it a special flavour. Here, for example, are some remarks by a lady who, having knocked about the Mont Blanc Chain a good deal with guides, might have known better. She is describing her feelings when she saw some clouds coming down during an ascent of Pillar. A companion is roaming Ennerdale below: 'Presently, however, it began to grow ominously dark, threatening, I feared, bad weather. I looked about me. To my horror there was mist on the tops of the mountains. Soon, slowly but surely, it came creeping down. What of her alone in this wild, inhospitable, deserted hill country, where people are lost for days together in the mist and only found when it is too late? My heart nearly stood still with fear.'[5]

These are hobgoblins bred of the fancy. No climber, with map and compass, who keeps his mind on the job, goes far astray on the British hills. Without map and compass, or in talk or dream, it is another matter. But the worst that can happen is a descent into a wrong valley and the ridicule of fellow climbers when you next meet them.

I wish I could steer a certain course among these memories. But time now seems a mist between me and those best early days, a wall that thickens and thins as capriciously and incalculably as any cloud. There are times at which it is no good staring in certain directions, times again when without reason the veil suddenly blows aside and there seems to be nothing between then and now.

So at one moment I am frowning up at Holland, grimmer and more piratical than ever in a red tam-o'-shanter, as he feels his way up the slabs of the South-West on Pillar. That must have been my first day of really hard climbing on Pillar. I remember that we had gone up the North-West. I thought I had reached the limit of delicacy there; how surprised I was to find myself on something still harder. What fluctuations! In another glimpse I am grovelling in trepidation round the simple step by the waterfall, an icy day with a boisterous gale sweeping up from the desolate snow-powdered gulf of Ennerdale, the thought of Owen Glynne Jones' winter ascent of Walker's Gully filling one with a blank sense of tragic wonder. Or again I am racing

---

5 *Mountain Madness*, by Helen Hamilton, p. 258.

desperately up the track above the bridge behind A. E. Field, ashamed to let such a senior observe how much too fast for me he was going! A blazing sun is above our heads and the rocks of the sky-line infinitely far off up the slope are shimmering in a drowsy haze. And another time I am lying among the bilberry tufts, glowing still with the enjoyment of having led the New West for the first time—the criss-cross traverses and the movements up the slab still alive in the fingers and toes like the last of a dance. But mostly I see Pillar with cloud whisking round it, a topsy-turvy country cut off geographically from the rest of the region, and the bulges of the cliff gleam wetly against a background below of grey opaque vapour. Oblique shafts of rain dash against the cliff and Linnell is stepping up the Rib and Slab as lightly and smoothly as though the rocks were dry and warm, and he were in rubbers. The deluge drowns the rest of the world, but he goes up the streaming spraying rocks as though they were a ladder.[6]

—

On another wet day, R. A. Frazer, my brother and I were going up Great Gully on the Ennerdale face of Great Gable. The rain had let up when we came to the little wall of rock that leads into the wide, funnel-shaped, amphi-theatre-like upper recess of the Gully. A still-ness had succeeded to the showers. The windless upper air might have been filled with cotton-wool for clouds; we might have been enclosed in deep soft snow, so quiet was the world. In this peaceful progress we were arrested by an extraordinary sound of bumping. Bounce, bounce, something was coming. We cowered down under the lee of the wall, and with a crash and a whir stones of all sizes began to spray past just over our heads. So much came down that it seemed as though the upper reach of the Gully were emptying itself. We stared at one another. I can still see Frazer's melancholy visage

6   M. Linnell's death on Ben Nevis, Easter 1934, has deprived British climbing of one of its most brilliant exponents.

looking as though this were, of course, just what he had been expecting
for years; no more than what those villainous enchanters, his enemies,
would naturally be doing. Will, on the other hand, seemed rather to
be tasting a confirmation of an opinion, which had for some time
been maturing, that climbing was a 'mug's game'. What I looked like
I cannot imagine. I felt as though I were under a kind of Niagara of
scree—that was only just missing me. However, it stopped at last,
with one belated angular fragment hopping down by itself as a rear-
guard.

The silence that followed was broken by 'Come along, darling,
this way'.

A gentle but very firm feminine voice replied, 'No: I shall just
stay here'.

'Oh but you can't, dearest, you must come down.'

'I tell you I won't. I'd rather be left here.'

'But it's quite easy.'

'I daresay, but I won't ever move again. You go down and leave
me.'

'Oh but we can't.'

'Yes, you must.'

The moderate tones of this argument rang tunefully among the
crags. Our astonishment made us stand up carelessly just as another
shower of stones began. Cowering down again under our very
inadequate shelter, we all three began to roar in very different
accents words to the effect of 'Keep still, you fools up there'.

They were greeted with a variety of surprised squeaks, and something like a mumbled 'I beg your pardon'.

It was not in a very forgiving mood that we hastened up the pitch,
but the sight that met our eyes drowned all anger in mirth. There,
sitting in a patch of steep scree, was a lady in a vast straw hat, long
pink sweater and high-heeled shoes. Beside her, in an anxious attitude,
stood a gentleman grasping an alpenstock taller than himself. Higher
up the Gully, seated, standing or asprawl in positions of varying
comfort and security, were the rest of the flock, all happily quite

unaware of the nature and steepness of the Gully beneath them. They thought they were on the main track to Sty Head on the opposite side of the mountain!

We soon told them where they were and what they had been doing. Then appeared the full richness of their situation. Right up at the top of the Gully is a little wall of rock easier to slither down than to scramble up. They had slid down it and now regarded themselves as hopelessly cut off, with the Gully below as their only way home to friends and fireside! Here we came to dash their last hope. Impossible to go up again, and apparently impossible to go down! Stern measures were obviously needed; Frazer took command and jumped up the pitch. We, for moral and physical encouragement, attached the rope to each member of the flock in turn, and while he played them up, we pushed and cajoled from below. When we reached the summit, the leader of the troop delivered a solemn harangue in the manner of an alderman on the duties and virtues of lifesaving and the gratitude they owed us. We tried hard not to look buffoons as we shook hands in turn with every member of the party. Then, seven times directed as to their homeward way, they set off again and their visionary forms melted into the silent encirclement of cloud.

On Gable is that Eagle's Nest Arête which, as I have related, used so to haunt my imagination. The moment when I found myself following Holland up the Direct Route was touched with solemn bliss. I watched him moving up with the crawl-and-pounce action that made his climbing so distinctive on his inspired days. Higher and higher he went above me, more and more merged into the sky-line, a grey-buff patch of motion on the buff-grey crag. Had he reached the most difficult step? It was impossible to say, he went so continuously and, in a moment, it was my turn. As usual the reality was quite different from my imagination; in one way it was infinitely less sensational, in another, being actual, it was much more so.

It was truly 'a grand bit of crag-work', as Ruskin might have been caught saying. Climbers remember him chiefly for his picture of the Alpine Club as 'red with cutaneous eruption of conceit and voluble with convulsive hiccough of self-satisfaction' and for his talk of 'soaped poles in a bear garden'; but he clearly had the true mountaineer's spirit himself. 'It is the finest thing I've yet seen, there being several bits of real crag-work', was his 1867 description of a ridge on Saddleback. Would that he were alive now to bring a voice outcarrying all others against the proposed road over Sty Head and other atrocities, and to reinforce the appeals of the 'Friends of the Lake District'.

The Napes Ridges make Wasdale the climber's paradise it is. They are the ideal practice ground for ordinary mortals. Near and accessible, they are what the Tryfan Buttresses are to North Wales; climbs that in one combination or another gave the half-days, the damp days, the cold days, the days when no one seemed able to climb, when even the first step of the Needle Ridge beat one, something, and much much more than a little, to remember them by. How they changed with the weather and with oneself! Upon them that connoisseurship which finds that the mountains are never on two days alike could be exercised to the full. The relative delights of degrees of wateriness could be tasted! The difference between 'A wet day' and 'Wet all day and *very wet*' properly appreciated. Or the odd affinity to the eye between the appearances of the cliffs in a hard frost and in the heat murk of high thunderous summer. And with what changes of apparent scale would they respond to a clearing of the air. How they would flatten out under the slope rays of a sun declining in glory beyond Wastwater over the sea! How they reared up when sharp-edged white clouds that gave away their motion to the crags fled above them through a blue and lofty heaven.

Round the corner from them is Kern Knotts, a more gymnastic ground. At Easter in those days T. C. Ormiston-Chant would take enormous caravans of moderate climbers up and down Kern Knotts Chimney, and a selection of them up and down the famous Crack, since superseded by something more spectacular each year. What jollity and backchat, what gaiety and good humour even when the

Chimney took a score of climbers five hours in a drizzle! 'Everybody happy?' a voice would hail from above; and 'Champion', someone would reply. Climbing, sometimes accused of withdrawing us from the world, has in its lighter hours a social side.

What a sight it was when, just at the point in the Crack where the climber should swing himself into the Niche, a rollicking eighteen-stoner in a prize-fighting white sweater suddenly dangled clear of the cliff on a very elastic rope! Up and down he danced, almost reaching the ground, almost regaining the Niche, like a toy on an india-rubber thread. What scenes again, when, in full view of a devoted wife, a man with an artificial leg jammed it only too well above. The more they tried to lower him, the more upside-down he turned, and a rescuer had to be lowered to unstrap it before he could be released.

Across the valley on the slopes of Lingmell is Pier's Ghyll, that vast cleft, which seems in some lights a baby Grand Canyon tilted up. Climbers avoid it because of a chilly stream that disputes the use of the holds with them. But in the midst of the draught of 1921, on July 10, a party of three[7] thought that their chance had come to make the first descent. The whole Lake District had been ransacked for weeks for a Mr Crump. What was their astonishment to see him in the gorge sitting sideways on a ledge and gazing down the Ghyll. He had been marooned there twenty days with an injured leg, without food, maintaining life on an intermittent drop of water! Happily, he was still able to walk and was nursed down to survive unharmed.

Such incidents in scores are in every climber's head. They were the staple of the climbing talk when we stretched weary limbs and roasted illegitimately bruised knees by the fireside at the great Easter Club meets at Wasdale, or lounged under the trees round Thornythwaite at Whitsuntide while light lingered on the slopes of Glaramara. How well I remember the moment when burly,

---

7   A. R. Thomson, W. A. Wilson, A. Walters.

indomitable Philip S. Minor, then President of the Fell and Rock, told me at Burnthwaite that perhaps now I might become a Member. We were all doing traverses of the Barn Door and I had just fallen off! Enheartened by this news I tried again and succeeded with flying colours. These 'stunts' were part of the regular evening entertainment at Wasdale. Through a cloud of smoke, when the clamour of that extraordinary game, billiard-fives (now, alas! a thing of the past since the table has been mistakenly banished), died down, strained figures could be seen—hands on the edge of the table, feet up on the wall—working their way round it.

Over these antics presided the portrait of Owen Glynne Jones, hero of innumerable unemulatable acrobatic feats. There always seemed to be some new story attaching to him. That he could pull himself up on the top of a door ten times by the tips only of those slim fingers which show so well in the photograph on the head of his axe, I had known for years. But that he could make a standing jump in climbing-boots from one platform to another across a single line of rails was a new and wonderful item of information. The Station Bobby at Euston was said to have once been a victim of this gift. Jones' irresistible flow of chaff had led him to threaten to come across and make Jones 'give over'. Pressingly invited, he got down on to the rails and then was at Jones' mercy. Before he could climb up out of the trough, the climber flew over his head like a bird. It was no good turning round, for Jones at once sprang back again! A more elaborate use of the same tactics put to rout all the constabulary of London when Queen Victoria opened the Albert Hall. Jones, wishing for an unrestricted view, shinned up the face of the building and took his seat high up over the centre of the main gate. When ordered to come down he feigned giddiness. There was nothing for the police to do but to wait until the proceedings were over, send for the fire brigade, and prepare for a well-merited arrest. But when the ladders came in sight, Jones suddenly recovered from dizziness, ran across the face and slid down round the corner to vanish in the arms of an uproari-ously sympathetic crowd. Whether to believe these stories I never knew, though I was told them by a venerable member of the Alpine Club. Still, they fitted the man.

Hereafter, until travel and life in the East broke the continuity, these meets were milestones in my mountain life. At the Coniston Dinner Meets 200 or more would congregate from all parts of the country, men and women of every walk in life, gathered in a happy-go-lucky, care-free comradeship which glows in retrospect and cheers one's cynical hours. Odd leaders who have taken one on their rope, willing parties who followed one with a bracing faith, stray wanderers who sat with one a windy hour in a corner of Honister Slate Quarry and cooked one bowls of cocoa. Friendliness, kindness, sympathy, good fellowship and behind it an inexhaustible enjoyment of simple things, the smell of the air on the damp fells, the passage of the day under the sky.

One glorious May morning there was a stir at Wasdale. Eustace Thomas was expected at early breakfast-time. He was to drop in for refreshment on one of the preliminary surveys or trials for his famous Fell Walk. 'Drop in' indeed he seemed to do. Pat and H. M. Kelly—who gave me so many memorable climbing days—were lounging with me in the lane on the look-out, our eyes straying over the slopes of Yewbarrow. Suddenly, like two little, rolling, hopping balls, he and Wakefield (who held the record and was pacing him) came dashing incredibly down the fell. In the Complete Walk the following times for this section are recorded: 'Yewbarrow Cairn was reached by Dorehead and Stirrup Crag at 7.13¾. Doubling back obliquely on course 65°, a good run of small scree was struck, and Wasdale Head was made at 7.30½.'

No one who saw them would consider this counting of split-seconds a mere pedantry. There followed a pause for a bath and rub-down. Then off they went for Scafell. It was an exquisitely clear morning and they came out, as sharply as shadow-figures in a Chinese silhouette-show, against the sky. All the way up the sky-line the eye could follow them till they vanished over the top. It was hard to believe that Wakefield was teaching him not to go too fast!

In 1922, having learnt this lesson, he completed the round from Keswick, over Robinson, Hindscarth, Dalehead, Honister Hause, Brandreth, Green Gable, Great Gable, Kirkfell, Pillar, Steeple, Red Pike, Yewbarrow, Scafell, Scafell Pike, Great End, Bowfell, Fairfield, Helvellyn, Great Dodd, Saddleback, Great Calva, Skiddaw, back to Keswick in 21 hours 54 minutes. The estimated height climbed is 25,500 feet! Unsatisfied, Eustace Thomas continued until the 30,000-foot mark had been reached by ascending all the peaks of the Grasmere group.

I have left Scafell, that transcendent cliff, to the last. It is surrounded for me by a peculiar halo, partly due no doubt to accounts from Holland before ever I came to Wasdale of his early explorations of the Central Buttress and Pinnacle Face with Herford. And Scafell is fitly associated with Herford, the climber on whom, in the years just before the War, the mantle of Owen Glynne Jones seemed to have fallen. With him the standard of superlative performance seemed suddenly to have taken one of those puzzling upward leaps which make men say, 'This was never thought possible before and beyond this there is no going'. But looking back one can see that in a cycle of some ten years the leap comes again and where the limit of possibility lies cannot yet be known. Nowadays, with the new climbs on Scafell East Buttress and Clogwyn Du'r-arddu[8] in mind, he would be rash who pointed to any line upon a cliff, however overhanging, grassy, slimy or loose, as beyond the power and taste of some future technical 'tiger'. Praise, in fact, of climbs which possess 'natural hazards'—disadvantages which used to be known as 'objective dangers'—is beginning to be sung. A. B. Hargreaves, in a spirited comparison between Welsh and Lakeland climbing, has indeed suggested that the 'best' Lakeland climbs are too sound, too clean, too well provided with belays! He writes: 'When once one has tasted

---

8   On these cliffs—long reputed impregnable—a series of extraordinarily severe climbs have lately been achieved. Leaders: J. M. Edwards, A. T. Hargreaves, C. F. Kirkus, M. Linnell, J. L. Longland, A. S. Pigott.

the joys of negotiating in conscious safety pitches which, in the Lake District, would be written off as unjustifiably dangerous, one is inclined to be bored with climbs the only reason for falling off which would be just letting go. However!'

Nearly all the classic routes on Scafell, it must be admitted, come into this last category. Some of the easier ones tend to be a little slimy, Keswick Brothers as I remember it in a rain-storm, or Collier's, even mossier; but the Pinnacle Face on a dry spring evening, with the late sunlight staining it, as it seems, an inwrought crimson, has an almost unbelievable perfection of clean structure. One wants to pat the rocks, so keen is the pleasure of moving over them! As to 'just letting go' as a reason for falling off them, I tried that once. Holland and I had been wandering happily up and down the Pinnacle Face all day and to finish off we traversed across to the 'Oval', the ledge immediately below the famous Flake Crack where many climbers have stood and wondered. Looking upwards at that overhang I shared their feelings of awe and reverence. The shadows of the boulders in Hollow Stones were sharp-etched upon the golden grass and a tiny figure was wandering among them as we climbed down. In the valley at Wasdale dinner was calling; but could I hurry down those smooth rocks? No. Holland's hunger grew and he began to wonder audibly whether I was developing a paralysis. As he became more urgent, so my balance perversely diminished. A voice from aloft said, 'If you can't find any holds, just let go!' I did. Down I went through clear air. An incredible experience, more surprising than unpleasant. Time to wonder what landing would be like, but the shock was quite swallowed up by satisfaction at nothing serious having happened, as Holland lowered me gently but firmly the last few feet to Rake's Progress.

On another day which, for a better reason perhaps, stands out in memory, H. M. Kelly led Morley Wood and myself up Central Route, Deep Ghyll Slabs. It was raining hard. We had done Jones' Route to Low Man and were coming down Jones' and Collier's when it occurred to Kelly to wander up a shallow slab in some rocks which no one had particularly noticed before. He came back in a meditative mood to suggest that we attempt an entirely new route up the slabs. In such casual fashion are new climbs discovered. As Kelly wrote, 'Ascents of an existing route make one acquainted with the surroundings of that climb, and, by observation—there is plenty of time for observation in rock-climbing—one can locate rest-places which, if only linked up, would provide pitches for a new climb!' The patient leader, waiting at the top of a pitch for his companions to join him, has leisure to look about him. From each fresh vantage-point the perspective of the cliff changes. What from another stance seems a vertical wall, is revealed as a slab not too repugnantly inclined, and the speculative eye divines a course to be taken upon it. But it is not usual for the course to be followed on such a rainy day as this. I recall my sympathy for Kelly when, after some of his most magnificent climbing, he had at last to get Morley Wood to make a detour and lower a rope to safeguard the three or four remaining feet of the hardest pitch. This, of course, made our climb not legitimately a first ascent. But Kelly had his revenge later in the year and added to his long list of discoveries a route that only 'just fails to reach the sublime'. (A category reached, I suppose, by his Moss Ghyll Grooves, climbed in 1926 with Mrs Eden Smith.) Under the then conditions, I felt that it almost passed it.

It was a pity Pat Kelly was not there, but she, as so often, was leading another woman up a neighbouring climb. This passion of hers for independent women's climbing was just then, in fact, bringing the idea of the Pinnacle Club into actual being. It had been a long conspiracy, prompted by the feeling we many of us shared that a rock-climbing club for women would give us a better chance of climbing independently of men, both as to leadership and general mountaineering.

This was no mere feminist gesture, it was a rooted sense that training in the fullest responsibilities of leadership in all its aspects is one of the most valuable things that climbing has to offer, and that women could hardly get such training unless they climbed by themselves. A women's club would make such climbing seem normal, would collect those who shared this aspiration, would help them to form real climbing *ropes* as distinguished from strings of people who happened to be climbing together. And for those who did not lead, but still desired to take the share of responsibility which falls to any genuine member of a *rope*, a club would help. The qualification for membership, ability to lead an ordinary difficult climb, was designed not to force those who are not naturally leaders into undertaking more than they should, but to ensure competence in route-finding, in estimating the character of a terrain, and in the management of a rope.

But from the idea to the reality seemed a long step, and without Pat Kelly's powers of inspiration it might have been indefinitely delayed. Or have never been made, we may think, if we take the anti-feminist tendencies visible in Germany seriously as a contemporary world-trend. I do not know if even Pat ever really hoped for a club as vigorous and successful as the present Pinnacle Club with its eighty members, its Hut in Cwm Dyli and its brilliant galaxy of leaders, among whom Evelyn Lowe and Brenda Ritchie shine out. Thanks to them the standard of women's climbing has leapt up with a remarkable suddenness, and climbs are now being made regularly as a safe and normal thing which ten years ago were thought of as suited only to the strongest parties of men. But, indeed, with many types of climbing there is no reason why a woman should find them any harder than a man. Her balance should be at least as good, since her centre of gravity is lower. Her hands and feet are smaller, which means that the holds are relatively larger for her. When sheer muscular power is necessary, she will be at a disadvantage, but such places are rarer than would be expected. It is not the force available but how it is disposed that counts.

Solitary climbing was a speciality of Pat's. She enjoyed it for the peculiar heightened consciousness it gives, and she was so complete a mistress of the craft that with her even very difficult solitary climbs were perfectly justified. Here is Holland's comment about one such climb. 'On a certain day on Scafell, a party of men, of whom I was one, sat under "Jones' from Deep Ghyll" and succeeded in finding quite a number of excellent reasons why it would be most unwise for us to climb it, the real reason being that the day was rather cold and we all funked it. So we proceeded to the top of the Pinnacle by the easy way. While seated there, a solitary figure emerged on to the Low Man; it was that of a well-known lady climber who had done "Jones' from Deep Ghyll" alone. I am thankful to say that my feeling of smallness has long been swallowed up by my admiration for what was a very gallant performance.'

And here is a letter from Pat herself about the same climb. 'As a rock-climber, you will understand the joy of getting to THE pinnacle, the greatest pinnacle, surely, in the world—the Scafell Pinnacle. Not the greatest in size, you will understand, but greatest in that it gives the supremest rock climbs to be found on any pinnacle. Then think what it meant to climb up from Eskdale on a perfect morning, to reach that ribbon-like track called "Lord's Rake" (what a place it must be in snow, with its tiny cols between rocky walls!), to meet other climbers in Deep Ghyll. How impressive the Pinnacle looks from the West Wall Traverse, and there as of old we saw the bogey man, which I really must describe to you, if I can. It is formed of a light-grey patch of rock for face, legs, and pointed fingers of a *hand*—his right hand—and the hand is stretched out as if to do an enormous traverse. He is under and to the left of Herford's slab. He either wears a black cape or a black rucksack, as you wish (formed by shadow and incut rock); he comes out splendidly in a photograph, and I will send you one some day to see. With a vivid imagination and in twilight, one might see him take the long outward step with his right foot, then down he'll crash, and the grey face and skeleton legs will rattle, and a groan will startle one—in imagination! Doesn't it sound gruesome? But on Sunday he looked so friendly I almost waved my hand to him, and had he waved a hand to me I do not think

I would have been surprised. A bite of lunch in Deep Ghyll, some moderate climbing to get warm and to gain confidence, and then a delight which only a rock-climber can appreciate—to stand on a mere inch or so of rock and look down an almost sheer 200 feet: the awesome exhilaration of a delicate, airy, upward step to a toehold on which to balance before grasping a firm bit of rock securely with both hands, and so raising oneself on and up to the land of pure delight—out in the sunshine to sit on top of Pisgah and have a view to satisfy all hill lovers. Just across the way was the Pike, with its summit cairn and new War Memorial, Gable, Kirkfell, Yewbarrow, the Screes; the very names will call up the picture to one who knows.'

In one thing she was unique: she was as interested in other people's climbing as in her own, imaginatively able to enjoy what they had done. This, with a strange selflessness, inexhaustible energy and a clear-headed organizing ability, created the Pinnacle Club in 1921. She had, too, a gift for thinking of delicious surprises—stolen week-ends on the Derbyshire gritstone; she arrived, I remember, at the foot of Castle Naze with a basket of strawberries. A hundred slight incidents—nothing to relate in themselves—were framed in the settings she created, lighted by a grace of spirit as remarkable as her deftness on the rocks. Few have ever moved more lightly or surely, with better balance or more tranquil confidence. This came from the perfect realization of her own powers and the problem before her. She was a climber whom one watched not only with admiration, but without the slightest sense of that anxiety which frequently accompanies the watching of others in exposed positions. On easy and difficult ground alike she was always in complete command of the situation. It is an ironic commentary on human care and skill that, as so often in the mountains, one of the most prudent and expert of climbers should lose her life while the irresponsible and reckless constantly escape. The accident on Tryfan (April 17, 1922) was one of those startling and cruel calamities which are the more dreadful because unprovoked. A loose stone, like those

which every climber handles on every expedition, justifiably confident that the risk is negligible, moved and brought disaster.

> . . . Magnificent
> The morning was, in memorable pomp,
> More glorious than I ever had beheld.
> The Sea was laughing at a distance; all
> The solid Mountains were as bright as clouds,
> Grain-tinctured, drench'd in empyrean light;
> And, in the meadows and the lower grounds,
> Was all the sweetness of a common dawn,
> Dews, vapours, and the melody of birds,
> And Labourers going forth into the fields.

The Langdale Valley basked sleepily in the warm sunshine—or I
lent it the sleepiness, for I had motored up from London through
the night to be on Scafell Pike for the Peace Celebrations of July
19, 1919. But there were no beds to be had in Langdale to receive
us after a second night of vigil. So, after exclaiming at the cottage
gardens overflowing with sweet roses and larkspur, we turned about
to drive round by the coast to Wasdale. Through those endless
rambling, twisted, narrow lanes we wound, over ruts and through
boulders, to come in the middle afternoon into Upper Wasdale. It
had been dank and raw in the night as we threaded the black
country. All early morning it had been raining over a grey Yorkshire.
And now in the washed air the crags seemed near enough to touch,
the lilac Screes tipping down into the lake so grandly that we could
not but pull up to peer at them through a fringe of trees before
going on to the end of our journey.

Never was there such a day. A whole month the year before had
produced nothing like it. Whoever might talk of sleeping, I had
to go up beyond the pine wood that shelters Burnthwaite, to lie in
the scented bracken, gaze at the ridges clinging to Gable and listen
to the curlews crying, 'Ah! WAIT . . . wait . . . wait . . . wait, *wait,*

wait wait wait!' Well are they called the heralds, though what they announce and celebrate is for ever passing in their cry.

We started for Scafell at 7 P.M., the lens-like air and the strange hour stripping all films of familiarity from the accustomed path, so that the stone-walled meadows, the gorse clumps, the shallows of the beck, the sedgy banks, the birch groves, the high iron stiles, the hawthorn bushes, the teeth-clipped grass under the reddening, falling sun, were phantasmagoria through which we phantoms also passed, transfigured like them into a richer life. And to add to the unreality R. A. Frazer was half lost beneath a tree; a pine twice as tall as himself was riding up the Pike upon him. By Brown Tongue the air had grown cool and we came easily into Hollow Stones to find that a sunset worthy of the day was preparing. From Mickledore we looked back on the lower reaches of its splendour beyond Red Pike, but as we neared the summit all the sky and all the mountains of England and Scotland, it seemed, were flaming with every-coloured fire. White foam fringed the coasts, the Mull of Galloway, the Solway shores. The Isle of Man stood up out of burnished waters and the Yorkshire hills huddled under an oncoming purple gloom, starred, as night deepened, with the dim glow of early-lit bonfires.

People were coming up through the dusk from all sides. Before 11 P.M. more than 150 had gathered about the pole where the flag was flapping eerily above our heads in the chill breeze. Everybody seemed to be consulting watches. A bugle sounding the réveillé and the zipp of a rocket brought us all to our feet. Out the bugle burst again and on the last note, Fizz! Bang! down came the metal lid of the flare-canister on the rocks below, and up shot the white roar of the flame. In the terrific unwavering glare, the summit stones, the packed ring of awestruck or excited faces, the straining flag, had the unreality of a stage setting. On the bright, quick-moving clouds a vast dark shadow-flag was waving, and as we turned about to see what other summits were doing, one's own shadow vaguely moved over against one in the night haze. But there were the other flares responding to us. Silver How, Loughrigg, Wansfell in a line.

Helvellyn, Skiddaw with a mother-of-pearl canopy of clouds just above it. And farther and farther more and more lights, becoming at last mere elusive glows on problematical summits.

A rather ragged 'God Save the King' closed the celebration and mist swept up soon after. Some went down by candlelight, others sat singing and smoking themselves by a brazier inside the sheltering circle of the cairn. We dozed and shivered the night through in a hollow among the stones, under the blue-black, white-flecked sky, and moved down as the light came. Slowly the greyness grew golden. We made coffee on Mickledore and watched the peaceful dawn. Would it had been an omen that the days of war were at an end.

CHAPTER V

THE MISTY ISLE OF SKYE

*Derbyshire Gritstone—Yorkshire pot-holing—Planning for Scotland—
Clach Glas and 'Mountaineering'—The Ladies' Step—Night out
ruminations—The Ridge—Purple Islands—A new Cioch climb—
Parcel post—Tumbles best left to the expert—Technique in falling—Ben
Nevis.*

To go up to Wales or the Lakes had become a delicious habit; any gap in London duties offered itself to my imagination first as a chance to get in a day or a few days more in the mountains. The snatched week-end, the detour by which attendance as a delegate at the Annual Meeting of the National Council of Women, for example, could be made to cover the time between two night trains to and from Bangor or Windermere; the Christmas, Easter, Whitsuntide spells were regular practices, in danger, though I never saw it so, of becoming a routine. Sometimes it would be Derbyshire gritstone instead. Those odd, bulging little climbs on low bluffs of rock scattered about the Midlands are known, almost every inch of them, to their devotees, who chart and name and classify every possible and impossible course with an ardour and perseverance that may seem inversely proportional to the size of the crag. It was easy I found to lose both the skin of one's finger-tips and one's temper on these problems. For 'the smaller the harder' is a general rule with them. It is best to be either very light and agile or very long and prehensile, if one is to enjoy oneself on them; but about this I could do nothing.

I never mastered enough of the peculiar gritstone technique to develop the appropriate passion for them, and would catch myself sighing desperately for Lliwedd or the Pillar in the midst of abortive struggles to stay on some rounded holdless flange with a grass slope just beneath me and a bush marking the summit of the cliff just above. The true enthusiast may scorn me for an incompetent poltroon, but I never felt like scorning him in return. I was too full of admiring envy.

—

Once or twice I tried pot-holing. Those grim Yorkshire pits can give one plenty of wild excitement and there is technique here too to be mastered, as I realized fully enough the first time I found myself twisting and spinning half-way down a rope ladder in darkness with a deafening spout of water spraying invisibly past my neck. But one might as well, or better, I thought, rope down the waterfall of the Devil's Kitchen. At least there would be glimpses of Llyn Idwal to hearten one in between! And to come up again after hours of crawling and clambering by artificial light, to scent the bracken and see the shadows lengthening out on a perfect May evening, though it gave one a moment of heart-shaking sweetness, was for me to remember only too well what I was missing. The seaweed smell inside, the grease from the candle in one's tin-helmet, the reek of sopped dungaree, even the acetylene fumes, were no compensation. I just felt a water-rat. And majestic though the stalactite-hung caverns sometimes were, and however thrilling the chances of discovery; the crowbars, picks or pulleys were not for me. I soon came to the conclusion that the engineers, who rigged the tackle, really got the fun out of these ventures. But I am grateful to R. F. Stobart for giving me a sight of the horrific nether regions— Nick Pot and Hell Hole indeed!

—

When there was no climbing party available I would sometimes fit in a solitary ramble in the less known Welsh mountains—wandering over Aran or the Black Mountains, trying out the pleasure of a planned solitary bivouac at some point as remote as possible from habitations. I remember coming down hungry very early on a September morning through a *cwm* above Llanthony to sight an isolated farmstead that promised a possible breakfast. At a trough before the door an aged hag was wringing out some rags. Wondering if she would understand anything but Welsh, I approached and hailed her. The response was electrifying. Every hair on her head seemed to stand up. With an eldritch screech, if ever I have heard one, she wheeled and fled into her house. Bang went the door, and I could hear the bolts being rammed home and the scrape of a table being dragged up as a defence. She must have thought that it was I who was the witch!

These excursions were the fruit of an ambition to widen my mountain and climbing experience to the utmost. Dreams of other ranges—to be to Wales and the Lakes what they were to Almscliffe— filled my days. I haunted second-hand bookshops for climbing literature, going without a new hat or sacrificing lobster salad for a bun and coffee lunch. I would go far out of my way to look, for the hundredth time, at a photograph of the Meije or of Mont Blanc on a poster at Victoria. I showed, in fact, all the symptoms by which this obsession manifests itself. So, when out of these dreams the actuality of a visit to Skye began to develop, there was fuel enough ready to be consumed. And the project reproduced all the tensions, all the sense of venture and of struggling emancipation that had lapsed as climbing holidays in familiar Wales or in the Lakes while becoming dearer ceased to be such a novelty. A new world opened once more as Herbert Carr, John Hirst and I started thinking about Skye.

In planning the visit another peculiarity of the mountain passion at its height became prominent. To the really sublime devotee the fascination of the peaks spreads itself to whatever else can contrive

to become in any way ancillary to their attainment. Not only equipment, boots, ropes, lanterns, ice-axes, or maps and literature, but
even railway time-tables acquired a derivative but irresistible lure.
The letters my companions and I wrote to one another on the
choice of route, the stations where we changed, the stores we did
not take, the possible camp, would convince anyone who did not
know the secret that we were pedants born of the dreariest hue.
They went into incredible detail, they could not find too much to
treat—and all because in one way or another, by however remote
a transition, they were steps towards setting out for Sgurr nan
Gillean or Sron na Ciche, Alasdair or Blaven.

A day came when above a white fold of crushed water I leant
on the rail to watch the Black Cuillin, blue and surprisingly
smooth-looking at this distance, shifting and growing as we
advanced from the Kyle of Lochalsh. This was in weather of the
utmost perfection. The gay sunlight lingered on; it seemed far into
what should have been evening, as after tea we tramped the dusty
high road into Broadford. My memory has one thing at least in
common with the camera. It works incomparably better for
sunshine. I can remember more incidents from the two following
sun-soaked days, as pictures or as facts, than from all the rest of
my five weeks of wind and hail, rain, mist and snow; and there
was plenty to remember in them. In the first, a spell of pack-
carrying over to Strathaird by Torran, a new experience for me
then (how it made one's neck ache and does even now!); the
imperiously possessive attitudes of the local great lady, and lessons
in the importance, in these parts, of the deer. But there were things
better worth recalling. Baffled by deer in an attempt to go up
Blaven, that very evening I walked alone over a tussocky col and
down to the shore to bathe near Camasunary. How strange to find
great mountains massively silhouetted, simple and pure of detail,
between the clear sky and the glittering water. Light had almost
gone when I swam out from the sandy crescent of beach, into a
web of cool reflections and rippled gleams. The mountains might

have been any size or distance from me, but they moved as I swam, grew and shifted and turned with every stroke, so that after a while I hurried back to my beach, not because the water was cold but because the world I had entered was beginning to feel too strange. Exultation was threatening to pass over into panic. In comparison the dark woods through which my way lay back to supper seemed friendly and familiar.

On the way up to them, Clach Glas and Blaven seemed to me the grandest mountains I had ever seen, and when we roped at the foot of a long gully that led up to the right of the summit of Clach Glas, I could hardly have felt more solemnly happy. Mindful that these were the big peaks of Skye and therefore we must be mountaineers and not mere 'rock-gymnasts', that we must make progress and not go looking for hard things to climb, we took to easy slabs on the right wall. But soon, tempted back into the gully, we were struggling up three difficult and tiring pitches. They brought us to the foot of a really hard 50-foot obstacle with resistance enough to recall us firmly to these good resolutions. An alternative route proved equally hard, and when after some time we found ourselves climbing down again to escape out of the gully, I felt that I was at least thoroughly learning a lesson that I knew by heart already. Back on the slabs, 'mountaineering' was resumed for another 400 feet. Then the moment seemed to have come to take to the gully again. With what a gusto did I savour every such slight strategic debate! The balance of the visible advantages against the unseen and conjecturable mayhaps, the gambler's sense that now judgment is to be tested, and luck tried, were a dash of spirit in a cup already overflowing. The walker knows it at the point where the footpath unexpectedly divides; but the climber, with larger stakes in time lost or saved and toil incurred or spared, wins an intenser relish. It was these explorations throughout long stretches of easy climbing that interested me so powerfully. Herbert excelled as a route finder and zest would be added to the game by divergent views. I confess he was more often right than I was, but this was my chance of a fuller apprenticeship than could be had anywhere else in the British Isles.

In Skye the compass often errs, through magnetic rock, so that in immovable mist the problem takes on a stimulating aspect. The other two members of our party, John Hirst and A. R. Thomson, were to be caught out later in the summer on our traverse of the Dubhs. They separated somehow in the heavy golden mist, and then, while Hirst heroically searched, all a very watery night through, for Thomson's mangled remains at the foot of the crags, Thomson himself hit on the Sligachan bar—hours away—as an agreeable place to ransack for Hirst! Meanwhile Herbert and I went back to Glen Brittle and had the pleasure of comparing their accounts when they independently turned up next day.

We were remarking on the glorious solitude of these mountains and listening appreciatively to the silence, when it filled with voices. A party was lunching on the summit. In those days of few climbers you rarely met people you did not know and it was not surprising to be hailed. But we could not linger long, for we had hopes of reaching Glen Brittle by bedtime. Little did we guess, as we clambered along the ridge to Blaven's summit, and surveyed the intervening country, what that coast-line held for us, or that this clear view of the intricate twisting summit ridges was to be almost the last sight of them that the visit was to give us. Well it is called the Misty Isle.

At Camasunary there was more bathing, and a tea of bannocks offered with impressive Highland courtesy. No other form of food seemed to exist there. To travellers fresh from Thornythwaite or Gatesgarth tables, this seemed strange. Looking at the map in London I had assumed of course that Camasunary would be a village instead of just a crofter's cottage. I was to think of it later hundreds of times in China whenever I saw any especially impoverished hovel to remind myself that people live primitive destitute lives, down on the bare margin of existence, even in wealthy England. I felt that my efforts to imagine what life all the year round there could be like were hopelessly inadequate. I could believe what I heard of a town-bred wife who, unable to stand the solitude and conditions, had deserted. Everything comes there by sea, and stocks for the whole winter must be laid in.

We were beginning to suspect that Glen Brittle would prove a long way off as we set out for it through the fair evening to be checked at once by a tide-swollen river. We tramped round Loch na Creitheach, and began to follow the coast-line. Overhead seagulls swooped and wailed. Seals floundered in the smooth sea that broke lazily in the hush. Deer cantered in a herd along a distant ledge. The novelty of the scene between water and high cliffs was like a spell. But stretches of smooth 'boiler-plate' slabs came between them and needed all one's attention. The 'bad step' that we had heard of developed into many. Which among them, I wondered, could be 'The Ladies' Step' of the map? An island a little way out seemed never to be getting behind us, but we came at last to Loch Coruisk. It is indescribable. However late or uncertain of arriving anywhere, we could not hurry past its mouth. The sunset light high up on the surrounding slopes did nothing to soften its bleak inhuman beauty. When we went on, dusk had gathered. We hastened, as much as sacks which were perceptibly growing heavier would allow, over ground that seemed to grow worse the further we went! Boulders, holes, heather, ferns, all the ills that a slope is prone to, entangled our progress whenever we were not actually climbing.

> Up the cliff, down, till I'm lonely lost
> And the unseen water's ejaculations awe me.

Now by the water's edge, now high up above it, we struggled wearily. But it grew too dark to be safe, and giving up Glen Brittle we encamped for the night. It was warm and still, punctuated with cups of soup, and, for me, peering seaward from our perch, sleepless. I see in my Diary an innocent complaint that it gave one little idea of what a really bad night might be! It was in fact my first impromptu bivouac, and when an ashen light spread over the sky and we set off again, in the dewy beauty of the dawn, the seemingly unending five miles of heather that remained were beguiled for me by many minute observations on my sensations. Would I, suppose I were caught high up—on some Alpine ridge, for example—wet through and in a cold gale, be able to continue next morning? Just how much was I merely stiff and how much tired? Was this feeling of sickness that came and went important? Was it Oxo or Bannock or Sleeplessness? A deliciously refreshing bathe near Glen Brittle put a stop to these musings, and soon there were the clumps of trees and the white-walled cottages that were to welcome us back so often from hours of 'Sullen moor and craggy mound', from gaunt slabs and the desolation of stone-filled corries. My first twenty-four-hour expedition came to a contented end at Mrs Chisholm's door.

A day of innumerable meals followed, of dozing on the hot and lovely silver-strand, of bathing in the little waves, of staring up into the tremendous amphitheatre of Coire Lagan, of airy, cheerful planning for more than a month's climbing ahead. The diarist, I notice, adopts a somewhat apologetic tone about all this. She seems to think in her heart that we ought to have been doing some climbing, and has scruples about 'wasting' a whole day. Next morning large masses of cloud were drifting about Coire Lagan and clinging to the summits. The Misty Isle was living up to its reputation, and I remember even welcoming the sight as more characteristic, not dreaming in the invincible optimism of youth that I could be a victim of one of those rainy seasons without respite about which one heard. Those things happened to other people who somehow almost deserved them, who let themselves be intimidated by a drop of rain. If it did rain, no matter; *we* would still go on climbing and so weather it out. That blissful sense of time ahead, an ocean of uncounted hours to travel through, which comforts one's very bones through the first week of a long holiday, was strong in me. With day after day of deluge, each wetter and colder than the last, this feeling wore thin. But for the flowers in the cottage garden, I should have thought each morning,

> Outside it must be winter among men,
> For at the gold bars of the gates again
> I heard all night and all the hours of it
> The wind's wet wings and fingers drip with rain.

Every day we burst resolutely out of our prison to feel our way, each in his own world of 'dingy cloudage', to the foot of some climb: the Cioch Gully, the Sron Dearg Window Buttress, the Inaccessible Pinnacle, the West Buttress of Sgumain and the rest. But what is there to tell of them; to the non-climber they are but uncouth names, to the Skye habitué they are standard routes and ridge wanderings. We did them in poor conditions about which he is bound to know too much already. As we gained height on them it might indeed often have been winter, so bitter were the cyclonic whirls that cut through drenched clothes. And on the summit of Alasdair in mid-August it heartily and shamelessly snowed. The Cuillin, I still think, can be colder in summer than any other mountain chain in Britain. They seem more like great ascents than anything else in this country. Perhaps it is partly because one starts so low and goes up from the thick air and inertia of sea-level.

Whenever the morning promised better we would seize the chance to set out for some part of the Ridge. Those were days when the complete traverse of the whole Ridge was an ideal firmly niched in the imagination of every enthusiastic climber who visited Skye. Great authorities had conjectured that it was impossible in the twenty-four hours. But in 1911 Shadbolt and Maclaren had shown what a party could do without thought of records. And in 1920 Howard Somervell, then acquiring that reputation which was to be so splendidly confirmed on Everest, was to show the uncanny

knack he possessed of making mountains somehow shrink beneath
his feet (14 hours 18 minutes from Glen Brittle to Sligachan!).
Though we were not (or not openly) considering a one-day attack
on those miles of ridges, we were eager at least to traverse them
piecemeal. In the end we made three bites of them. The best bite
for me took us over the Am Basteir–Sgurr nan Gillean-Sgurr na
Uamha section. We had been held indoors by the weather, our first
day of complete imprisonment, and had resolved, however it
poured, that we would next day go by one way or another to
Sligachan. Up we went in thicker cloud than ever for thousands of
feet, until suddenly, there toppling, it seemed, right over us out of
the opaque air, was the Tooth. This always astonishing pinnacle is
cut by an extraordinary deep cleft, the Nick Gully. We scrambled
with some difficulty up the first overhanging pitch. This led us from
the outer density into a region of even greater obscurity. In almost
total darkness we began to explore the cavity of the Tooth for some
way up. While one read the guide book at the entrance and another
searched indoors with a candle, I, led by some pot-holing impulse,
pushed myself through an absurdly small hole in the remotest
corner. It led into a dark easy chimney. Up we struggled again,
thinking that we were probably lost, and (what tricky mountain
sprite could have planned it?) through another hole out into brilliant sunshine, with writhing wisps of vapour fading away on all
sides. There at last was the Ridge, with Sgurr nan Gillean riding
clean on a base of cloud, and out to the west, wonder of wonders,
purple islands without end floating on coloured seas. Beyond the
Hebrides a hazy leviathan must have been St Kilda. We were the
more joyful for all the hopes deferred that had been lying on our
hearts.

The rest of the day kept tune with this exultation, for the Sgurr
nan Gillean ridges were what I had dreamed they would be. Perhaps
in my visionary state I needed chastening. At least the manageress
at Sligachan seemed to think so. Even though this was after the
War she shook with fear lest I might 'be seen' in the hotel without

a skirt! She almost ordered me to borrow one from her, but as the place was full of climbing friends, I concluded I was being bullied and went down to dinner without her full, black emblem of respectability. Sligachan then was a simple inn-like place. I have not seen it since it has been brought 'up to date'.

How things have changed for women climbers since those days. Less than ten years later Lilian Bray and the Wells sisters were making their resolute all-women traverse of the entire ridge. On the first attempt they slept out midway, on the slope of Ghreadaidh, while through a Whitsuntide night their bottle of tea froze solid in their sack! The rocks in the morning were glazed with ice, a frosty curtain shrouded the scene, and without a dissentient voice they abandoned the ridge. On the successful day in 1928 they slept out again, largely because this time it was the hottest day of the year, too tropical to eat, and they nearly perished of thirst. The Pinnacle Club count this exploit one of their earliest triumphs. Mabel Barker, another member and the first woman up Central Buttress, Scafell, had been over it, with men, two years before.

Soon afterwards Hirst left and Holland arrived, bringing a fine day with him and burning with an all but unquenchable zeal for severe new climbs. The 'aetherialized muck-heaps' of the Main Ridge he found tiresome in comparison with the slabs of Coire Lagan. The fine day we spent dodging stones in the Slanting Gully, Mhadaidh. There being hardly more than ten climbers all told on the island, a perverse chance of course sent them to the same long and rather loose climb. All but the last man, amid cheerful vociferation, had to climb for hours with agonized care lest they should send something down to crack the crowns of those below. As to the last man, he, if spared this anxiety, had his own cares.

Rock-climbing pioneers vary immensely in their strategy. There are those, and Holland was among them, who prefer just to go and do the new climb, without wasting time in airy speculation as to where it will go and what it will be like. They hold that, as Captain Farrar used to say, 'You can't tell anything till you've rubbed your nose on the rock!' Others prefer a careful observation and survey, both from a distance and from neighbouring eminences. While data is being collected and the crucial attack is being prepared, they must preserve an innocent air of knowing no more than anybody else about the terrain. Among such wily and experienced experts none have been more successful or added more useful new climbs, both in Wales and in Skye, than E. W. Steeple and Guy Barlow. Indeed they had even then added so many that it was idle for them to pretend ignorance or absence of ultimate design if found near any attractive crag. If you heard they were about, you invariably went on to wonder what they were up to next. So when we met them, looking like Vikings, in Coire Lagan, with Holland intent on 'something new near the West Wall of the Cioch', some shrewd glances seemed to be being exchanged. On we went, to triumph in Holland's characteristically dashing fashion over a series of very exciting slabs and chimneys in gabbro. Gabbro, though it tears one's clothes and is too sharp for the fingers, is satisfyingly sound to climb on, above all when the exposure and the sense that one is clinging on nothing over nothing are as intense as they were here! The new climb seemed to us rather harder, on the whole, than the Cioch Direct. We noticed at the top that Steeple and Barlow had watched our proceedings and it was kind of them to break through their polite reserve far enough to remark that our climb was 'Very pretty'. Later they thawed so far as to entertain us, with the uttermost hospitality, in Mary Campbell's once famous den. This was a rival establishment, frequented only by the most courageous at Glen Brittle, a dark cabin with cupboard-like, shut beds in the walls. Here when a large meal ended, tea and eggs in dozens would appear. But Steeple and Barlow beat this. Not content with the tea and eggs in surplus, their hospitality produced a plum pudding boiled in their own billy. It had been gurgling therein succulently all through the meal. Whether it had come to Glen Brittle in one of their locally notorious parcels or had been somehow created by them there I never knew. These parcels were nicely calculated not to exceed either in weight or dimensions the maximum allowed by the Post Office Regulations and yet not to fall short of it. They were elegantly encased in a distinctive buff-coloured material and soundly stitched. You could recognize them a long way off. In a stream of such parcels their entire luggage, gear and provisionment would arrive, harbingers appearing some considerable time before Steeple and Barlow themselves. The feelings of the postman, confronted daily with the largest and weightiest parcel he had yet seen that was just *not* beyond the legal limit, may be imagined. The distance to Glen Brittle is nine miles.

> Cold's the wind and wet's the rain,
> St Hugh be our good speed;
> Ill is the weather that bringeth no gain
> Nor helps good hearts at need.

St Hugh seems to have been the patron saint of shoemakers. I had become in decided need of his aid, for the Skye stone-shoots had ripped my boots to pieces and the parts had to be lashed together round my feet. Rubber shoe climbs were a relief as adding *hours* perceptibly to the life of my boots. But on most days the rocks streamed with too much water for rubbers to be suitable. It was hard indeed as wet morning succeeded wet morning to see what gain such weather could bring, or what heart, good or not, could be helped by it. Ill it was indeed!

One day we were back in the Cioch Gully again, trying the top pitch, which we had cut on our first visit as seeming distinctly severe, though our only literature made nothing of it. The usual icy downpour was spattering on its flanks, and trickling down the great walls which framed the chockstone. Twenty feet up the left wall is a comfortable platform about the size of the seat of a chair from which Holland was making a series of determined attempts to gain hand-holds which seemed to be really out of reach. At last he got to them somehow and Herbert and I both thought that he was out of trouble. But no. Wriggle and strain as he would, nothing more happened. His feet were well above the platform and, if he couldn't pull up, there was nothing to take them back to it. There he was, on numbed hands in greasy holds, and the end of the gallant venture was fairly clear. The floor of the pitch, twenty feet beneath him, was large angular scree, not at all the stuff one would choose to fall on. And in the time available there was nothing we could do to help. A surprisingly calm and impersonal voice remarked from above, 'I'll be off in a minute'. Whether to try to catch him or not was a nice problem to solve in such a hurry. Perhaps it was as well that no one was in the line of fall when he came. Boots first and the rest nowhere, it seemed! Holland's skill in falling, of which he is himself rightly proud, was never better shown.

Here is his account: 'Just as I was congratulating myself on reaching the final pull-out all strength left my arms and the effort could not be made. Retreat and advance were equally impossible and the only thing to do was to fall. I am sure that those who saw this happen will agree that the performance was distinguished by ease and considerable grace, for I managed to turn round and do a sitting glissade down the big slab, while the delighted laughter of the rest of the party was ample compensation for my loss of dignity, if any.'

The laughter must have been that of relief, when Holland—skin unbroken and composure unruffled—rose to his feet and began to look for his pipe. Asked what it had felt like, he explained that the peace of mind that followed the agony of instinctively hanging on to the very last second was so deep that one felt nothing else.

My last day in Skye reserved for me an even more dramatic moment. It was ironically fine as Holland and I, in blazing heat, plodded up to the Basteir Tooth. All went gaily, until we were coming down the last pitch of Shadbolt's Chimney. This is another gloomy fissure that winds deep into the Tooth; at the bottom there is an awkward overhang where one is pushed out uncomfortably over the 200-foot drop of the cliff below. There is a roomy cave under the overhang. I had reached this with some ado and Holland was following. Somehow he got into the wrong position, a foot and knee on each wall on inadequate holds and all his weight hanging too long on those wonderfully strong hands. I came out beneath to see if I could hold his feet or help him to pull up again into safety. But he had been in a strained position too long. Even his spirit could not force his arms to take him up again. The labouring intake of his breath as he struggled was significant. Again a quiet voice remarked, 'I'll be off in a minute'. Desperately I scurried to the back of the cave, to squat down and brace myself, rope over the shoulder, against anything that offered itself. I was hardly fixed when . . . down he came. Somehow I was able to get the rope taut from him as he landed upside down on the lip of the cave to bounce out into the void and stop not more than six feet below me. Again nothing was amiss. As Holland describes it: 'After an abrupt descent through space I found myself hanging head downwards against the wall below, thus adding several feet to the climb. Although, theoretically, this unorthodox movement should have resulted in bodily damage, the contrary happened, for in bouncing on a ledge the last remaining adhesion left from a wound in the right arm was knocked out and the arm was afterwards considerably better from the shock. This falling movement, however, like crossing the feet on difficult slabs, is best left to the expert. The only occasion on which I hurt myself was when I fell two inches in the Black Chimney on Doe Crags, which seems to show that the secret of a successful fall is to make it a good long one.'

There is a small school which believes that some practice in falls is well worth having! Herford belonged to it, who practised long jumps down into boulders, and its modern exponent is A. W. Bridge, who has carried the necessary technique so far that, happening to fall off while leading the Flake Crack on Scafell Central Buttress, he stopped himself by putting out a hand to the chockstone as he passed by! An Alice in Wonderland episode. But to a moderate climber with no aspirations to join this class of

experts, these adventures were full of strange profit. It was astonishing how much they enriched the climbing-mood. But not at all
as plums to be fished out of memory's pie in a Little Jack Horner
spirit. These were no mere thrills to recall. They were rather an
indistinguishable ingredient in the sauces from which innumerable
later climbing-feasts were to get their savour. Risk was the salt, but
he or she would be a stupid cook who thought that the more there
is of it the better! Leading or following, there must be difficulties,
mental as well as physical, for effort and resolution and achievement
to measure themselves against. But climbing, I felt, was not a
gamble. That was a view that only desperate people could take. Risk
seemed almost always controllable, at least, in British climbing. It
was up to you to decide what was justifiable. And on the rare
occasion when it had threatened to get out of hand it presented
aspects (as in Herbert's cool pluck that first day on Lliwedd and
now in Holland's invincible nonchalance) that I could not but be
glad to have seen.

My only visit to Scotland closed with a quick climb on the
Tower Ridge of Ben Nevis. It gave me views of the greatest cliffs
in Britain that made me hunger to return, but they seemed to miss
the sheath of ice and snow that at Easter makes them our finest
Alpine climbing-ground. As we reached the summit a wintry cloud
drew over and a wild hail-storm drove us down. I have rashly
promised I. A. R. to go back some Easter to climb from an *igloo*
at the summit. He avers that when he slept in his snow-house there
he could keep the indoor temperature at any point he wanted! And
I will go back to Skye too some spring, to redeem those promises
that I had watched disappearing behind the watery veil.

CHAPTER VI

AN ALPINE NOVITIATE

(*1920*)

Alps at last—Alpine arrival—Numerals on the Buet—First steps on the glacier—Hut life—Drama in the Couvercle—A correct ascent of the Charmoz—The Géant—Frostbite on the Grépon—The traverse of the Drus—Into Switzerland—Petit Clocher de Planereuse—An erratic umbrella—Wasteful rest-days—Dream-walking—The Guide's roll.

One gets all the pinnacles, ridges, bosses, aiguilles and domes by the wrong names as one leans out of the train windows between St Gervais and Argentière on the morning of one's first sight of the Alps. But what does it matter and what would one not give to have that moment over again!

The train across France had been so crowded that even first class passengers had had to stand all night, but still the excitement was so great that I could hardly look at what appeared between the separating cloud masses. The upper regions were all an inextricable confusion of dazzling gleams and grey frowning baseless precipices, and I felt in a trance, already tasting that mixture of ecstasy and weariness and discomfort that from the beginning to the end is the basic quality of the Alpine experience.

I recalled I. A. R.'s description of his first Alpine hours. As a little boy he had gone up in the funicular to Finhaut feeling as though he was going up in a balloon. And there suddenly was snow—the Aiguille du Tour and some of the Aiguilles Rouges. The train had dumped him at a station. Where was the snow? Surely it must be melting! Up a burning street he trotted—no snow in sight, only house fronts—and then into a hotel. The snow he felt would all be gone before he reached an upper corridor and, running down its length, pulled the curtains aside and looked out. The Trient Glacier was, he found, still there! By Argentière a thin drizzle was already falling and the heights had retired behind a curtain of cloud. Mr and Mrs Culling Carr, Herbert and I walked up to the Planet Hotel, with a sense of illimitable adventures before us. I remember the wet path and my thin shoes. A gentle melancholy descended upon me. The hotel looked so huge, so sophisticated, and there was an echoing quality about its vast corridors. The view of Mont Blanc from here is certainly magnificent, but it was hidden; the mountains looked too big for anyone to go up. In short, the Alps are bewildering to a newcomer. One's feelings have been over-wrought. Ecstasy had evaporated into deep sadness.

With training the beatitude comes back, on a firmer foundation. Herbert and I set out next afternoon up the Col de Balme. I had been looking up at it from my window—an inviting grassy hillside. It had an accessible look in its grey-green familiar colouring, its moorland air seemed to make intimacy with it possible, in contrast with the strange forbidding aspect of the great peaks. The grass was springy under foot, the aromatic savour of the dwarf rhododendron filled the air and the plateau was boggy like a Lakeland fell-side. But oh, the million new flowers. Up on the Croix de Fer I looked across to Switzerland and the little emerald-green saddle of La Forclaz. Over above me was the Aiguille du Tour and far off, beyond the Verte, the fortress of Mont Blanc, but as yet I could not measure or much realize those immensities. We made plans for a journey of discovery into Switzerland before the season was over and turned homewards. Half-way down, two sombre figures, the man in a dark blue suit, the woman ahead in black, were rushing with short deter-mined dashes up the slope. Mind was dominating matter and in time they would infallibly arrive. We approached, and I perceived that the man was carrying a book as big as a family Bible under his arm. Something struck me as familiar about them in their earnestness. At closer range there was no mistaking Beatrice and Sidney Webb, whom I had never tried to imagine away from a platform. All the way down I thought about H. G. Wells' conception of an Alpine holiday in quest of inspiration. Did it not give him his *Little Mother on the Mörderberg* who rolled down thousands of vertical feet to emerge on the glacier 'a little thing like a black-beetle struggling in the heart of an immense split ball of snow'?

The Belvédère was our very first Alpine expedition. It heightened the sense of adventure to be seen off by Mrs Carr, to be carrying an ice-axe up an 'ice-mountain', and a sack with things for the night, dark glasses and glacier cream up to a *real* hut! It was a little hotel really, hardly a hut at all, with beds and sheets and a three-course dinner. These high hut-hotels in France specialize in extortion. Because we were hungry we managed the tepid water soup, the goaty stew, the sour cream, but what food to give heroes! The submissive tolerance of the climbing world is strange. When you consider the plenty, flavour, cleanliness and variety of the fare in the Austrian hut-hotels, it is nonsense to pretend that these French inns do the best they can.

But of all this I knew nothing then. All for me was *couleur de rose*. How exciting it was to be getting up 'in the middle of the night', starting off on a *proper* expedition! I remember it as a long, long snow slope and how I began a trick of counting steps first in English and then in French to beguile the way. It stayed with me for a season or two, as a dodge for making snow-grinds endurable. Toiling over the glaring surface, I wondered for the first of many times what enthusiasm made one labour so and what was the recompense? Your face streams, your temples pound, your breath is short, you feel that another step and you will lie down on the snow and quickly expire! A dogged determination forces you on. But what was this state of utter mental blankness that came upon me in place of the anticipated raptures? The summit, I fancy, was of reddish

shale. Both guides shook hands with us all and said 'Good-morning'
in their comic way as though they had not seen us before and by
way of mutual congratulation. We went down by a long easy ridge
and a snowfield that landed us near the Flégère. There were wild
strawberries in the upper forest slopes and swinging harebells, and
we lingered among them, broken in at last, and by this time well
content with our first Alpine peak.

After a few days we went up to the Lognan Hotel—to me then
full of romance through its association with *Running Water* and
my first imaginings of the Alps. The path up follows a moraine. I
had seen plenty of grass-covered moraines in Wales but never a
living one, if any such negation of life can be so described! The
pebbles, the stones, of every size and colour, half buried and inse-
curely set in a matrix of what looked like finely pulverized cement;
the giant boulders askew on the ridge, streaked and splashed with
the pervasive glacier grit; in all this the desolation was beyond any
that British cliff or scree-shot could show. A strange kingdom! I
felt then that it could never—like other deserts—grow to be a
mental home. One would always want to be off the moraine—either
down on the grass or up on the glacier. It is just a means to an end.
Does anyone relish moraines?

The glacier here, though, hardly looked as though one could get
on it. This was my first close view of a big ice-fall, and it held me
spell-bound and somewhat aghast. The waves of the ice near to me
are not like water's waves. These towers, split and splitting, and
leaning forward one behind the other in close-packed ranks over
the valley, were all the more terrifying for their beauty of clear
white and palest greens and blues against the sky. As I watched,
one tower far up shifted and then disappeared among its fellows
with a surprising echoing roar.

We had hoped to go up the Aiguille d'Argentière or make the
circuit of the three cols (Chardonnet, Saleinaz and Tour). But the
weather was unkind and we had only a chance of practice walks
on the glacier. This was thrilling—to walk across the curled and

knife-like edges between crevasses or across wider gangways of snow. How the chips from the steps echoed down and down in the depths of those blue-black gulfs below! What matter if it were a little undignified to be held up by the belt by the guide as I slid and quivered across the abyss. It was deliciously terrifying. I felt like a novice tight-rope dancer and I was seeing the Alpine world.

What I knew about glaciers all came from books. The actuality surpassed even my well-fed expectations. What a variety of kinds of crevasses there seemed to be! There were chasms and there were cracks; there were open clefts, evident except that you could see no bottom; there were fissures bridged across by masses of snow very palpably wedged in their mouths. The guide poked them with his axe, and sometimes then we just walked across, sometimes we made a long detour round them. What could be the difference he noticed? Their lids of snow were sometimes white or faintly yellow, more often various shades of grimy grey and it was hard to make out why. More puzzling still, there were very similar-looking streaks of snow that were not lids of crevasses at all, but only drifts choking up runnels in the honeycombed fretted ice. These he seemed to recognize at sight. Higher up, they ran together; a continuous white blanket spread out—slashed, it seemed, capriciously, over long, narrow, sea-green or indigo gulfs whose brinks were overhung with unsupported flaps of snow. It was obvious enough that one should not walk on these. But where could one walk? Here was Ferdinand probing cautiously across a smooth unbroken stretch. In reply to a question, he pointed away to the left where an innocent sort of wrinkle seamed the slope some distance off. Apparently an entirely invisible crevasse stretched right under our feet. How carefully then I stepped in his footprints; how advisedly I kept at the full distance of the rope, the twenty feet of it taut between us; how friendly felt the slight pull from it at my waist, as Herbert, behind, did the same. I should not go far if the ground opened under me! This mutual insurance seemed a delicious extension of the climbing co-operation. I began to realize the point of not carrying loose coils of rope in my hand, for obviously every coil meant a yard further to drop.

There was much else to learn from close observation of Ferdinand, and I plagued him with unanswerable questions. Where stones and ice avalanches fall; why one tempting slope would cost hours in step-cutting and why another, that looked so similar, would be no more than a steep walk; the difference between soft snow that compacts itself under foot and that other snow that melts into slush and gives no hold; the changing colour that sometimes shows in what thickness the snow clothes the tilting ice and whether it is fast bound or will slip away. Little by little some understanding of these things comes to you with experience. And there is no greater pleasure than discovering that your technique has grown.

On the human side I was learning, I hope, some less dignified items of Alpine lore. How to keep the rope between me and my companions from being a nuisance to them. How not to bound on, after making an awkward step, without giving the next man the extra seconds in which to take it. Not to breast up the grass or moraine slope parallel to the leader who is setting the pace. Not to tread needlessly out of his steps in the snow—thus setting those behind an endless series of petty problems as to where they in turn will set their feet. All these things together constitute rhythm. They seem trivial to a beginner. But if you neglect them, you break it, and by the end of the day the cost of such fractures, in extra effort to the party, is enormous. How maddening I must have been, prancing off down, as soon as the difficulty was passed, with a huge tug upon the man on the pitch behind; picking improved lines of my own that tangled the rope all round the crags; and thrusting up past the patient legs on the path in front. No doubt I still have many vices that I know as little about; but not these!

We soon went round to the Montanvert, where I was to go up the Moine with Mr Lewin and his guides. So I came to my first experience of a real hut as opposed to a high inn. It was very different from my ideal imaginings. The tiny Couvercle of those days was crowded to the limit. I had never seen so many tramp-like figures of all nationalities—ragged, dirty and unshaven—as were lolling about the platform, smoking and gossiping, when we trudged up the wooden steps towards them. To my intense relief, the tall form of Mr Solly emerged from the crowd of wild men and with him Noel Rooke, who had been making some striking drawings of the Tacul and the glaciers. The reason for Mr Solly's extra special welcome was at once made plain. He had a big pipe and it was unconquerably blocked. What he most needed in life was a hairpin, and what use was woman on the mountains unless she could instantly provide one?

Through the crowd I penetrated into the dark interior of what was evidently an eating- and sleeping-room in one. It was perhaps good training to start with one of the worst huts in the Alps. Now, much enlarged, it has become a semi-hotel. Beginning so, I was well placed to develop, at leisure, a taste for hut life—that queer existence in between the luxuries of low, well-found camping and the hardships of the high bivouacs of the pioneers. This compromise gives you a roof, a stove and an enamelled *batterie de cuisine*, though this tends, in Latin districts, to be as much missing as present. There will be pails, or tin tanks you sling on your back, to fetch the water with from the spring or collect it, drop by drop, from the recesses of a crevasse. Or you may have to melt snow. So parsimony in the use of water is common. 'Where does one wash?' friends ask; and Alpine novices even take up sponge-bags and bath-towels! But a cat's lick will be the best you can hope for. Dressing is little more than putting on your boots. Cooking is as simple, for extravagances are checked by your capacity to carry. In good huts and weather you take up provisions for three days and, unable to drag yourself away, make them last out five! Friends picture one concocting tasty dishes, or preparing the sandwiches. Actually you eat bread and cheese and sardines and ham and jam and drink tea in gallons. But I have forgotten Maggi—the mainstay of the evening meal when the day's exertions are over and the hungry climber sits down to

restore his forces. And what is Maggi? No one knows! You buy it
in yellow packets under innumerable names—Petits pois, Tomate,
Légumes, Julienne—but the flavour is the same. This may be partly
because most Alpinists get into the habit of heaping their plates of
Maggi with any stale scraps of bread they may have, fragments of
butter left in the tin, and of slicing into it ancient bits of cheese.
Almost anything edible may get into this mélange. Non-climbing
walkers who visit huts seem to marvel most at the soups their guides
concoct, not realizing what usual Alpine fare it is. Appetite altering,
alters all. High on a peak one looks forward ravenously to such a
dish and pictures with relish *le potage bien tassé* that one is travelling towards.

Maggi is indeed the great Alpine comfort. You consume it on a
bare board table stained with decades of use, by the flicker of a
candle mounted in the neck of a bottle, sitting on rough benches
or little square stools. Beyond its glimmer, under solid beams and
strong braces that hold the hut up against the tug of the tempest,
is the communal bunk, a dim recess laid with humpy mattresses
stuffed with straw. If you are lucky, it may nowadays be silk waste—
the rats will not eat this. Here you sleep, side by side in rows, packed
more or less densely, under blankets that, in the day-time, are piled
in square stacks or hung, in more provident huts, on wires out of
the reach of rodents.

When you have supped down several enormous bowls, you kick
off the great wooden sabots that in most huts are provided for you
to wear while you dry your boots, and roll up in your blanket—or
better, in several, if you have the hut to yourself. Those are the
golden hours when, thousands of feet above the rest of the world,
you can look out at evening from your nest upon mountains that
then seem peculiarly your own. Then you are indeed, as the Club
notices tell you, '*Chez vous*'. It was harder to feel so in the Couvercle
that evening. It was in one of its most congested states.

A partition split off a space at one end the size of a small bathroom. This was the hut *gardien's* sanctum, but so great was the

crowd that, for a consideration, he had turned it over to the only two other women there, a Comtesse and her maid, and he suggested that I should arrange with them to share it. When I went in, I was dazzled to find a Parisienne beauty in pale blue *costume de sport* with a jaunty little cap perched at the right angle. She had in front of her a fitted dressing-case open. Gold-topped, monogrammed vessels seemed everywhere, a faint perfume of jessamine filled the air. Scents, powders, paint, eyebrow-pencils and lipsticks were in fine disarray. The Comtesse graciously permitted me to have the floor if I cared to. Seeing that the men were sleeping that night on their sides on the floor of the main room, and even so some had to sleep outside in great cold, I thought myself very lucky.

In high huts you sleep in your clothes and have to be off before dawn while the snow is still hard with the night frost. I had heard much of the rules of hut life. The vigorous 'Lights out!' and the silence that falls at nine. The Couvercle did not come up to my picture. A riotous racket went on till after 11 P.M., and cooking was in full swing well into the night although a party was starting at 1 A.M. for the Aiguille Verte.

No sooner were the lights out at last than My Lady and her companion started an animated conversation about a shipwreck—exclamations and screams of horror echoed above me. I felt through the wooden partition the hatred of the masculine mass for feminine frivolity. Presently what I expected happened. A rap on the wall and an exasperated '*Voulez-vous vous taire?*' I writhed in shame on my floor. Half an hour passed quietly. Then on my horrified ears came the sound of high-pitched, tremulous groans. What could be the matter? They grew louder and more insistent. At last the companion woke up and declared that the Comtesse must be *souffrante*. The Comtesse clearly was. She cried out that she could not breathe and that she was going to die! At this the companion collapsed in despair. It seemed to me that a light would be helpful, but find the matches I could not. The quieter I tried to be the more things I knocked over. Soon I felt sixty-odd angry men would be growling furiously next door. At any moment might we not be described as *la limite sanguinaire*? It needed all my courage to creep out and slip over the sleeping bodies to find some matches, Mr Lewin and his brandy-flask. When I got back and lit the candle, the Comtesse disconcertingly sat up, still groaning, and faintly screamed that she saw red cows on the ceiling! Soon after this the companion divulged that Madame had a husband and that M. le Comte was even outside among the would-be sleepers. So out I crept again, feeling absurdly like an Elementary French Phrase-Book, to whisper '*Où est le mari de Madame?*' across the resentful huddled forms. Soon an ineffectual little wisp of a man appeared. I gave him the brandy-flask and he tried feebly to make her take some. At which she sharply accused him of attempting to poison her. His reply was to take her hand and stroke it gently, murmuring the while '*La, la, ma chérie. La, la, ma chérie!*' After a little of this I decided to become a firm sick-room nurse, turned him out, gave Madame a dose of brandy and propped her in a sitting position in bed. Sitting up she soon breathed better, and after a short while happily fell asleep. The hardest part of the whole thing to me was that the men never realized that she really had been ill and needing assistance, and simply lumped the three of us together as 'silly women—always making a noise at the wrong time!'

The Moine was a delicious climb. Perfect weather attended my first inside view of the Mont Blanc chain. I remember being unfavourably impressed by some of the local guides. Two of them were making fun of their clients, merely inexperienced young men, all the way down. But in Chamonix, more than anywhere else, you must not confuse the really admirable men with the general ruck and riff-raff of the profession.

Back at the Montanvert, Mr A. R. Thomson, who was taking an off-spell, kindly lent me his guides, the Summer-matters, to traverse the Charmoz. It was my first big Alpine rock-climb and I was a-quiver all night with expectation. The path round to the Nantillons Glacier runs, on a level, high over the Chamonix Valley and there was the famous cross of the Chamonix lights spread out right across the valley like a nether constellation. But soon, with evident steps, the dawn came; as though the light were being turned on in gushes at some central source. The glacier itself was in a horrible condition, though I did not know this at the time and supposed our antics to be normal. A thin flange of ice, diagonally dividing two huge crevasses, had to be walked. Midway of the narrow ridge, a bollard of ice barred progress. Each man in turn had to loop his rope round it and slide down the other side, with the cold vacancies of the under-ice world below him. By this time dawn was full in deep rose on the flame-like peaks about us.

I may have needed it, or the guides may have assumed I did, but never since have I seen anything like the elaborate devices to make pitches easier for me and prevent my having to do any real hard work. Now it was a rope balustrade outside me on the traverse, now a loop supplying the place of a distant hand-hold, now a shoulder for my foot from behind and always a helpful 20-lb rope-pull from in front! I realized once for all that with a light and docile novice two strong, capable guides can make Alpinism a very gentle sport indeed. In spite of all this I had a splendid day and we were down again at the Montanvert by noon. This is a guide's idea of a correct mountain day. They get to bed to sleep and rest for the morrow. Later when wisdom has come, the amateur may do the same. In a first season one is apt to sit on the terrace and drink innumerable cups of tea and tell whoever will listen about one's climb. There is this also in favour of the guides' policy: it is probably far less tiring for the novice to go down quickly in the glow and energy of the achievement, than to linger until the reaction comes.

The guide, with his immense boots, giant axe, coils of rope and thick duffle suit, is an Alpine institution which fascinates the non-climbing tourist. He is often regarded as an infallible superman whose absence from a party spells Foolhardiness at least, and probably Disaster. But he may be an incompetent ruffian with a licence

won Heaven knows how! Or he may be a genuine Hero with every
fine quality. I was to find out later that all grades between these
exist. The ordinary, well-recommended man is just a very strong,
capable, professional mountaineer with a thorough knowledge of
his local peaks. As such he deserves every respect. Like any other
professional man—a doctor, for example—he carries serious responsibilities. And if one thinks of the incompetent parties he takes
care of, his risks are considerable—even when he confines himself
to a few peaks in his own district of which he knows every yard.

The really eminent guide has gifts of a higher order. He takes
intense pleasure in the subtleties of his craft, combines shrewd
judgment with daring, and to watch him is an education to his
followers. Between him and them a comradeship grows up, tested
through years of joint expeditions. It is then that really big climbs
become enjoyable and safe. To the enterprise the guide brings a
lifetime of experience on the hills. One has only to watch Alpine
peasant children playing about on the snow-sprinkled rocks in
winter, almost as soon as they can walk, or to think of the years
they spend scrambling about broken precipices as goat-herds, to
realize what reserves of inbred aptitude they have. No amateur
coming late to the game can learn to rollick down cliffs with a
tenth of the ease of a first-class guide. And, obviously, few can wield
an ice-axe as well as a man who spends his winters cutting down
trees, building chalets or working at the forge. This does not mean
that the amateur is a passenger. Besides being a capable Alpinist he
may be the strategic brain of the party. He has ten or eleven months
of the year in which to pore over Alpine Journals, maps, and photographs, in preparation for the next climbing season, and usually
knows much more about the mountain's history than his guide.
Generally he is the initiator, and his, in any case, is the ultimate
responsibility. But, inevitably, in any danger or emergency, the
decision lies with the man who does the leading.

Our next scheme was to go up the Grépon, but the weather
went bad and all we could do when it half-cleared up were the

Montanvert training climbs, the Petits Charmoz and Aiguille de l'M., and exercises in roping down from a telegraph post. At last when the weather seemed a little more settled, we set out, Herbert and I with Ignace and the Summermatters, for the Grépon. At the foot of the far-famed Mummery Crack it began to snow! Two Italians ahead of us, however, continued, which was an extra reason why we should not turn back. So up we went, for my part not entirely self-propelled. My hands grew colder and colder in my gloves and I lost sensation in two fingers of my left hand. They were putty-coloured and lifeless by the time I got to the top, and Ignace had to rub them hard and long with snow to bring agonizing sensation back to them. Whenever it was at all cold that season the two frost-bitten fingers went dead again at once, and they did not go quite right again for a couple of years.

After this it was hurry-scurry through the storm, with the snow-flakes silting into the holds. On the Chemin des Bicyclettes the Italians stopped to watch me come down the Grand Diable. This is a colossal holdless boulder over the left-hand corner of which you pass your rope and slide down. Both the Italians below and Ignace above were full of advice and instructions, and the mixture of German, French, Italian, with English from Herbert, was a most bewildering, Babelish sound! We struggled up the last pitch to the summit and swung down the other side as quickly as possible, for the storm was getting worse. We felt the more exuberantly delighted to have managed the traverse in such weather. The rock is so sound and the pitches so full of character that I was filled with a longing to do it again as soon as possible on a fine day. Paradoxically, I have never been back.

The Montanvert is a big hotel with a terrace; at the end of the mountain railway 3000 feet above Chamonix, and it is crowded in the day hours by tourists coming up to experiment with the Mer de Glace. But there was excellent company there: Mr and Mrs Helburn from Boston, Messrs O'Malley and Newton. And when Mr Culling Carr came up next day, we started off for the Col du

Géant in stupefying heat. The ice-fall was twisted and intricate that year and I clambered in steps up and down pinnacles and along the sides of crevasses for a long time with great content, feeling myself now really in the Alps, for there are few finer routes than the Col du Géant. But the plateau above was grilling hot, the snow soft, and I was back counting steps again, first in French, then in English, before we came to its edge, and there, over the roof of the Torino Hut, were endless Alps and a hint of the Italian plain.

That astonishing spire, the Dent du Géant, was our climb for the next day. An exceedingly cold wind blew, and climbers from the Torino often delay starting till late. The Géant is in places festooned with ropes and dotted with *pitons*, the reason being that they are very useful in bad weather. They were talking in the hut of replacing these ropes, which were old and rotten. When we reached the second rope, which goes up a slab supplied with quite nice holds, we found a cluster of humanity hanging on to it, headed by a dilapidated ancient guide. They were clinging to it, grim, determined, without attempting to use the hand or foot-holds that were there. At their request we passed them, went up to the top, where an enormous silvery Madonna stands, a wonder to all who behold it when they think of the ground up which it has come. We rested, ate, and enjoyed the view of the Italian Alps with the great sombre clouds of the plain behind them. Then we went down to find the same pleasant old party hanging in the same old place! They seemed undismayed. The sight of their efforts gave us a great respect for the strength of the worn-out ropes.

At the foot of the peak on a sunny verandah of rock was Mr O'Malley, recovering from some inland fish which is one of the chief dangers of the Alps. He and Mr Newton came with us on the morrow in a great caravan that walked up the snowy plateau of the Aiguille du Midi and down to the Montanvert. There I spied Mr Geoffrey Hastings and worshipped. Was he not the doughtiest hero remaining from the Mummery Epoch? He did not let my expectations down. An enormous sack jutted out from between his shoulders. When he lowered it the ground shook and he divulged that he made a practice of filling it with boulders to keep himself in training!

The peak that dominates the Montanvert is the Dru. It looks so colossal from the terrace when in the reddish evening light its cliffs seem to draw near, that I felt very presumptuous to be thinking of it my first season. Still the weather had now turned perfect and what a climax its ascent would make to the year! As we (Herbert, Ignace Zurbriggen and Ferdinand Summermatter) toiled up the zigzags towards the Charpoua under well-filled sacks (the Charpoua is a cold hut with few blankets and you have to take up wood with you for the stove), I could at least feel I was approaching in no rash, light-hearted spirit. To be honest, I was rather frightened. One's idols are daunting when one comes close to them. A mixture of awe and admiration filled me as I craned my neck to look upwards. After a while I felt I knew why good-mannered Chinese people may not direct their gaze higher than a superior's girdle.

The last hour up to the Charpoua Hut is very steep and hot and the sun is on one's back. A little below the hut are some slabs. Just by them we met a young man who had done what one is always expecting to do. He had tripped on the path, and unable to recover himself with his enormous sack, he had plunged down the slabs and taken a great deal of the skin off his face. He was not an encouraging sight but luckily was not much hurt. There were several parties in the hut, and among them Mr Bowen, who sat on the bench at the foot of my bunk describing the climb and earnestly recommending me to wear white kid gloves, as he had done, to protect my hands. After supper, an enormous moon came up. Mont Blanc shimmered under it as though lit from within, and its light made the enormous walls about us look higher than ever. A search-party went out, up into the maze of *séracs* of the Charpoua Glacier, to look for two climbers who were late in coming back from the Dru, and brought them in towards 10 P.M.

We still had the moonlight when we climbed up the glacier. It is extremely steep. How I longed to be wearing crampons, those iron ice-claws that are nameless in English. Americans sometimes call them creepers. To a novice they seem to make all the difference between safety and suicide! Without them I felt that I stayed in the steps chiefly by miracle. Ferdinand kept telling me to stand up straight, and this is certainly the clue to the good ice-man's ease and security on steep slopes. This slope was as steep as a ladder, and it seemed fantastic to be feeling for one's steps there half-awake in the dreamy dim light—especially when one's shadow fell across the places where one's feet should go. The ice runs up into a bay in the cliffs. With the first daylight we were off with a will up the wall of the crags. How they soared and soared above! I thought at times that we should never get up them, but the going was glorious. My chief memory is of the need for speed—the continuous saving of seconds that a really long climb requires. My diary notes only that we reached the summit of the Grand Dru at 9.07 A.M., testifying to my interest in the flying minutes. Alas that one recalls sitting on the terrace of the Montanvert gazing up at the cliffs so much better than the actual climbing. One is so busy seeing that the rope goes out smoothly and getting ready to follow up the next pitch. But a general impression of height gained and air and sunshine, and of a rhapsody of swift movement, remains for ever. Corners of rock one swings round, steep narrow scoops to wedge up, a place where there is a little descent, come back. And then suddenly, quite near, are the summit rocks.

From the Grand Dru one looks down across a gap to the Petit Dru, where is the silvery gleaming Madonna that Ravanel le Rouge, with a little company of the strongest guides, had taken up the previous September. The ridge between took an hour. We dropped over the edge into the gap, down a smooth overhanging wall, on a spare rope.

Down the Petit Dru one goes very largely on a spare rope to save time. The route in 1920 was extremely difficult to find from the summit. We did not discover it without a good deal of scurrying about, looking down various possible and impossible chimneys. Nowadays the ascent of these chimneys is often made, but it is strenuous, for they are steep and narrow and with small holds. On a spare rope one slides down with less effort—but Mr Bowen was right, a pair of kid gloves would have saved a lot of skin! Down we went from storey to storey, as it seemed, hurry-scurry, helter-skelter, though not hugger-mugger, for the rope has to be kept in order, no matter what happens to one's clothes. The breeches work up over the knee and the coat gathers round the neck; one feels a bunch of garments as one swings on a rope that pulls and pulls as it draws out round the thigh and over the shoulder. This friction checks the rapidity of the descent, but, after a bit, the wear on the person begins to tell and I wondered whether a permanent set of grooves would be left with me as a memento.

This roping down—an *abseil* or a *rappel*, as it is usually called— is a trick one gets used to. There are several methods. As a rule you wrap the rope round you, under the knee and over the shoulder. The chief secret is to put your feet on the rock and lie well out over the void. To the beginner the sensation is soul-stirring. But it is still more moving when, on an overhang, you dangle, like a spider spinning on a thread, free from the rock. Unfortunately, a human being, twisting on the end of a line, cannot wind himself up again and so gets it over as soon as possible! The last man pulls the spare rope down after him. It has been passed round a belay or through a loop made fast and left behind.

—

It was on a glorious September morning that I went for the first time into Switzerland. The grass of the Col de Balme was fresh after the rains, the air was cool. How suddenly, with each break in the weather, towards the end of the season the temperature falls. The distances were crystal-clear, the colours of the lichen on the rocks were vivider, the shadows crisper, the freshly snow-sprinkled

Glacier de Trient whiter than anything I had seen before. Across the Trient Valley the little green saddle of La Forclaz was emerald-bright in the morning sun. That was Switzerland—to me the land of enchantment, the climber's paradise, the legendary country where the great knights of mountaineering had vanquished those dragon-glaciers and won their proudest castles. To many, Switzerland is the home of sterling but not very exhilarating virtues, a somewhat dull, business-like but efficient region of personally-conducted tours, cheese, chocolate and watch-making. But to me it was the land of heart's desire, and Herbert and I dashed down into the Trient Valley as though we were the doughtiest of adventurers. The other two of our party, Gedling Bradley and B. F. K. O'Malley, being hardened mountaineers, had unromantically but self-sacrificingly gone round to Martigny by the electric railway, taking the luggage with them. Incidentally our passports were not visaed for Switzerland, and we dared not go by train. At every turn, as we approached Trient, we seemed to see a *gendarme* stepping out into the path from behind a boulder. We had all the thrill of boy-scouts breaking through a cordon. It was the first international frontier I had ever walked over, and the surreptitious feeling heightened and exaggerated all my perceptions of differences. Here were wooden chalets in place of the dusty stone houses of France. (I forgot the chalets I had seen on the other side completely!) Here was, it seemed, a new flora—pale mauve autumn crocuses were piercing up through the short wet grass. The villagers of Trient wore an air which seemed new and strange. No doubt many of the differences one detects are illusory, but every mountaineer knows the feeling of intense freshness and novelty that comes with the crossing of a frontier ridge. It is one of the emotions that Alpine experience never stales. I shall feel it, I know, as strongly when I am seventy, if I am lucky enough to be crossing high cols on foot at that age. But why not? Did not M. Paillon lead up the Meije Orientale at the age of seventy-five? Does not M. Brulle, at eighty, still derive real pleasure from *une belle promenade de montagne*—which meant over Mont Blanc in a blizzard? And is it not on record that, when Mr Claude Wilson, Mr E. H. F. Bradby and Christian Klucker ascended the Ago di Sciora, 'Klucker, at the age of seventy-one, led like a careful lamplighter', and that 'the average age of the party was sixty-four'? These, indeed, are leaders to follow.

On the Forclaz saddle the last hay-crop of the year was being scythed. The grass was only a few inches high but the swathes lay in parallel curves about the smooth meadows that undulated like the soft-flowing slopes of a snow-field. The cut of the scythes had left a pattern everywhere. Old women were out raking under the hot sun and the air was charged with the scent of the hay as we tramped across to the path that leads down towards Martigny. How ravishing are these scenes after a course of the upper snows in the lifeless region—where only a patch of silene or a cluster of rock anemones lightens the waste of moraine dust or the harsh angles of the granite.

At Martigny, at the little hotel with vermilion chairs opposite the station, there was trout wonderfully cooked, and as we ate we made plans. O'Malley, who had been up almost every peak between Chamonix and Zermatt except the Vélan, felt that he must add it before the season closed. So he arranged to go for it by himself with a guide. Bradley, who, like that other elegant climbing connoisseur, G. R. Speaker, has many favourite severe rock-climbs scattered over the Alps and likes to introduce his friends to them, offered to take us up the Petit Clocher de Planereuse. We jumped at the chance. So next day saw us at Champex, all the big hotels empty and the dinner-gongs booming dismally one after another across the still waters of the Lake. At the end of the season, when one has the lake-side to oneself and the Hollow Land below the outlets to wander in alone, there can be few more lovely places. The ground is threaded with subterranean rivulets, the bilberries stain one's clothes as one lolls among them, the Grand Combin soars into the sky across the valley and the lake waters fill with more and more mysterious shadows as the early evening closes.

To go down a thousand feet before going up six thousand, with a heavy hut-sack on one's back, may be later an occasion for good jokes but in itself is a bad one. Towards evening we passed our peak, the Petit Clocher de Planereuse, a sharp fang of superlative rock. At its foot is a large overhanging rock, La Gare, in pioneering days used as a *gîte*, or sleeping-place. We had played with the idea of trying it ourselves, but nights are chill and long in September, so we trudged on up the remaining thousand feet to the Saleinaz Hut.

We had it to ourselves—a welcome change after my experiences at the Couvercle. I had a chance to examine a first-class Swiss Alpine Club Hut and admire the economy of its planning and the orderly completeness of its furnishings. After supper I went outside, wrapped in blankets, to watch the moonlight moulding the backs of a sea of clouds in the valley and cutting the upper glacial world into heraldic simplicity of sable and silver.

We were up at dawn, but so luxurious were our preparations and so conscientious our cleaning of the hut that we were not away till 8.30 A.M. It is only a step, a thousand-foot step, to the foot of the climb. Leaving everything, except a little food, we went up in rubbers. The climax is an extraordinarily hard crack midway up what the French guide-book rightly calls *une paroi vertigineuse*. It starts from *un replat minuscule* and is very much harder to climb even than it looks. Bradley, as chic as ever in his debonair brown corduroys, went up with deceiving ease. When my turn came, I thought the place more difficult than the famed Mummery Crack on the Grépon. You jam your right leg in the fissure and try to find rugosities for the left foot on the wall outside. Then you struggle and somehow, in time, you get there. It is one of the difficult places I recall with most pleasure. Herbert soon came up with the sack and we continued, enraptured, up some extremely steep but not difficult rocks above. Soon our heads came out into welcome sunlight, and a little way on was the summit.

There in the cairn, of all things in the world, was a decayed umbrella. Fortunately, Bradley knew the story. As Herbert recounted it shortly afterwards, it runs as follows: 'Once upon a time when a crowd of climbers was gathered at the Saleinaz Hut there arrived a large party of tourists, those parasites of Alpinism as I am tempted to call them in less liberal moments, one of whom had been careful to furnish himself on his perilous journey with a stout umbrella. After the manner of their kind, these good people contrived to make themselves unpopular by talking and singing late into the night, despite all protest, a criminal offence in the sight of men who are going to start on long expeditions at 3 A.M. He of the umbrella seems to have taken a leading part in this ill-timed revelry: in any case certain wicked men singled him out for punishment, and, having taken counsel together, at dead of night they carried out their plan. When morning came and the tourists prepared to return to the valley which they had been so ill-advised to leave, the umbrella was nowhere to be found; the hut was ransacked without success. Disconsolate, they began the descent. All at once they lifted up their eyes unto the hills and behold! There, far above them against the sky they saw the missing property, standing upright and open upon the very top of the Petit Clocher de Planereuse. And there its skeleton remains. You can see it in the illustration; behind Bradley's hat.'

This ended my first Alpine season. I had learnt a lot, much of which I shall have to relearn every year. For example, that the swollen face, the baked eyes, the headache, the qualmy inside and uneasy lungs of the first few high snow-climbs are the price to be paid for the amazing well-being that follows. Aching muscles and bruised feet turned next week into balance and resilience. There was nothing surprising in that, nothing out of the range of my experience in the home mountains. But that the novel discomforts and afflictions of the first Alpine days should also change into something new and strange, into clear vision, that was a point much harder to grasp. I thought indeed that in this I was just, once for all, getting used to the Alpine scale—much as I formerly thought that I was definitely learning how to climb rocks. It was not so, I was not paying a kind of entrance fee; and I was to find out that for the Alps there is no life subscription.

I had developed a hearty scorn for those supposed pleasures of rest-days about which senior Alpinists, I noticed, grew sometimes so enthusiastic. To me then a rest-day was an unfortunate necessity, almost a shameful concession to mortal weakness. However lovely the valley, however serene the far-off peak, I fretted to be back on the snow and the rocks. The beatitude with which, on the fine rest-day morning, I gazed at the flowers, the waves in the corn, the sun-dapple under the boughs of the fir, or the spread of its needles against the blue, I reinvested instantly in impatience; my heart leaping with anticipations as I thought of trials, deeds and achievements to come. Every colour, every sound, every taste, every breath of the fragrant meadow air came sharper, richer than ever elsewhere, each straying random thought carried its fresh, clean-washed charge of lively inexhaustible feelings. The inner world of associations and reveries stirred and pulsed, and imaginings flowed limpid and full; but, as I lolled about with stiff muscles and scorched cheeks, I longed to be up above the moraines again. I felt that a couple of such rest-days would be awful waste and would imperil my standing as a mountaineer!

Without the toil, the driving effort, of the active days, there would have been but a sleepy torpor, the merely pleasant doze of too much sun and air and food. Nothing of this other joy would have been. But in those days I did not see the account so. The rest-days were by no means a reward for work done; they were defects in my ideal of a tireless climber. And by the scale of the performances which the Alps had shown me were within ordinary human compass, I tried now to measure big days on the home mountains. It is a persistent puzzle how much more one can do at the moderate Alpine levels. Snowdon is quite a longish walk up; in the Alps an equivalent movement may be only an incident in the *approach* to a mountain. The usual explanation, the quality of the air, seemed hardly enough; the whole mental setting too is changed, the mood in which you move. In the Alps you can sometimes walk up thousands of feet in a reverie almost without noticing them. Handing over the whole business of where to put your feet to automatic centres, a semi-dream, full of delicious memories of all the nicest things that ever happened, or equally beguiling visions of castles in Spain, floats you up. Rare and fortunate days these, for you reach the top of the slope and wake up, almost refreshed. How different, more frequent, the days when every loose pebble offers itself to the conscious eye as a tiresome problem to be dealt with, when the moraine slips maliciously and the ripples of the dry glacier will not take the foot. I have never found out where cause is and where effect in this semi-sleep-walking. Do you dream because you are walking so easily? Or do you walk so easily because you dream?

The guide's gait, that labour-saving roll, I had been sedulously cultivating. It makes one comically recognizable in a city street at some distance; a greater disadvantage is that, in time, it becomes hard to speed up without disproportionate strain. It becomes a habitual easy ambling. This perhaps was the firmest of my first season's acquisitions. But at the time I thought I had gained permanently a quite new level of balance and endurance. My first walk taught me otherwise. It used to be a standing joke with us that the steps of the bridge from platform to platform at Crewe were easier to cross before than after a climbing holiday. I was to have a similar surprise the first time I tried out my Alpine feet across English fields.

CHAPTER VII

EXPERIMENTS AND DISCOVERIES

(1921)

Alpinism sans hommes—*The Egginergrat—Dress-parade—A great thunder-storm—Women Pioneers—Over to Zermatt—The Zmutt Arête—A grim museum—The Bétemps—Waiting for the weather—Ferpècle—A dragon—The Bertol ghost—The Za and an important encounter—Arolla—The Aiguilles Rouges—'I believe I'm in a crevasse!'—Sunset on the Évêque—The Ferpècle Ridge—A new ascent—Swinging in the void—Route-finding* in excelsis—*Fourteen hours' sleep.*

In 1921 guideless mountaineering for women, *sans hommes*, had hardly started. Such feats as Mrs Le Blond's traverse of Piz Palü had been hushed up, in a Victorian era, as slightly 'improper'. Even ten years later criticism of such undertakings was not infrequent. The *Alpine Journal* wavered between incredulity and stern disapproval, announcing the first woman's lead of the Grépon with a hesitating 'it is reported' and declaring that 'Few ladies, even in these days, are capable of mountaineering unaccompanied'.

While sympathizing with these signs of shock, I suggest that the question is mainly one of the right choice of expeditions. No sensible woman will imagine that she has the strength of a first-class man. But she need not lack judgment and the capacity to limit her enterprise to her powers. This too is a man's problem. One has only to watch a few score average Alpine parties of men to be convinced that a large proportion of them are utterly unready to meet a real emergency if it should arise—to bring up a companion from a crevasse if he really goes in, to get down a ridge plastered with snow which an hour before was pleasant rock-climbing, to deal with a broken leg high up on a peak. Yet, if this makes their expeditions unjustifiable, where would Alpinism be? I find it an alarming thought that when all goes well the party is to be congratulated on a fine climb. A single touch of really bad luck and they are open to the charges of incapacity, levity or culpable negligence. What came home to me from these reflections, as Lilian Bray, Annie Wells and I discussed a programme of guideless climbing to open the 1921 season, was that we must be unusually careful to incur no legitimate criticisms. We felt ourselves to be pioneers. The doctrine that women could and should take full responsibility for climbs within their powers was to be tested. So for the first experiment our plans were very modest. We had a week and hoped to do three expeditions, each of us taking the lead once.

We were going to Saas Fee and kept our intentions a dead secret until we arrived. At Stalden it was Sunday and no posts were going up the valley to Saas Fee until the morrow. True, we were offered six mules, but only at a vast expense. There was nothing for it but to repack there on the platform and carry up what we immediately required ourselves. A group of curious prying porters and officials gathered round, as we bashfully opened our suitcases. The entertainment was a frost. Instead of frills and furbelows, out came tins of herrings in tomato sauce, worn corduroys, woolly mufflers, battered aluminium saucepans and spirit stoves, a box of Keating's and mud-stained leather gloves! The audience sniffed in disgust and dispersed, though the six mules continued to be pressed upon us until we escaped from the station into the appalling midday heat of the valley. Bray had been inspired with the idea that everything for the three of us should be packed in one rucksack, which we were to carry in turns. When it came to her turn to carry it she seemed doubtful about the source of her inspiration and pleaded that she had meant it for the best.

At Saas Fee, when we divulged our plans, we were enheartened
by sound advice and encouragement from Mr Sydney Spencer,
who was there with Rudolf Lochmatter. The Carrs, with whom
I was to climb later, were also most helpful. Our first choice was
the Mittaghorn-Egginergrat. Except for the heat and our thirst,
nothing could have gone better. Bray persuaded us to let her lead,
on the specious ground that we would enjoy leading the harder
climbs to follow, but actually (as she confessed later in the *Pinnacle
Journal*) for the reason that, as an experienced Alpinist, she was
expecting the weather to break (it did soon afterwards) and
wanted to have a run for her money. On the top of the Mittaghorn
we roped, Bray joyfully throwing everything she could to us to
carry, for, as she persuasively said, 'it's always understood that the
leader carries nothing but responsibility'. The last chimney, which
we had expected to find difficult, Bray led without noticing. The
day was dreadfully hot, without a breath of wind, and we lay
gasping like fish out of water in a tiny scrap of shade among the
summit rocks. But pangs of thirst drove us down before long
towards the Britannia Hut, and when we found a cave with water
dripping from the roof we soaked ourselves inside and out. Soon,
refreshed, we were tramping round on the path towards the Plattje
triumphant at having accomplished our first feminine guideless
climb.

Bray, being herself in an immaculate buff corduroy suit with cap
to match, was naturally critical of her companions' attire. Wells, in
dark blue, escaped with the remark that *that* wouldn't last long
under Alpine conditions. But I came in for a heavier attack. The
point focused upon was an unfortunate lilac sun-bonnet with which
even then I was hoping to defeat the malevolent influences of the
sun. It was frilly and stuck out to throw a grateful shade—altogether
the very thing for a milkmaid in an advertisement. But such a
bonnet was unheard-of on an Alp, no one had ever climbed a
mountain in one before. It simply was not done! The whole status
of the sport was imperilled by it. On my next expedition, the

Portjengrat, I meekly reverted to my coloured handkerchief, not to upset the balance of the party.

Times have changed and women of all nationalities now crowd the Alpine centres. Thirteen years have sorted out the styles, and a stratification has developed that tells you fairly clearly what kind of climbing the wearer has in view. Here is a lady in vast cinnamon plus-fours, a parti-coloured bolero showing vivid sleeves, and to crown all a dashing picture hat. The face is made up with the same verve. She, like her rival in the musical-comedy cavalry breeches—enormous at the hips and tight at the knees—is frankly in fancy-dress and no one expects to meet her on the heights. Shorts occasionally appear on girl campers; they also are not going up to the glacier line. Preponderant is the democratic ski-ing girl, wearing out her last winter's kit—long, navy trousers, rather baggy at the ankle, and short-sleeved shirt—an outfit suitable perhaps for the snows and mild sun of winter but not in summer. Every time she sits down on a boulder the dark blue picks up the white glacier grit. These skiers generally walk well, but, though they carry ice-axes, they do not often go higher than the 8000 ft huts. There they eat a spirit-stove supper, sleep and look at the sunrise, and a few ascend some convenient belvedere. The genuine woman Alpinist is rarer. She can be recognized at once by the wear on her sack and axe and the tough texture of her clothes, fit to stand the scullioning of hut-life and the attrition of long descents over rocks.

The Portjengrat is a more serious climb. We started for it on a perfectly clear balmy morning and all was going excellently under Wells' leadership, when we were surprised by one of the most sudden and violent thunder-storms I remember in the Alps. Other climbers may remember it too, for it swept with amazing speed right across the Alps. I. A. R. was driven down by the same storm from a peak in the Valpelline, and my brother John saw it pass in the Dolomites. It came up in a few minutes from the west—a high, level, clean-cut wall of darkness, olive-green in colour. Before it, white against the gloom, tiny puffs of cloud like shrapnel-bursts were forming and disappearing in an extraordinary agitation. Our axes began to sing, and we scampered off the ridge in great haste, laying them aside while we cowered under the lee of a crag. Soon the wind was lashing past, covering everything with a blinding veil of hail and snow. But the storm passed as rapidly almost as it had come, and before long the sun was shining again. The storm looked, however, rather like coming back and we decided to make our way down while the interval of fair weather lasted.

As the storm came up we had been joined by Herbert Carr and John Hirst, who were climbing the mountain by another route. When the sky cleared, we went with them, down, as it turned out, a peculiarly uncomfortable wall which involved us in three long and rather spectacular *abseils*. Unhappily for me, this break in the weather prevented us from completing our programme, though the other two traversed the mountain successfully a little later. I joined the Carrs, with whom I had a glorious day traversing the Weissmies, and with that my time at Saas Fee was at an end.

Since those days expeditions *sans hommes* have become less unusual. This rather provocative slogan has been recently introduced by members of the Groupe Haute Montagne. I say 'provocative' simply because the registers in Club Huts show that the vulgar find this phrase an irresistible occasion for ribald comment! The standard of achievement has risen, and parties of women now have many first-class ascents to their credit. Among them are the Peigne (Miriam O'Brien, Winifred Marples; 1929), the traverse of the Grépon (Alice Damesme, Miriam O'Brien; 1929), the traverses of the Mönch (Miriam O'Brien, Micheline Morin) and Alphubel (Miriam O'Brien and Jessie Whitehead; 1931), the Tour Carrée de Roche Méane and the Matterhorn (Alice Damesme, Miriam O'Brien; 1932), traverse of the Meije (Alice Damesme, Nea Barnard Morin, Micheline Morin; 1933), the Blaitière (same party; 1934). After this, who can foretell what the future holds?

Already on British crags severe routes are accepted as within a good woman leader's power. But a great ascent in the Alps is another matter and a much bigger strain. You have hours of approach. You reach the difficulties already tired. You have to watch the whole time to secure the party against the unexpected. You have to move together quickly much of the day to cover the ground before night. You may have steps to cut. You must be ready to face crevasse emergencies on the glacier in the afternoon. For all these reasons a successful all-women's party has reason not to be displeased with its record.

Exceptional women, since the earliest days of climbing—about the middle of the eighteenth century, when a few wandering eccentrics and curious naturalists were discovering Mont Blanc and the Bernese Oberland—were occasionally members of men's parties. In 1809, only twenty years after the first documented ascent of Mont Blanc, the Chamonix girl, Marie Paradis, was taken to the summit of the mountain. I have to say 'taken' because she was more or less hauled up to the top—but then, on the other hand, how many men amateurs who preceded her were not treated by the hardy local peasants in the same way? Did not the immortal De Saussure himself require the assistance of countless guides?

But Marie's performance was admittedly a financial deal, so I will not dwell on it. Henrietta D'Angeville, having made her will (but they all did that in those days), went up Mont Blanc in 1838. She was a genuine pioneer—for she climbed in knickerbockers. Her good sense was shown in her entire outfit, since, unlike Captain Beaufoy who climbed in what was practically a suit of pyjamas, she had sufficient appreciation of the sort of rude climate she was going to meet in the higher altitude, to go thoroughly well equipped. She therefore donned the following warm and comprehensive kit. Lots of red flannel underclothes, heavy woollen stockings over silk ones. Scotch tweed knickers lined with more flannel, a thick woollen blouse reinforced with pleats on the back and chest, fur-lined gloves and bonnet, also a straw hat. These were insufficient for the arctic conditions she expected to encounter on the snow-covered summit, and in reserve were a velvet mask to protect the skin of her face, and a plaid and a fur-lined pellisse.

Her perturbation before the ascent will move a sympathetic throb in every climber's bosom. She experienced 'Une telle angoisse, une telle anxiété, une si complète insomnie, une tension de nerfs si fatigante, un point si fixe, que je puis assurer qu'un tel état, s'il se prolongeait, userait le corps vingt fois plus que l'ascension si désirée, quelque pénible qu'elle puisse être'. How she burned for the great hour to arrive! 'Oh! quand donc viendra-t-elle? Vrai, c'était là mes pensées, et en me les rappelant, je me sens toute prête à plaindre et excuser le délire de l'amour dans certaines natures exaltées. C'est une monomanie du cœur, comme ma passion pour le Mont Blanc, une monomanie de l'imagination. Quel bonheur de n'être éprise que de la tête et pour un amant glacé! la curieuse chose que de nous?'

Mlle D'Angeville was a permanent case of mountain mania, for she climbed the Oldenhorn when she was sixty-nine. In the early days even Royalty seems to have been attracted to the peaks. How many people know that the Empress Josephine, with the aid, it is true, of sixty-eight guides, went up to the Montanvert? And Queen Margherita of Italy, early in the present century, spent the night at the Refuge named after her on the top of Monte Rosa.

In the later 'sixties, mountaineers were conservative and thought it impossible to climb without guides. Yet it was in that decade that the first really great feat of climbing by women was performed. This was the first descent of the Sesia Joch in 1869 by the Misses Anna and Ellen Pigeon. This expedition, down the appalling South-East precipices (average slope 62°) of Monte Rosa, is all the more wonderful for one of the ladies coming down as 'last man' on account of the incompetence of the porter. A fine feat at any time, but especially remarkable in view of their voluminous skirts and the superstitions of those days.

During that period too, in 1867, the guide Carrel's daughter got within 350 feet of the top on the Italian side of the Matterhorn and described the ascent as a trifle! But these were forerunners. Not until the 'nineties—with Miss Lucy Walker, Miss Brevoort,

Madame Charlet-Stratton, Mrs Aubrey Le Blond, Mrs Jackson, Miss Katherine Richardson, Mlle Mary Paillon and Miss Gertrude Bell—had women won a recognized place in the front rank of *guided* mountaineers. Parties with women in them became as likely to make new climbs as anyone. This is true still. But the standard peaks were not as easy then as now. There were fewer huts and therefore many climbs were longer. More important, being as yet uncleaned by the passage of hundreds of parties, the ridges were littered with *débris* and the Classic Climbs had not that polish they have to-day. Miss Richardson, the first woman to go up the Meije, was also the first person to start for it from La Bérarde, leaving at 9 P.M. and getting back again at 5.30 P.M. the next afternoon! Mrs Aubrey Le Blond specialized in first *winter* ascents—a branch of the sport in which women have made a notable mark.

What has been done by Englishwomen more recently may be read in the *Year-Book of the Ladies' Alpine Club*, and the other nations are now not behind us, as the great careers of Eleonore Hasenclever (Frau Noll), who was killed by an avalanche a little below the summit of the Weisshorn in 1925, after climbing more than 150 peaks of 12,000 feet, and Mme Debelak, who led the first ascent (1926) of the great North face of Spik in Yugoslavia, have shown.

—

Zermatt was beckoning, a Zermatt I knew only through the pages of Whymper, Tyndall, Mummery and Leslie Stephen, a Zermatt dreamed of for years. It lay behind the ridges of the Dom and Täschhorn, on the other side of those dreadful, stone-swept slopes that, even before I visited the Alps, had terrified me. And I longed to be there. Every climber no doubt has his pet centre, and to many Saas Fee is an Alpine paradise; to my friends Walter Roberts and the Carrs it was so. Though I realized its charm, I remained unmoved and I never quite got over the feeling of being crushed by that western barrier towering up and taking the light of heaven from me. Breath-taking though its beauty is, I was overwhelmed and sympathized with those plainsmen who feel a touch of claustrophobia in the hills.

Different visitors to the Alps develop strangely different conceptions of the mountains about them and about this same face of the Dom there are some odd stories. Some non-climbing hotel acquaintances were full of a story of a girl they knew (or a friend of theirs knew) who got up one morning *very early* and went up the Dom from Saas Fee and down again by breakfast! They explained the feat by the fact that she was an extraordinary girl who was always doing things like that! It seemed hardly worthwhile to tell them that the fastest time imaginable for a racing party of guides from Saas Fee to the summit might be over seven hours.

My way to Zermatt was over the Alphubel Joch. Packing, as everyone knows, instead of taking half an hour, keeps one up till 11, and the knock on the door came at 12. We (Mr Carr, John Hirst and the two Zurbriggens) were away by 1.15 under bright still stars in an amethyst sky. As we toiled up the Langenfluh we seemed so shut in by the mountain walls around we might have been in a pit. For some hours the small circle of candlelight in which one walks seemed to be wandering incomprehensibly. Only when we came out on the crest between the glaciers, did the lines of the summits begin to show up hard against a changing sky; and soon the dawn was striking the crests with flaming red.

It was sweltering on the snow-slopes, lack of sleep made them seem long, and I was not too sorry when a proposed ascent of the Alphubel was cut out of the programme and we went down direct to Täsch. The train by which Mrs Carr was coming round had broken down and we had a long wait, which we beguiled by what I seem to have described in my diary as 'a childish game of presenting arms to greet her when she arrived'. When the train appeared, however, Ignace Zurbriggen, in an agony of self-consciousness, implored us to enact 'no such fooling' since it would reflect on his guidely dignity!

So I came to Zermatt and the Monte Rosa Hotel, that focal point of the glamour of my Alpine visions. There was the Table where the Mandarins of the Alpine Club ate in awe-inspiring state. How small and humble I felt whenever I dared to raise my eyes towards those venerable presences. There outside was the famous Wall where the guides sat! Beyond, a large bare square, with dusty trees about a bandstand, seemed less satisfactory, and the vast façade of the opposite hotel cut off a sad amount of the landscape. But round the corner the meadows were abloom, the scent of hay was in the air, and one could perch on an old timber railing to look at the mountains. Ruskin has described the Matterhorn and I dare not aim my words so high. But, in appraising its transcendent form, I always see its noble company. If you except the Dom and Täschhorn, any one of that royal circle of peaks would automatically take the first place in another Alpine valley. Nowhere else have all the summits in sight such individual character, such hardy grace, such unforgettable outline.

The Zmutt Arête of the Matterhorn had taken hold of my imagination, no doubt through reading Mummery. In 1921 it was still a climb with exceptional prestige. Later, the dry season of 1923 made it almost a popular climb and the route was much improved, though it will always be hard and long. From Zermatt you see just where you hope to be going with an almost overwhelming clearness. The long, swooping snow-ridge, which your feet will tread, and the leaning upper section above 'the galleries' form the mountain's right-hand profile. Seen later from the Schönbühl Hut, in cold light after sundown or before dawn, the route hides itself in the intricacies of the high-hung shadowy crags and the scale of the mountain makes the expedition seem impossible.

Sunday, August 7th, passed in deliberating upon my favourite jams and cheeses, in consultations with the Zurbriggens and ordering provisions. We got off immediately after lunch. The Zmutt valley is adorned at one point by an amazing cascade. The heavy masses of water crash down beside the path, spraying the passer-by and sometimes bringing large boulders down with them. This year a good deal of the path had been demolished and we zigzagged up for a few minutes through a local rain-storm of spray. Higher up, a shallow sun-warmed pool between the moraines caught my eye and I sent the guides on while I took rather muddy dips in its grey-green waters. Up at the hut were several unexpected old friends (Messrs O'Malley, Pryor, Newton and Robertson Lamb—also bound for the Zmutt), a pleasant encounter, for I was feeling strange and lonely with a team of guides and a crowded hut to manage for the first and last time alone. Also, there is no denying that a really big climb creates, just before it begins, feelings that make cheerful companions very welcome.

The morning was clear and cold and we were away at 2.30. Progress at first was a series of unpleasantnesses; several big moraine slopes have to be descended without a path. One slides in the darkness from one gritty knob of rock to another, not sure what will give way under-foot next or how big 'the fall' beneath is. Then, through hummocks of boulders heaped on ice, to the open spaces of the dry glacier. The Zmutt Glacier here is almost buried in *débris*. On the other side of it we put on crampons to go quickly up to the rocks— across some crevasses whose bridges looked horribly spectacular in candlelight. Dawn found us at the foot of the first great cliffs.

All the lower part of the mountain felt like preliminaries. Intricate route-finding but uninteresting going. From time to time Ignace would shout down directions to the guideless party below. We went up an unpromising couloir and breakfasted at an old bivouac site (whether Mummery's or not I did not discover, though it gave some overtones of memory to the morning). Then on, over shaly ground with a long sideways movement along *débris*-littered shelves. It was intoxicating after all this tedium to reach the snow arête (6.30 A.M.) and feel myself on the spot I had looked at so often and for several winters imagined myself on.

The arête itself was sharp-edged and felt steep and the drops on both sides are tremendous. One feels as though on a colossal roof-pole. The vast white blade sweeps down from a kind of handle of jagged rock-pinnacles that have to be climbed over or turned. We ate in a sheltered nook among them (8 A.M.). Then comes the Nose, very steep and exposed but easy climbing and with everything rather too loose for comfort. And the wind was growing steadily stronger. As we mounted we found more and more *verglas* (an all but invisible film of ice) and loose snow on the sloping ledges. Icicles detached by the gusts came tinkling down upon us. This light bombardment was making us feel jumpy and the guides began to hurry and urge that bigger stuff might fall. The Tiefenmatten gulf—the most terrific hollow perhaps in the Alps—was filling like a witch's cauldron with opalescent fumes beneath one. Above loomed a wall that looked as though there could be no way up. We seemed to rush at it. The pitches grew steeper and steeper until I would have sworn they were perpendicular. Haste on such ground destroys contemplation and my memory is hazy until we made off back to the left and joined the sky-line ridge again, up which we finished. What a sense of space it gave. Nothing to fall on your head. In place of the rocks one had been plastered against for so long—the universe, as it were, at one's feet. At midday we reached the summit. The marvellous view was cut and distorted by quick-moving clouds that swept across it, now hiding, now framing Monte Rosa. It was cold and we were glad to shrink into a cleft below the ridge to rest and eat in shelter. The ropes at the Shoulder of the Zermatt route were iced. It is easy to deplore them at a distance, but it is grand to have them to slide down when conditions are bad. The Solvay Hut, *ca.* 13,000 feet, that port in a storm which has served so many parties, looked infinitely pathetic, a mere match-box lost amid the immensities of the crags, as we went by. But when Herren Franz and Toni Schmid of Munich gained it after their thirty-four hours up the deathly North face of the Matterhorn in 1931, to rest there through two days of falling snow, its shelter and supplies must have seemed paradisial.

My diary records that the 5000 feet down to the Hörnli Hut, 'which it seemed we should never reach', were 'rough, dull and loose'. A meal and down another 5000 feet to Zermatt, finishing from the Schwarzsee by candlelight, staggering and prepared to be very pleased about the climb on the morrow. As it was, I was infinitely grateful to that Good Samaritan, Walter Roberts, who happened to be in the hall of the Monte Rosa Hotel as I came in, for taking my ten-ton boots off and ordering me a brandy and milk. When next I looked out the noonday rays were on the Zmutt Arête. It seemed just as remote, just as challenging, just as inaccessible to mortals as ever.

Now the weather, which had been remarkably steady, broke badly and I had my first long spell of Alpine impatience. But there is much to be done in Zermatt. There is the Pâtisserie where you take more cakes than you can eat and eat more than you should, and where all your friends conspire to aid and abet you, and you sit and listen to a good orchestra. For one afternoon this life has a tang of pleasant contrast to glaring snows and angular rocks. After two, you forget the defects of the heights and ache to be on them again!

For one afternoon there is the Alpine Museum, with a vestibule containing a few moth-eaten stuffed fauna. Beyond is a Chamber of Horrors which must do much to preserve the young and thoughtless from their rashness. I at least have never been the same since my first visit. There is the boot (only one) of Lord Francis Douglas. There the piece of sash-line that broke between him and old Peter Taugwalder at that hideous moment on the first descent of the Matterhorn in 1865; there the bits of torn garments and twisted frames of lanterns, flotsam of perished parties; mournful mementoes enshrined among a host of portraits of the victims of Alpine disasters. There they are—mostly in their Alpine kit, full of energy and excitement and hope, and in a moment without warning it is all over. The stone falls, the cornice crumbles, the snow-bridge breaks away beneath the feet and the irrevocable has happened. To those who let their imagination develop the hints that these exhibits provide, the Museum is a terrifying place. One turns to the relief-models of the district and of the Matterhorn as though escaping from a vision of the Tomb.

But it would be morbid to continue this strain of thought or to stay too long in the Museum. After a few words to the living exhibit, the well-known and gossipy Rudolf Taugwalder, who lost his fingers in 1908 on Huascaran (22,205 ft) in the Cordillera Blanca of South America, one rushes out again into the sunlight.

Outside, the cosmopolitan throng streams up and down before the shop windows, filling the narrow canyon-like street. For them, life between the post-card store, the bandstand and the Bier-halle seems very much as in any other international rendezvous. In spite of which, one can step into any side street, its balconies hung with geraniums like vermilion velvet, and drop back seventy years to find oneself peering between the old rust-toned timbers of the chalets up at the same outlines that gladdened the hearts of the pioneers.

Then there are the guides to consult about the weather, and plans to make, a lastingly fascinating pursuit. Engaging them is something of a gamble. You can either take a guide by the expedition at a high tariff worked out by the guides' associations, or engage him for a period at a daily rate. If the weather stays fine, you obviously gain by the last arrangement as much as you lose if it breaks. Hence an added restlessness in bad weather! In a fine interlude, I did the Matterhorn couloir of the Riffelhorn with Mr Lewin and then paid off Ignace as the rain began again. All the time the Rothorn was tantalizing me. It would show up between cloudy spells looking almost ethereal with the white sprinkle that, alas, powdered its rocks.

On August 14th, though the weather still looked dubious, Ernest and Walter Roberts took me up to the Bétemps Cabane. I believe Monte Rosa was in the background of our hopes. Everything was quiet when we arrived and we thought to have the place to ourselves, when suddenly thirty members of the Italian Alpine Club burst in. The uproar and atmosphere drove me out after supper, to sit wrapped in blankets on the bench by the wall of the hut. Over the Lyskamm an immense white cloud was streaming up, endlessly moving yet always in the same place, and lit with orange gleams from a moon that was still hidden by the mass of the mountain. A confused racket reached me through the wall of the hut; but here outside everything was queerly still. A black band of cloud silvered above hid the upper half of the Matterhorn, and from the Zermatt Valley, beyond the slopes of the glacier, a few scattered lights twinkled.

Four o'clock next morning showed rather like an English winter morning, much damp grey mist breathing around. It was my first serious guideless glacier expedition, and perhaps I took note of the conditions, the scene and the routè more particularly therefore. The scene, say I, but in fact we hardly saw anything all day. Our goal by this time had dwindled to the Jägerhorn, the lowly prominence in the plateau at the head of the Gorner Glacier under the prodigious north wall of Monte Rosa's Nord End. I recall a glimpse of the lowest reaches of that precipice and a passage through an area covered with pieces of fallen ice. But the rest of the day was compass work. We felt our way through a mist so thick that it was hard to tell whether we were going up or down a slope, except from the feeling in the legs. The snow got softer all day, we sank in to our knees, and as we came back a fierce wind arose. Our last hour or two was through a blizzard. I admired the style in which Ernest Roberts found his way back to the hut for tea.

That night we turned in early with the hut all to ourselves. We were just going to sleep when there was a din at the door and in came a very bad-tempered Swiss with an enormous sack, which a bit explained his ill-humour. He clattered round and disappeared swearing. A long interval elapsed before he reappeared, still swearing, with a second still more swollen sack and a miserably exhausted companion. The sacks contained, one could not help seeing, as they were violently unpacked between the candles on the table, four cameras as well as enough tinned foods to last, it seemed, for weeks. A horrid dispute was very evidently going on! The exhausted companion was declining firmly to start at 1 A.M. for Monte Rosa; the swearing Swiss grew more and more incredulous and disillusioned. However, the painful scene subsided in time, and later I discovered that the companion had started from Munich early that morning, had walked up to the hut from Zermatt on this first evening of his holiday. He simply could not go on upwards after only two hours' sleep.

Hopeless conditions drove us down, but on the 18th the three of us went to the Gandegg Hut and up the Breithorn and the Klein Matterhorn. Company was polyglot in the hut: Swiss and Germans, a Dutchman looking like Judas, a Russian and an Italian, two plump French girls and an incredibly smart American party. Their brand new climbing costumes from Paris were a subject of much discussion and a young boy named Lincoln kept on calling his mother out to observe a bigger and yellower moon than had ever been seen before. He was proud and ambitious and often informed the company how glorious it would be when he stood on the summit of the Breithorn. It was a pathetic small boy who lay on a rug on the glacier about an hour out from the hut, very mountain-sick and wishing no doubt he were back in Boston. His sister went up all right. Little did I think that in 1925 she and her mother would walk into my tent at the Canadian Alpine Club Camp, or that Lincoln would become a leading light in Harvard mountaineering, or that Miriam O'Brien would later dazzle the mountaineering world with her exploits on the Aiguilles du Diable, the Grépon and the N.E. face of the Finsteraarhorn.

The weather was blustering in the morning, and the wind whistled uncomfortably through chinks in the stone walls of the hut. Waking at 3.30 A.M. we had some disgruntled conversation, which is apt to occur on a bad morning at that hour, and promptly went to bed again to reappear more sweetly later on. The sun came out about 6 A.M. and we started, though clouds hung heavily about. For a while nothing was to be seen but the beaten track of the ordinary way. From the summit we started off along a beautiful ridge eastwards with the snow in perfect condition, after a little turning down to the Breithorn Plateau to make our way over to the Klein Matterhorn in a rather cold wind. A hundred feet of rock was a relief to the monotony of snow and we really had a view. The Oberland showed up well in the gap of the Nikolaithal and Italy was covered by a sheet of level cloud. Ramparts of rock and snow surrounded us in all other directions, and far below, but close at hand, were the great creamy slopes of the Théodule Glacier broken only by the tracery of crevasses. We discarded the usual route, made a direct way down the N.W. face on a fairly steep slope of excellent snow and were back at the hut at 2.40 P.M. drinking welcome weak tea. Lingering often to shelter from the wind and to let the green of the valley seep in after the wilderness of ice and snow, we tramped down the mule-track and across the meadows to the luxuries of the Monte Rosa Hotel.

This was to be the end of climbing at Zermatt for that year. The barometer fell. Far from being about to do the coquettish Rothorn, I could not even get over the Col d'Hérens to Ferpècle, where I was awaited. Though I engaged a guide and porter to make up the three they insisted on having for the crossing, I only managed to discuss the weather with them and then dismiss them.

Down into the Rhône Valley it had to be. The Breithorn and Klein Matterhorn were a sublime spectacle in their new snow, framed between the forests of the lower slopes as the train crawled down towards Visp. The Rhône Valley was at its most stifling. A wizened old man from Neuchâtel was ecstatic over its somewhat monotonous beauties. He told me that he spent his Sundays taking train journeys along it to various places ever since his wife died thirteen years ago. To every one his own pleasures.

—

The diligence from Sion to Haudères turned out to be a little yellow post-chaise. I was the only passenger and felt like a travelling princess as we changed horses at Euseigne. We took most of the day to crawl up the long valley, and the too gallant postman-driver, when not trudging beside his horse, beguiled the way with anecdotes and attempts at flirtation. The end of the long drive is Les Haudères, a maze of muddy passages between overhanging wooden chalets. The post gallops in in style with a hissing and jangling of bells. The horses are brought up sharp in a space no larger than a room and all the idlers stand round to watch. I collected a much too heavy sack from the boot of the chaise, tucked my ice-axe under my arm and promptly lost myself in the labyrinth of narrow alleys of the village. After some circling in the half-light I gained the path. Once out of sight of the village, I ate some bread and cheese, took off my travelling skirt and, as the night fell with surprising suddenness, hurried on up the valley.

The path up to Ferpècle is extra romantic and charming—even among the best Alpine paths. It threads an undulating park-like country, passing sometimes close above the roaring milky torrent, sometimes under the eaves of unexpected chalets, round grassy knolls and beneath vast overhanging boulders. Fresh-cut hay rustled under foot and the fields breathed scents of clover.

But the lights which should have gleamed round some corner seemed slow in appearing. The sack was *very* heavy. A blot of double darkness above the path looked rectangular but deserted. So, after going on till the glacier seemed near and the prospect of lodging for the night looked poor, it appeared best to turn back. The black blot, on a second inspection, looked more promising; a trickle of light came through a shutter, but I had to bang at the door many times, feeling rather hopeless, before voices came out to say 'But this *is* Ferpècle!' Inside, round the lamp in the tiny stuffy salon, were the friends I had been travelling to meet: Mrs Daniell, R. B. Henderson and I. A. R.

Ferpècle was quite a new kind of place to me. At Chamonix and the Montanvert last year, at Saas Fee and Zermatt there was big luggage in the hotel, different clothes to choose from, cotton frocks for off-days and silks for the evenings. I had never before stayed in a simple Swiss chalet where one could go into the kitchen to gossip in the evening. No tourists, no fashion; it was delicious. Madame was a very human sensible woman. Her husband seemed to do little more than conduct the mules up and down from Les Haudères and take a *petit verre* there. A marvellous set of efficient, self-possessed children helped her to run the place. Julie, only fifteen, looked after the Bricolla Alp Hotel, a tiny stone hut 2000 feet above on a bare alp between the glaciers. Pierre (fourteen) was butler, postman and other responsible personages. In winter he went to school in Sion—a child again, with scholastic ambitions. Then there were the twins Rose and Marguerite (about eleven), long-legged, grave-faced little apparitions speeding up and down the path to Bricolla or leaping after goats among the moraines—their straw-coloured pigtails flapping behind them.

The one thing wrong was the weather. When it cleared we scrambled on the Mont Miné, the graceful little point that divides the Ferpècle Glacier. From its summit we looked across at the smoke from the chimney of the Bertol Hut, hidden on its knob of rock in the midst of the glaciers, and I. A. R. told how with two equally inexperienced companions he had once waded across to it by night from the Mont Miné without a lantern. They had come up from Evolène and lingered so long gazing at the Dent Blanche from the slopes below and bathing in a moraine pool, that night caught them before they reached the ridge of the Mont Miné. So the three of them sat down to let the snows harden! But they soon found it cold and set out without more ado. Their safe arrival towards morning, seeing the route they took, still makes I. A. R. wonder why crevasses are so incredibly kind to the young. Even then the sight of their track in the morning light had made them ready to believe in miracles.

After going up the Pointe de Bricolla, we all moved up to the Bricolla Alp, a grey little box of a place, stone without and wood within, perched on the edge of the pastures that hang over the Ferpècle Glacier. From its windows you can look down on the furrowed and hummocky ice several hundred feet below, or up to the Dent Blanche, which from Bricolla seems to lean over wildly to the left as though under the pressure of a great wind. Its northern precipices and west ridges seem so near in their stark clarity that, to an inexperienced English eye, its summit appears only an hour or two's scramble away. The near grassy shoulders of the Bricolla Alp cut off the intervening moraines and glaciers and the white peak seems to soar up unsupported out of the meadows.

Our first expedition, on the Grand Cornier, was, as it deserved to be, a complete failure. It had been snowing most of the night, the very meadows were covered with slush and the rocks plastered. As soon as we had reached the main ridge up the westward spur which drops towards Bricolla and had looked over into the Mountet basin we cheerfully gave it up. There across the Zinal Valley were those three giants, the Weisshorn, my longed-for Rothorn and the Gabelhorn. There were the ridges and faces—to ascend which was my greatest ambition in life. I had read of them, gazed at them in photographs, talked about them, gone up them in imagination a score of times under impossibly good conditions and in record time always! Now at last I saw them. Unlike most anticipated things, they exceeded my wildest fancies in their scale. They were transfigured in their fresh snow. But closer and more overwhelming than any of them was the North face of the Dent Blanche. As we looked up at it, following with the eye the great unclimbed ridge that falls to the Col de la Dent Blanche, the germ was planted of an enterprise that was to dominate our Alpine plans for eight years. We waded down the snow swamp to Bricolla, and that evening exuberantly went up the pretty little rock-ridge of La Maya.

Next day settled weather seemed at hand and I. A. R. and I rushed down to Les Haudères. The Ferpècle meadows were shrill with grasshoppers and the valley colours were at their brightest, fresh-washed with the rain. But our business was provisions, sardines and such, including cognac for the flask. This last item led us into what an American would call a 'dive'—a cellar café which is the centre of social life in Haudères. At three o'clock in the afternoon it was empty except for the very shaky proprietor. As he had not what we wanted, we were led to sniff most of the many bottles on his shelves. What we got proved to be in the end mostly burnt sugar and water. But the mixture of exhalations from his bottles was absurdly intoxicating. In spite of the leaden sacks destined for the Bertol, we floated up to Ferpècle and stopped for tea. Madame came out smiling to tell us stories about the dragons that lived in the glaciers. Once she had really seen one. One night she had looked out about 10 P.M. and there was a light coming down over the brow of the snowfield. A smuggler perhaps? But soon there was another. Two smugglers or, more likely, a very belated climbing party? But another appeared and another and another. Soon a long chain of glowing points was undulating like a vast illuminated spine down into the valley. By this time the whole hamlet were collected in a panic-stricken group. Was it the dragon's phosphorescent backbone at last? The relief was unspeakable when the boldest of the men went out to meet it and came back with news of the Swiss army on manœuvres.

On our way to the Bertol next day we groaned and often decided that too heavy a price can be paid for tinned peaches and luscious pineapple. And to this day we go dry and empty rather than carry any tin larger than a sardine. As Mrs Le Blond notes, the introduction of the small tin was a revolutionary aid to Alpinism. Later I was to discover the virtues of fresh-washed salad, taken up with a flask of oil and vinegar. A priceless addition.

The Bertol Hut (11,155 ft) is perched like a medieval castle close to the summit of a spire of rock just where the westward glacier falls away to the Arolla Valley. A bergschrund (that crevasse where the glacier joins the rock-face) guards it most years, so neat and evident that only one person is known to have fallen therein. This adventure is a standing joke among the guides and porters of Arolla.

His shouts soon brought the Guardian out, who looked everywhere except in the crevasse and went in again. But the shouts went on and were so near and so mysterious that the Guardian became persuaded that the hut was haunted. Fortunately another party soon came along and fished the ghost out unhurt in a few minutes. Up the rocks a thick rope has been fixed and square steps hewn as footholds. It was a constant *divertissement* to watch parties coming up this stairway and diagnose their mountain experience from their behaviour. In those days the hut itself was small and the edge round it narrow. Here one could sit in an Indian red blanket skirt while one's breeches dried. We had sunk waist-deep in the new snow crossing the glacier, and now basked contentedly in the sunlight.

Round the corner from the Bertol, two hours or so away, is one of the prettiest peaks in the Alps—the Aiguille de la Za. I. A. R. had climbed it *en face* from Arolla as an undergraduate, with a reluctant companion. Betrayed by a Libby's Little Lunch Tongue whose tin nearly sliced the tip of his finger off, they wandered nearly all over the extensive face of the mountain in quest of a gentle route fit for the fingerless.

Our route was up the usual short stretch of amusing rocks; it has the concentration and neatness of moderately difficult Welsh climbing. I watched Mrs Daniell strolling last down the famous slab and admired the pretty balance which has given her so many conquests in Wales. The glacier on the way had been heavily cut up with crevasses. To vary the return and avoid the soft snow we followed the enchanting but long crest of the Douves Blanches, which sends down an easy spur to the North Col de Bertol near the hut. It was evening as we approached the Col. Two tiny black figures had been standing on the snow shoulder where the track from the Za leads round to the hut. They seemed to be observing us. Presently, to our relief, they vanished; but soon a single figure reappeared and came rushing with remarkable speed towards us. We were annoyed. Horrors! An officious search party! Such things can be a great nuisance and expense. We were prepared to be haughty; there was no occasion for a search party. It was only just dusk and we had no distance to go. All such feelings, however, were instantly dispelled by the charming smile with which we were met. This Imaginative Unknown produced a bottle of freshly made hot tea—casually, as though such Good Samaritanism were the most usual thing in the world. A slight antagonism often exists between guideless parties and professionals; but this young guide with an upturned nose and bright blue, slightly mocking eyes evidently did not share it. While we drank his tea he explained that he and the guardian of the hut, having nothing to do, had come out to see whether we were coming, that he knew how interminably long the Douves Blanches ridge was and guessed we might be thirsty. This sympathetic intuition we learnt later to be characteristic of him. The meeting was fateful for us, for this was Joseph Georges le Skieur, who was to be our guide and friend thenceforward. By the end of the season we had made two new ascents with him and an association was cemented which has lasted ever since. That evening in the hut he was very helpful, and such a mutual liking sprang up that I made half an agreement with him to go up the Dent Blanche later in the season if the weather still held. He was called the Skieur to distinguish him from innumerable other Joseph Georges, and because as a boy he made himself some ski from a picture he saw in an illustrated weekly, and was for years the only ski-runner in the Val d'Hérens. It must have been a little before this, when he was eleven, that he carried a sack to the Col de Seilon for Mr Girdlestone. Who then told him to go home. But the young mountaineer had other notions. He had seen the 13,000-foot Mont Blanc de Seilon! So he hid behind a rock until the coast was clear and then traversed it, axe-less, taking to the rocks to outflank the ice-slopes. He showed less prudence when he reached the family chalet that evening, and the story ends sadly!

Next day we were in Arolla. To the English this is probably the best known of all the remoter centres of the Alps. Perfectly situated amid pungent scented *arolles* and at just the right altitude

(6500 ft) for general purposes, it offers an extraordinary number of interesting peaks.

But not the Za, nor the Bouquetins, nor the Aiguilles Rouges, not Perroc, Collon, Pigne nor Petite Dent de Veisivi, explain the passion with which so many return year after year to Arolla. Something behind all nameable and describable things holds the secret; and it is better to attempt no explanations but to recognize the fact that many have been in love with such places, have cherished a passion as seemingly simple and unresolvable as any other 'elective affinity', so that the sight of a name or even of letters capable of forming part of the name make the heart jump and the world lighten. A thousand things might afterwards seem to be part sources of the spell; they were merely its vesture.

Into this henceforth enchanted region we now descended to be greeted by M. and Mme Anzévui, gargantuan host and hostess. They showed a remarkable interest in their regular customers. They even remembered which peaks one went up from year to year! M. Anzévui's pride in his kitchen was shown by his having electric stoves almost as soon as such things were known. His gastronomic understanding and his care in the choice of *chefs* have refreshed the frames and raised the spirits of many famished climbers. The long tables of the 'Mont Collon'; the stone stairs so steep after a 'first day'; the crowded glass-walled verandah where one sits on cane chairs to gossip, to read detective novels, to play cards on wet days, with the feet against an electric heater; the miscellaneous rooms in which one interviews the guides over coffee and liqueurs; the Salon which has the red plush chairs and sofa and the regal gold-tasselled curtains and the piano, but in which one may not smoke— what is there in all these to hold the fancy? Or about the derelict tennis court, the terrace where you lie in deck-chairs under the pines and order *thé complet* to your detriment on off-days? The Guides' house, the Cordonnier's shack, the practice Boulder and the path that turns up to pass by 'the Smuggler's Chalet' and across two wet patches to the village, the Poste and the shop with the aluminium eggs—strange how magical all these become in the memory. To those who have not been there, a dull list of things needing to be transposed into another idiom, into that of Saas Fee, for example; but to those who have, keys to feelings that remain as long as life itself. Such places hold a deposit, an effluence of youth and eagerness and energy, and in memory give it back to one.

The most interesting of the more familiar Arolla rock-climbs is the traverse of the Aiguilles Rouges. It was new to I. A. R., who had been over many of the other Arolla climbs in previous years. We felt the excitement of novelty as we set out late, the weather only clearing definitely at dawn. It was the end of August and the grass up by the Praz-Graz chalets was glittering with hoar-frost. There was an autumnal tang in the air, and the Bouquetins, across the bend of the Arolla Glacier, looked their highest in the morning light. Invisible from Arolla, they leap up gigantic as one reaches the cross-crowned boulder at Praz-Graz. But the tips of their raven-wing crest were shimmering with new-fallen snow in the sunshine. An irrigation channel carries an almost level path right round from Praz-Graz to sandy flats laced with rivulets right under the Aiguilles Rouges, and we halted there to discuss our route. Fearful of missing any of the delights or difficulties of the traverse, we chose in the end to begin at the extreme south-east end of the ridge, that is, at the tip of the Mangette, a kind of tail to the main ridge tucked in sharply beside it, like a lobster's on its side. The legs would then be the pinnacles of the Middle Peak and the claw the North Summit.

I put on rubbers to speed myself up a bit, and we left our axes and my boots at a well-marked spot, as we thought, and launched ourselves impetuously at the rocks. They were disgustingly loose and confused. We were soon climbing through what seemed an abandoned quarry. We learnt later that this Mangette part of the ridge is never done, and with good reason. When we struck the main ridge, however, the rocks became all that a climber could desire—firm, varied, aerial and amusing. Over the South and Central Peaks we scampered in high glee, after a while realizing that we had a lively rival to race against in the sun, whose steps towards the horizon were alarmingly rapid as we rushed from pinnacle to pinnacle. The pinnacles of the Aiguilles Rouges are legion. All went well until the moment when the sun and we both simultaneously decided to go down. We knew enough not to try the descent between the South and Central Peaks. This is a well-known trap that has caught several parties for the night. Our way lay over the Central Peak and we mistakenly thought that a route straight down from the summit to the east would be shortest. Somehow we found ourselves overlooking a very steep place down which stones were humming. There was nothing to be done but to hurry back up to the summit again, high and lonely now in the light of late evening, and take the longer, more orthodox route. But half-way down this we came to a broadish channel of hard snow. Axeless, we felt extremely stupid here, or I did in my rubbers. I. A. R. had to kick some sort of steps in the tough stuff and bring me across like a fish on a line. But our troubles were not over yet. Even when we got off the main peak we had awkward patches of snow to cross in the now gathered darkness, and a wilderness of moraines to slide down and hobble through that were no great fun in rubbers. To find my boots and our axes was evidently a hopeless job, so we made as straight as we could for the sandy flats. A number of anecdotes now came to mind to guide us. The ground here above the Cascade des Ignes is famous as a place for benighted parties. There is the remarkable story of the man the search-party could not find. When in despair they went back to Arolla, there he was sitting in the hotel garden. 'Wherever have you been? How did we miss you? Didn't you hear our shouts?' they asked. 'Yes,' replied the benighted one, 'but they sounded so terrible and angry that I hid under a rock until you had gone by!'

The usual mistake of late parties, we knew, is to get too low near the Cascade des Ignes and be caught in the crags. So we kept high.

After a time something showed in the dim lantern light exactly like a main road beneath us. It looked as though it were a long way off down a very steep slope. A few steps towards the edge and the candlelight flashed on running water. What we had seen was the irrigation channel, the *bise* only a few yards away from us! We jumped across it, on to the path, in high spirits—out of our difficulties and safe from the threat of a night out. So ended, in a cheerful jog-trot down, a completely satisfying expedition.

We now engaged Joseph for a week and fetched the abandoned boots down from under the Aiguilles Rouges. September is not a very likely time for long expeditions. Not only are the days short and cold, but the peaks do not recover quickly from new snow. Joseph had to take a party over to Zermatt before he could join us, but arranged to meet us at the Bertol the next day. We filled in the time with an exploration on the Douves Blanches' West Ridge. It is rather surprising that this ridge is not more famous, as the rocks are impeccably sound and the situation glorious. We were rather pleased to find a new way on to it, more in keeping with the rest of the climb than the earlier route which went up to the ridge near its foot and included a lot of not very interesting scrambling. Some way up there is a remarkable formation like the keel and flank of an immense inverted boat, which everybody going up to the Bertol must have noticed. Our exploration led us up a convenient ladder of steep rocks on to the flank of the boat. Content with it, we came down the same way and went on up to the cabane.

The guardian was a pink-faced and cheerful *gaillard*, a good friend of Joseph's. I had climbed into a bunk to take a nap or rest my eyes from the glare of the snow-fields, when he woke me with the exclamation, 'Voilà Joseph!' Jumping up, I followed the line of his pointing finger. Far, far away, near the slope of the Tête Blanche, a minute dot was just perceptibly travelling across the blinding white waste. For more than an hour we watched its approach and magnification; it came astonishingly quickly, until we were looking down on a short figure trudging knee-deep in the snow, and a moment later his simple-seeming face was grinning at us as he swung up the rocks to the platform at the hut door.

Joseph nowadays takes a very different view of glacier dangers. He says it is prudent middle-age and strange experiences that have changed him. 'When I was young I thought I was infallible with crevasses, I could always tell where crevasses were; now I am never sure they are not going to play me *un vilain tour*,' is his present doctrine.

In 1921 we were all three in a youthfully care-free state of mind about glaciers. If you fell into a crevasse you were fished out again, that was the theory. It was not until two years later that we discovered what a difference there is between half going into a crevasse and falling right down into it. I. A. R.'s account of his undergraduate adventures with crevasses amused us. He was going one afternoon over the Col de Collon with a novice friend. They were walking confidently in some party's morning tracks. Suddenly he found himself with his chin level with the surface of the snow, hanging on somehow by his elbows and unable to touch anything with his feet in any direction. Just as he was hoping that the other man would begin to pull him out, he heard a puzzled voice remark, 'I say, I believe I'm in a crevasse!' Looking round as well as he could, all that was visible was another head with its chin on the snow. The great problem was, were they both in the same crevasse or in two different ones? It was never settled; but after he had somehow wriggled up on to solid ground again, he got a very stiff shoulder 'sounding' the snow with his axe every step of the way home!

There was still too much new snow on the Dent Blanche, so next morning we did the North Pointe de Bouquetins, going up its east ridge instead of the ordinary way. It was one of Joseph's most appealing traits that he was most willing for us to lead if and as we wished, but we soon found out that when we wanted to save time Joseph must go ahead. Snow was sprinkling the rocks as we reached the summit, so we hurried down. Back in the hut we found that more provisions were needed if we were to wait over a couple of days for better weather. A consultation led to Joseph going down to Arolla for them, with an arrangement to meet us next morning on the Plan de Bertol if the weather were good enough for a try at the Évêque. The weather did clear, but only with sunrise, so it was late when we met and we did not get down again from the Évêque till dusk. We went up by the rocks of the south-east ridge, reaching them by some intricate wanderings among séracs. We came down at a scamper, having watched the sunset from the summit with a delicious nonchalance quite new to me in guided climbing. Without malice I had always found that the guides' idea is to get you up safe and down quick—with a view to going to bed themselves to recuperate for the labours of the morrow. And who shall blame them for such good horse-sense. But Joseph was as ready to enjoy the present as any amateur. We picked up our sack of provisions on the Plan de Bertol without difficulty. Above, the surface of the Bertol Glacier had frozen to a glass-like slipperiness. The slope is not steep enough for one to fall far, but we all felt more like embryo skaters than Alpinists by the time we reached the welcome hold-fast of the fixed rope up the rocks to the hut.

I had a rest-day after this. I. A. R. and Joseph did the Douves Blanches South-west Arête at a run and came down enthusiastic about it. Then we turned in early to be ready for the Dent Blanche.

The night was the finest I remember. A sky of extraordinarily deep royal blue with the edges of the vast Ferpècle snow-basin black against it. One could see a great deal in shadowy outline without being able to tell in the least how far off it was. Joseph's hat and the tip of the Matterhorn were objects in the same plane floating in and out of a dream. The slope ahead looks like a five-minutes affair. Five minutes pass and it is still the same. Then you suddenly wake up to find that you have been walking for three-quarters of an hour in a blissful doze and it is still the same! What moved a little as we advanced was Orion spread out in unspeakable splendour before us over the dim shoulder of the Wandfluh.

Suddenly we stopped. Joseph waited for us to join him, gathering in the rope as we came, and asked 'Which would you rather, the Ordinary Route or the Ferpècle Ridge?' The generosity of the proposal would have taken my breath away if it had not been evident that Joseph was aching himself to make his first ascent of the Ferpècle Ridge. He had been down it as porter some years before. On this occasion a night was spent out near the foot, during which the amateur beheld a guardian angel hovering over the head of the leading guide, a well-known Arolla figure, who by all accounts needed one! Joseph evidently had very definite ideas of his own as to the route that should be taken. The ridge has a bad reputation for throwing stones down on parties who linger in the introductory couloir and Joseph had a short-cut in mind to reduce this danger. Needless to say we jumped at the idea. (To the non-climbing reader, the fact that the tariff for the Ferpècle Arête is 180 francs and for the Ordinary Route only 80 francs may help to convey roughly the difference in scale between the two expeditions. Joseph was travelling with us at the regular engagement rate of 30 francs a day and was out quite simply, as we were, for the best sport.)

On we went at a new angle and the bulk of the mountain grew rapidly over our heads. There are several shelves of broken glacier which cut in towards the foot of the arête and Joseph was taking us from level to level of these in the darkness without a second's hesitation. We at once began to learn all kinds of new tricks. It was still quite dark and the night was frostily silent. I recall descending an extra-steep couloir gravely with a sense of the importance of making no mistake. We were walking crab-like, Joseph ahead, down a half-inch crust of snow on ice. We traversed to the north and Joseph hewed steps out up a snout of hanging glacier. Then, with the first light, we came to the unpleasant couloir.

Conditions were perfect at that hour. All was still and the rocks were plastered with iron-hard films of snow—not ice. With the palm of the hand on the adze of the axe and the arm straight out like a leg below one, a kind of pegging progress could be made. Only a couple of nails in the toes of our boots bit into the snow—

too thin for a step to be kicked—and the main weight was on the axe. I felt that a second axe for the other arm would be a heaven-sent luxury! Your unweaponed hand feels so helpless as the glove rubs against the unyielding knobbly snow. Mixed feelings jostled; but exhilaration from the quick movement came uppermost. Climbing all together we were very soon high enough up the couloir to take to the rocks to the left and pass out of the zone of danger.

The slabs were icy and not easy. There was the usual *débris*, but the underlying rock was firm. The cold of the dawn-hour lingered long into the morning as we climbed in the shadow up one grey furrow after another. I. A. R. produced a vicious stimulant he had carried on every expedition so far but never used—a tin of Brand's Essence of Beef. The effect on him—I didn't fancy the chill look of it myself—was better than a bottle of brandy.

Looking up at the cliff ahead, where the sunlight was slowly gaining in fine lines on the outjutting flanges of crag, and looking down to the wastes of glacier, beginning now to lie out like a flat map below, I felt as insignificant and lost at moments as when one lies to look up at the stars. Climbing in the centre of the rope, it seemed as a telegraphic channel as well as a link of surety. Joseph's confidence and enjoyment travelled down it to me and almost his reflections on the progress of the day. So did the magical effects of the Brand's Essence quiver up from below. Round a tired climber the rope seems to catch everywhere; round a fresh one it looks after itself and its coils flow in and out of the hand automatically. Most of the time we were climbing together. Close by on our left, just before reaching the sunlight, we passed the difficult buttress where the 1899 accident occurred. The scene of Owen Glynne Jones' death had a special melancholy. He was the chief of my early climbing heroes. Introduced by *The Complete Mountaineer*, he had been the complete mountaineer. How often had I looked at that little brass plate under his photograph at Ogwen or Pen-y-Pass or Wasdale Head, and wondered about him and his end? And here was the place itself, though it was impossible to say just where the slip happened which cost four people their lives. It was hard to imagine how the solitary survivor, Mr F. W. Hill, reached the summit in one and a half hours or how he struggled down through two days to safety.

Once in the sunshine, though the way seemed long, it went merrily. From time to time we paused to look across and down to the unclimbed North Arête, of which we were already talking to Joseph. There was not much to be learned from our inspection, for the chief difficulties would certainly lie lower down, hidden from our sight by the proud but evidently climbable upper reaches. We were a gay party on the summit. Joseph had turned away from us on arrival in a secretive fashion, working away at something he held out of our sight. In a few moments he displayed, with an air of a magician producing a rabbit from a top-hat, an enormous open tin of pears. An amiable trick he had on big expeditions.

The descent stays in my memory chiefly for two stretches of difficult going. Soft slushy snow lying on ice seems to me the condition which bothers English climbers most in the Alps. We have nothing like it to practise on at home, and I was glad when they were past. We were hoping that Bricolla Alp would still be open, but it was close-shuttered and empty when we knocked and so was Ferpècle, but we hurried on, rejoicing, through the valley to Haudères. Our ambitions of the morning had been utterly surpassed. Joseph, who was spending the night at his chalet in La Forclaz, had shown himself all and more than the companion we had hoped for. And he seemed every bit as happy as we were. Already we were spinning dreams of North Arêtes and other oddments in that ecstatic moment of accomplishment that every climber feels after a great mountain.

The next evening we were back at Arolla with the weather very doubtful and only one more day left. I. A. R. had long been fascinated by Topham's brilliant explorations with Pierre Maître of the Pointe Sud of the Bouquetins, or Petit Bouquetin. The outstanding problem of its ascent from the Arolla Glacier seemed the right kind

of thing to look into with Joseph, who joined in the plan with
avidity. So, in spite of a series of sinister filmy wisps of clouds curled
dolphin-like one above the other in a sky that flashed a horrible
blood-red at dawn, we set out up the Bertol track on a reconnaissance. Autumn seemed to have come suddenly into the Alpine
world. The Mont Collon Hotel was almost deserted. On the glacier
the temperature was so low that a bottle of tea in Joseph's sack
tinkled with the ice forming inside it as we halted at the foot of
our peak to attempt a breakfast. It was too cold to linger and we
worked up the little glacier that flanks the Pointe Sud under a sky
that had turned leaden. But we were so keen to try our first ascent
that we would not turn back unless things looked very much worse.

A tortuous gully rises in a bay of the cliffs all the way to the
crest just to the south of the Pointe. It was a gloomy-looking recess
nearly free from snow, but lined for a large part with *verglas*. We
had a new lesson in mountain-craft as we followed Joseph up one
tough pitch after another, looking, at each move, for the edge or
patch of rock that poked itself through this atrocious, slippery,
almost invisible film. The infection of the assault carried us a long
way up, over most repulsive ground, before we paid much more
attention to the weather. It was not promising. But we were nearing
our goal. One more slithery and desperate-feeling pitch and we
were on the sky-line ridge and in a few minutes more the Pointe
was ours.

Then and not till then we really looked about us and intelligently
took note of the weather. It was disgraceful, as disgraceful as our
own neglect of it hitherto. Quite clearly the quicker we got somewhere else the better. At this moment Joseph chose to produce out
of his sack a thing that looked exactly like the judge's black cap.
When he assumed it, this put the finishing touch of grimness to
the scene.

We ate hastily, while Joseph reconnoitred a little along the easy
ridge, flinging himself down here and there to crane his neck over
the eastward precipices. There was a general feeling that almost any

way down would be better than the way we had come up, and when
Joseph returned with a bright light in his eyes and the announce-
ment that he had seen a better way down, we cheered up. Losing
not a moment we hurried off along the ridge to the place indicated.
It was only a very short distance to the north of the Pointe. As we
did so, clouds closed round us. The chosen spot certainly looked
most unpromising. However, time meant everything and discussion
was out of place. As I. A. R., with an expression of mournful resig-
nation on his face, started down, he looked just like a man dangling
out of the basket of a cloud-wrapped balloon. All below had
vanished and the crags we were on seemed actually to overhang.
Of course they didn't, *yet*! But the climbing, even at the start, was
as steep and exposed as any it has been my lot to meet. Fortunately
there were holds—at immense distances it seemed—and the rocks
were solid on the whole. What was so *impressionant* was the difficulty of seeing what was coming next. I. A. R., warmed by the
excitement of the chase for a route, came into fine form in spite of
a surprisingly bulky sack; and Joseph above seemed to grin the
wider, the smaller the holds and the more ferocious the cliff. I have
seen this expression since on other diabolical occasions. All through
the descent the rare ledges were less than footstool size and by some
trick of the cliff's perspective one could hardly ever see more than
thirty feet ahead even when the clouds parted for a moment. All
one saw was the edge of a vertical slab tilting under. Before long a
moment came when to climb down further was evidently impossible. It was the turn of the *corde de rappel*. We had a particularly
long spare rope, 180 feet of it, which I can't help thinking I. A. R.
had carried about all the season in hopes of such an occasion as
this. He had his reward, or his punishment. The spare rope came
out in what looked suspiciously like a tangle. Joseph—we were all
three more or less standing on one another's feet here, in a ridiculously tiny niche—took over the responsibility of the unravelling.
'*Ça peut facilement nous coûter une heure*', he remarked sardonically.
At this moment a fine flurry of snow began to brighten the scene.

However, the rope came out reasonably quickly, and I. A. R. was despatched rather like the plummet on a sounding-line into the snow-storm below. The rope gyrated prodigiously before we heard him call up that he had found a lodgment and I could follow. I took the two fine cords of Alpine line—they look pitiably frail and inadequate on these occasions and are always uncomfortable—wrapped them round under a knee and over the shoulder and desperately committed myself to the abyss. If it had been the moment for a fuss there would have been one, but it wasn't. When I got to the end of the rope, there was I. A. R., on a smaller ledge than ever, some three yards to the left of me. He had had to swing himself into it, since the cliff here overhung, and he drew me in like a bale.

To do an *abseil* on the Grépon or the Dru, at a recognized place and for a recognized destination, is rather a pleasant sensation. But here, as one didn't know where one was getting to, matters felt otherwise. Each time that we all three gathered on our tiny perches, we could see nothing definite to aim for below: only the edge of the crag tilting over still more steeply a few feet beneath us and beyond it the vacancy of cloud or, through a swirling gap, the streaked glacier a thousand feet below. One could see neither the bottom of the pitch nor the bottom of the mountain.

I don't remember how many times this performance was repeated. It seemed endless; but at last, just as a marked darkening of the scene hinted of night, as I slid over a bulge of rock I saw I. A. R. not this time clinging to another bulge but actually standing freely on an ordinary steep slope. We had reached the *glacis* below our Wall. And just in time. The last of the twilight was only enough for us to gallop to and fro down its shelves. And the last stretch of all to the edge of the glacier had to be done in the dark. The principle on these occasions is that anything a little lighter than the darkness is a hold and you put your foot on it. We had so settled our minds down to the prospect of a night out on the Wall above that it was with a sense of cosy unreality that we found ourselves sitting on a boulder in a *bergschrund* to eat something by the light of our lantern. All three of us were now privately convinced that we had only exchanged a night out on the cliff for one on the glacier. If so, we would do 'a-ring-a-ring-o'-roses' to keep ourselves warm till we all fell down or till daylight.

It was too arctic to sit where we were, and snow was falling thickly. Joseph, after a spell of his peculiarly tense reflection, declared that he would not be sure of finding his way either to the Aosta Cabane or round by the Col de Za de Zan, as I. A. R. had suggested; but that he was sure he could find the Cabane de Bertol. We were sure of nothing; I, anyway, was thoroughly befuddled in the driving snow. It seemed to me nothing short of a miracle that anyone in such a storm should keep any sense of direction, avoid crevasses, or in fact see anything. However, we might as well spend the night trying this out as sit freezing. So we set out.

The next two hours might, it appeared, so far as Joseph was concerned, have been clear calm daylight. For us they were a confused nightmare—of the exhilarating kind in which magic is at one's disposal. We wandered among séracs as large as the Bouquetins. They drifted by as though we were at rest and the scene in motion. Or crevasses floated past under our feet like leaves on a stream. We were wafted up slopes like disembodied spirits or the snowflakes that blew with us. It was all as unreal as unreal could be. What was real was progress somewhere. We scampered through a narrow rocky funnel where the wind roared overhead. Soon afterwards we were on a level plane where Joseph exhorted us to keep the rope *very* tight. He lengthened it and made himself a stirrup. He also was most anxious that here we should keep an exactly straight line. We had two lanterns burning, one at each end of the rope, but I remember being bothered by not being able to see where the footprints were.

Suddenly Joseph halted and signalled for us to join him. Dimly then, half buried in new snow, we could see an old track trending away from us. A track from the Central Bouquetins to the Bertol, declared Joseph. He had triumphed.

Supper in the deserted Bertol Cabane about midnight was a festive affair. The bulkiness of I. A. R.'s sack was explained when, among other delicacies, he unpacked a bottle of champagne. He had taken it up to drink on the summit after our first ascent and had felt ashamed to mention anything so frivolous in such a desperate situation. He produced it now with the seriousness with which he might bring out a new view on the meaning of meaning. Next day the jovial and rather noisy Gaspard, coming with a caravan over from Zermatt, woke us up with a tremendous bang on the hut door at about 3 P.M.

Arolla was shutting up for the year and we shared a diligence down to Sion with the chef (whose efforts the night before had surpassed all our dreams). He told us all the scandal of the Arolla staff—which was racy. He, however, as an artist, was above these things! He gave us lumps of fat ham, pink, semi-transparent and greasy, not easy to appreciate, until he added a glass of Monsieur Anzévui's best red wine. Washed down with this nectar, the ham became ambrosia. I can remember now the satisfied smirk with which our artist noted the success of his recommendation. And so to Sion and that night into the train for Calais.

CHAPTER VIII

CORSICA

(*1922*)

Young Napoleons—Soft snow on Monte d'Oro—Three thousand feet of glissading—'The sea-blue stream of the gulfs'—Treasure-hunting—Bandits—Hard snow on Monte Cinto—Storm-bound—Wild piglets—A ghost country—Man-hunt.

Wet weather at Christmas had chilled us about going to Wales at Easter, a season which has a trick in bad years of being even wetter and colder. A hankering after sunshine and new peaks and some general mountaineering in a new range laid hold of me. I hardly know how it happened. On one day the Pyrenees were gleaming in my imagination, on another Norway, but Corsica won in the end. I knew little about it except that there were bandits there and *maquis* and a few other items gathered from the *Corsican Brothers* and *Colomba*, through which I had struggled page by page at school.

Fortunately, Dorothy Thompson and my brother John were free and inclined to try the venture; and I. A. R. soon set to work to look up the available mountaineering data. The journey was full of delights and the little boat from Marseilles found the sea calm. The bare hills of the Mediterranean coast filed by in beautiful, monotonous succession. At night we lay in our sleeping-bags on deck absorbed by the star-pierced void. It is true that in spring you can smell the flowering Corsican *maquis*—a heather-myrtle *mélange*—before you sight the island. By dawn Cap Corse lay on the water near at hand and, as we came round the headland, Bastia in its garish colours was taking the early sunshine like some unbelievable bank of blooms.

At Bastia we got into a train, in which, from the look of the map, we expected to stay some three hours. But it lingered among eucalyptus trees—how naked they looked with the strips of bark peeling off them!—and sauntered by banks of prickly-pear for half the morning before it turned off into the hills. At Corte, on the station platform, the young men stood about before our incredulous eyes in the very postures of Napoleon—crossed arms and all; and the peasants in the train showed bearded faces more noble than any we had ever seen. Up above the thick, overgrown slopes, at the heads of long valleys, utterly Alpine heights of dazzling snow gleamed from time to time. I. A. R. nearly fell out of the window in his eagerness to identify them, and took innumerable pictures (chiefly of telegraph lines!) as the train swung round the curves. However long the journey, and evening was advanced before we reached Vizzavona, it was packed with pleasure, and if we were tired as we got out it was with the exhaustion of happiness.

The hotel at Vizzavona itself (there is another one, in some ways better placed but closed in early spring, on the Col de la Foce above) is a tall white building with a terrace before it. On the terrace were those mounds of melting snow, slid or shovelled from the roof, which are one of the characteristic signs of spring in the mountains. As we came up the steps water was dripping from the eaves. Round about were forests, and above the tree-tops the white summit of Monte d'Oro (7767 ft) stared down on us with a challenge that we could lose not a moment in taking up.

So the rising sun next morning found us on our way. To set one's gear in order overnight, lay out the alarm watch on the most resounding surface in case the hotel staff were untrustworthy, to pad down the dark stairs, boots in hand so as to awaken no one, to sip tea and nibble rolls by candlelight—all this was like stealing another year, that is, another Alpine season, out of life. As we beat our way up through the bushes, we were already certain that, however it fared with our climbing in Corsica, we had done well to come.

The snow was soft, the ridge was long—we took the most direct route we could see from the hotel—and our feet near the top grew dreadfully cold, being wet through with hours of snow-wading. But from the summit there was all the island spread out about us, Ajaccio showing through a cleft between two boulders, the snow-coated central range over against us in all its splendour, the hills of Cap Corse stretching far out into the sea, and, could it be? Elba and Monte Cristo itself and, under a pile of rosy, cumulus cloud, a dim hint of the Appenines. Descent was a simple matter: we walked a little way along the ridge and then sat down. About 3000 feet lower we were still sitting down, though beginning to feel a little damp, and the scenery was still flashing past at a comfortable rate. Down we tobogganed into a gorge. Here I. A. R.'s miscellaneous Alpine reading came to our assistance. He suddenly remembered a sad story of the watery death of somebody somewhere and brought us all to a halt. Under our snow surface was a torrent and at certain points, not easily detected from above, the snow-bridge had fallen in. It would have been an easy matter to splash down into the water and be swept, never to reappear, into the dark tunnel below. Nasty thought! So we stood up and returned to a slower and more tiring mode of descent!

Monte d'Oro, in such soft snow, is a long climb, and in spite of our rapid descent, it was late evening as we threaded our way through the close-growing, solemn beach forests and tramped along the logging road back to Vizzavona.

We lay about in those forests all next day, by the banks of the Ruisseau de Fulminato, cool, soft-floored, whispering solitudes, ate oranges—they stand about in vast straw basketfuls at Vizzavona—sprawled over maps and made plans which the weather was going to cancel. Even our next attempt, on a rock ridge of the Migliarello, had to be abandoned early on account of rain and we beat a retreat to the Col de la Foce. There, over wine, John suddenly realized that he had left the rope he was carrying beside a waterfall about two hours away through the deluge! As we had picked it up and hidden it in I. A. R.'s sack, we could pitilessly enjoy his consternation before assuaging it.

In Corsica, when the weather breaks, there is the coast to see. From Vizzavona the railway goes through a tunnel and down to Ajaccio, where the waves break phosphorescent in the evening, and there is Napoleon's house to inspect. After this you can get on to a motor-bus and enjoy wild driving over giddy roads slung up and down the headlands where the mountains break down to the gulfs, by ochre beaches where the sea froths:

> Is not the sea the peacock of peacocks?
> Even before the ugliest of all buffaloes doth it spread out its tail;
> never doth it tire of its lace-fan of silver and silk.

Cape by cape they pass, Capigliola, Cargese, where Greek refugees of the fourteenth century still talk Greek—they were singing under the almond blossom as we went by—Punta d' Orchino, Punta d' Arone, Cap Rosso, Piano, with a modern little hotel under a terrific pinnacle of red rock, Porto, a harbour out of a fairy-tale. You see it from a height, its gap of quiet water held mysteriously between spurs that stretch out into the wrinkled sea and are edged with a pale fringe of foam.

And when, since it is spring and higher roads are closed by snow to motors, you leave your bus, you can (or could) charter a little victoria whose driver has blue-check shirt-sleeves large as a bishop's, to take you up through country so tangled, abrupt and choked with *maquis* that, away from the road, you could hardly travel a mile a week, over to Evisa, the town of the region known as the Spelunca.

Here in the inn we dropped into a wedding feast. A great lady from Paris had arrived to be present at the marriage of her god-child, the innkeeper's daughter. Down we sat at the long table to eat trout and chestnut fritters while a strange music was throbbing in the courtyard.

From Evisa to Calacuccia a road goes, by the Col de Vergio, through forests. For us it was feet deep in snow. We set out fairly early to trudge over it, but not too early to find the road-menders at work. Road-making seemed the one industry of the Corsicans— an impression later explained for us by an approaching visit of inspection by the French President. And what a people! At sight of us they would drop their tools and, running to get out their wine, beg us to sit down with them for a glass and a cigarette. So many were the road-gangs and so hospitable that we began to wonder how many days it would take us to get over our pass. Even the postman on his way to some upland village would sit down for a chat. Our Alpine gear was a deep mystery to him. 'What did we find up there? Diamonds? Nothing? No, that was not true! We must find something, it was evident, or why did we go up?' Such logic was irrefutable. I wished then, and have wished many times before and since, that I could give him or give myself the name of the treasure.

Higher up the pass we were knee-deep in soft snow between long walls of black-green glistening pines. Our foot-steps made hardly a sound as we ploughed along. These forests are immense and uninhabited except for an occasional *garde* or bandit. Alas! poor picturesque outlaws, they were all rounded up in 1931—or said to be, but I doubt it. Apart from one or two who had gone to the bad, no Corsican I met had anything to say against them! They had acted as they should according to the local code of morals—and, more, they supplied in their contest with the police the equivalent for our league matches! It is true there was another species of 'bandit', racketeers who held up Ajaccio, to be sharply distinguished from the true bandit—who lived a hidden life in the *maquis* only because he was a man of honour.

Calacuccia is at the foot of Monte Cinto, the highest point in Corsica (8033 ft). Night caught us some miles short of it and we turned in at a small hamlet, Albertacce, where the accommodation was really rough and we all became certain that we were being given *cat* and not rabbit for supper. It was not on the whole quite as nasty as we would have expected. Morning found us trying to make a cross-country, sloping ascent of Monte Cinto. The route was not a success; the snow was too soft for such a distance to be covered, so we retreated and installed ourselves in the Hotel de France, Callacuccia, a house that deserves and has a considerable reputation.

Why we started so very late as 8 A.M. for our ascent of Monte Cinto up 5000 feet of soft snow I find it hard to remember. Perhaps we only intended to reconnoitre the approaches to the mountain. But at evening we were somehow on the summit, as surprised as we were happy. Another quick glissading descent for thousands of feet was made memorable by the almost complete disappearance of the seat of I. A. R.'s breeches. We all suffered a good deal, but he most, through going at high speed over a crusted area on the lower slopes that had unexpectedly frozen iron-hard in the shade! But I. A. R. carried a four-yard silk scarf with which to meet all emergencies. I never saw it put to better use.

The next morning passed necessarily in a search for garments, and by afternoon he was looking resplendent but peculiar in a pair of skin-tight, orange, cotton cavalry breeches with the braid taken off. We then wandered across the valley to inspect Casamaccioli, a village opposite. It consisted of a few enormous white buildings each housing some dozens of families, like Venetian palaces that have sunk to become slum property. The narrow paths were troughs worn by water and human feet out of the friable large-grained granite. Here and there one passed huge boulders hollowed out by some mysterious agency so that they looked like the empty eggshells of the Roc. The blossom was just opening on the plum trees, and over Monte Cinto and Paglia Orba the bright sky was banded with long dark fish-like clouds.

These, as usual, foretold trouble; our planned ascent of Paglia Orba, shapeliest of Corsican peaks, ended merely on its shoulder in a storm. But we saw the Viro Valley with the five heads of the Cinque Fratri looking into it, and we passed through Calasima, another village of huge buildings grouped fortress-like on a knoll, their deep-set windows blinking goodbye to us through the smothering snow.

Time was up now—we should in fact have sailed that very day—but news came that the Ajaccio boat had broken her rudder in the tempest. The Bastia boat to Leghorn did not sail for two more days. So we went to the post-office to telegraph 'Storm-bound in Corsica'. It was one of those all-too-true statements that nobody believes, and that take so much living down, thanks perhaps to a tendency to cry 'Wolf! Wolf!' on occasions when another mountain day could thereby be gained.

Our way to Corte and so to the boat was by the Bois de Cavalla Morto, the Col de Rinella and the Tavignano glen. Up and down, up and down endless little hot troughs it led, to come out on to glorious upland meadows, with short crocus-stabbed grass in which lay, oddly enough, the skeletons of horses. Then it plunged into a deep interminable ravine, precipice-sided and hung with scattered pine trees. We were ambling gently down when a peculiar noise brought us to a standstill. There under a tree was a Beast. Its little wicked eyes glared at us, but what was most horrible was the width of its jaws. They seemed at least as broad as those of a man-trap, and tusks showed that brought a sinking of the heart. Near-by some comely little mottled piglets were gambolling on the cliff and demonstrating that if the pig did not grow heavy with advancing years the chamois or sheep would have a serious rival. In our ignorance of the nature of wild boars we merely grasped our ice-axes firmly and waited to see what happened. Fortunately the enemy decided to retreat, for I doubt whether our axes would have had much more effect than switches on the creature's gristly head. After a moment's glaring he trundled away surrounded by a leaping crowd of offspring. And almost simultaneously, we took the other direction!

Of its kind there can be nothing lovelier than the Tavignano glen—it rivals the gorges in Sung paintings. The industry of a vanished population has paved the path through many miles of valley with enormous flagstones. All over Corsica you can see these signs of a departed people. Terraced hillsides where no one goes now. Paths untrod and irrigation channels long disused. Where are those people? Some say their descendants are in America. Whoever they were, they were more energetic than the moderns. Their works lingering on long after them make the empty hillsides and valleys a ghost country. As everywhere in China, one senses under-foot the past.

In this case the past was extraordinarily hard to the feet, which came to burn on those endless flagstones. We felt as though we had been bastinadoed before we came out on to a great built-up bastion at the mouth of the valley. There, immediately below, was Corte, huddling within its walls. We hobbled gratefully down an earth path towards it. Unlike most of Corsica, Corte smelt unpleasantly, but it was correspondingly picturesque.

Bastia had one or two surprises for us. It was the moment of the Genoa Conference and all officials were on tiptoe to protect Lloyd George and the rest of them from their would-be assassins. So, passports had to be specially looked to. Mine and I. A. R.'s were deficient in Italian visas and for a long while we were certain we would miss the boat. We rushed up to the Italian Consulate. It turned out to be a little private fortress with a steel gate and a furlong of approaches to keep the petitioner from his Worship the Consul. We rang. After a long time a small panel opened in the gate and we were severely inspected. Unluckily I had not had time to change out of climbing kit and a scarlet handkerchief on my head was hardly a recommendation. Also I. A. R.'s new cavalry breeches made us look like musical comedy figures from Ruritania. Obviously our appearance was not distinguished enough to carry things off with a high hand. The Consul was dining and could not be disturbed. No! No message could be given him, none. Official hours were 9 to 12 in the morning, unhappily, and it could not be helped if we had to wait a week for the next boat! Click went the panel and we began to feel positively certain that the boat would go without us. Fortunately an intelligent hotel porter suggested that His Worship's Clerk might be approachable when His Worship was not, and gave us his address. Again our nailed boots, slipping all over the cobbles, woke the echoes of Bastia. This time matters went very differently. We were royally received, escorted down many more streets, locked offices were flung open, seals were appended. More perambulations back to the Consul's house. Here, after much whispering, we ragged ones were left outside while the clerk braved the dangers of the Presence at dinner for us. The minutes ticked by, the steamer was hooting in the harbour, there was nowhere to sit down, the cobble-stones were hard, and our feet were still burning from the Tavignano glen. This was altogether too much of a comic opera for us! At last! Brandishing our passports in one hand in triumph, the clerk reappeared. In the other was a far heavier item, a bill in which his trouble on our behalf was not forgotten. It was assessed at a very fancy price. Still there was the steamer to catch, so we paid! With only half a hope left that the boat would still be in sight of the harbour we tore down the hill.

But our way was not clear even yet. Suddenly the most formidable-looking *apache* dashed in the darkness out of a squalid alley with outstretched arms to bar our way. His sickly, green, expert face watched us craftily as he made some unintelligible remark and seized I. A. R. by the shoulder. I had pictures in the quiet night of one or both of us being carried off to South America or some unknown destination. We got ready for a fight, when from nowhere a still less attractive figure jumped up behind us. Dressed in a tight black uniform it brandished an enormous whip! Corsica was indeed giving us a last taste of the Romantic!

Fortunately the man with the knout was more intelligible, in speech, than his fellow. After a close inspection of our faces under a dim lamp, his face fell. '*Allez-vous-en!*' he growled. We were not the people he was looking for! Merely harmless *Inglese*. On we clattered over the quay. And there was our steamer, an hour after her sailing-time, as tranquil as though it were going to stay there a week. And so it might be, we feared, when we got on board. The Captain and the Mate were playing cards under a lurid and smoking oil lamp. They looked as bold and bad as pirates but showed no such spirit. In fact the Captain was not certain of the weather and was waiting a little while to see if a storm would not begin to threaten. But none did, and we had a perfectly calm crossing when, an hour later, we set off for Italy.

Tryfan at sunset from the Llugwy.

Llyn Ogwen, Y Garn and Foel Goch.

The famous slab of Slanting Gully, Lliwedd.

Alf Bridge ascending a steep section of Roof Route on the
East Peak of Lliwedd.

Gashed Crag, Tryfan. The overhang is turned on the right.

M. G. Bradley on the Terrace Wall, Tryfan.
The Capel Curig road is seen nearly 2,000 feet below.

Top left: Daloni Seth Hughes on the Far West Buttress, Clogwyn du'r Arddu.
Top right: Brenda Chamberlain on South Arête, Tryfan. *Lower left*: Daloni Seth Hughes on Hope, Idwal Slabs. *Lower right*: Penelope Seth Hughes on Yellow Slab, Central Buttress, Tryfan.

A steep wall with uncomfortably placed holds on Dow Crag.

Climbing Arrowhead Ridge Direct, Great Gable
(C. F. Holland, Violet Pilley, A. G. Macfarlane).

The Scoop, Castle Naze. Pat Kelly on one of her favourite gritstone problems.

A typical old-fashioned Hut: straw bedding, large cooking stove, shelves for provisions and black Hut-register on the table.

This was thrilling – to walk across the curled and knife-like edges between crevasses or across wider gangways of snow. The bridge here is substantial.

Roping down the Grand Diable on the Grépon.
The Bâton Wicks appears on the left.

Matterhorn. The Zmutt route goes up to the snow ridge on the left and thence near the edge of the sunlight to the summit.

Summit of the Petit Clocher de Planereuse. The umbrella appears behind
M. G. Bradley's hat. Aiguilles Dorées and Col des Plines in background.

At over 11,000 feet, the Bertol Hut is perched like a medieval castle. The Petit Mont Collon is seen beyond with Mont Gelé in the distance.

Chalets of La Forclaz on the way to Ferpècle. The Dent Blanche has her little black imitator, La Maya, to be seen over a chalet roof.

Joseph Georges, Le Skieur, of la Forclaz.

Mont Blanc. The final ridge of the Bosses du Dromadaire is steep and very exposed to wind. Several parties can be seen descending.

Above the Géant Icefall. How the rope is worn on a safe, well-trodden track.
Fewer coils would be held on a soft, unknown glacier.

Dôme de Rochefort with the Col des Grandes Jorasses on left. Mont Mallet
on right. In the foreground the Périades.

The great red gendarme on the Wellenkuppe–Gabelhorn ridge. The summit of the Obergabelhorn is seen beyond.

N. E. Ridge of the Jungfrau seen from the Mönch. Matilde is the little snow hump at its foot. The ordinary route ascends the snow basin on the left to reach the left skyline at the Sattel.

Col d'Hérens from the Dent Blanche. Between the Téte Blanche (R) and Tête de Valpelline (L) appear in the distance the Grivola (R), Becca de Luseney (low and central) and the Grand Paradis. In the foreground tracks are seen avoiding an immense but evident crevasse.

In the daffodil fields under the Pic du Midi d'Ossau at evening.

Dent Blanche seen from Trifthorn, showing the north ridge
in outline on the right.

CHAPTER IX

THE MONT BLANC CHAIN

(1922)

In step with the storms—Rival rockets—Descent into Italy—Down came the top of Mt. Blanc—Lilliputians on the Bosses du Dromadaire—Officialdom—Joseph starts his travels—The Blaitière—Miaow!—Dent du Requin—A raging descent—A conscientious night—The Rochefort Ridge—Murderous rivalry—The sense of direction—A benighted family party—Movie mysteries.

My first two Alpine seasons had spoilt me with too many successful days. I was now to experience an average season with its mixture of weathers. Often a party's fortunes will depend upon getting into step, as it were, with the storms. If you can rest when the snow falls and be ready to start on the one fine day in four, all goes well. But if you start on the day that the weather breaks, you may have nothing to show at the end of the season in spite of a good deal of exertion. To choose the right days to start and to rest is not so easy as might be supposed. One starts before dawn, before the day has shown its character; or one toils up to a hut on some hot afternoon and a storm breaks before morning. There is nothing to do but go down again as patiently as one can. Often to a visitor staying at the mid-Alpine level, and rising at a normal breakfast hour, such a season will appear full of good weather. The peaks, in their extra-white mantle, seem unusually lovely. But the climber up above, who has to wait till the fresh snow has melted off the rocks, will be in despair. It can be said, perhaps, that such seasons add the excitements of a lottery to the climbers' sport. But that is poor comfort to a loser.

1922 was a broken but not exceptionally bad season. My plan was to take a long spell of training and guideless climbing before joining with Joseph for some ascents in the Mont Blanc chain, which he had never before visited. I went out to Lavancher—a little white hotel perched on a grassy terrace not far from the snout of the Mer de Glace. Mr and Mrs Culling Carr had kindly invited me to join their party, and my first training days were spent wandering about the Aiguilles Rouges with a couple of novices who trusted me not to lead them astray. We went up the Aiguille de la Floriaz and several small peaks and to the Col de Balme and the Croix de Fer.

Other climbers must have noticed too how the first few days in the Alps, after the felicity of arriving, are filled with a queer moral and physical lassitude. You may even think for a time that you no longer care for 'these horrible mountains', they seem too large, too steep, too threatening, too strenuous altogether. The poor strained machine recoils from them. On rest-days one gapes at them uncomprehendingly. And the sunshine in which they are bathed seems a mockery. Next week 'the eye altering alters all'—unless one should rather say 'the leg'. Every season, when this mountain gloom falls, one must remind oneself sternly that the rewards are worth the early penalties.

When fitness came, Herbert Carr asked me to join the Oxford Mountaineers in an attempt on the Blaitière. I remember that the snow was in perfect condition and that the Nantillons Glacier this time was a walk. But there was much snow on the rocks and the weather turned against us.

Soon afterwards my own climbing party, I. A. R. and my brother John, came out. Off we went to Lognan and next morning took a training walk up to the Col d'Argentière. At the cabane was the famous Chamonix guide, Joseph Ravanel 'le Rouge'. He took us aside and pointed out the well-beaten track up the snows to the Tour Noir. 'Those', he said, 'are *my tracks* for the ascent'! Ravanel's idea about his tracks seemed reasonable. A party running down a snow-slope in the soft afternoon snow can soon reduce a nice ladder into a series of miniature pot-holes. Ravenel was at that time at the height of his career, leading all the great climbs. Later in the season he was with M. Albert, a name which hardly hid the identity of the King of the Belgians. I had seen him once at the Montanvert, tall, distinguished and relaxed among a group of guideless climbers. He climbed almost more with the leading amateurs than with guides. Lilian Bray recalls seeing him, or one-third of him, in his bunk in the Albigna Hut. The royal *hosen* had been rent on the rocks and were being repaired!

It is not hard to understand why such a King should have a craving for the simple, unsophisticated, unpolitical action that climbing offers. He hushed his passion for the mountains up as much as possible—hating publicity as few do and loathing above all '*les tremolos de la presse sur le Roi Alpiniste*'. To maintain courage by measuring oneself deliberately against danger and the fear it may arouse, his companions say, was a principle with him. He had done most of the classic Alpine routes. In the end he was killed (February 1934) on a practice ground, les Rochers de Marche-les-Dames, near Namur. He was alone, had finished all serious climbing and was about to go up a little pinnacle nine feet high, on the summit ridge, when a huge loose block he touched came away and flung him down the cliff. Such are the chance strokes of Fate.

The Col gave us a marvellous view. The north flank of Verte, Courtes and Droites shows all its height; the Mont Dolent towers at the end of the Glacier d'Argentière, whose width is so dwarfed by the heights that it looks like a corridor. Down the east slope of the pass the ghastly recesses of the Neuvaz, all grey crumbling glacier and stone shoot, made a spectral contrast to the glories of the upper snows. As we looked at them we remembered with appreciation Raeburn and Ling's guideless expeditions here. All these slopes in the main Alpine chains have nowadays their stories to an eye that has looked through Alpine literature.

Our next expedition, in thick cloud all through, was up the Petite Aiguille Verte. In a break we had our recompense in a close-up view of the Aiguilles du Dru powdered with snow and seen from the least accessible side. Near Lognan on the way down we caught sight of three outsize men with outsize sacks hung on Canadian pack-boards. They were Odell, Frazer and Stobart going up to sleep under a rock with designs on the north face of the Verte. This was a sequel to their great attempt of two years before when they had to huddle together all night on a block wedged in an ice-slope two-thirds of the way up, and make a very fine descent in a snow-storm next morning.

We were now out of step with the season, but toothache inter-vened to get us back again. '*Il faut certainement l'arracher!*' said the sympathetic folk at Lognan as they saw I. A. R.'s cheek palpably swelling. So down we went to Chamonix, where a Greek dentist took the same view and called in a Bulgarian anaesthetist. Only ether was available, but a climbing-rope came in handy to tie him to the bench on which the operation was performed. After this the Aiguille du Chardonnet seemed better than any Dent. We only got up as far as the Pic Adams Reilly, partly because so many stones seemed to be trundling down all the obvious ways up.

Then we moved round to the Montanvert, where Bentley Beetham, Meldrum and Bower appeared, fresh from Zermatt by the High Level Route. An enjoyable day took us up to the Refuge Torino. The proprietress remembered me and my pig-tails from two years before, which won us places in the dormitory. There were seventy people with room for forty, very noisy indeed. The Alpine air smelt worse than ever! We sat for hours in the little kitchen waiting for our beds. M. Henriot was there on one of his attempts on the Aiguilles du Diable and Grand Capucin, then unascended; and told us a great deal about the rival merits of the French or English rockets by which he had been hoping to fire a line over the Grand Capucin. Apparently English rockets go straight but are not sufficiently powerful; French rockets go far enough but you never know which way they will take! These technical specialities and an account from him of the delights of a voluntary night-out sitting on the summit of the Matterhorn, whiled away the time.

Next day, from the summit of the Tour Ronde, we watched a thunder-storm coming up out of Italy and beat a hasty retreat to the Refuge. O'Malley, Newton and Pryor arrived from the Graians. The bad weather continued, and we decided to go down to Courmayeur.

This was my first descent into Italy. The pleasure of going down into a new region—especially into a new country—remains the sharpest and possibly the most durable of all the Alpine delights. Each time the difference in language, costume, architecture, flowers, even the soil and earth itself comes home with a fresh tang. All this is heightened after a spell in the universal no-man's-land of the snows. The very grass seems greener and softer after the dazzle of the glacier and the grit of the moraine. Under the Col du Géant on the Italian side, the little Pavillon du Mont Fréty stands in its grassy basin, with mossy ancient rocks poking up out of the meadows. Streams meander among them. Then, below, the pines begin—not in close forests that hide the view but in scattered twos and threes. The path sidles and turns, at every bend the valley scents come stronger, the crimson dwarf rhododendron bushes offer themselves as cushions.

Courmayeur was *en fête*, crowded with gay people. After buying several kilos of peaches for a few pence, we set off very late to sleep at Pertud—the tiny hotel in the entrance of the Val Véni on to which 'the summit of Mont Blanc' fell suddenly some years ago. Wild raspberries conspired with the peaches to delay us deliciously still more. And when at last we crossed the bridge to Pertud it was to find that some hay in a barn was all we could have for the night. But they gave us sheets with the hay, which seemed some protection against the vast spiders I feared must haunt the place. Before turning in we sat in the garden feasting on chicken and mulled claret. Behind the bench at which we sat, near enough for us to lean our backs against it, was a boulder half as large as the hotel. This was one of the pieces that had come down from near the top of the Mont Blanc de Courmayeur. It had landed there without damaging the bench we were sitting on. The people at the hotel were still full of the miracles of those awful hours. They told how the mountain had groaned and rumbled for a week before the fall. How the warning grew so plain that only the *propriétaire* had stayed up there. How the world suddenly grew dark, as at its end, to an awful tune of thunder. And how the rising water from the river, blocked by the debris just below the hotel, had nearly drowned the man whom falling mountains had contrived to miss. A shepherd minding his flock above was said to have been blown unhurt (along with hundreds of trees which were not so lucky) over a neighbouring ridge. A French guest at this point enquired whether the *patron's* hat had not later been found on the roof of Milan Cathedral!

All this while our plans had been unsettled. But as we got up from our hay the obvious idea occurred to us, 'Why not Mont Blanc?' We seemed to have got back in step with the weather. It looked very much on the mend and the odds seemed in favour of a really fine day on the morrow. And a fine day is necessary for pleasure on Mont Blanc—especially for a guideless caravan on its first visit to the mountain. So we wandered gently up through the young forest clothing the moraines to the Combal Lake—a tranquil sheet of grey silt-clogged water, islanded with light green tufts of grass and thronged with frogs.

The way up to the Dôme Hut, our sleeping-place, is a long one. The Miage Glacier is paved with stones which are wearisome walking. Above, where the path zigzags for a while on the slope of an Alp, we spied a party of two ahead of us. Presently we overtook them. They were halted in apparent despair before a little rock-wall barely ten feet high up which the path mounts with two easy steps on rough ledges. We could hardly believe our eyes when we saw that these young Italians were stumped by this. That they should dream of attempting Mont Blanc and be done down by such a staircase seemed preposterous. I can only describe them as vexed at my appearance. We did our best to find some difficulty in the passage for their sakes, but it was impossible. Above this was an easy snow-slope and then a short spell of broken rocks led to the hut.

It was a clean, neat little shelter with a wonderful flanking view of the vast south-east Brouillard Ridge of the mountain, from behind which brilliantly flashing stars later kept appearing. Six people were there when we arrived and supper was our first care. From time to time someone would go out on a neighbouring promontory to see if the Italian pair were arriving. And we were beginning to be a little anxious lest they should be benighted, when they turned up, pale and not a little weary.

The night was rather a squash, as it usually is in small huts. Someone seemed in the middle hours of darkness to have unlimited supplies of tissue paper to rustle, until with unladylike vehemence I exclaimed 'Do shut up!' I. A. R. had a dream about a non-existent watch which he thought was lost under John's pillow and his search again provoked expostulations. However, morning came in time and at 3.40 A.M. we were off. The glacier, though much crevassed, was frozen beautifully hard, the weather was faultless and we marched on through the dawn in fine spirits. When we came to the Col de Bionnassay we could see far below two dots, like tiny insects, which were the Italian pair just starting out. Hours later, from far above, they hardly seemed to have advanced at all. How far they got in the end we never learnt. Probably not beyond the Col de Bionnassay. Though whether later on, at Naples or in Rome, they felt they had been up Mont Blanc, is a point that it would perhaps be unkind to look into!

Mont Blanc in fine weather is hardly a solitude. As soon as we began to go up the magnificent steep snow-ridge that leads from the Col de Bionnassay to the Dôme du Goûter, we could see Lilliputians everywhere silhouetted against the sunlight. Their yodels rang through the golden air. Up on the Col du Dôme, a wide plateau where a regiment might manœuvre, we spread our sacks on the hard, still-frozen snow and made a second breakfast. Little strings of figures were converging from all sides upon the Vallot Hut and already going up and down the final ridge of the Bosses below the summit. And a very aerial-looking party was tight-roping along the knife-sharp Bionnassay ice-ridge. All this distant company at such a height, in the perfection of such a morning, gave a very pleasantly social spirit to the scene.

At the Vallot Observatory, these dots solidified into full-size figures—very individual indeed. A whiskered Solitary, of no precise nationality, lay stretched X-fashion on a broken door in the sunlight beside the carcase of a chicken. The Observatory disgorged a *savant* with his young daughter, small dog, some experimental guinea-pigs and a cohort of guides and porters. I was reminded of early engravings of De Saussure. Everything, indeed, seemed in keeping with the day and mountain. However, there was still the Bosses du Dromadaire to be ascended. Even on so fine a day there was a stiff, icy wind on the ridge. It is airy and spectacular enough to be *impressionant*. And it is my private opinion that we should hear much more about it if all the tourists who 'ascend Mont Blanc' actually went further than the Vallot Hut.

I found it really true that the view from the summit is disappointing. However, it does give a queer sense of exaltation to be at the highest point of Europe. Once it was my sad fate to appear in the American press, photographed on a pinnacle under the rubric 'Dot's on top!' One does feel very much 'on top' as well as a dot at the summit of Mont Blanc. And though the view is flattened like an aeroplane photograph, its geographical interest is extreme.

It was too cold, even in the sunlight, to linger long on the summit and we went down to the Vallot Hut for our rest. The hut itself—not to be confused with the Observatory, which is a locked up, well-kept place lower down—was dirty, dilapidated and half full of wind-blown snow. It must offer most uncomfortable quarters to the many tired parties who have sheltered in it from bad weather.

Downwards, the snows were stamped deep by descending parties. The route passes through the finest snow scenery in the Alps. Enormous ice-cliffs tower, at a safe distance, into every form of fantastic pinnacle. They lean about like city churches in an earthquake over the glittering snow-fields below. Young climbers sometimes affect a disdain of 'the ordinary way' up Mont Blanc, as 'not serious mountaineering'. I can plead guilty to passing through such a phase. But few things in Alpine travel now seem to equal it in splendour. And its quantity matches its quality. In fact by the time we came to the Grands Mulets, a shanty perched on a rock where food and beds can be had—at the highest imaginable prices—we felt, as others have before us, that we must be nearly down at Chamonix. Actually one is a long way off, as we found when we set off after an hour's rest.

There are two ways down from the Grands Mulets. One goes by the Pierre à l'Echelle, but across this route at a certain point stones fall on hot afternoons. We took the other route, down the much crevassed Glacier des Bossons and out on to the rocky promontory of the Montagne de la Côte. Along this crest the famous M. Vallot (several generations of Vallots have devoted themselves to the mountain and the neighbourhood) has designed a path. Dusk was falling as we trotted along it. Every time we expected it to drop at last into the valley, it would suddenly gather itself *up* to climb a minor summit and catch what is known in America as a 'scenic view-point'. I fear we hardly appreciated these treats as we should! We stopped for supper in a chalet. It was delicious to walk in the cool darkness through the woods of the valley, to come out into the lighted streets of Bossons and sink, the moment one's head touched the pillow, into that deep sleep which crowns a long successful day in the mountains. It lasted unbroken till eleven o'clock next morning.

At Chamonix we ran into a striking example of local callousness and bad organization. I found Miss Nicholls, a fellow member of the Ladies' Alpine Club, at her wits' end in attempting to organize search parties for her aunt, Dr Sophie Bryant—the distinguished headmistress of the North London Collegiate School. She had disappeared on Monday the 14th of August. It was now Friday, and no trace had been found of her. Her niece and party had assumed, when she could not be found, that she was coming down by train from the Montanvert to Chamonix while they walked, but she never appeared at the other end. The paths round the Montanvert are few and she was not likely to have left them. But there was just a chance, since she had been suffering from occasional loss of memory and had known the district well in her youth, had been, in fact, a keen climber, that she might have gone down another way and have been seen in some village of the valley. Thus a descriptive notice to be posted throughout the district was an obvious step. Unfortunately this required orders from the responsible official, and, while she talked to the search parties, I visited him. The reception I got was extremely odd. The official had gone to bed—before nine o'clock! At first he refused to hear anything about it. When the urgency of the matter was stressed, he sent out a message that it behoved elderly women to stay in their homes and not cause trouble in the mountains!

More than one visitor to Chamonix, when rescue or search parties have been needed, have commented upon the unsatisfactory spirit of those whose duty it is to organize such things. Many famous Chamonix guides have shown extraordinary devotion in this unpleasant and often dangerous duty, but there is a lowly class of Mer de Glace 'conductor' (it seems hardly right to give them the honourable title of Guide), who sees, in such occasions, no more than an opportunity to pick up handsome payment for nothing, often by what amounts to false pretences. This question of charges has, in fact, recently been noticed in the *Alpine Journal* and taken up by the French Alpine Club. Seeing Miss Nicholls' distressed condition, I took over some of the negotiations with the men who had been engaged in the search. Their attitude made me miserable, though later, I understand, they behaved better. A fortnight passed before Dr Bryant's body was found. She had diverged on to the Les Praz path, and probably stumbled into a fall which, at her age, seventy-two, proved fatal.

We were now expecting Joseph to join us, and realizing after awhile that he was delayed, we decided to try the Aiguille du Blaitière. The Nantillons Glacier was completely changed from the snow-walk of a month before, and was now plentifully cut up with big crevasses. The ridge up to the peak is a pleasant aerial scramble. At a point where one descends a little, the Rocher de la Corde, it is usual to leave a rope fixed in a chimney to help one on the return journey. As we came back, after a wonderfully clear hour on the summit, we saw the only other party on the mountain having such a spectacular time climbing up their rope that our hearts failed. We chose rather to turn the obstacle by a little excursion to the left on ice.

Joseph arrived while we were having dinner after this expedition. We were much excited at the thought of meeting him again. His wide turned-up nose and bright eyes gave him an air of rustic youthfulness and eager expectation as he came across the lounge to take coffee with us. It was the first travelling he had ever done and we feared for his simplicity among the quick-witted hangers-on of the great tourist highways. Quite unnecessarily. Far from being shy and lonely, he was soon at home at the Montanvert and very anxious to uphold the honour of his Val d'Hérens among these foreign guides and mountaineers.

We were rather tired from the Blaitière, but afraid to miss the fine weather, so we started latish for the Tacul to show Joseph the chain and choose among its expeditions. In the middle of the glacier an extraordinary sound met out ears. Could it be a ghost? Or was it a cat? Round the shoulder of a hump of ice came a minute grey kitten cramponing along the edge of a crevasse with great skill, all claws extended, as if it had lived there all its short life. Its pads were bright pink with cold and it shivered and purred in turn as we took it up. Filled with pity we offered it cheese, as the nearest thing to milk! It would not eat and Joseph declared that it wasn't really hungry to be so fastidious. He took it back to the path while we continued up the glacier.

The Tacul, which stands like an island between the main ice-streams that combine to form the Mer de Glace, is an unexcelled view-point and has a compact little rock-summit very attractive to lie on, while the eye wanders round all the innermost recesses of the Mont Blanc Chain. From here, perhaps better than from anywhere else, the intense individuality of the Aiguilles appears. I thought, as I gazed, that out of a hundred peaks there was only one commonplace form—the Aiguille de Leschaux. The dominating masses, Mont Blanc, the Grandes Jorasses and the Verte only bring the lesser heights here into greater salience.

It was boiling hot on the descent, boding little good for the morrow, and sure enough the weather broke at dawn in a thunderstorm that raged itself out before we got up. Joseph, as a kind of busman's holiday, had jumped at the idea of doing the Grépon with my brother, who had had an off-day and was leaving us for Sicily. They had a stirring climb in the tempest, though somehow, in the crisis of the storm, which caught them at the Grand Diable, Joseph forgot his ice-axe. It was brought down in a few days by another party. Till it came, its absence was a constant theme of lamentation. How he ever came to leave it behind remained an insoluble and torturing problem for Joseph. It has ranked since with a later incident as an opportunity for badinage in our party. We had settled down ravenously to a meal on the summit of the Ecrins, when our one and only loaf escaped from his fingers to bound 4000 feet down the South face. Vain for him to pretend that he was feeding an imaginary caravan below. An imaginary loaf would have done for that!

Two days of bad weather followed. Then we went up the Dent du Requin, that famous and entrancing rock-climb. Cloud gathered and snow began to fall as we got off its rocks, but we had had a good look at the lie of the glaciers between it and the Col du Géant.

We were confident we could take a high-level line well above the séracs of the ordinary Col du Géant route. So we felt our way round and between and above and below what seemed innumerable ice-falls, each more like a bombed or quaked area than the last. Our way would be barred by gulf-crevasses whose ends, on each side, vanished in the falling snow. At other times we would pull up on the brink of ice-cliffs that might be twenty or two hundred feet high for all we could tell in a curtain of mist as blind as a London fog but dead white. Little by little we made sure progress through the labyrinth, and in the end, as we rounded the head of a shallow valley in the ice, there were the Col du Géant tracks just where they lead off without difficulty to the hut.

Joseph has a queer way of staring at tangled country from summits, almost as though he were about to spring at it; and we have noticed on plenty of occasions that he seems to carry no ordinary impression of it away with him after these fixed intent gazes. These miles of broken glaciers were quite new to him, yet through all the scores of blindfold turns we took he never hesitated. Each had a place in some comprehensive plan of our course that he somehow carried in his head. The difference between this kind of route-finding and mere experimentation in a general direction is hard to describe but recognizable at once. Joseph on ground he has not so surveyed goes just like anybody else: tentatively; after a survey, he has positive convictions that work out uncannily well even when (as here) he could not possibly have *seen* what was there. It is as though some guiding principle had become clear to him. A mysterious matter, but all highly skilled route-finding is mysterious.

Could anything be more provoking after this than to find the hut crowded beyond all chance of finding sleeping-places, largely by sight-seers. There was nothing for it but to dash through the darkness, in a rage which gave our feet wings, down to the Mont Fréty. Three thousand feet are no joking matter after a tiring day, and a good deal of snow had fallen on the upper part of the ridge. As we ran we hurled curses like avenging spirits of the night.

At Mont Fréty, that charming Pavilion hanging on the slope and overlooking half the Italian Alps, we were comforted. Sleep caught me, as I plunged into bed, before I could blow out the candle. One of three Alpine occasions on which I have awakened in the morning to find it burnt out in the candlestick!

We lay about on the grassy knolls next day. Idyllic hours! The sun baked us gently; the breezes fanned; the cowbells clanked, now near now far off, along the slopes; gentians starred the turf with their aching blue. From time to time parties would pass, on their way up to the Torino Hut. But we had engaged places up there the night before and felt no need to hurry. Not until the evening shadow crept out from the slopes above us did we gather ourselves and our things together, shoulder our sacks and set off uphill.

There is no trusting anyone's word out of Switzerland. Such at least was Joseph's wrathful opinion when we discovered, on reaching the hut after dark, that our promised places had long ago been given away to newcomers! We were tempted to go down again to the Pavilion, but we had a long-coveted climb—the Rochefort Ridge and the Mont Mallet—planned for the morrow. So, making the best of what we felt was bad business indeed, we borrowed some very rat-eaten blankets and went high up to the derelict hut dedicated in the name of Queen Margherita of Italy. This is a windy structure, whose comforts are limited to a little straw. Draughts search it so thoroughly that a night there feels only one degree better than a night on the rocks. I at least got no sleep there. I could thus observe to the full the working of Joseph's supersensitive conscience. Our alarm watch had ceased to function and no dependence could be placed upon promises from the hut people to wake us at the appropriate hour (3 A.M.). Joseph therefore was tormented by the fear that we might oversleep ourselves. The result was that he woke up regularly every ten minutes or so—each time to go through the same performance. A hasty reach for matches; a furtive striking of them; a search for his watch; a blear-eyed scrutiny of it; incredulous auscultations of its ticking; a disgusted grunt; instantaneous slumber again and the same antics repeated ten minutes later!

The Rochefort Ridge in a snowy season is one of the finest in the Alps. It stretches from the Dent du Géant to near the rise of the Grandes Jorasses. I say 'in a snowy season' because in dry years this entrancing series of snow and ice-crests can shrink enough to leave a tedious pathway of broken rocks clear on their flank, and parties at such times may find the former great reputation of the arête hard to account for. In fact I was made to suffer for recommending it in 1928, when Winifred Marples, who has a nice taste in climbing, asked me 'Do you really like miles of dull, rotten rock?'

Not so in 1922. It was then a sublime expedition. Like a mile-long wave about to break, its tense white edge curled and twisted ahead, a foreground to stupendous views on either side as one followed it. Only on the flank of the Dôme de Rochefort, where we turned off to Mont Mallet, was there rotten rock. It did not last long but the steepness of the wall and the drop below made care extremely necessary. Once across it, we were soon lolling on the summit of our mountain.

Mont Mallet looks across a gulf to the Dent du Géant, which shows its most miraculous, least believable, profile from this angle. We could see parties on its summit and at its foot, no larger than mites. Their voices came clearly to us in the now still air as we lay and rested in deep content. It was broiling hot and the idea of returning over the softened snow of the ridge—with probably a long bout of step-cutting—was losing its attraction. Below us, under the mighty North walls of the Grandes Jorasses, the Glacier du Mont Mallet tilted steeply downwards. What we could see of it looked very inviting. If we went down that way we could be at the Montanvert that night and ready for the Aiguille Verte should the weather hold good. The decision was soon taken and we scrambled down the Mont Mallet and waded off over the soft snows of the glacier towards the Col des Grandes Jorasses.

We looked up at their appalling North face and speculated, as every party does, on the chances of its ever being climbed. Nowadays they are being only too grimly tested. Since 1930 a dismal series of fatalities upon its *verglas*-coated, stone-swept slabs and overhangs has stained Alpine history. The sensational press has taken it up and articles under such headings as '*Un émouvant duel franco-allemand*' are turning the conquest of this terrible wall, '*entièrement française*' as it is, into an international struggle. Hitler is alleged to join in with telegrams of condolence to the relatives of perished young climbers, celebrating each '*fait d'héroïsme accompli en terri-toire élranger*'. More lamentable even than the deaths, or than the waste of so much courage, is this corruption of a sport which once promoted sympathy and understanding between peoples. But with all this paper-heated folly and vain recklessness the precipices were then untouched, and we could wonder at them without smelling the reek of a battleground, as we plodded on.

After a while we came to a sudden dismayed halt. Before us the glacier was cut, at first it seemed completely, by an ice-cliff some hundred feet high. Our hearts sank; should we have to go back after all? We scouted along its brink to right and left, and there was even talk of hewing out a belaying bollard in the ice round which to fix a loop of rope and of a descent on a doubled cord, before we found a fault in the rampart. A narrow crack cut into the face sideways, and it was possible to jam into it and more or less slide down between its vertical walls of rough sticky ice. In a few moments we were standing, rather to our own surprise, knee-deep in the soft powder at its base.

Cheered by this gracious miracle, we went on at speed, taking a wide curve close under the Jorasses. But soon we could no longer avoid entering the fantastic chaos of the main ice-fall. Hundreds of crevasses, criss-crossing one another, here cut the glacier up into a jumbled confusion of towers. The movement of the ice tilts these towers till they fall one over another at all angles. The result is a three-dimensional maze of not too stable material that can easily feel like a nightmare to a party that is pressed for time. There is always a good chance that there may be no possibility of further progress—but it is remarkable how rarely you are actually prevented from advancing somehow.

From time to time we would assemble on a pinnacle to survey and discuss the line we would attempt to follow. As a rule one cannot see very far ahead. The convulsions of the ice are too tortured. Time passes quickly in such dramatic travel—however vigorously and neatly the steps are cut. Suddenly from a last eminence the glacier smooths out below, the crevasses run together and close up. You sidle in steps down a last slope and then, with a few zigzags round the closing fissures in the ice, you are walking down a normal glacier stretch again.

Here, to my surprise, the sleepless night took its revenge. We came to the first stones of a moraine and, as we sat down, it seemed clearly quite impossible to go a step further. Food, an obvious remedy, seemed as impossible to swallow. I decided, quite definitely, never to move again! I. A. R. was in the meantime fumbling in the sack and presently produced a strawberry ice made of jam and snow. This, within a quarter of an hour, acted like an elixir. Strength flowed again in my limbs, my eyes opened on a new world, the encircling peaks changed from horrors into a delight. Fresh energy welled up and soon we were striding at a round pace through the confluence point of the glaciers, along the banks of the surface torrents, past the ever-thrilling ice *moulins*—echoing awesomely with the fall of waters through their hidden depths—and down the homeward reaches of the Mer de Glace.

This to us was the expedition of the season—to be celebrated with feasting and champagne. Days of snow-fall put other projects out of the question as we kicked our heels desperately at Montanvert and Joseph's time with us drew on to a close. On a too fine morning some days later we set out for the Col du Géant once more, to go over to Courmayeur and see him climb a stage on his way back to Arolla. Just above the ice-fall of the Géant Glacier we sat down for some lunch. A little mist was drifting on the gentle slope above us.

'*Que ferrons-nous!*' exclaimed Joseph in burlesque terror. '*Le brouillard descend! Revenons dans nos traces!*'

Later we wished we had. In an astonishingly few minutes a really bad *tourmente* was upon us. The wind, shifting its direction continually, drove impenetrable snow clouds past. It was impossible, without feeling, to tell whether the slope trended up or down, or tilted to right of us or left. The next hour finally converted Joseph to a belief in the virtues of the compass. Like many people who have a very strong sense of direction he had been inclined to regard it as a prop for weaker brethren. But no one in such a blinding welter as this could possibly walk straight without some guidance. A moment came when I. A. R., as last man, stood still to watch Joseph and me circle at the rope's length almost right round him under the impression that we were heading directly for the Col!

Sense of direction is, so far, an inexplicable gift. I remember once, when climbing in the American Rockies, Jim Howard, one of the last of the old-time cowboys, telling me how amazed he had been when one of his friends had lost it. They were out on 'night-hawk' duty. Two cowboys as 'night-hawks' ride ceaselessly round and round the herd which itself roams, often in circles, over the featureless prairie all night long. The riders circle in opposite directions, passing one another twice in each round. A mile or two away is the cook-wagon. Every so many hours a relief comes out and the relieved cow-boy will ride off at once without hesitation, no matter how dark the night or how thick the weather, and 'make' the wagon by a direct line without thinking about the matter. One night, when relieved, Jim's friend had surprisingly lingered. Jim thought he was ill. What had happened was that he had quite suddenly felt doubtful as to just where the wagon was and Jim had to ride with him to see him home. The friend never came out as a 'night-hawk' again. He had lost his sense of direction for good.

Such a feat reminds one of the firmly attested power of the Chinese porter to know North, South, East and West automatically under all conditions. Chinese labourers digging at the bottom of thirty-foot wells, turning round and round for hours, are reputed to be able, when asked, to point accurately in any direction! Such a gift would be useful if one could retain it in a whirlwind on a glacier.

Failing it we had to rely on the *boussole*. And being now not at all clear just where we were, we resolved, to remove all doubts, to turn north-east when we reached the frontier line and find the unmistakable foot of the Dent du Géant and then follow the ridge southwards again to the Torino Hut. Our plan worked out admirably, but our eyelashes were iced over and our *passe-montagnes* crusted till we looked like Esquimaux before, with a shout of delight, we laid hands on the first rocks of the Dent. Lightning-flashes played all about us on the way back to the Torino Hut, and we were glad to get into its shelter and warmth and to find it empty except for the caretakers. No words will represent the contrast between the battle with the *tourmente* outside and the peace and comfort within.

The storm continued. Early next morning a prodigious racket awoke us. Two Chamonix guides who knew the region well had wandered, with a numerous French family of ill-equipped novices, in the opposite direction from ourselves. They had spent the night partly perambulating the upper plateaux of the glacier and partly lying in a human pyramid on the rocks of the Tour Ronde, a little way above the hut. Soon items of the caravan were stumbling and being helped down the snow-covered rocks. They were very lucky to have survived such an experience. Mama wore a claret-coloured cloth dress with trailing skirt and flowing georgette sleeves; sons and daughters and their attendant young men were as unsuitably dressed. It was curious to see how much better off those were who had been in the middle of the protecting pile. They emerged flushed and bonny. The others looked pinched and putty-coloured. I remember rubbing the younger girl down, and the pale tint of green she had turned.

We went down to Courmayeur and by autobus to Aosta; it was

Joseph's first ride in such a vehicle and he enjoyed the thrill immensely. In an Italian driver's hands it can be no mean one! It was sad to part for another year. We left him buying coloured ribbons for his sisters at La Forclaz and an olive-green velour hat which would make him look very debonair at Arolla. Alas, it was blown away next season!

We had a look at Cogne. The valley on the way up was all ancient castles and trees bright with red apples. But the mountains were hidden and we came down again through soaking rain to find Aosta in the gaiety of a fair. The deep trench of the valley was roofed with cloud and Aosta was cool. Under the Roman wall we sat watching a blue-robed woman raking late hay and carrying it in great loads to a hidden gateway under the apple-laden boughs, and the end of the season seemed to have come.

We started home by the Grand St Bernard. At the top there was no corresponding post-bus, and we had to make a bundle of all our luggage and carry it slung between us on our axes down Napoleon's road. At Orsières next morning the weather cleared. This was Fate. So, instead of returning home, we could not refrain from going up for a final weekend at Champex and round by the pretty little Col des Ecandies and the Fenêtre des Chamois to the Julien Dupuis Hut, an admirable place in the uncrowded off-season.

As we arrived, a paralysing apparition appeared in the doorway of the hut: a tight-waisted creature in a royal blue and canary sweater with a rakish tassel to his (her) cap. To a nearer view, the androgynous being showed the big-boned grotesqueness of a low comedian. The face was daubed thickly with yellow grease-paint. We were more than a little alarmed at the prospect of such company until we discovered that a movie party was in possession. The fair heroine spent her time in a bunk, recovering from the ascent to the hut, and the figure which had so scared us was an actor deputizing for her through the perilous episodes of the picture. We spent much time admiring their methods. A scree-slope just outside the hut was made the scene of most daring feats. Under the fire of a tilted camera perched on the hut roof, roped quartets in leather motor coats toiled and leapt and saved one another at the word of command. The chief energies of the outfit seemed indeed to be expended in shouting. They said it was the first picture to be taken in the Alps. Certainly their publicity methods needed no development. A basketful of imaginary carrier pigeons was their sole means of communication with the Geneva papers during their sojourn in this inaccessible eagle's nest. Morning and evening a flutter of wings could be fancied carrying news of their survival to an anxious world. The great moment was the 'accident', when the villain, or perhaps it was the hero, had to fall down a frightful precipice. I. A. R. sacrificed a worn-out climbing coat to be sewn to some breeches and stuffed with straw. The choice of the cliff it should be flung down was a subject for hours of conference.

These entertainments filled in the leisure hours for us between climbs on the Aiguilles Dorées and the Aiguille du Tour. Fresh snow fell almost nightly. The heroine rarely appeared and complained much of the cold when she did, but cavalcades of porters constantly brought up the steak and onions she required for supper—much to our suffering, while we were living on *gruyère* and Maggi.

The season was over. We parted from them in mutual envy—they longed to go down instead of us and we longed to stay up instead of them.

CHAPTER X

INTO SPAIN AND BACK AGAIN

(*1923*)

Winter conditions—On planks—Grande Fache—Morals of the Rope—Spring magic—François Bernard Salles—The Port de Boucharou—A Marquis—Trapped—A grave choice—The tour-mente—The frogs' progress—Back safe by the hearth.

Corsica had been so successful that in 1923 we decided to go abroad again for Easter. So off we went, Dorothy Thompson, John Hall Paxton, a new American recruit, and ourselves, to the Pyrenees. On the map the great barrier between France and Spain offers an easy and alluring field to explore. We made scores of plans. In imagination we penetrated all the valleys, ascended all the peaks in that wild romantic country—about which we knew no more than the map and Belloc's book could tell us. In such amiable planning space contracts; time expands like a concertina; handholds are plentiful everywhere; snow bears your weight; difficulties vanish and the weather is always perfect. Soon, alas, our schemes came up against the immutable laws of real mountaineering in late winter conditions. And of that host of dream expeditions a few minor summits and a crossing of the frontier into Spain were alone to materialize.

At Easter the Pyrenees are a country of deep snows and varied weather. Many expeditions that are simple in August are frankly impossible and avalanches are a serious problem. We began at Cauterets. In summer it is thronged with tourists who, with the

peculiar French taste for curing themselves, parade the Place aux
Œufs and hopefully drink strong smelling sulphur waters. The place
was now completely deserted. This made us objects of interest—of
pitying interest, when it was known that we had actually come to
climb! A young guide was recommended to us. Largely, we
suspected, to see that no harm should befall such irresponsible
cranks. In engaging his services we made a tactical error. He was a
ski-expert and he soon had his novices under his thumb, assuring
us every few minutes that the peaks were unclimbable at this season.
The village echoed the refrain. And so a meek party laden with
those unwieldy planks was led off to practise that sport so painful
to the beginner.

He was a nice youth with one eye, a very active one, and as soon
as he had put us on ski we were at his mercy. The insuperable
difficulties of shuffling along and rotating—evolutions later to be
known by more dignified terms—absorbed us. We paddled about
in soft wet snow at the Pont d'Espagne while our teacher, sublimely
unconcerned, sat on a boulder reading a yellow book. A young
Frenchman with a cheerful dog—how we envied his free cavort-
ings!—came down the valley with news of avalanches further up.
Altogether our mountaineering prospects seemed very gloomy.

Ski-ing continued on a practice-slope in the Cambasque Valley.
When every bone ached, we left Tommy and Paxton to continue—
having skied before, they were more resistant to its fatigues—and
went in lovely sunshine up a not very distant rock-peak. As we
mounted, a whizzing in the air developed into heavy bumpings.
An enormous boulder was flying down towards us. We had only
just time to skip out of its way. This scare past, we were soon at the
summit—a jolly little rock-nook above the snows—and I felt I had
climbed my first Pyrenee.

We all revolted from vigorous drill next day to go up a 7000-
foot summit, the Viscos. Muscles stiff from their new exercises were
in murmurous protest as we ground up behind our scampering
guide. A pretty little snow-ridge led us to the cross on the summit.

Here our young companion, as a boast, left a signed and dated card tied to the cross-piece to show that he had really been there. He said that, otherwise, no one would believe him! As for us, we were in a paradise after our ski-ing purgatory. We could look across a hundred miles of wave-like white summits. And until the wind grew chill we basked in the passing sun-bursts and practised the not difficult art of drinking out of a Pyrenean wine-gourd. For this charming pastime boldness is all that is required. Throw the head far back and squeeze the goatskin bag firmly. A long fine jet of wine squirts out, and the cool spray can be directed just to those parts of the mouth or throat which seem most parched. The only disadvantage is that the wine tastes so strongly of goat and of the tar with which the gourd is lined. A new gourd is easily picked up; but is apt to prove an expensive pet to keep at home. It needs seasoning with repeated charges of brandy!

The descent introduced us to a less pleasant Pyrenean speciality, steep grass—dry and glassy, it shot precipitously down, and across it we crept with exactly the opposite of the famous movement of the cat over hot bricks. In the evening *petits verres*, counted only by the *patronne*, were consumed in the smoky café underneath our hotel. Bad weather threatened, we needed a rest day; why not view Gavarnie in the next valley, celebrated for its *cirque* and for the highest waterfall in Europe?

The day was full of motoring thrills. We skidded about wet roads—as edgy and precipitous as any in Switzerland and inconsiderately seamed with slithery tramlines. Our driver had no hooter and was content to whistle occasionally when charging round particularly blind corners. He enlivened us with accounts of charabancfuls of tourists flung down hundreds of feet into the green water below. On one occasion twenty had been hurled over together. One Dutchman, tossed higher than the others, landed last on top of the human mattress and survived undamaged. We felt too few to hope for any such good luck as we grazed the low wall twice in the course of an especially complicated skid.

Half-way up to Gavarnie we lunched at Gèdre. The innkeeper, an old *chasseur* who had wandered with British clients over large parts of the world, gave us Pyrenean pictures, remarking that they might not interest us much now 'but in old age, yes! When, like me, you will live with your memories!' The *cirque* at Gavarnie was roofed with cloud and hung with rain. We trailed up into it, feeling, in walking-shoes, skirt and mackintosh, that peculiar paralysed 'cut-off' sensation that is the hard fate of the tourist. To feel that one is *in* the mountains but not *of* them is a torment to the climber. The heart goes out of the day, one is 'out of touch', and it is best to hurry back to the car and return another time in the right costume and with the right intentions.

Next day at Cauterets a brilliant spell of weather opened. We got away late to toil on ski under a broiling sun up to the Marcadou Cabane. It was a whole day's journey for us. But the snow was evidently too soft for plain walking and we felt recompensed for our hours on the practice slope. At last we began to see the point of ski.

The cabane stands in the middle of a wide upland basin among scattered pines. Valleys radiate in all directions—towards Spain, towards the huge western slope of the Vignemale, towards the Balaitous. Here all next day we practised our ski-ing, seduced from our proper purposes. At nightfall a near-full moon swam up and the snow hardened into a perfect walking-surface. Outside, the pines cracked and cracked again in the frost with startling explosions as we sat round a Pyrenean blaze that roared up the hut's wide stone chimney. The smoke made us wipe our eyes, our middles ached after hours of clumsy kick-turns, there was no more kick left in us and we thought of all the surrounding peaks up which, on such a night as this, we might have strolled.

These are, of course, the mere beginner's attitudes to ski. Even then we did not doubt the service they could be—on proper legs— the new possibilities of adventure they opened up, or the glory of movement their mastery could confer. But we were novices with impatience for the summits gnawing at our hearts; we were getting no instruction to make our preliminary efforts interesting; they were sheer hard work—trial and error, with error exhaustingly predominant. And, with Corsica in our minds, we knew that we could accomplish much more, in a limited time, without ski than as ski-ing tyros. It was hard to take the long view and sacrifice our precious ten days to the practice slope. But it was soon clear that the two purposes—learning to ski and getting up mountains—could not be combined. Next day, whatever happened, we must get up something.

As it was, the ski went up and down the mountain on us, not we on them. The snow was as hard as loaf-sugar right up to the frontier col at the foot of the Pic de la Grande-Fache, and the only grooves cut that day were in our shoulders. The Pic was a sharp little affair of disintegrating rocks patched with snow. We left our ski and started up. Here and there a thin layer of soft snow was only too willing to break away from harder stuff below under an incautious tread. As there were biggish cliffs below and the ridge itself was steep, the rope seemed to us a most evident and natural precaution. Not so to our guide. When he saw us produce it, his jaw fell. '*La corde! Jamais de la vie!*' He became highly indignant and positively stormed at us for our reckless suggestion. But we had two beginners in the party. A slip might happen at any step and the need of the rope was obvious. Our guide, however, surprised us with the high moral tone he took about it. '*Si quelqu'un tombe, tout le monde sera emporté!*' he shouted with deep conviction. Expostulation was useless. To him our idea of roping was criminally foolish. In the Alps, as everybody knew, innumerable fatal accidents were due entirely to the use of the rope! In fact, he would not be responsible for us on any difficult rock if we insisted on using the rope. This threat was singularly unavailing, for by this time we, on our side, were certain that he would not be with us on any such rocks.

But the incident filled us with reflections upon the different traditions in the Alps and the Pyrenees. The Alpine pioneers of the 'sixties and their guides developed a technique for safety that now seems to the climber an obvious and inevitable procedure. Mere common sense in fact. It does not seem at all extraordinary until one comes across a guide who point-blank refuses to share in the corporate responsibility of a roped party. One hardly realizes what complicated moral issues the rope brings in, or how easily its practical advantages can be overlooked until it has been tried.

To a good guide of course the rope is an invaluable means for getting his party safely and quickly over the ground. So far as he is taking responsibility for them, it is a source of safety to himself, for it is much easier to hold up an uneasy tourist on the rope than to jump down and steady him ropeless. No one who has taken novices about cliffs has any doubts as to the advantages of the rope to everyone. The point really narrows itself down to the question of whether the members of the party feel any real responsibility towards one another, and how much. In this light the creation of the Alpine tradition is a phenomenon worth the notice of the social historian. It does not, for example, take root quite naturally in the Far West.

We roped, then, in the face of all expostulations and made our own way up the peak. From the summit we looked into Spain for the first time. To the south-west the high ridge of Las Peñas Coloradas shut in the prospect, and deep haze-filled valleys parallel to the frontier ridge wound down too confusedly to be followed by the eye. After an hour or so of delight we came down smoothly except for the interferences of our independent companion, who could not at all understand why the rope should be hitched whenever awkward steps were being taken.

At the Col we thought at last to take profit from our ski. But it was 4.20 P.M. and already the shadowed slopes were frozen and covered with an icy surface. To such novices as we they gave only one method of ski-ing progress. A wild, uncontrolled, uncontrollable swoop and then crash! This proved too emotional and painful for three of us; but Paxton appeared to relish hard falling. So while he was lustily shouting, turning somersaults and furiously scratching the slopes, we other poltroons took off our ski again, loaded them on our tender shoulders and stalked down with dignity, our heels biting into the crust. Suddenly Tommy's impatient ski fled from her like a spear through the midst of us down the slope. Our guide, in his element at last, leaving us to continue by ourselves, dashed off after it, and in an instant had swooped out of sight. By the time we gained the valley floor the moonlight was sparkling from the snow ripples. Nothing broke the soundless peace except the crunch of the snow underfoot. From the cabane as we approached firelight flickered and a savour of grilling steak was wafted to our nostrils.

But before morning the peace was broken and there was uproar in the hut. A large party of skiers from Toulouse arrived. Though they only turned in at 2 A.M. already by 5 A.M. *chuchotements* had begun. Their energy evidently enabled them to do without sleep. We were not so lucky, and, as the hut was now overcrowded, we went down to Cauterets to find that spring had meanwhile made one of its sudden leaps forward.

Below the snow, the path was fringed with daffodils and thronged with evening sight-seers. It was Easter and Cauterets too was crowded. In the morning a procession of the Assistance Mutuel, in black, with banners, doddered round the main streets; the town-crier with a big drum announced the evening's ball; charabancs from Lourdes discharged pilgrims every hour; the female popula-tion in their gayest clothes sauntered in the Place aux Œufs. We felt out of place in our old climbing-gear and left quickly for Gavarnie, where, over the Port de Boucharou, was our best hope of crossing into Spain.

How changed was everything under the spring magic. The Pierrefitte Valley was filled with cherry-blossom, but the hills in a haze of sunshine seemed exasperatingly remote. The magnetic attraction of 'the other side', which had gripped us in the Alps before, became intensified. 'Spain' echoed in our minds as we raised our eyes towards the skyline. It was hard discipline to spend so much of the perfect afternoon in a gloomy provision store even though it contained everything from decayed cheese to fly-blown face-creams.

For safety this time we took the train from Pierrefitte. It was a rattling box with little glass windows through which the limestone cliffs of the gorge looked terrifying. At nightfall we arrived at Luz. In vain the hotel people insisted that we could sleep admirably at their establishments. In vain they praised the views we could enjoy from their windows in the morning. Our plans for the morning were very different; our visions were of castles in Spain.

Accordingly, to the bewilderment of the crowd which had gathered to see the strangers, we bargained with a motorman and drove off, amid a universal shrug of shoulders. To go up towards the fearsome mountains while you could revel in the town was incomprehensible to Luz; to us it was the first step towards Spain.

At Luz some sort of market or fair had been held. Now and then we swept, an incongruous apparition, past dark figures wending a nocturnal way back to their remote upland dwellings— men and women in long black cloaks and hoods, glimpsed in the dazzle of the headlights and throwing out an atmosphere of privacy and secrecy. Not hostile but alien to the high-powered car with its valley implications. Often with them would be their mule, a woman riding, the more sombre figure of the man pacing by its head. Biblical shadows in the scenic glare.

They were gone in a moment as we went steadily upwards. The openness of the sky overhead, now deep blue and shot with the glimmer of the mountain-hidden moon, brought, after the shattering din and vibrating oppression of the train, an indefinite relief. The walls of the gorges towered incredibly upwards in the impregnable and repelling way of limestone. Before long we were passing through the Chaos. Here half a mountain has fallen and lies in huge pieces. On a far bigger scale, they are like the boulders which strew the Devil's Kitchen above Llyn Idwal. The road winds among them sinuously to spring up again beyond and pass through a winter avalanche. We sped down a cutting between high gleaming walls of snow, and so out into the comparative openness of the Gavarnie basin. Here lights blazed out from one point in the otherwise dead scenery and deserted village. The Hôtel des Voyageurs was expecting us.

After dinner we had a glimpse of the family sanctum, a room at the end of a passage whence firelight flamed. A room, or a rather widened end to the hall, where behind curtains a great table stood on red flags before a chimney with space for a whole gathering round the logs. Here the *propriétaire* and his brothers (we never found out how many there were), their families, and friends came and went with a welcoming smile. The *patron*, very much of a joker, regaled us with accounts of summer tourists scrambling out of their cars to exclaim, '*Voilà Gavarnie!*' before driving off again in the opposite direction!

We made enquiries about guides. Presently there entered François Bernard Salles. How our hearts sank! With crude, unseeing eyes we looked at him. Tall and bowed with a stoop which brought his head far forward of his knees, his shoulders, drawn together, gave him a narrow broken-down appearance. Indefinitely old and worn-out he looked. His hands, gnarled and corded with great veins, drooped low as he sat, fidgeting with his ancient beret. But a grim, peasant strength was in his haggard face, in the great hooked nose, the narrow, high, bony forehead fringed with ragged, short grey hairs, and in the hollow toothless jaws and indrawn burnt-out mouth stained at the corners with tobacco juice.

We looked at one another wildly but sympathetically. His responses to our questions were mainly made up of grunts and *patois* exclamations. Yes, we could get over to Spain if the weather were good. Yes, he could use ski; but why need we worry about them, we could get on better without them! If we started at 6 A.M., not later, we could be in Torla by the evening. No need to take provisions with us. Something to eat on the Col, yes; but we could get all we wanted certainly on the other side. He rose and we shook hands, wondering at his gaunt aspect, his strange bony frame poised in a curious way as if he were about to spring. He went and we did not know what to make of him. We might hope for the best but it did not look very promising. At least we could get over and have a look at Spain.

In the morning he surprised us. Between grunts and expectorations we gathered that he could lend one of us (who had been improvident) an axe—he had a spare one. Had we a rope? This was a different kind of guide from our Cauterets friend, and as we followed him out of the village in the early light over crisp snows, we could see that here was a guide of the old school—one who, instead of displaying his own agility, concentrates rather on setting a steady, rhythmic pace. Salles walked with a masterly gait; it had a strange swing, almost a stumble, in it, which ate up the slopes but never seemed to be fast, was easy to keep up with yet would have been hard to outstrip. Up to the sun we mounted.

The Col de Boucharou (or Port de Gavarnie) is a long trough in its upper regions, flanked by fine peaks, the Gabiétous and Taillon on the left, beyond them, on the French side, the Cirque de Gavarnie, the Pyramide and Mont Perdu—great limestone precipices banded with shelves of glacier. There is an easy, frequented mule-track here in summer, but now all the hollow valleys and all the slopes, except the sheer rock walls, were deeply clad in snow. We mounted smoothly. The perfect day wore on, but not faster than our journey. Up the long floor of the trough in well-judged tracks, with a few steeper zigzags at its head, we followed; exhilaration, hope and a sense of well-being steadily growing greater.

On the top the old man was pleased, unmistakably. In the brilliant sunlight he looked even older, sixty-five we thought, as he grunted with satisfaction. We made out he was telling us that it was an extraordinarily beautiful day and that we had come very fast, much faster than usual, and that the snow was good. The snow indeed was perfect, firm to walk on and crisp, so that granules of ice chased each other over the Port with a scurrying sound. Above us the gloss on the ice of the Gabiétous was almost too bright to contemplate in the sunny, limpid air.

Beyond was Spain, the country we had longed to see. It stretched in a deep valley at right angles to the one we had ascended, though we had no sight yet of the ground below the snow-line. Opposite, limestone ranges sharp but tremulous in the brightness of the early sunshine stretched away, more and more yellow, into the distance.

Soon, wishing to escape the wind, we set out again at a little run bearing along and around the hollow curves of the flank of the Gabiétous. Suddenly brown leafage poked up over the edge of the snow-drifts, and we were in a bare, tawny, grassless region where box bushes grew in tangled masses and a narrow stony path, cut by water channels from the melting snows, led steeply down to a wasted, trench-like valley far below. Through this, like a twisted ribbon, wound a river bordered on either side by burnt-out levels. Nowhere was there any sign of life. Nothing below the snows but the reddish earth, red rocks and dark patches of the box bushes. Heat struck up from the ground; a full, almost pungent scent rose from it—aromatic, southern, a smell of Spain.

We ate, and drank from the streams and from the wine gourd— that rank drink tasting of goat and tar grows upon one with experience. Then we went down and round the corner. Boucharou appeared. We had heard much about this 'village'. Here, so Salles said, we were to find all we could want: wine, bread, sausage and cheese. Now we saw it—a barn-like hovel with an unfinished stone building beside it. Picturesque certainly but hardly encouraging to our hopes of pastoral banquets.

Between us and it a narrow humped-backed bridge spanned the river. We went down, to be struck at once, when we reached the level, by a hot blast which seemed to rush out of the ground. Much conversation now ensued between Salles and a number of men; a confused, prolonged grunting from him, violent gestures from them. An old, very dirty patriarch appeared, dressed exactly like a pirate, a red handkerchief about his brow, and white, strangely clean expansions of linen hanging out at his knees and flapping about his calves.

We were glad to go inside into the cool darkness and were led upstairs to the main dwelling-room. This was a large space surrounding a central, blackened, circular chimney-shaft through which, thirty feet above, the sunlight could be seen slanting diagonally downwards and shining through the little streamers of soot which clung to its wide stone cowl and supporting pillars. A small fire was burning, its wisp of smoke spiralling up through the sunrays. Three days later we were to see all this under very other circumstances. A suppressed disappointment fell on the party on account of the non-appearance of the promised baskets of fresh fruits and cold delicacies. True, we were given anisette, said by some to be a cooling and refreshing drink, and we bought a piece of garlic sausage which looked so terrible that we all silently and independently resolved to leave it to Salles—who devoured it with avidity.

Down the valley the heat increased out of all measure. We could understand now why the landscape looked so bare, yet it was only April. Only the dark box bushes throve; they surrounded us as we went on, following the winding, deep-worn, narrow path towards the forests. We passed a chapel set high on a knoll and almost hidden by surrounding fir trees, and in time came into the shadow of a cliff beside the river, now foaming through a series of rapids. Here hours passed. When at last it seemed as though it must be cooler we went on, stumbling along a stony way which wandered round shoulder after shoulder of the hills, sometimes with great drops and overhangs below—gorges where the river disappeared in roaring plunges, and always with greater and greater precipices rearing themselves above.

At last a final shoulder threw us out to where, commanding the opposing side of the ravine, we could look over it and into the main valley soaked with a rich, stain-like sunshine. Black, small and remote, upon a slight rise in its midst, stood Torla, a huddled patchwork of roofs above low walls, rising in the centre to a square, dark tower. Green meadows lay about it; beyond, to a vague horizon, an unbounded corridor stretched between declining hills. At our feet a bridge—the Pont des Navarrais—stretched across the gulf. Up to our left another higher-level valley ran back at right angles, walled (few other valleys have so strict a right to the word as the Val d'Arazas) on both sides by mind-shaking ramparts of smooth, sheer limestone, banded in ochre and russet; streaked, where streams dissipated themselves into air upon them, with black and purple. Every shelf and all their crests were overlaid with snow.

In the little town we went to the house of the Marquis de Viu. Its courtyard swarmed with pigs and poultry. Up a flight of steps, a vast cool salon received us from the broiling heat. The Marquis— no longer a Marquis, taxes explain his abandonment of his title—was out when we arrived. Salles vanished. No one understood a word of our French. We pointed to the poultry and made clucking sounds but without effect, till we drew an egg and a frying-pan. Then omelettes and a peculiar thick wine, coloured and flavoured like beetroot, soon came.

Afterwards we went over to the church to look at the silver reliquary which is its treasure, and sat on the battle-mented terrace before it, watching the haymaking. A grandmother toiled and a baby grandchild scattered all the ricks behind her. Nowhere was a man in sight. Later the 'Marquis'—a good-humoured man and positive as to the virtues of a mule if one had to travel any mountain path—explained that a Spaniard was too sensible to allow himself to undergo fatigue.

Our programme was to go up to Ordesa in the Val d'Arazas and round the Mont Perdu to the cabane behind it. Failing that, a return to Gavarnie by the Brêche de Roland would have satisfied us. But the next day was filled with a queer lassitude. We wandered, listlessly, up into the Val d'Arazas—the primroses and violets by the wayside were unusually beguiling. What odd things one remembers. Our American friend surprised us by saying that there were no primroses in America! At the opening of the valley a whole forest was lying flat—cast down by the wind-pressure of an avalanche which had not reached them. Higher up a deep clear pool attracted us irresistibly. The icy shock of our dip was followed by a dreadful lazy faintness. Bathes in the heat on the way *up* anything are a temptation to be resisted. So we lay about on the grass while Salles spent half an hour hiding the rucksacks from the chance discovery of any Spanish 'brigand' (*i.e.* peasant) who might pass. He found it necessary to cut down a whole grove and replant them over the bulgy sacks before he was fully satisfied! Then we lit a giant bonfire and toasted ourselves round it in the woodlands before turning back to Ordesa. This is two small whitewashed cottages standing on a grassy knoll under some of the most appalling cliffs in the world. We went to bed, dragging ourselves away reluctantly from one of those wood fires which by themselves make a Pyrenean journey worth while.

We awoke in the morning with a sense of bewilderment that turned to dismay. The ceilings of our rooms shone with a 'strange, unheavenly glare'. Leaping up, we saw snow all about the little house—snow not in any sprinkling but in beds and layers. All day long it rose higher and higher. The wind moaned and roared, and two-thousand-foot-high cataracts of snow-dust fell from time to time from the almost invisible cliffs opposite. By evening the problem of returning to France had become serious. But we had hardly any alternative. For two of our party time was up. The only other route, by the Canfranc tunnel, meant two days lost and trouble and delay for lack of passports. After much discussion we resolved to attempt the recrossing of the Col de Boucharou, though we knew it would be no easy matter.

At dawn we set out through a blanched, obliterated world. Nothing to be seen through the veil of falling particles. The new snow filled in the gaps between the lower bushes and covered them leaf by leaf with little soft light heaps which clung to one another. To step through them or between them was much the same. Here and there a clump of trees had kept the ground clearer, and the dark pine-needles, showing through, might be an indication of a path. We went on steadily, almost swiftly, winding without halts downwards across the broken hillside. A stumble broke the silence from time to time: broke rather the steady, low roar of river and wind which seemed to come up heavily to the ears and blurred. With his coat collar turned up, Salles appeared more bent forwards than ever. He seemed all the time as though screwing himself through some narrow place, head down, shoulders drawn, legs bowed and knees bent, feet together.

After a while we turned more steeply down—there was less snow here—and came out at the bridge from which we had first seen Torla. There was little to be seen now as we took the upward way to Boucharou—except coloured rocks rising into a yellow opaqueness out of which snow-flakes steadily silted downwards, the darkness of the roaring gulfs below and the laden, uneasy forest trees. As we rose again we began to take notice of the wind. At times the boughs above us would thrash together, swinging and swaying with a hoarse angry sound and brushing thick clouds of accumulated snow from their needles to fall in blinding showers. Above the nearer noises we could hear—high, sustained, almost note-like in quality—the prolonged rushing of the gale against the upper ridges. The same thoughts were in all our minds.

Above the gorges, where the forest gives way to open, bushy country, the wind seemed less menacing. From time to time wild white clouds of snow-dust would sweep by, twisting and writhing upon themselves and sucking up all loose snow from the ground to pile it up in the sheltered sides of bushes so that the path became almost free. With the cessation of the forest noises our hopes rose. We were warm, making quick progress, and Boucharou was at hand to retreat to, if need be, from the upper reaches. It was true that, even at the clearest moments, only a beginning of vague slopes rising into impenetrable obscurity showed; but the snowfall seemed to be diminishing, or were the flakes merely passing by more thickly at a higher level overhead? We did not know, but cheered by the now near loom of the houses we pushed on rapidly, enjoying that peculiar pleasure which people who have been out enduring a storm feel at the thought of encountering fireside folk.

Inside, a truly Pyrenean fire was blazing. Half a dozen four-inch saplings were laid together across the wide dogs in the middle of the room and piled high with lighter pieces and bits of charcoal. As it burnt, the numerous population, crouching on low stools, pushed the wood forward, sending swarms of sparks upwards to the wide aperture above, through which fell to meet them a ceaseless stream of snowflakes, dwindling and vanishing before they reached the flames. An occasional hiss would indicate the survival of a giant. Through the aperture the wind entered, catching the smoke streams and whirling them in spirals about the chimney. However, few of these gusts got into the room, which was astonishingly free from smoke. Here amid three generations of mountain dwellers we sat to dry ourselves, to eat a little and to listen to the storm outside. The prospects of crossing, we presumed, were the topic of conversation. Not a phrase was intelligible. Even gestures— we were watching Salles closely now—meant little. They consisted of shrugs for the most part, accompanied by grunts of violent though entirely vague emphasis.

Suddenly Salles turned, and without any diminution of his grunts made a statement in his patois: '*Moi, ughah, ça m'est égal! Périr la haut, ça m'est égal. Moi, je suis vieux ughah! J'ai vécu, mais vous, ughah, vous êtes jeunes, deux jeunes demoiselles périr la haut dans la neige! C'est dommage!*'

The choice appeared grave.

We did not know what to decide. From time to time it seemed that the wind might be dropping, but soon its flurrying would begin again. In the end we agreed to start, taking with us a Spaniard, who might be supposed to know his own side of the pass, sloping up as it did from his very doorstep, and thus should have been an added strength to our party.

He began by calling to his aid a singularly light-headed and incompetent dog who gambolled about in the most carefree fashion in and out of the track—pushing past us in the awkward trough which we were ploughing through deep snow-drifts. The next moment he would get lost and have to be called in by his master, most of whose small energy was dissipated in strident shoutings and whistles. Encumbered by a flapping overcoat, he took turns with Salles at breaking the track, already no easy business. As we mounted it became more and more arduous. Sometimes for a few yards we would find a streak of hard surface which the wind had swept clear of powder-snow, crusted, glistening and slippery. But in a few steps we would be in the waves again, plunging thigh-deep through an element which offered no resistance except when we tried to extricate ourselves or to advance. In the brief trances of the blast we could see dimly a circle twenty yards across of streaky white surface ending in mist. Then the wind would begin again, the circle would close in, and we would be drowned in a whirling tide of hard, stinging particles. Eyes closed, half choking, we could only just stagger on against it.

After a while the slope steepened and we came to a halt. The Spaniard had already complained a good deal of cold. We had in fact to lend him our gloves. Now it appeared, through Salles' disgusted gruntings, that the Spaniard was afraid; he wished to return home to safety. Salles was doubtful himself and was scrutinising his party for signs of fatigue. '*Ça va? Hein? Faut essayer encore? Que pensez vous?*' The dog had long ago given up the expedition and returned, reasonably, to the fireside. How often during the hours that followed we were to envy him! After a moment we sent the Spaniard after his dog, rather relieved to be rid of him.

We were now, we reckoned, about half-way to the pass. Though the old man showed no signs of flagging, it was time to relieve him of some of the toil, and from now on we all took turns at going ahead. The drifts became deeper. It was often no longer possible to walk. The only way to make even a yard of progress up the slope was in a peculiar spread-eagled, frog-like position. Sometimes we crawled on all-fours for a hundred yards together, trying desperately to keep on the surface of the yielding welter by spreading our weight upon shins and elbows. Every few moments the blast which roared endlessly overhead would drop upon us, and the slope would dissolve into a race of white writhing smoke that seemed to eat one's skin. All sense of where we were and even of what we were doing vanished at these moments. A lull would come and we toiled on.

Every fifty yards, at most, a new leader was required. Following exhaustedly behind in the track, we waited for our turn to come again; changing slowly from a feeling that another step as leader was impossible to the sense that after all there was not much difference between going first and following! But we realized that Salles' spells ahead were longer than we could any of us achieve. Buried to the hips or flopping like a huge frog on the billowy surface that old man seemed to belong to a race of giants. His strides were immense and unfaltering. His hunched shoulders seemed to bore into the storm. We gradually grew to feel a puzzled wonder at his stamina. He had seemed to us, on account of his age, a liability. Now we felt instead a thankful reliance in his strength.

At last the drifted snow thinned; we could walk again, and with a final zigzag we came to the pass itself and a glimpse of downward stretching snow-slopes in place of the blank unending whiteness into which we had been pushing. It was time: one at least of the party, less experienced than the others, had been feeling that despair which precedes breakdown, and a collapse here would have been a desperate business. How transformed from the gentle walk of two days before.

We plunged down in a completely changed mood, thinking that now our troubles were nearly over. One thinks indeed that downhill over easy slopes one can always contrive to travel somehow. It took perhaps half an hour to disillusion us! On the French slope the drift was even deeper and seemed even stickier. The downhill going drove our feet in still further, and our spells at leading became shorter and more exhausting. It is a strange experience to lie in the snow unable to take another step, to know that prostration must come again and again before there is relief.

Half-way down, on a little hummock, stands a Pyrenean cabane. It had brightened our imaginations for hours with a promise of shelter and rest. But it bore no resemblance to any of the cabanes of the Alps. Not high enough to stand up in, built of loose stones and roofed with insecure slabs and more used by sheep than by men even in autumn, it offers little protection and no comfort. Yet we reached it at last almost with a sense of home-coming. After ten minutes' rest a chill struck which drove us out shaking from head to foot. We had to go on or collapse.

The wind at this lower level had moderated. Up above in the dim, white, cloud-hidden heights it was still howling. We held fast to the thought that it must be packing the new snow above fairly tight, for we had now to cross the mouths of many gullies to emerge out of the funnel of the valley on to the more open slopes above Gavarnie. It was a place evidently much exposed to avalanches. Following in the track, we had ample time to gaze up into the vagueness above and imagine the drifts piled up on tilted ledges which hung above us ready to fall. Across the gullies we moved singly. By so doing we ran less risk of disturbing the equilibrium of the slope, and there would be some left to dig out the engulfed should anything happen. The danger under the circumstances was not too great, and it was carefully weighed. If the weather had been clearing up it might have been prohibitive. The place has a bad name, and the tales of lost Spaniards which we heard that evening in the village made us feel lucky.

Beyond, on the wider, gentler slopes which hang over Gavarnie, we thought once more we had reached the end of our toiling. Again we were tricked. But now it was more exhaustion than the depth of the drifts which held us up. We were tired as no ordinary mountain expedition in fair weather can tire climbers of some experience.

We found ourselves back in a state familiar to those wandering for the first time in mountains. There below loomed the valley, blackness working unevenly through the mist. Now and then, as the wind cleared it away, we could even see the village church and separate houses, and, after awhile, lights glimmering here and there in windows. We toiled on and they seemed to come no nearer. A kind of impatience and fretfulness which belongs only to one's very first expeditions assailed us. Our legs seemed to have become the wrong kind of things for walking downhill. Even Salles, fighting through the snow to the last with an energy worth all the rest of us put together, seemed to feel the same weakness. We limped and lumbered down, stumbling and slipping. When the snow ceased at last and we came to grass and scree, we went no better; we had almost reached the limit of our resources.

As we joined the valley path two men came out unexpectedly, looking like two ravens in long black cloaks that trailed the ground. They stood and watched us with curiosity. One of them was Salles' grandson, that year's champion ski-runner of the Pyrenees. He greeted his grandfather in a peculiar fashion. Calverley was once asked by the Dean of his College how he regarded the Decalogue. Not knowing precisely what it was, he replied, 'With feelings of reverence mingled with awe'. It seemed to be with similar feelings that François Bernard Salles was regarded by his grandson. But it was no uncertainty that inspired these feelings. Later on, rested and refreshed, and sitting in a glow of congratulations by the fireside, we had it impressed upon us that no other man in the valley would have dreamed of crossing the Port in such weather. He had done it before when younger, but no other guide had cared to risk the expedition. We enquired his age and were told that he was seventy-two.

Already in his own valley he is a legendary figure round whom tales of exploits worthy of Samson or Milo of Crotona have gathered. We had seen enough ourselves to credit them without difficulty. Mr Haskett-Smith tells the story of how a stove which no one else could lift was carried by him up the Vignemale to one of Count Russell's grottoes. All the other porters had gone off with lighter loads. Salles looked at the stove a moment then went off to collect a load of wood with which to fill it! 'What's the use of a stove without wood?' he had demanded. And there were other tales. How a mule which collapsed under too heavy a load on a cliff path had been caught as it fell and hoisted back into safety by him alone. How it was he, when no one else could, who had taken the great bronze Virgin up to the Touquerou. To-day's performance, they said, was just like him!

Sitting by the great log fire listening to the hiss of the still falling snow in the wide chimney we thought of what would have happened if he had not been so remarkable. The chill of the cabane, though now a distant memory, had lost none of its vividness. With an ordinary man we should still have been there if lucky; or, if unlucky, in the snow on the Spanish side. The thought was sobering. That night we went to bed with a profound feeling of respect towards the grand old man who had preserved us from that necessity. An epic figure from a vanished age.

CHAPTER XI

ALPINE TRAVERSES

(1923)

An ideal hut—Au secours—*A crevasse disaster*—*The Rothorn*—La course la plus chic de la région—*A lost alarm*—*The tour of the Monte Rosa summits*—*Back to the Dent Blanche*—*The Witch*—*Flight to the Oberland*—*Aletschhorn and Mönch*—*The Northeast Ridge of the Jungfrau*—*Loose rocks*—*A crazy cornice*—*Leap-frog in the lightning*—*Schreckhorn and Strahlegg*—*Petersgrat and Oeschinen See*—*Théodule and Valpelline*—*A civilized chalet*—*A new climb and a glacial night.*

My memory of this year's doings is helped by an article that I. A. R. and I wrote, immediately after our return, for the *Alpine Journal*, and with the sympathetic consent of the Editor I propose to avail myself of it liberally without further acknowledgment.

For some reason, probably something to do with a theory of recurrent spells of bad seasons in Alpine weather, we went out expecting to be endlessly frustrated, and resolved never to wait about for peaks, as I had waited at Zermatt in 1921 for the Rothorn, but to travel and at least see the Alps if we could not climb them. Kind fate gave us instead a long spell of magnificent weather, but our resolve had this effect, that we traversed our peaks and managed, with one exception, to come down on the opposite side of the mountain.

Dorothy Thompson came out with us to start her first Alpine season, and we began with a cloudy and rainy training day on the

Aiguille de l'Allée—easy rocks growing steadily more interesting as the ridge dwindles to a sharp edge. Broken weather continued. *Par un temps menaçant* we toiled up to the Mountet, and though strengthened by hot grogs on the moraine we found the walk long and the sacks heavy. But then, *of course*, from Moore in his Diary onwards, all Alpinists have grumbled steadily at everything—food, inns, paths and, above all, the sack—yet are quite happy! We stayed a day or two at the Mountet Hotel and then moved with advantage to the Constantia Cabane, the ideal hut in every way, with grass slopes about it to loaf on.

The next day a bitter wind caught and paralysed us above the Col Durand. A crimson dawn had bathed the towers of the Viereselgrat in ill-omened glory, and now the sky was suddenly blurred with multitudinous rapidly moving cirrus wisps. Discs of snow-crust, torn up by the whirlwinds, flew glittering by but stung painfully, and skins not yet hardened found the blasts unendurable. We turned back from the Pointe de Zinal and hurried down to spread ourselves lazily in sunshine and shelter on the Roc Noir and watch the manœuvres of a guided party on the wall of the Col. '*Deux dames,*' they exclaimed, on seeing the three of us, '*et point de guide, qu'elles sont courageuses!*'

In the basin below, crevasses muffled over with snowdrift made us proceed with a caution which at the time we thought perhaps unnecessary. Next morning we saw dramatically the possibilities of the place. It was 2.30, and we were preparing in the little hotel to start for the Grand Cornier. A party from the hut had passed at 2.10, and as we laced up our boots an iterated cry came faintly up from the glacier. It might have been yodelling, but, as we listened, the cries were more distinct; indefinite alarm grew to certainty, it was '*Au secours! au secours!*' Seizing axes, rope and lantern, we dashed out and down on to the glacier. Red lightning was flashing behind the Gabelhorn, and the filmy moonlight shed an indistinct illumination. On the dry glacier all the hollows, watercourses and crevasses were filled with lingering spring snows. Here and there

rocks and holes made dark blots on the dim expanse. Less than a
hundred yards out, in a place where many experienced parties might
not have roped, three such spots in a line seemed to be the place
the cries were coming from. The word *crevasse* detached itself. A
boy crouching with ice-axe fixed, a girl prone, immobile through
the tension of the rope. The third blot was a jagged opening like
the mouth of a well from whence came heart-rending groans of
pain. It was not easy to find where the crevasse began or ended.
Still more difficult to lower a spare rope to the suspended guide
owing to the thick overhanging eaves. If they broke away they fell
on his head. And the rope he was hanging from was cutting into
him too much to be pulled upon. Before long further help came
down from the cabane, and soon seven people were grouped on
both sides of the crevasse. A third rope was lowered, so that he
could be lifted from two directions at once. While I played an
electric torch down into the depth, a desperate bout of hauling
took place. None the less, more than half an hour of strenuous toil
elapsed before we got him to the surface.

Fortunately a doctor was present, and broken ribs and a perfo-
rated lung, the sad effects of this accident, could be attended to at
once. We heard later that he made a fair recovery though he could
never guide again.

All this was a great shock to one's preconceived notion that an
elderly, experienced guide simply cannot go wrong on his own home
glacier. Here was a man of sixty, of good reputation, dropping in
at the very edge of the glacier with coils of rope in his hand and
all but dragging his party with him. Later in the day a party hunted
down the crevasse for his axe and found no bottom after descending
150 feet! The morning was frosty and cold, the surface of the snow
hard; nevertheless a bridge had collapsed beneath his feet like a
trap door just as he was testing it. All this was disquieting enough.
But what shocked us most was the extreme difficulty of getting
him up again once the rope had cut through the snow-eaves. The
notion which all Alpine novices entertain that a strong pull is all

that is needed was dead for good. We never were to feel quite as light-hearted on a glacier again.

Thenceforward, when in our wanderings we were *à deux*, we set aside the ordinary Alpine rope and used 120 feet of Alpine line doubled and furnished with loops so as to form a rope-ladder. Mercifully I have never had to try it out! This lesson taught us to walk warily and delicately in places where before we should have suspected nothing.

After this excursion, the Grand Cornier, for which the unlucky party had also been bound, lost its charm, and we wandered tranquilly up the Besso instead, feeling uncommonly tired and short of breath. Running hard and hauling ropes is especially tiring before dawn. Tommy now joined her guide for the Matterhorn and we chose the Rothorn as the expedition least involving crevassed glaciers. I was eager to lead it as a revenge for my disappointing days of waiting in 1921. A guided party on *le Blanc* seemed rather surprised at this. But as we reached the shoulder clouds swept upon us; a black mist was coming up from the west and blotting out Mont Blanc and the intervening ridges. We went on to a sheltered nook by *le Rasoir*. Here the three parties on the mountain assembled, trying to keep warm in spite of stinging hail-storms which swept by. For an hour and a half we waited, the weather clearing and thickening in tantalizing fashion. An elderly man in thin trousers was shaking from head to foot while his guide tried to induce him to dance, ejaculating, '*Faut se remuer! Faut se maintenir!*' but in vain. At last the situation but not the weather became clear, and we followed the rest of humanity on the downward track.

Next day Joseph Georges joined us. We lay in the sun and watched him descend from the Rothorn with a party of our friends, remembering with vivid pleasure how we first met him on the North Col de Bertol.

In the evening forty school-girls arrived. Their harassed mistress could not keep them quiet. They effervesced. And all through the night spluttering giggles went off like fire-works. But we were off early in the morning, with a farewell to the *gardien*—a man of remarkable charm who handled even the unexpected *pensionnat* with perfect aplomb and equanimity.

Once again we attacked the Rothorn, Joseph deriving much amusement and pleasure from the fact that 'Mademoiselle' was acting as his guide. I found *le Rasoir* thrilling and it was fun to be greeted by *'Elle est épatante!'* from a French party on putting my head over the last rocks at the summit. The other side fully came up to our high expectations until we reached the notorious moraine which leads down to the Trift. It was horrible to leave a wake of dust like any motor-car, and worse still to follow through one!

Midnight, and impossible to start for the Ober Gabelhorn; the thunder awakened us just in time to save us from getting up! But it was sunny in the morning and the flowers in the Trift glen, as everywhere that year, seemed richer and more plentiful than ever before. Descending to shop in Zermatt we lingered too late over ices and chocolate cakes and made the usual foolish rush back up to the hut late in the evening. But we brought a new item for the provision-sack, Basle Leckerli (a super honey ginger-bread which never goes stale), henceforth a staple article in our climbing diet. Incidentally we succeeded in eliminating all tins from our sacks with great benefit, not only to the tins and the sacks but to ourselves!

The long spell of fine weather started that evening and we were away at 2 A.M. for *'la course la plus chic de la région'*, as a Swiss enthusiast described it. The traverse of the Wellenkuppe Ober-Gabelhorn Arbengrat, I felt, deserved this tribute. The Trift Glacier itself, as the crystal clearness of the sunrise crept down upon it, was a thing almost too exquisite to walk upon. On the first rocks of the Wellenkuppe a chough kept us company at breakfast, pursuing, with hops as singular as they were absurd, our crumbs which bounded down the snow slope. *'Je me demande'*, ruminated Joseph, *'ce qu'ils trouvent à manger ici en hiver?'* We halted under the snow-cap of the Wellenkuppe to put on all the clothes we had. On the other side a draught from the north had made the fresh snow crisp and bound it tightly to the old snow beneath. At first broad and gently sloping, the ridge gathers itself together to rise as a high-pitched roof and abuts on a great red *gendarme*, smooth-sided and clean-cut like the spire of a church. From its most repellent corner we found hanging an immense cable. The ascent of this was the least attractive and most fatiguing section of the day. Beyond, sweep after sweep of the clear white ridge, rising and falling and lipped to the left over the Zermatt valley like a frothing billow, led up to the final rocks. Along this snow-ridge, as along the edge of some cloud hung in the sky, we made our leisurely, effortless and exciting progress. At the summit we met a party whose hats, appearing intermittently above the ice bulges of the North Arête, had from time to time been a comic distraction.

After some conversation we began our descent. About the Arbengrat we knew nothing whatever except that parties following it sometimes returned very late. We therefore made some haste down these magnificent rocks, nowhere very difficult, but continuously interesting.

High up on the first steep drop, I. A. R.'s new and cherished alarm-watch—purchased but the day before—escaped from his pocket. *Clang* it went on the slabs and the gong escaped. The glittering fragments dwindled to specks too small for the eye to follow in their leaping, but the faithful departing gong kept up a mournful music. Long after we had decided it had reached the snows at last, a sudden plaintive tinkle would come up to us. And so on, it seemed, for ever. It would be fun to take a supply of tiny gongs and drop them down other great unfrequented rock-faces; the sounds given out have a very pure timbre. But not gongs housed in alarm-watches! Recovering from this diversion, we clambered downwards for some hours.

On the Arben Glacier, Joseph, seeing an opportunity for an intricate glacier descent, a branch of the sport which he particularly favours, left the usual route and cut straight down through the middle of the ice-fall, which pranced in vain.

From Zermatt we were soon away to the Bétemps Hut. The way thence in the darkness before morning was complicated for us by an attempt to follow the meanderings of some lanterns ahead. Eventually we ran down their bearers perched on some rocks which they declared impossible in all directions. Passing them, we saw them again from the summit not much farther on. Although no wind was stirring, this was for me the coldest day of the summer. Before we reached the sunlight Monte Rosa justified its reputation for chilliness. On the rocks of the East Ridge of the Nordend were an immense coil of cable and several hundredweight of iron *pitons* hidden under a boulder. I wondered what they were intended for and soon found out—nearly pulling my arms off getting up the overhang above them.

The tour of the summits of Monte Rosa to the Signal-kuppe was enchanting. The vast gulf on the Italian side filled as the day grew older with huge towering masses of cloud which seemed always approaching us without ever coming nearer, the steep snow couloir to the Ostspitze, the hour of slumber on the Dufourspitze, the discovery of immense steps leading up the ice of the Zumsteinspitze, the ant-like, aimless wanderings of tiny figures on the plateau below the Margherita Cabane, the arrival at the cabane with its *garde-fou* and special *lucarne*—all these made up an unforgettable impression. Especially the hour of slumber, since the sun then caught me off guard and skinned my nose! We rested in the cabane next day, distracted by streams of visitors from the Gnifetti Hut, which is evidently during the holiday-time a place to be avoided. Our second night was less successful than the first as far as sleep was concerned, the window being sealed by national feeling in a manner familiar to Alpinists. Only when our hearts almost ceased to function and a medley of snores reassured us, did a surreptitious loosing of the shutters restore respiration.

There are few places more perfect at dawn on an orange and primrose morning than the Lysjoch, with the pyramid of the Parrotspitze half lit, and the rich blue gloom of the ice valleys contrasting with the lustre of the near ridges. The Lyskamm on this day was unbelievably simple. The celebrated cornice, whose reputation through relics in the Zermatt museum had a little intimidated me, was harmless this year, less formidable than some on the Gabelhorn and the Nordend. The whole ridge was an ethereal walk, curving, rising and falling in great sweeps which passed by without effort and without even that slight mental strain which accompanies so many glorious expeditions. On the Felikjoch we were in two minds about the Zwillinge, those Heavenly Twins, so gleaming and so shapely. After some debate we hurried over Castor. Pollux we cut, because its rock ridge looked uninviting. We came down by the Schwarztor, the final ice-bulge of which was awkward that year.

Two days later we were on the Tête Blanche. Whether it was our two nights at 14,965 feet in the Capanna Margherita, or whether we were going too continuously for our condition, certain it was that we were out of form. We sat on the Col d'Hérens listening sympathetically to a young Swiss praising some special brand of pills which made him feel very fit, he said, every third day. We had come to 'have a look' at our North Ridge of the Dent Blanche. The goal of how many dreams was near, yet as we plodded across the snow plateau towards the Bricolla Alp, our leaden limbs seemed to turn the airy lightness of those visions into a mockery. Though we hardly realized it, we had, temporarily, 'run down'.

The history of the North Ridge is wrapped in a good deal of obscurity. The mountain is too conspicuous from Zermatt, and the frequented Val d'Hérens to the west, for any of its main ridges not to have caught the eyes of passing climbers. Rumours of attempts and explorations by many noted parties were current in Alpine circles. We had picked up new gossip about it at Zermatt but not as much as we should have liked. An intriguing silence usually attends unsuccessful expeditions, and my curiosity was insatiable.

We too had secrets to keep about our interest in the ridge. There are mountains which haunt individual climbers like a passion, or an obsession, so that it is sometimes difficult to decide whether to envy these devotees or to commiserate. They seem to be bound to their pet particular object as though by some spell, almost against their will. While other climbers wander care-free through the Alps, suiting their region and their programme to the season and the weather, they hang about their mountain cursing fate and becoming mystery men to their friends who are not in the secret. So it was with Whymper and his Matterhorn, and so it has been with countless lesser climbers and their lesser goals. It is as if they were bewitched.

Certainly the Dent Blanche is a witch. Her name alone shows it. To one who has fallen beneath her spell, no Horn or Needle in all the Alps can carry half so sharp a suggestion of sweet ferocity as that gleaming Tooth. I. A. R. she enchanted while he was still a schoolboy, in the days when he thought she soared up quite near-by out of the Bricolla pastures, and he set out to vanquish her in twenty minutes or so from the Bricolla Alp! She caught him again as an undergraduate while he was bathing with a wanton disregard of all mountaineering decencies on the slopes of Mont Miné at five o'clock in the afternoon as a preparatory to crossing the glaciers by night to the Bertol Hut with two still more innocent friends! For the third and fatal time the irrevocable spell was cast, that day in 1921, when new snow smothered everything a foot deep on the lower rocks of the Grand Cornier and we loafed a morning away under the Witch's northward face. Thenceforward the thing became a part of one's destiny. The Witch lurked behind our plans each season, thwarting or favouring them and shaping our climbing lives.

And now, after a fried sardine on a toast briquette, we looked up at our enchantress with desperately unresponsive eyes. Instead of going to bed and getting up refreshed to look at her again, we let the cold feelings of the moment over-come us. Instead of alluring glances, she seemed to flash resentment; and, filled with bitterly confused feelings, we fled from her down to Haudères and thence, as soon as Postes would allow, to the Oberland.

The queer lassitude hung upon us still, or the Rhône Valley

reinforced it. We were silly enough to try to dash up from Brigue to Belalp at noon on the hottest day of the year. A gloomy party collapsed exhausted on some ant-heaps under a tree just above Naters. '*Quelle charogne de bêtes!*' groaned Joseph every time he woke up. None the less, not till dusk did we toil on up the interminable path, sack-straps cutting through the shoulders, one foot dragging after the other. We remembered stories of the legendary wisdom of Hope and Kirkpatrick who lightened their sack by inventing the aluminium collar-stud. We all agreed that this promenade was the hardest expedition of the summer!

In general, I have noticed, there are few climbers who do not suffer from even a brief immersion in low-altitude air between spells on the heights.

At the Aletschhorn Hut we were welcomed by two cheery Swiss climbers with the best coffee in the world. They were lamenting that they had brought up too many provisions to be able to make any traverses. Their sacks would not allow it! When we saw the baskets overflowing with their tinned food we could believe them. Our own sacks at the beginning had been fairly well charged, though not with tins. Aneroids, telescopes, verascopes, 100-foot coils of Alpine line, Pyrenean wine-gourds, cooking apparatus and heavy reading; this kind of thing was left behind at every halting-place as we became wiser. By this time we had reached the Spartan limit and were travelling fairly light.

The Aletschhorn up the South-west Ridge I found monotonous. The boulders and shale of that slope, which never develops into even moderate scrambling, seemed even more tiresome and uninteresting than perhaps they are. And at the summit Joseph and I went to sleep instantly. The other side was a different matter. A beautiful snow-field, with beyond it the peaks of the Oberland, now seen by us all for the first time, led down to a narrow ice-ridge. The level floor of the Aletsch Glacier, far down to the left, looked singularly unapproachable, until, beyond a broken chaos of overhanging séracs, we could see a thin rib of rock rising towards us in low relief upon the great wall of ice. Gaining this, we scrambled quickly down, but the way seemed long and hot. A tiny caterpillar caravan going down to the Concordia from the Lötschenlücke came into sight and vanished before we left the rocks, crossed the bergschrund, and waded out into the middle of that vast snow-corridor which is the most impressive feature of the Oberland. Far away down it the Concordia looked like a little hanging village on its bluff.

The immense scale of these glaciers and the peculiar lure of the passes, which are so often seen indefinitely remote, as at the end of immense avenues, we felt again as we went up from the Concordia in the morning towards the Jungfraujoch. The restaurant there was an odd place, a cross between a cowshed and the Trocadero, with flavours of the Bakerloo Tube and the caverns of Cheddar. We came down to it from the Mönch, which we traversed, up by the pleasant South-west Ridge and down by the East. The glacier was strewn with prodigious masses of ice—a large part of the covering of the Mönch must have fallen away earlier in the year. They formed three long curving piers from twenty to a hundred yards wide, their vertical walls sometimes thirty feet high. Joseph no less than ourselves was amazed at the sight and suggested that we should photograph 'ce spectacle unique'.

It was queer after this to enter the Jungfraujoch Hotel by walking a plank stretched from an ice-slope, down which stones were trickling, to a window-sill. We hopped through into a roomful of cosmopolitan Asti-drinkers and post-card fiends. Water, by the way, was unprocurable at this establishment, the reason *given* being that it would be snow-water and therefore unhealthy!

All day the fascination of the great North-east Ridge of the Jungfrau rising in four great sweeps from the Jungfraujoch had been growing upon us. We had read of its descent in 1903 and we heard now of its first and only ascent in 1911. By this time we had recovered and were feeling in great form, ready, as we had not been lately, for an exceptional expedition. To make sure of this we took a rest-day, but Joseph's enthusiasm was too great to restrain, and he went off early alone on a reconnaissance, about which we were sworn to secrecy. The afternoon was shadowed with an accident. A girl we had seen going off gaily at about 11 A.M. was struck just below the summit of the Jungfrau by an errant stone. Joseph's quick eyes were the first to see the signals, and within twenty minutes a party of guides with stretcher and sledge was *en route*. Their careful descent with her was a wonderful sight. The sledge swung down among them like a flying-boat. But the curiosity of the pushing crowd, when she arrived, was horrid. We heard that it was a head-wound and that she was conscious; she was taken down the railway immediately.

The next morning we started at 4.45 A.M. up Pt. 3560, nowadays known as 'Matilde'—a little snow-peak on which the day before we had seen so many tourists first find out what snow-steps feel like under foot. This sport could not have been more amusing to them than the game of guessing what their aptitudes would be was to us as we watched them set out. Up the wooden gangway from the Hotel they flowed, like animals disemboguing from the Ark. But which would prove a butterfly on the slope and which an elephant? Each towed by a solid phlegmatic guide, they came to the ridge and then—we might have lost a lot of money if our bets had been taken! It was not always the lizards who darted up or the camels who broke away the steps.

Beyond 'Matilde' the ridge begins at once and rises, at first snow, then moderate rocks, to the foot of the great *gendarme* or Sentinel which guards the ridge. This Sentinel we found the main difficulty of the climb. '*Ce n'est pas un gendarme, c'est plutôt une montagne*', as Joseph remarked. It is impossibly direct and has to be turned on the north or Wengern side. Here the rock is broken and deeply disintegrated. There must that year have been far less ice than when Herr Weber climbed it in 1911, for our route lay wholly upon rock, or rather, upon rocks. No leader without great delicacy of movement and an instinct for the handling of loose blocks could have made the passage, as we found it, with safety. It was hardly ever possible to secure the rope in these exposed situations. Every peg came out, so rotten was the face. We could only advance with extreme slowness and caution, one at a time. Every few yards we had to mount straight up, and here the problem involved by the presence of those below called for very careful placing and clear thinking. I would put my head over to the left and I. A. R. would crane his neck to the right and Joseph would drop his bricks between us. None the less, such was Joseph's prudence that he managed to avoid dislodging any stones accidentally, although for some steps wheelbarrow-loads of *débris* were tipped into the void. Of course we had made sure of the absence of any parties below. I shall never forget the rising drone from those dreadful flocks of humming-birds as they swooped down to the Guggi Glacier. During these two hours the horrible temptation to the imagination offered by those stones, as I watched them leaping farther and farther and dwindling in size beyond the power of the eye, was the most alarming feature of the experience. I was not altogether surprised when a later party asked where my loose stones were. We had thrown most of them down to the Guggi! And in less dry years than 1923, the ice-cement and snow-plaster would bind this crumbling masonry together.

By nine o'clock we reached the crest of the Sentinel and breakfasted with a distressing sense of eyes behind telescopes. Thence, by pleasant, reasonably sound rocks, we advanced rapidly over Pt. 3788 until a *gendarme*-studded rise led up abruptly to a snow-capped summit (Herr Weber's 'huge secondary summit'). These *gendarmes* again forced us to proceed one at a time; they gave admirable sound climbing, and, unlike Herr Weber, we did not find them at all comparable in difficulty to what had gone before, although at one point we were again forced, as he was, to take to the dangerously rotten north flank. The snowy point to which they led assumes great prominence from the Jungfraujoch station and appears almost equal in height to the Jungfrau. The whole ridge divided itself for us into four sections: first, from Matilde to the Sentinel, roughly south-west in direction; second, from the Sentinel to the point now gained, the 'huge secondary summit', south-south-west; third, from this point to the Wengern Jungfrau, south-west; fourth, from the Wengern Jungfrau to the summit, south-south-west.

The continuation of the ridge gave us the most dramatic piece of snow-work imaginable. A sharp ridge, corniced on the left, ran ahead for seventy feet, then turned at a right angle and became still sharper, with an immense dilapidated cornice overhanging the snow-gulf below. Joseph proceeded across the first stretch, knocking off the cornices, which hissed like dragons in their descent. Then I joined him at the angle. Here I sat astride the edge, watching the rope, while Joseph made further progress. A crack of uncertain depth separated intermittently the crazy cornice from its supporting ridge. Astride, one knee in this crack, the other over the Giessen Glacier, Joseph warned us not to be startled by the probable fall of the cornice. Indeed, the situation was such that if this occurred nothing more than a shock to the nerves need be feared. Whoever was moving would be left safely straddled, however aerially poised, with vertiginous walls falling on either side. Though we clearly realized this, the thought of the sudden disappearance of so large a part of the landscape caused a lively perturbation. It was almost with a sense of disappointment that I. A. R., as last man, shuffled off without a cataclysm having happened.

Now began the best rock-climbing of the ridge, culminating in three *gendarmes* which, progressively more difficult, led in steps to the Wengern Jungfrau. The last of these is a very wonderful affair and caused Joseph some surprise. '*Je me demandais où diable ils sont passés*' he confided to us later. Very steep slabs sprang up, holdless except for small nicks, invisible from below, near the right-hand uppermost edge. No more exposed climbing than this could be found.

It was about half-past three when we reached the Wengern Jungfrau, Pt. 4060, and the end of the serious difficulties. For some two hours the darkening sky and the sound of

The archangels rolling Satan's empty skull
Over the mountain-tops

had been disquieting. To the peculiar feeling in the muscles which
tells of a big electrical disturbance was now added music from the
axes. The party was reassured by discovering that one was rendering
'Home, Sweet Home' and the other 'Rule, Britannia'. What Joseph's
axe was doing we had no means of ascertaining. It was probably
something inspiriting, for we advanced with remarkable *élan*. About
this time a sable cloud enveloped us, and as we hurried in crampons
over the snow-ridge which links the Wengern Jungfrau to the
highest point it was impossible to see more than a few yards in any
direction. Suddenly we found ourselves apparently in the bowels
of an ice-fall; in and out, up and down, through gigantic schrunds
Joseph led without any bewilderment. There was a dream-like, or
perhaps nightmarish, quality about this which a blinding hail-storm
accentuated. A singular suspense, as though the storm were gathering for a climax, caused us most apprehension. An ochreous fume
seemed to be growing thicker and thicker. We struck rocks again,
which were rapidly whitening under the hail, and suddenly we were
passing through a net-work of iron struts—the signal on the
summit—just then by no means a welcome neighbour. It felt, if we
clasped it, much too much like a gigantic lightning conductor.

Down the opposite slopes of shale we scuttled as if the ghost of
Satan, in that darkness, were at our heels. We were hardly a hundred
feet down when what we were momentarily expecting happened.
It was so violent that I dropped my axe and sat down, to the
consternation of the others. In a blue glare, to the sound of the
heavens falling, a companion tumbling prone on the snow seemed
to disconcert them. Nothing was amiss, however. I had only had
one of those convulsive spasms which other climbers have reported
in thunder-storms. Did not M. de Lépiney, to the horror of his
companions, once dive off the Brouillard Ridge as though practising
leap-frog? We went on fast, although drifting hail smothered all

the ice-steps and the blinding wind seemed strong enough to blow one over into the depths. Bad accidents have happened here even in fair weather. This is the slope from which a strong English party slipped, wearing crampons, in 1931, to disappear, over the edge of the Rottal cliffs, before their companions' eyes.

It was a relief to find ourselves over the Sattel and to eat in comparative shelter. Below, during these hours, the hotel had been occupying itself with gloomy expectations. They had made up their minds that we should spend a night of storm in some crevasse. *'Nous n'y avions pas pensé!'* Joseph said. It seemed only a few minutes (actually sixty-five from the summit) before, wet through, we reached the hotel, the thunder still raging. A crowd flocked out on the wooden gangways to see us come in and made us feel as though we were finishing a Marathon! After this, since so serious a break had occurred in the weather, we decided to cover as much ground as possible, giving a miss to big peaks.

We went down to Grindelwald through a dull, dark tube, to find the pastoral scenery most refreshing. The chalets looked like immense ornamental toys, fresh as paint, after the rough-hewn structures of the Val d'Hérens. What carpentry and what finish; but how costly too, commented our expert Joseph, who has, for many winters, been building himself a chalet. How soothing the velvety grass to our feet. How curious, if not dulcet, the tones of the cowherd's trump! I was hardly prepared for the magnificence of the Bear in Grindelwald. We relished its baths after so many days of cabane life, but were drawn back as early as possible next day to the Strahlegg Hut. Here we were lucky enough to get up the Schreckhorn, in poor conditions, before another heavy snowfall. This is a most attractive climb; our only regret was that the cold forced us for once to break our rule of coming down by a different route, preferably into a new valley.

So much snow now fell that we began to wonder if we should even be able to get down from the hut. All the other parties cleared out and we had packed our sacks and locked the shutters when we spied a patch of blue sky. This sight and a new card game we had taught Joseph, from which it was difficult to tear him, turned the balance. We risked some days of short commons and remained at the hut. Our reward was to go over the Strahlegg in a snow-storm, a day made memorable by the addition to our party of two unknown boys who had arrived the previous evening. They fed Joseph with pieces of cheese, his favourite food, and hung around like retainers. Half-way up, at the Gagg, they imagined they were already at the pass! Clearly they would be happier and safer tied on to our rope. It was bitterly cold, they had no gloves and had to make shift with our spare socks. As to their methods of descent, these were elementary and, unchecked, would have been speedy. The schrund was gaping widely and, though they might possibly have shot it headlong, this seemed unlikely. So, when they spread themselves on their backs in the couloir, we held on like a tug-of-war team and told them to kick steps. This they could not manage, so Joseph left us to hold them and went down to do it for them. After some explanation they began to see the advantages of more orthodox methods. Reaching the glacier they turned delightedly to Joseph to ask if he had ever done anything more difficult. Joseph, who is the soul of tact, did not disillusion them.

At the Grimsel, the time came to say farewell to him. A melancholy moment. Links formed when toil and stress, ease and triumph and disappointment have been shared in common, grow firm, and are hard to sever. How intimate is the quality of companionship given by adventure in the hills. What a journey we had been together! Merely from a technical point of view the traversing of a dozen 4000-metre peaks, quite unknown to the party, without a moment's confusion or the slightest check is not an ordinary man's performance. And when to the quiet and daring mastery of every incident of high mountaineering is added an uncanny insight into the moods and half-formed feelings of others, a whimsical play of humour, a gift for friendship and a fund of natural feeling, a devastating shrewdness and the crispest modes of expression, the personality that stands out becomes both vivid and appealing. We watched him striding up the slopes to catch his train at Gletsch, to join friends of ours, with much more than the usual regret that a party which had been happy together should break up.

Hereafter we continued our scheme of travelling light and wandering. At nightfall we were walking in the moonlight up the Lötschental, which, wonderful though it is by daylight, was then like a fairy tale. With W. M. Roberts and J. H. Hollingsworth we had hoped to do the Bietschhorn and other expeditions, but broken weather frustrated our undertakings. From the Mutthorn hut we went on a cloudy morning to the Lauterbrunnen Breithorn, dividing at the rocks into two ropes. The sideways thrust of the wind on the final snow-cap made us glad of our crampons, even though putting them on involved an ordeal for the fingers. It was a day for rapid moving, and no sooner were we back in the hut than snow started falling seriously and continued heavily all night and the next day. A bitter cold filled the hut and the blankets we wrapped ourselves in felt damp. There was a Swiss there supporting life under these rigorous conditions upon raw carrots and unsweetened lemon juice. To see him gnaw and sip them redoubled my shivers. The second morning saw us descending the Kanderfirn under a fading moon. On our right the south face of the Blumlisalp, so black two days before and an object of our ambition, was pure white from crest to base. We were glad, when we saw the crevassed state of the glacier, that we had not endeavoured to go down during the storm. Coffee and the first warmth of the sun at the chalets put us in the mood to appreciate the stupendous scenery of the Gasternthal. That evening we were at the Oeschinen See, so beautiful a place that it is hard to believe it real. The sheer stream-stained walls under their crowning snows, the fringing pines, the slant green of the Alp, the hues of the cliffs, seem as visionary and insubstantial as their images in the still water.

How, after this, we went back to Zermatt and, with that inde-fatigable wanderer, A. E. Field, over the Théodule into Italy, and the rest of our way to Chamin, may only be sketched. We crossed in the evening, rocks and snow dyed with a carmine sunset. Thence by the Col de Vaufrède and down through a strange chaos of boulders among which the Lac du Dragon and nine other lakelets ranging from turquoise to indigo lie bound, to the Col de Bellatsà. A little way down the glacier we overtook a party without either crampons or step-cutting ability. They were apparently expecting to come across the Rifugio d'Aosta, three valleys away, at any moment! It was then towards six, so they did wisely to return to Valtournanche, whence they came, as soon as they saw what was ahead.

From Prarayé we made an attempt to fit in a scramble on the Sengla before going up to the Rifugio d'Aosta, but merely got a soaking for our pains. Then it cleared and we bent ourselves under four days' provisions and more wood than we could burn and went up to the hut. We gazed rather resentfully at the whitened faces of the Bouquetins, for that pale glory meant the ruin of many cherished hopes and dreams. The wind continued high, and next morning, when we had walked round by the Tête de Valpelline to the Col du Mont Brûlé, its icy breath soon made clear to us the impossibility of serious climbing. It was some consolation to crawl into shelter and look up at the wall of the Petit Bouquetin and recall details of our descent two years before. Now in the clear light, with the ledges picked out by new snow, we could see better ways. But they needed dry rocks. It was annoying to be debarred from trying them. We came down to the cabane by the right bank of the Za de Zan Glacier, a much quicker way than walking round the snow. The Za de Zan Alp on the right, to which the cows mount after an hour's walking on the glacier, was alive with marmots and starred with edelweiss.

That night snow fell again. It was plainly idle to wait for better weather. Leaving supplies behind with more patient friends in the hut, we were soon running down the valley below Prarayé.

But half-way down was Chamin, an old haunt of I. A. R.'s, and

the sun came out as we passed it. The temptation was too great and
we stopped. Chamin is a group of three chalets with low-hung,
wide eaves and balconies, the summer home of Madame Buissonin,
who owned the herds in the Val Sassa and made a wonderful marmot
ragout and multitudinous other good things over the embers of an
open hearth. Here, with the step across her threshold, one entered
the life of a vanishing age. A life of fine manners and clear discern-
ment, settled ways and a knowledge of good and evil ranging from
food and wines to national policies. With her cluster of grandchil-
dren about her, Madame Buissonin was indeed a lesson in
civilization. And how they had learned it! '*C'est de la Vandalisme!*'
declared twelve-year-old Victor of the present use—as a cowshed—
of that astonishing medieval refectory at Prarayé, a relic of the days
of the great fairs up there when cattle were driven over the Col de
Collon. They were full of speculations about the old life of the
Valpelline when there were villages, now no more than low swellings
in the turf, a thousand feet higher than now. The weather must
have been much warmer in the centuries before the Great Plague
came—the same that hit Pepys' London—and the people hurried
down from their high villages to pray in crowded churches to the
saints. Few of them managed to get back again. But the Valpelline
and the whole Aosta region kept its character. I ignorantly asked
when it first belonged to Italy. Madame Buissonin drew herself up
gently and said: 'It has never belonged to Italy. Our Duke became
King of Italy also in 1861', and I was abashed. On the modern
attempt to make the Aosta Valley speak only Italian they had firm
opinions but seemed to remain surprisingly unembittered.

That evening the autumn bonfires were to be lit, in honour of
a local saint it was understood; but when we went out on the
promontory to sit by it, Madame Buissonin pointed out the vast
numbers of insects that flew up into the blaze and wondered
whether perhaps *that* had not more to do with the institution of
these fires than any saints? We sat late watching distant cliffs leap
with the flying gleams across the shadowy valley. The children

danced in a ring hand-in-hand round the embers, shrieking in hard, thin voices trivial ditties of the town.

We traversed the Becca de Luseney, a model of what a small peak should be, coming down to a little pass at its south. Our hearts sank as we looked out upon an enormous *clapier*, a mile-wide, mile-long chaos of tumbled boulders which we must cross to return home to Chamin. But there was a pleasant surprise in store for us. The little pass nowadays leads from nowhere to nowhere, no foot crosses it from year to year except perhaps an occasional cowherd's. But none the less there was a clear convenient track over it and through the *clapier*, the sort of thing that only the feet of many generations can wear out, no parvenu improvisation like the King's hunting-paths in the Graians, but a solid, everlasting, deep-worn, communal path through the settled boulders. It might have been there when the Romans came.

First ascents of merit, not altogether too difficult for ordinary mortals, are almost undiscoverable nowadays in the Alps. But two years before I. A. R. had picked out a big unclimbed ridge running alluringly from the Val Sassa up the attractive rock spire of the Becca Rayette or Picion Epicoun, as the Italian and Swiss maps respectively call it. We were in great spirits when we found ourselves quickly gaining height up it upon rocks that could not have been sounder or more interesting if we had designed them ourselves! One aerial span of the ridge led to another, each pinnacle we passed revealed new ones. And always there was the thrilling doubt as to whether the rest of the climb would 'go'. In these excitements time speeds fast and in September the evening shadows lengthen out with unexpected rapidity. We realized, with something of a shock, as we scampered up the last few yards to the summit, that dusk was filling the vast trough of the Otemma Glacier. We should have to move very quickly indeed if we were to get off our mountain by nightfall.

Unfortunately the map was very sketchy and thick masses of evening mist were obscuring the view just where we most needed to see clearly. The little Upper Chardonney Glacier seemed to offer the quickest way down, but not till we were on its slopes did we discover that it was scored, under a soft coverlet of new snow, with an endless series of large crevasses. We charged as fast as the crevasses would allow down the glacier, hoping vehemently that each chasm we crossed in the misty growing darkness would prove the last.

Crevassed glaciers *à deux* are always anxious going. In darkness they become a nightmare. I, as the lighter and presumably the more easily fished out, went ahead. I do not know how near I came to going into some abyss. Again and again I seemed to be crawling on all-fours across frail snow-bridges, sounding with my axe in a wet, invisible, yielding, substanceless mush and almost despairing of finding solid ground. Only the knowledge that a night actually on the ice would be a very serious business drove us on from one risky passage to another. The whole thing had become unreal, like a dream, by the time the glacier smoothed out and we could creep, now in complete night, down the final ice—to find ourselves on the edge of abrupt cliffs of glacier-worn rocks. Our last candle was almost burnt out and it was obvious that we could go no further. By the final flickers of the wick we managed to find a cleft in the rocks with a chockstone. Under this roof, on a bed of sharp boulders, we settled down to watch through the night.

We were lucky to find so much shelter. Such cold as this soaks in quickly to the very marrow. Your teeth join with all other unemployed muscles in a counterpoint of chattering. When, at times, back-broken by our restless turning and stretching, we emerged from our hole, the searching of the glacier breezes and the exposure to the clear frostily glittering stars were scaring. We would crawl hastily back into our cranny again until cramps drove us out once more. Mercifully a kind of stupor descends to dull the senses. After I had felt several times that the night would never end, came suddenly the first faint light of the dawn. Then it seemed that the vigil had passed quickly. How stiff we were as we struggled down the rocks below and stumbled across the moraine chaos! In time the sunlight came and our joints loosened. We made all speed down through the fragrant alpage, sprouting with lilac colchicum, to relieve friendly anxieties at Chamin.

This finished our summer's climbing. By the Col de Berlon and the wilderness of the Otemma moraines we crossed to the Chanrion Alp and hunted long in the early dusk for the cabane. We had no taste for another night out! We found it by accident at last. The next day, as we hurried down the Val de Bagnes under a cloudless sky, we were keenly conscious of the truth of a remark which Joseph was fond of making, 'We may none of us ever have such another season again'.

CHAPTER XII

THE PYRENEES REVISITED

(1924)

The poetry of motion—Palm Sunday celebrations—Midnight mysteries—Drunk on the Vignemale—Soup or swill—Pan's Hostelry—Benighted on the Route des Pyrénées—No loitering—Round and up the Pic du Midi d'Ossau.

Our first visit to the Pyrenees had left us with all our chosen peaks untouched. Ski and spring weather had frustrated us. We were the same quartet as before. Especially had we designs on the Vignemale.

It is best approached up a side valley from Gavarnie, on the French side of the Pyrenees. In summer it is a straight-forward enough climb with a small glacier to cross and a convenient hut on a shoulder where another way comes up from Cauterets, and nowadays severe routes are being developed. Its summit was once renowned as the summer abode of Count Russell, who bought it and caused a number of grottos to be excavated up there for his use. In winter the mountain has another character. The snowfall is deep and the valley approach is threatened at several points with avalanches.

The two of us started our season by struggling up the Piméné, a sharp snow-peak that gives superb views of the whole *massif calcaire*. On a first day it felt a most desperate feat of endurance as we burrowed thigh-deep up the final slope!

Then, with the same party as before, we had two training days on the snow-slopes under Mont Perdu. The second of them was with François Salles, who looked not a day older. He looked indeed as he did then, as old as possible, already in fact an immortal. His strength and fortitude passed all praise. Even his weaknesses, as will be seen, were on the heroic scale. To this day the French Pyrenees resound with stories of his exploits. He led us over the Col d'Estaubé. A ravishing day of snow scenery and sunshine. The crest of the Col bulged with double cornices many feet thick, and the old man's repeated warnings and expressive shoulders as he worked a devious way about and through them brought back vivid memories of our fearsome adventure with him on the Port de Boucherou the year before. We were early on the Col, so early that it was still the boundary between the chill of night with the hard frozen snows of the dawn-hours and the blazing radiance of a sun that topped an opposing ridge and glared levelly into our eyes. We warmed ourselves in the blaze and ate, looking down a very steep wall of snow that swept undulating down from our toes for some thousands of feet into a still-shadowy snow-filled valley. When we had eaten, Salles picked his giant limbs up and took a sitting dive into this valley. Down he swept, with a brave crest of snow-spray shooting up on either side of him, and soon he was a mere black speck winding away and away from us. Diffidently we sat down to follow him. The pleasures of a really long, steep, sitting glissade have points of advantage over even the best of ski-ing. The ease of the thing, the absence of all call upon one's prowess! Careless of Telemarks, Christianias or even Stemming turns, one floats in cushioned ease! Snow-foam does, it is true; work its way up one's sleeves and down one's neck, but this seems better than the giddy somersaults of the would-be ski-runner and no more wetting! And when at last the glorious motion slackens, there you are down in your valley, your point of departure hangs behind you almost out of sight in the sky and a rivulet is bubbling over mossy pebbles at the snow's edge only a stone's-throw away.

After this we wandered down a broad, dry river-bed to a deserted village. Only two years before an avalanche had smashed all its houses into flinders—leaving only the tiny white chapel on its little knoll intact.

The next day was Palm Sunday. Sitting on a low wall in the village street we listened to the singing and watched the black-gowned women come out of church each with her piece of palm and her black shawl over her head. The rest-day seemed a proper preparation for an attack on the Vignemale. Little we knew that the feast was, for Salles, inevitably quite another kind of celebration—a thirty-hour affair in which his annual prowess with the flagons was legendary in the valley. The *patron* of the hotel did indeed give us—so he said later—some broad hints about this, but in the peaceful Sabbath atmosphere we entirely missed the point of his winks and shrugs. In fact we took him to be merely an anti-clerical, or Freemason.

We went to bed with all arrangements, we thought, fixed. Midnight was to be the hour of departure—to give us plenty of time to get through the dangerous narrows of the Val d'Ossoue before day would awaken the avalanches. Grumpily we rose at the thunder of the Boots on our doors. Downstairs the hotel seemed cold, the candles dim, the coffee flavourless. Worst of all, there was no Salles to be seen or even to be heard of. What could have happened to him? We wasted many speculations about his alarm-clock. We must have kicked our heels for more than an hour before, in desperation, we set off to find his chalet in the upper village. No sooner were we out of the hotel than there he was, in a great fume and like nothing so much as a bear with a sore head. He had been knocking violently, so he said, for two hours at the hotel door! Seeing that we had been all this time in the hall, or peering forth for him into the night, this passed our comprehension. Later we found that he had been knocking at some other door! However, at this stage we still suspected nothing and the party set off at a *pas gymnastique*. But we soon slowed off, and I passed the word back that there was a very funny flavour in the atmosphere of the night. In fact the more I sniffed the more it seemed to smell of *eau de vie*, white wine and anisette! Suspicious movements of Salles' arms ahead—his rolling gait was more marionette-like than ever—suggested that the Pyrenean wine-gourd he carried on top of his sack was not being left in that proper and provident position. It was little surprise to me, though staggering to the rest of the party, when after twenty minutes he sat down on a rock and suggested a rest as the morning was *accablant*.

Hereafter the rhythm of the march was broken every twenty minutes or so. It is idle to pretend that our Great-grandfather Guide in his merry condition was not a responsibility! However, he seemed happy; seemed too to be 'walking it off', which we thought was perhaps the healthiest thing for him to do. The day promised to be glorious in a non-convivial sense also; and as long as I. A. R. went ahead making the steps in the deep snow, there seemed no reason why our Guide should not come with us. Indeed we should have had no slight difficulty in persuading him to go back—for strong reasons, in his sack, which we were only to discover at eve.

The valley is a long one when choked knee-deep in snow. As soon as we could, we climbed up out of its trough and circled over the more open terraces on the south. From time to time we would cross the tumbled *débris* of an avalanche, its packed snow-boulders giving a welcome rest to the toil of deeper and deeper wading. We had lost a good deal of time and had now no intention of trying to go further than the hut—the Refuge Bayssellance on the Hourquette d'Ossoue. Salles was vague about its beds and blankets and in fact about everything, but we hoped to rest there somehow and catch the summit by dawn.

In the evening light the sharp opal peaks around took on an amazing elevation as we kicked and toiled up the last steep shoulders to the hut. It was a blow to discover its door wedged feet deep in solid ice. It had been left about two inches open, so that the main room was half full of drifted snow. As we peered into its dark recesses, the sun sank behind the Vignemale and a fierce wind began to bluster round us, with driving showers of snow crystals. There was nothing for it but to work a way in through one of the windows. By the time we got in night seemed to have fallen.

The prospects for the night were far from festive. It was bitterly cold and for a while we were all scurrying about the hut like a mad menagerie. Firewood, cooking utensils, beds, blankets alike were missing. There was nothing but an empty, sooty stove, two benches and a rickety table—besides snow and ice—with which to make ourselves comfortable. It needed all our cheerfulness to pretend that we were having a good time. In the sacks were bread and cold veal, normal spare sweaters, socks and two oil-silk *ponchos* which were to be our salvation. Salles pretended to know of a *cave* full of wine bottles and all kinds of good things, firewood, kettles and blankets. We listened to him with high hopes until we discovered him grubbing for the trap-door to it, like a dog after a bone, in some hay in the *upstairs* sleeping loft! When we found that our bottle of brandy for emergencies and a large reserve gourd of wine as well as Salles' own super-large gourd had mysteriously emptied themselves on the final slope, we guessed the source of these hopeful visions! Disturbed from grubbing, Salles plunged down the ladder to the main room and began to whirl the benches about like catherine-wheels. It took the four of us, hanging on to him like terriers, to prevent our Grandfather Bear from breaking them into flinders for firewood. These exercises at least kept us all warm. We found the lid of a packing-case for him to smash and with it kindle a brief blaze. A zinc pail was the only receptacle in the place. In it we put snow and—with dreams of a piping-hot nourishing soup—we recklessly flung our veal and bread in too! With a most mournful result. Snow takes an unconscionable time to melt, and as to getting warm! The swill produced never rose to more than ten degrees; the veal floated gelidly in the scummy froth! An amateur cook stirred the stuff with a pine stick, adding a sauce of resin and splinters. The bucketful in the end looked unfit for a pig's trough and we had to drink in turn from its lip. Our enjoyment of this joke has made us all difficult to amuse since. Soon replete, we carried more than half the pailful up to Salles, now couched on the hay upstairs and groaning fantastically. To our immense relief he lapped it up with gusto.

After this we settled down for the night. Leaving Salles to his hay, we packed ourselves in a corner upstairs and spread our *ponchos* for a coverlet. Snow sifted through cracks in the roof and rustled crisply on the oil-silk surface. But we managed to sleep when our teeth were not chattering. The board floor was iron-hard, and we were stiff in the morning—stiff enough not to be too downcast to find the Vignemale wrapped in a blizzard. Our coveted peak would have to wait till yet another season. It still waits. Waking Salles, who seemed a giant refreshed after his sleep and no whit the worse for yesterday's doings, we packed up quickly and set off down. The only reminder we had of the Salles of our ascent was that at every avalanche track he paused to assure us, in spite of our footprints, that it must have fallen over-night. We were in Gavarnie by lunch-time, glad to forget the taste of that soup at the *patron's* excellent table.

Storm-clouds hung over the Cirque next morning, so, acting on the sound principle of moving one's centre when the weather goes bad, we left for Gabas. Our plan was to motor to Arrens and thence walk over to Eaux Bonnes. We soon left the rain behind as we swooped through the masses of sunlit blossom below. By the pretty squares of Argelès, up steeply to the miserable little village of Aucun with its big squalid stone houses, their roofs splayed out to the ground, past churches squatting down like hens, we wound, and came about lunch-time to Arrens.

Here a spell fell on us; we wandered about the village finding each sight lovelier than the last. An ancient mansion full of carvings was standing derelict in the main street, its roof falling. Inside were rooms of perfect proportions with immense fireplaces, twisted staircases and lozenged windows. Entering the church we met a procession of nuns. Their voluminous robes and air of grave surprise made me feel bashful, and knickerbockered legs are hard to hide!

We must have lingered long over lunch. The wine seems to have been overlooked by Mr Belloc but would have deserved his attention. When we left, we seemed to walk with the lightness of air. High up the slopes, however, doubt arose as to what path we were on and whither we were bent. Fortune, or perhaps Bacchus, sent Thyrsis and Pannychis to our aid. They showed us a short cut and beguiled the way with local legends. When, regretfully, we said good-bye to them, we were on the Route des Pyrénées, and confident that we could at least follow it to our destination. So, for some miles, we tramped on unsuspecting any problem.

In this care-free mood we were startled to find that evening suddenly seemed to be coming on fast.

We had encouraged ourselves all day with the notion of the motor road. We had looked forward to a quick march in a lingering clair-obscure. Perhaps there might be a few inches of snow, but surely, we imagined, however much the natives might say '*Beaucoup de neige. Impossible*', a stretch of the famous Route des Pyrénées could offer no serious route-finding difficulties. Now we halted for a few minutes with some miles of the celebrated highway before our eyes.

It ran, a thin climbing braid, round the head of a long, trough-like, grassy valley. The point where we stood was perhaps a mile and a half short of the turn. There, we were horrified to see, it crawled beneath a series of snow-hung crags. Scores of obvious avalanche shoots cut across it and the fan-shaped piles of *débris* down below in the valley told their own tale. Beyond this belt of crags the road gathered itself up and climbed boldly on to whale-backed uplands where, as well as we could see, it vanished under deep beds and rounded banks of snow.

Seeing all this so clearly in the evening light we hesitated. Should we turn back and sleep in Pan's Hostelry at Arrens? Or take a chance, cut across the valley, so outflanking the avalanche zone, and try to get over to Eaux Bonnes before darkness fell too heavily? Tommy, cheerful and enterprising as usual, Paxton with his dyed-in optimism, were for pushing on. After some deliberation we were all agreed. What we none of us realized was that a great road could on occasion be no road at all. So hypnotic is a last-year's schedule of daily motor services. Hitching up our sacks, we set off at a canter down the 600 feet of smooth sheep-bitten turf into the depths of the valley. The last sunshine was still glowing brightly on the green slope, our hearts were high, and with the quick blood singing in our ears we tore down into shadow and up the opposite slope. It was crowned with a birch-tree spinney and dotted with clumps of box—points whose importance we little realized as we threaded our way through them. Where we rejoined the road stood a house to which we paid scant attention. 'A road-mender's shelter!' said Tommy. We were too intent in getting on towards Eaux Bonnes to trouble much about it. The road now developed to the full its disappointing quality. Soon it was filled with steeply sloping snow of the squashest character. In a little while we were walking in single file along the crest of the wall at its side. Huge, dim, white slopes fell from the mountain above and continued until they vanished in the dusk of the valley below, and we made our way across them along the thin black line of the coping-stones of our wall. Here and there, where the wall was buried, the top layer of snow had a nerve-racking tendency to slip away with a hiss when touched and slide off into the now invisible depths below. This soon brought us up short for a consultation. Paxton remarked that a night *à la belle étoile* looked likely. We looked at the stars that were beginning to appear. They were too cold in their glitter to make the idea attractive. Tommy then recalled the road-mender's house and suggested that they might have a fine hot soup for supper! At this, with one consent, we turned in our tracks and went back, hoping that nothing would come hissing down from above upon us and rather wondering that it didn't.

Dark on their journey lour'd the gloomy day,
Wild were the hills and doubtful grew the way;
More dark, more gloomy and more doubtful showed
The mansion that received them from the road.

The 'road-mender's house', when we examined it by the light of our
lanterns, proved an empty shell of a place. However, it looked better
than the Vignemale Hut—having no snow in it, though equally no
road-menders, no soup, no supper and no beds. A vast chimney-
place frowned into an empty room. An old boot and a few charred
logs on the earth floor were the only signs of human habitation.
We could only hope it wasn't haunted.

The night was a very long one. The earth floor was too cold to
lie on with any comfort. Our unsupported backs froze, while our
eyes watered at the smoky blaze. The door was too decrepit to shut
and night breezes searched the place as busily as the rats. But
thickets below offered stores of firewood, and while Paxton and
I. A. R. descended to gather it, Tommy and I went through the
sacks for imaginary provisions. Every few minutes, a fresh sortie
had to be made to the thickets for fuel. A trial for Romanticism!

A bitterly aloof full moon was sailing through a cloudless sky
and the cold outside shot an ague tremor through one's limbs. After
the Vignemale Hut we could not even pretend that the experience
was a novelty. Our supper had to be divided between itself and
breakfast, and was made up of Tommy's raisins and four dates. We
had never contemplated anything so silly as delays on this expedition. We congratulated ourselves on our fire and roof, though the
smoke went every way except up the chimney. All our store of
conversation was exhausted early and our tales—ghost stories being
barred—only just lasted out the night. Unfortunately they sent
none of us to sleep and it was a bleary-eyed party that came out,
at the earliest possible moment, to salute the pristine purities of
the dawn.

The road was no trouble in the morning. The snow was frozen

hard and took our boot-nails with a crisp crunching. Very soon we came out into sunlight on the whale-backed uplands where the road buried itself in the drifts. What in the night had been a vague loom of various shadows to the north was now fair provinces of France seen over a sparkling sheen of snow. Above us sharp little peaks leapt up in the sunlight like white flames incredibly steep and pointed. We longed to turn aside to climb them but Eaux Bonnes and coffee called too strongly.

We had dreams of some really grand hotel with a table-cloth white as the snow to welcome us. But when we passed down the fresh budding avenue, in the gay glitter of the spring morning, the place seemed a town of the dead. Vast façades of closed hotels, so still, so lifeless they seemed abandoned mausoleums, faced us round the central *Place*. Further down the main street we found an eating-house where last season's paper napkins and an equivalent coffee were given us. A drowsiness came on us as we breathed in the soft air. Once again we had discovered that to cross a mountain pass toilfully and come down into a new region and climate was the best of all ways of recapturing the spring. In a haze of content we drove up through Eaux Chaudes (dimly wondering about Henry IV and La Belle Fosseuse) to Gabas.

The inn at Gabas is a strange building which looks like an abandoned church or meeting-house with a railed-in garden very like a charming graveyard. Inside, the long corridor, lit at the far end only, gives into vast bare rooms whose floors tilt drunkenly and bewitchingly. The river rushing by the side of the long building fills the air with a subdued uproar: 'Aragon a torrent at the door!' indeed. We at that early season were so happy as to have this Paradise to ourselves. Madame, in charge, was an excellent cook; remarkably good wine came up from the cellar; a spirit of gaiety pervaded the place that matched with the crystal-clear spring sunshine.

The village itself was crowded with Spanish workmen employed higher up the valley in some mine or hydroelectric undertaking. We were amused to find that the local opinion (always on the

French slope of the Pyrenees very contemptuous of *les Espagnols*)
considered this work—which was described as highly dangerous—
very suitable for Spaniards. No Frenchman, we were informed,
would touch it. We were reminded of those tribes of wandering
Italian masons who do most of the engineering and building work
in Switzerland.

The *exploitation* seemed more or less to have commandeered the
road, including the village street, for its uses. A rickety miniature
railway-track was laid on the roadway to the inconvenience and
danger of all other users. Perhaps private interests in France have a
stronger pull over public utilities than elsewhere. On our first
morning, in fact, we were nearly wiped out by a side strain of its
activities. With no more warning than a few screams of habituated
terror from groups of villagers in the main street, a runaway truck
came hurtling round a bend just as we were crossing the road to
the post-office. It sped through the children of the village, spraying
out its load of stones as it swayed round the turn on two wheels.
We had hardly recovered when we were nearly annihilated again
by a motor-car full of engineers in wild pursuit. All this relieved
us of any sense of rashness in attempting what we thought was a
first winter ascent of the Pic du Midi d'Ossau.

If there was one peak which we wished to climb more than the
Vignemale it was the Pic du Midi. It is the Matterhorn of the
Pyrenees, shapely, isolated, commanding, romantic, and in summer
a pleasant but not difficult rock-climb, either by the South or
North-east Ridges. Other harder ways up can also attract the cragsman. We had very little idea of the best route for the snowy, spring
season. So when, after a rest day, we set out for it at 2 o'clock on a
perfect morning, it was rather with an intention to reconnoitre it
than with any definite hope of an ascent.

Perhaps for this reason the party dallied over its start. Anyhow
the scheduled hour of 1 o'clock had been scandalously overpast
before boots were on, forgotten lanterns discovered and lit, the
rope re-coiled, and the party collected at the door. At this point

I. A. R., usually no aggressive disciplinarian, burst out with a diatribe on the culpable waste of precious sleep caused by early morning sluggishness. He pointed out that anyone can dress—*for a mountain*—in ten minutes and breakfast in another ten and still have ten good minutes in hand for loitering! By reflection on these figures, a whole hour could be saved either for the difficulties of the mountain or for downy rest. A meek, rebuked and surprised party then set off after a still fuming leader.

The road turns up a thickly forested valley, choked in spring, where gullies come down from the heights, by vast accumulations of avalanche *débris*. Above this the valley opens out into the wide basin of the Lacs d'Ossau. Here the woods in the dawn-light were glimmering with crowds of daffodils—thick as bluebells in an English wood. These fields of daffodils, as we mounted and the sunlight began to blaze in the clearings, combined with a blistered heel to turn Paxton's desires from our peak towards a fuller leisurely enjoyment of present delights. Tommy too seemed to incline to contemplation rather than exercise. We decided then to divide and leave all attempts on the mountain to the morrow. We two would go up, to survey possibilities only, while they gave the heel a good chance to recover and enjoyed the country under the snow-line. So, with no definite plan, we set off. Our day was a series of climbs and swoops, for in the end we circled the mountain. First we went up to the foot of the Northern Ridge—too hung with ice, as we saw it then, to tempt us, though it has since been climbed under spring conditions by two Cambridge mountaineers. Then came a rushing sitting-glissade into the next valley, which we decided would be our proper approach to the mountain next day. Then another ascent in a sunshine which was beginning to scorch and over snow that was growing moist and heavy. From the ridge so gained we planned our probable line of ascent—first by an easy-looking ridge which gives the simplest of the summer routes and then by a series of snow gullies to the summit.

Followed a very wet sitting-glissade indeed, after which we lay like seals on our faces for some time on a warm boulder and discussed sardines and Feminism. Sardines—not, under a city régime, a food I consume by the tinful with pleasure—acquire a strange relish at high altitudes. Even bread dipped in the oil they are packed in is appetizing. With them for me, as a perfect mountain food, goes jam. On very hot days it can be mixed in a cup to give a sherbet. When over-tired, feeling sick through strain or heat, I can take this mixture, I have discovered, when even biscuits and acid-drops repel. The Feminist argument, which was linked to the sardines, is less easily summarized.

All the time the presence of the mountain, as it turned fresh facets to the quadrants of our circle, brooded over us. This form of expedition is not easy to find. There are few big mountains that can be circled close up under their cliffs in a day's march. Spurs and satellites hide them, the continuity of their presence is broken. Or you must go too high and near to see them, as with Mont Blanc, or too low, as with the Ortler. Fuji Yama, it is true, manifests itself continuously, but is a freak mountain shining alone like a miracle in the middle of lowlands.

The last quadrant showed us the South Ridge—with too many mushroomy cornices, we thought, to be healthy. The snow by then was thigh-deep and the going toilsome, and we were not sorry to come out of it into the daffodil fields at sunset. We jogged down to supper at Gabas more captivated than ever with the Pic du Midi and ready for a special effort on the morrow.

A more than military promptness marked our departure next morning just after midnight. The lecture had done us good. Perhaps as a reward the day was a series of happy chances. I had the luck to hit the very confusing line of ascent up through the cliffy, snow-muffled forest slopes by lantern light without losing the party as I feared I would. At the base of the North-east Ridge an icy wind was blowing off the Balaitous. It was too cold to breakfast and we roped in some uncertainty. The first half-hour was a battle against the *tourbillons* of a gale that drove blinding cold showers of snow into our faces and down our necks. But once well up on the mountain we came into shelter. Very little of the usual route was recognizable under the deep white mantle. The chimneys described in the guide-books were buried. But the snow for the first half of the day stuck solidly to the rocks and could be kicked and stamped into steps without much trouble. Higher up it softened and corners came where very tender and solicitous stepping was needed if the staircase were not to slip away and a whole section had to be worked out again.

Spring snow on such ground gives a charming sense of security to a leader. If his step breaks away there is a soft snow blanket to catch him (as the net catches the trapezist). With a well-managed rope there is no chance of his endangering his party. The gully that falls away so steeply beneath him is not, as in summer, all sharp boulders or slithery ice; it is a bed into which if anyone plops by mischance he will at worst get a wetting. However, no one plopped on this occasion. We might, if we had hurried here, but the weather was now impeccable, the dawn-gale had quite subsided and we had all the rest of the daylight to play in. So not till afternoon did we come to the last gentle slope that leads up to the northernmost of the twin summits. The length of our toil perhaps heightened the lifting exhilaration with which we trudged up the last little ridge—gazing southward into a Spain now hung with a mysterious violet haze. The precipices of the Balaitous to the east glimmered with rose and purple gleams under a rising moon before we turned away and sought out the longest, gentlest gully for our descent. Too soft and clinging for rapid progress, the snow gave us leisure to watch the coming on of night in all its stages. Moonlight was throwing shadows over the snow-waves round our knees as we waded down the valley reaches. Once again we found by lantern a quick line through the forest.

At midnight we reached our inn. A faultless welcome awaited us. A piping hot ragout, a fine wine, a bright fire, a glowing lamp, drawn curtains, comfortable chairs and smiling handmaidens made a fitting close to a day near as possible to perfection. When we turned in, Hilaire Belloc's *Tarantella* was more than ever thrumming in our heads:

Do you remember an Inn, Miranda?
Do you remember an Inn?
And the tedding and the spreading
Of the straw for a bedding,
And the fleas that tease in the High Pyrenees,
And the wine that tasted of the tar?
And the cheers and the jeers of the young muleteers
(Under the vine of the dark verandah)?
Do you remember an Inn, Miranda?

CHAPTER XIII

MAINLY ITALIAN ALPS

(1924)

Over the edge—Guiding, guideless—Glacier nine-pins—Nearly shot soon after dawn—The Val de By—Royal paths and Alpine gloom—Herbetet—The Paradis traverse—The Piantonetto Hut and a dreadful truth—A night out with a brigand—The Tour St Pierre and a cataclysm—Ardua Grivola Bella—40 x 25 steps in ice—Falling stones—The Witch again—Disconsolate Alpinists—A body on the Col de Collon—Marmot-hunting—Eastward—Penalties of wealth.

This year we began earlier than usual and as a larger party. Patrick and Patricia Blackett and my sister Violet came with us, and later we were joined by Muriel Turner, the daughter of Sam Turner, the well-known New Zealand climber.

At Vallorbe we went into the clouds, and even the Dent du Midi was shrouded in mists. But, whatever was happening on the summits, at Sion it was scorching hot. We went straight up the rocky hill where the castle stands, and ate cheese and tomatoes with fresh rolls on a grassy promontory where aromatic air was stirring. Thence we gazed up at the dim cloud-hung outlines of the Arolla peaks huddled behind the seamed and patched knees of the Val d'Hérens.

What a grand drive it is up to Haudères! The vast yellow postcars, manned by a special race of imperturbable drivers, to whom no one may speak, swirl up round hairpin bends to a fanfare which thenceforth forever echoes through one's imagined approaches to the Alps. They have the privilege of the inner position whenever any other vehicle has to be passed on the road. As this time the Poste was full and we hired a car; we had the outside edge. It can be a strain on the nerves and I. A. R. insisted on telling us a story of his first visit to the valley. In those days one took a landau and gave up the whole day to the journey. They were trotting gently along the level section towards the Earth Pyramids of Euseigne when suddenly, with a jangle of bells and a crash of wheels, round the next corner came charging a two-horse timber-wain with two very drunken drivers bumping up and down on the fore-carriage. It went by outside with an inch or two of road to spare, the drivers singing uproariously, oblivious of the 500 feet of gorge beneath them. That evening news came up to Evolène that at the very next corner the timber-wain had gone off the road, horses and men alike crashing down to destruction. It was a story to keep our attention awake as we swung, apparently, over the void—the intermittent buffer stones or wooden railings looking ridiculously inadequate. But the valley was full of flowers, the sky was clearing, the sun gleaming here and there and the higher air filling our lungs deeper and deeper as we swept upwards to fresh delight.

Haudères seemed unchanged, but there was little time to linger. Evening was not far off as we went hurrying by the Chapel of St Barthélemy, passing the sad little iron crosses that show where some herdsman of the valley has been suddenly overwhelmed by avalanche. The mule pack-train with its bells singing out of other years crossed us as we toiled up the steep piece above the Victoria Hotel and M. and Mme Anzévui, unchanged and undiminished, welcomed us into the Mont Collon. As for how many others, that hotel had become for us a mountain home.

Above Arolla are some of the most pleasant pastures in the world. Clear streamlets wander gently among them and single *arolles* throw soothing shade on the sweet grass amid the clumps of short heather and bilberry. Here a group of nymphs belonging to our party were surprised by a cowherd next afternoon bathing in a secluded pool. They fled in the approved Greek manner behind the shelter of diminutive tree-trunks. Meanwhile I. A. R. sat in a scholarly nook correcting the proofs of *Principles of Literary Criticism*. All day the Pigne—a wave of white surrender—beckoned to us to hurry before the perfect weather fled. So next morning, rather injudiciously, our long caravan, desperately out of training, but provided with two lanterns and a torch, was puffing up the long curving moraine to the Pièce Glacier and across the snows to the Col des Vignettes. A lovely saffron dawn came on, but it was too early in the holiday for us to pretend that we were enjoying ourselves. Three of the party had never set foot on a glacier before. No doubt some smaller training walk would have been wiser, but it would have lacked the pull that the Pigne was exerting upon us. None the less when we came to the little, new, corrugated-iron hut that Arolla owes to Stuart Jenkins' generosity, we were all glad of the excuse for loitering a while. We came later to talk of it somewhat irreverently as Jenkins' paint-box, for it had been newly daubed a bright red; the paint was hardly dry, and we were reminded of it the rest of the season by splotches we carried on all parts of our persons.

A veil had perhaps best be drawn over the rest of this ascent. Every Alpinist knows that the boasted joys of his sport can be imperceptible on the first trip of the season! Later in the day the unheroic spectacle of five Alpinists lying in all attitudes of lassitude and abandon on the snows might more than once have been beheld near the summit. No other party was on the mountain and we could be shameless. We did peep down one at a time over the huge cornice to observe the group of toy roofs that is Arolla 6000 feet below. But the sun had been blastingly hot and storm-clouds gathered in the afternoon, so we made our best speed down and home over the Pas de Chèvres.

The trip showed me how much difference there is between guided and guideless climbing. A guided party will walk up so easy a peak as the Pigne as though it were nothing at all. A guideless party, with novices to look after, will find its slopes, especially on the descent, gaping with gulfs and undermined with hidden traps. This makes it much more interesting of course, but much more tiring. It is not the absence of local knowledge which makes the difference but the responsibility—much heavier through a whole Alpine day than on a British cliff. Though one knew it imaginatively already, this first actual consciousness of Alpine possibilities was another thing; and the sense that we *must* be ready to act *instantly* if any mischance occurred, had supplied a ground base for the whole day's variations. The prudent leader in Britain, even though he may be called a 'grandmother' by the young tigers of the sport, has a definite technique. Through it he can feel perfectly at ease about the safety of his party. He sees that the belays are in order and then can forget his party for a spell, if he likes, while he gives his whole mind to the pitch he is climbing. Afterwards he can secure himself and bring the others up without a trace of uncertainty as to how to deal with whatever may occur. By contrast, the guide or amateur leader and his party on a big mountain will be moving almost continuously. The rocks will be far less stable, with loose pieces far less cleaned away. Shortness of time prevents belays from being used systematically. The guide while moving must keep an eye on the whole party, and must be ready to take violent, immediate and effective action to meet a slip, a dislodged block, falling stones or any other emergency. The sense of strain is even greater on glaciers. Their tricks are inexhaustible and unforeseeable. And if anyone goes into a crevasse—not always, as some solitary climbers have averred, an avoidable mischance!—no ordinary strength may be needed to bring him up again. Still more on steep snow-ridges; the average guide's power to stand on thin watery snow overlying ice and hold up a whole party of novices that has no secure attachment to anything is little short of miraculous. I found amateur guiding a very good lesson in respect for the guide's profession.

No doubt one's point of view changes with years. Joseph was telling us the other day of his first visit as a young porter to Zermatt from Arolla. His uncle told him to go home by the railway in the Rhone Valley, but he disobeyed and set out alone to gain a thorough acquaintance with the Findelen Glacier, and toured all the upper bays of the Gorner Glacier under Monte Rosa and The Twins, before finishing up *via* the Col d'Hérens and the Bertol. He summed up tersely: 'When I was young I thought all glaciers safe and simple. Now I'm old I never know what I am standing on!'

But to get back to my story. The weather that season went by alternate days. If one knows this ahead it is a very restful and convenient arrangement. But like all Alpinists we had a dread of getting out of step with it—of setting out at dawn on all the days that begin to rain at 8 A.M. and waking up at 9 A.M. on all the perfect mornings!

So the next day but one, though the rest of our party took the risk of staying in bed, we two dashed off to traverse the Perroc from the north, if we could. We could not. It was too long for our second expedition and a rainstorm stole two hours at the Col de Zarmine. We seemed to traverse miles of ridge and got about two-thirds of the way up from the Grande Dent de Veisivi. But at 12.20 P.M. we were still that fabulous half-hour from the summit, and as the way down from the Perroc has a bad reputation for benighting parties, we turned back. By this renunciation we probably missed a miserable night, for as we reached Arolla again it began to rain.

A return of promising weather saw us, with Pat Blackett, passing again, but much more cautiously, by Jenkins' paint-box. Our intention was the Mont Collon, but signs of coming trouble in the heavens led us instead to the Petit Mont Collon where it rained intermittently throughout the afternoon. With re-established weather, next day our complete caravan visited the North Aiguilles Rouges. On the upper Aiguilles Rouges Glacier a large boulder slipped soundlessly from the retaining wall far away and came for us down the glacier-slope like a three-foot cannon-ball. Strung out, the five of us made a fairly easy mark for it. The rope on these occasions is a distinct embarrassment! One never knows which way those in front and behind are proposing to run. Telepathy would be useful. This cannon-ball had a bias like a bowl and curved in its flight beyond computation. We were merry *after* it had whizzed through the ninepins without touching them, though we felt the mountain unkind to assail us so from an ordinarily irreproachable slope.

Our next adventure seemed at one time likely to involve missiles also—of a more human and lethal character. My sister and Muriel Turner had gone ahead over the Col de Collon to climb the Dent d'Hérens with Joseph; the Blacketts with us were to follow an hour later. In the interval a violent *tourmente* developed on the Col and we could not follow till the next day.

We had left the glacier and we two were ahead scuttling down the Combe d'Oren on the other side, when two short, wispy and venomous-looking lads jumped up from behind a rock and called upon us to halt. They were in Italian uniform, Neapolitans, and they wanted our passports. That was in the days when Mussolini was beginning his closure of the frontier against Alpine travellers and we quite failed to understand the serious intentions of these grey-green hobbledehoys. So when, after some jesting with them in no particular languages, we discovered them holding the passports upside-down, we went blithely on our way. For a few steps only! The unmistakable sound of breech-blocks sliding brought us quickly to a halt. There were the two negligible scamps, all a broad eager grin of delight, getting ready for a little shooting. Fortunately, before we had stood there at attention for long, the Blacketts caught us up. Patricia is half Italian and could find her way, if anyone could, even to the hearts of such young ruffians as these. But they were hard to appease. We had flouted their dignity and disappointed them of their shooting. In vain we asked whether they thought we had Matteotti's body in our sacks. In those days all Italy was seeking for his body to prove him murdered. Down we all had to march four miles to the tent of an officer superior enough to be beguiled by Patricia. Only so was imprisonment at Turin avoided. Then back we trooped in the evening downpour to Prarayé.

This closed the season's climbing for the Blacketts. A bitter wind howled dismally round Prarayé on its bare, exposed, rocky knoll. Thin iridescent clouds hung in the sky, dappled with all the colours of the rainbow. This perhaps worst of all Alpine weather-signs was not displayed in vain. Rain and wet snow fell for the next three days. It rained again as we went back by the Col de Collon to Arolla to set them on their way to England. At 1 A.M. it was a clear starry night, windless but warm. I. A. R. went downstairs in his silk scarf dressing-gown to look out of all the windows. When we set off at 2.30 A.M. with only one lantern it was through a very dark night that was overclouding already. I remember it being difficult for the last man over the rough and pathless way. Snow began to fall about 4 A.M. but we got over by lunch time without trouble.

We were due to start out with Joseph for the Paradis Group in a few days, and filled in the time of waiting by going, on our own, over the Petite Dent de Veisivi and up the Roussette in deep snow, scowling at the sky (but it made no difference) and giving Joseph liqueurs in the evening. He had never tasted Chartreuse, grimaced amiably, and found it far from *doux*. Then one threatening morning we joined up and set out. There was a stuffiness in the night as we plodded up the grass-slopes towards the Pas de Chèvres. We all suspected the worst from the start. At the Col snow was falling and the Seilon Glacier looked grey and spectral under a low black cloud-canopy. Soon we were trudging, in a white mist, heads down, *passe-montagnes* lowered, against a whirling drift of vast snowflakes. A little later we might have been inside a snowball, and were rather pleased with ourselves when we struck the Col de Lyrerose and could gallop down to surprise the folk in the Chanrion Hut. We came in to them at breakfast, like snow-men—plastered from head to foot and eyelashes bristling. Then we had the joy of making up for our early start by going to bed again—an indulgence that the Alpinist often sighs for in vain. At eight that night we regained consciousness in order to sup on Welsh rarebits soaked in wine. The hut was as spruce as ever. All through our Italian tour it hung in our minds as a contrasting model of how things should be.

Plans for our next day were of the well-known kind that look better on the map than on the ground. Baggage for our Italian tour

had been sent up to the Grand St Bernard. One of the great conveni-
ences of tramping about Switzerland is that you can go over a range
and find your change of clothes waiting for you in the village to
which you come down. The Swiss Postes take all the bother off your
hands in an easy fashion that makes one marvel at the primitive
absence of organization in other countries, in Italy or England, for
example. How often have I wished for a similar arrangement in the
Lake District. But how few good ideas, after all, are really international! The transhipment of this baggage into Italy had to be done
by ourselves at the St Bernard. So, we thought, why not walk straight
across there? An arrangement with this additional advantage that
Joseph, who did his military service at the hospice and has retained
very cordial relations with the monks, would be able to revisit his
friends and spiritual pastors. We counted, alas, without the wiles of
the Val de By.

This immense green bowl fronts the south. Valleys within valleys
find room in it, their recesses smoothed out under the midday
sunshine to an eye looking into it from one of the surrounding
peaks. Channelled by a thousand rivulets seeping down from the
fifteen miles of its rocky rim, and chased all over with delicate
thread-like grooves of cattle-tracks, its great slopes, when you are
in them, fold you into private worlds of their own. Here a white-
walled chapel crowning a long shoulder invites you to incline your
route past it. There an abandoned summer visitors' hotel lures you
out across a space of level meadows. One brown village signals to
another up on the height or down in the glen, and between them
is thrown a tangled web of paths: main contouring paths, transverse
occasionals, chance directs, occupational loops, every kind of path
in every direction except one suitable for a passage from the Col
de Fenêtre to the Grand St Bernard. Much of our day was spent
listening to Joseph shouting in one incomprehensible *patois* to
distant cowherds who replied in another. The sound from Joseph's
powerful chest would pulse off into the blue air and a time would
elapse before the tiny black upright mite on the shoulder of the

next vast green slope would begin to agitate itself. A faint thin creaking sound, only just audible to us, would come back. These local peasants must have had perverse natures, or the paradise in which we were wandering made us careless. We lunched again and again by different streams, gazing up at the steep red Faudery peaks or the Fiorio or the Combin or the Vélan. It seemed to make little difference which we neighboured. Our paradise had no confines, or the later part of the day seemed to bring us no nearer them. It had its serpent, however. Something was quick in the grass and Joseph was bounding forward, axe upraised, before we had time to exclaim. The adder was dead in a moment, and only a few yards away a lad lay sleeping on his back in the sunlight, sleeping so soundly that he was hard to waken. At last we struck a really impressive irrigation *bise* and bathed our feet, heated with so much contouring on steep grass. The path at its side led us away into a forest, soft and cool after the glare without. But, some hours later, it seemed, as evening advanced, interminable as the green hummocks of By. Dusk was falling when we spied an entrancing village with a lovely campanile some 1000 feet below us. Through it ran, unmistakably, a motor road. We felt we could almost read the milestone which showed it to be not less than 15,000 paces from our destination. After a short struggle with Joseph, who hates to be defeated, we dropped straight down. A *festa* was in progress; the village was illuminated, musical and gay. The church was lighted, and its clock struck nine three times over. The porch of the inn was hung with vines. To-morrow, quite against our principles, we might use the motor road, but not to-night.

What actually happened was that Joseph rushed off early to fetch the luggage while we strolled down towards Aosta. Dust lay on the road, and the Italian sun was hot, so we went into a cool dark cottage to enjoy the sunlight, and the flakes of the Combin above, through the trellis of the window. Into this quiet came an old, wandering, grey-bearded vendor carrying umbrellas by the score up the St Bernard. This odd apparition drank wine and rested and tried to sell us large cotton gamps. If I had known then what I know now, I would have bought one to ward off sunstrokes. Then, I could only think of them as summit souvenirs or parachutes!

That afternoon we honked and rattled into Cogne. For all its beauty of setting in a fair open basin of meadows with the Paradis gleaming occasionally out of a chaos of clouds beyond, it pleased us no better than before. Scores of Italian families were exhibiting to perfection the ideal bourgeois holiday. Mama knitted in her best afternoon frock in a canvas chair. Papa, rather too plump in the wrong places, played ball with his offspring or fiddled with field-glasses. Quarrelsome muslin-dressed children shrieked. Why the mountaineer should feel so desolated by these scenes is hard to say. Perhaps the lack of imagination and enterprise shown by staying for six weeks in a chair in an hotel garden depresses one? The children at least might make mountains out of mole-hills or find other conceits. Two spirited urchins completely happy with a clothes-line on the Arolla boulders came to my mind! Or perhaps, as a candid friend once suggested, 'It is simply your climber's snobbishness that makes you feel so!'

If so, the next morning took the pride out of us. Once again, as in 1923, we were taken aback by a mysterious lethargy. A leadenness in the legs and an utter disinclination to walk uphill assailed us. It was worse than starting a holiday afresh. Recognizing the symptoms after a while, we put them down to our descent into the low air of the Aosta Valley. Twenty-four hours takes the poison out of the system and puts all right again but until then it was as if one were sickening for a fever!

We had set off early for the Grivola. At the point—only a mile or two from Cogne—where the steep path turns up, rain began. We sheltered in a cowshed, a picturesque scene in the lantern light, while the shower passed, and then began to crawl painfully upwards. When heavily-laden peasants, under forty kilos of wood, took to passing us as though we were standing still, we had to admit that we were badly out of sorts. We gave our mountain up early—too weak to be even resentful! When we reached the King's Hunting Lodge on its lovely plateau we were horribly tempted to ask for beds—at 8 A.M.! But we had had nearly three weeks in the Alps with so few fine days! Instead of resting, we foolishly trudged on in a villainous temper till we topped the rocky crest which holds in the Grivola Glacier. Here we lay down and gazed at our peak. It pleased us not at all! True the Grivola is not especially attractive from this angle; but almost anything would have displeased us then. We were suffering from a bad attack of 'mountain gloom', which is certainly a disease more frequent in the Alps than climbers' accounts often confess. All slopes looked toilsome and just the very places for stones to come trundling down! The more we looked at the shallow gullies and ridges of this face of the Grivola—the ordinary usual route—the less tempted we were. In the end we ran away—crawled rather—in the direction of the Col de Lauzon.

Our intention was to find some high cheese-maker's chalet and sleep in it for the traverse of the Herbetet next day. From the Lauzon Hunting Lodge you are too far from the Herbetet; it only serves for the Grivola, and we were in a mood to turn down any near-by peak in favour of something else farther off! The Col de Lauzon path is a sad exhibition of the vanity of vanity. Originally it was a kingly path for the use of le Roi Chasseur. As such it had to be five feet wide and smoothly graded for mule-back mountaineering. When new it must have been a fine witness to the thews of the Italian Army. But, alas, its zigzags were built up full in the path of all the spring avalanches. Irresistible forces had swept its turnings away. As we scrambled among the tottering boulder piles that now represented all that labour, it was irritating to reflect that a perma- nent footpath close under the cliffs to the north could have been arranged with a tenth of the trouble. Such a path would have remained secure for all time, to win the gratitude of every traveller over the Pass. We hearkened therefore with malicious pleasure to Joseph's *patois* as he carolled away at a scurrilous Aosta song about the Royal Sportsman:

Umberto! Umberto!
Il Re d'Italia!
Buffare la polenta
Tutto le giorne.

The cheesemaker's chalet was unspeakably filthy and much too high. A mixture of decaying cheese and manure seemed to be daubed all over its dark interior. Joseph's indignation—his brother is the famous *fruitier* of the Upper Arolla Chalets—at *ces sales gens* was a relief to us all. If it had come within his code he would have written to *The Times* about it! There was nothing to be done but go down quite a thousand feet to the little white-walled cabin of the *Garde-chasse* that was gleaming on a green shoulder at the very edge of the depths of the Val Savaranche.

The *Gardes-chasse* are a fine set of men, as even Joseph admitted, who, being himself once a mighty hunter of chamois, is naturally of the other party. The welcome of the *Garde*—a tall swaggering man with a magnificent moustache—was courteous in the extreme. He was going down to the valley and gave us the place for our own until he returned. Cosy and comfortable it was, so putting down our gloom to fatigue we decided to spend a rest day in these soothing surroundings.

The morning after saw us happily on the Herbetet. It was sprinkled with new snow and the rocks were cold, but we scampered over it in high spirits being thoroughly refreshed. The climber's mood often changes as suddenly as the weather and as mysteriously. In contrast to our mountain gloom we were close to exuberance. Even a sinister wind roaring through the summit rocks and a black storm threatening us just as we passed the spectacular difficult step on the South Ridge did not depress us; and the long contouring movement that leads across the glaciers to the Vittorio Emmanuele Hut was sheer joy and seemed too short.

The hut, as we found it, was a disgrace to humanity. Only the most confirmed Alpine Romanticism could overlook the polluted state of the environs. A slope of garbage tippings fell from the door-step into a rancid little lake. It is hard to excuse such a condition when any Boy Scout or Girl Guide knows how to arrange things with decency. With all nature in their favour, with sun and wind and water to keep the site clean, it is sad that people should mark their presence by filth and stench. There are plenty of clean and beautiful huts in the Alps to show how things can be done. Early the next morning we were glad to escape from it on to the Paradis—far from paradisial with a regiment of soldiers upon it. Alpine recruits were being put to the test and taken up at a pace that few could withstand. The weaker brothers—pale blue or faintly green according to their complexions—were turning back at all stages of the ascent. Counting the two who were in each case deputed to see the sufferer safely down, we estimated their casualties at over fifty per cent!

One other guided party was on the mountain. A very young man who was determined not to let a woman rival him in prowess. He was obviously out of training, but he and his local guide stormed past us again and again like the hero of *Excelsior*. Each time he got a little ahead he collapsed—each time a little paler. It was pathetic; but what could one do? His guide was too stupid to see that, by going at our humdrum moderate pace, his client could have been quite comfortable on the mountain and would probably have wished to give him further engagements. As it was, the young man was lying on his face with heaving shoulders at the summit. He would have called it 'mountain sickness', but speed, not altitude, was his trouble.

We roped up at the summit—so down-trodden had the track been—and put on our crampons to go along the vertiginous series of corniced snow-ridges that leads to the Piccolo Paradiso. A local guide on the summit amused me by saying it was very unfit for a lady because of the cornices, though why feminine feet should disturb them more than masculine weight it was hard to guess.

Few arêtes are more splendidly spectacular than this, nor when the party comes to the little rock pinnacles of the lesser Paradiso is any very obvious way of escape visible. To the east is the enormous

Tribulazione Glacier with its endless labyrinths of crevasses and ice-falls. To the west is a very tall precipice that looks a deadly haunt of falling stones. A climber without a sense of time might easily be tempted to continue along the ridge towards the Herbetet rather than try either way off. A fierce wind continued under a clear blue sky and the rocks were plastered with frost feathers. The cold, however, had helped us down the ridge, freezing the snow hard. Crooking the knees, one frog-walks down with a determined reliance on the spikes of the crampons.

We lay with our chins over the western precipices for some time before deciding upon the safest line down. In the end Joseph skilfully made out a series of ridges which could be linked up by side movements under the shelter of over-hanging flanges in the cliff. Most of it went very well, though I find in my diary mention of taking 'a swing at a corner'. And so with a final dash out of the danger zone— but without hearing or seeing a single falling stone—we came down to the glacier. The western sun had thoroughly melted the snows. *'On risque de prendre un bain!'* said Joseph as we splashed across it. He was right. Pools of all depths had accumulated under deceptive lids of thin snow-slush. Such an icy plunge was not to our taste either.

Next day, however, when we were idling in the warm meadows, we taught Joseph that a dip in a glacier stream does not entail *danger de mort*. Like most peasants he had deep misgivings about open-air bathing even in the most tempting pools. Encouraged by our example, however, he did on that afternoon take the decisive plunge, and since then it has been hard on sunny days to keep him out of the water.

Later that afternoon we learnt a new Alpine lesson. I. A. R. went to sleep in a hollow where the growing shadows caught him before he awakened. The result was a violent chill. Joseph was full of stories of wearied haymakers killed by such carelessness! He treated the complaint vigorously and successfully with infusions of herbs which he seemed to gather from under every rock.

The sufferer was well enough next morning to set out for a rambling crossing of the southern valleys of the chain to the Piantonetto Hut. The local guide was in attendance on his frail young monsieur who was still groaning in the ladies' compartment. This, in fact, had by this time become an infirmary for him and two young Italians, who had tumbled that afternoon down a face of the Ciamarella. He pretended to know all about this hut. He told us how fine it was, of its excellent blankets and the stores of wood that it contained. We believed him for some inexplicable reason. There was no malice behind his romancing, merely ignorance. Probably he never went anywhere but up and down his Paradiso. However it was, he made us confident that our long walk would land us in snug quarters for the night. Long it was! The beautiful white glaciers that appear on the map have receded to leave wildernesses of trackless boulders. Snowless stony corries radiate into upland fastnesses to which the red retaining walls give an unseemly appearance of toothless jaws. After a whole day's marching up and down over these boulders, we came at last into a grassy horseshoe looking down a long valley choked with cloud, out of which distant voices and dog-barkings mounted.

Somewhere on this slope was the Piantonetto Hut and we were in a great hurry to find it, to change, and make ourselves comfortable. Evening was at hand, so we separated to scour the slopes. Nearly an hour had passed before we found some foundations and part of a pair of bellows. Slowly the dreadful truth dawned upon us. This had been the hut. A memory came back then to I. A. R. of reading in some past *Alpine Journal* of some remote Italian hut swept away by an avalanche. '*C'est malheureusement trop vrai!*' sighed Joseph, picking up a scrap of broken woodwork. We were more angry with our stupid romancing guide than anything else. But what was to be done? We were some seven hours from the nearest village. The south was flickering with lightning and dark clouds were shutting off the last of the twilight.

Far, far below—about 2000 feet down—we had glimpsed

cowsheds with cows around them. Joseph proposed to go down, borrow any coverings he could from them and some kind of cooking vessel. We meanwhile would find a sheltering hole in the rocks and collect some fuel. So off he went like Mercury, sparks flying beneath each foot, while we groped about for firewood. The avalanche seemed to have been singularly destructive. Hardly a particle of the hut of any use to man had survived. And the darkness was falling fast! However, we did in time collect a few flinders of matchboarding. Happily too we discovered a grotto, if a narrow crevice behind a rock could so be called. About this time a thunderstorm rolled up and rain started. From time to time one of us would crawl out of our grotto to scout for Joseph. At last his lantern was to be seen not far below and a sound of vituperation came up to us.

He arrived in a towering passion—a quite new Joseph to us who had never seen him even mildly out of temper before. He was wrapped in blankets and carrying a large pail of milk and had been running hard uphill. Behind him panted a surly, frightened peasant in another blanket. Joseph's account of his adventure, punctuated with explosive exclamations, justified all his high feeling. He had reached the chalets very quickly—found them crowded with '*une espèce de brigands*' enough to make any stranger nervous. He had explained the whole matter to them and asked for the loan of some blankets and a vessel. These '*voleurs*' had begun to make trouble at once. They had even suggested, '*quel sales gens!*', that he would never return them. He, a Swiss guide, wearing his badge there before their eyes! Apparently these '*infâmes*' thought nothing of Swiss guides, knew nothing except how to rob travellers. The whole chalet was full of the furniture of the Piantonetto Hut, carried down there by that avalanche, '*hein*?' In the end he had offered them ten francs for a pail of milk and the loan of blankets that in La Forclaz would be burned by any villager at sight. Not enough. They asked a hundred and wouldn't take less till Joseph started to look dangerous. Then they compromised at fifty, and even so wouldn't believe that people who would pay fifty for their vile blankets wouldn't carry them off with them over the Tour St Pierre! So this worthless scoundrel—here the accompanying peasant winced and shivered under Joseph's eye— had to come up with him, stay the night with us and see that we didn't thieve their filthy rubbish. On the way up the '*vaurien*' had actually tried to drive a bargain of his own—another twenty francs for coming up with Joseph as a kind of policeman. Ah! he had been a lucky one, that '*forçat*', not to get a thick ear, a good one, for that. He, Joseph, had the milk pail in one hand and the lantern in the other, otherwise—!

All through this tirade Joseph was actively at work fixing up the night's quarters. Before the rain began we had done our best to mattress the floor of our cranny with wild hay. Soon a brisk fire was crackling at the grotto's mouth under its overhanging eve, hissing and spluttering as the raindrops were blown into it. How the four of us were to pack in was a difficult problem. There would have been little enough room for three. For a time we tried again to persuade our involuntary companion to go down to his nice bed at the chalet. But it was clear that however much he feared us—which seemed now not a little—he was still more afraid of something below. Once while Joseph and I. A. R. were seeking more wild hay, I was left alone with the trembling wretch and tried to achieve by soft words and soothing gestures (we could none of us understand any of his *patois*) what more violent attempts had not won. But when with reassuring smiles I pointed to my Ladies' Alpine Club badge, he replied by crossing himself! At this I tried a volley of furious English. And the others returned to find him on his knees with his hands clasped (and me with hair flying, hands waving and eyes flashing in the firelight), afraid for his very soul and convinced that I was a witch. In spite of his terror he was immovable. There was nothing for it (short of murder) but to let him into our tiny grotto for the night.

Joseph's tender care for him now was a lesson in Christian charity. First he made him sit and scorch his back dry at the fire lest, after running so fast up the mountain, he should catch a chill! Then in the thickest of the blankets he stowed him away by himself, since no one wished to be close to him, in the narrowest, further end of our grotto. Then we three *en échelon* got as much shelter as we could in its mouth. The night was not easeful. Flanges of rock in our floor grew sharper as it wore on. Grey dawn was almost a cheerful sight, the storm seemed to have passed and we were not long in creeping out, handing his blankets and pail over to '*le misérable*' with an irrational tip, and setting off. With not a word of thanks he slouched into the mists and we began zigzagging up the drenched grass-slopes towards the Tour St Pierre.

Stiffness wore off about the time that the sunlight burst through the valley clouds. We were working up a long snow-slope by then and coming close to a raw looking mass of crag that led, we hoped, conveniently into the upper recesses of the mountain. We had had no chance to reconnoitre, and felt in fact quite lucky, on such a shrouded morning, to be actually on our chosen peak and not some other by mistake. The cliffs we climbed on for the next few hours were firmer than we expected, but they looked like a newly abandoned quarry and we were glad enough to strike the main dividing ridge, to look over the Northern glacier-clad slopes and feel on ground more traditionally Alpine. Here we breakfasted. Perhaps it was our sleep-starved state, but the Tour St Pierre more than most mountains seemed to offer us its summit and then churlishly withdrew it. However, in the end we sat on it and stopped its antics.

The descent went merrily—until we neared the bergschrund. Then suddenly a beating, flapping roar burst out above us. '*Attention, une pierre*,' shouted Joseph. We shrank as best we could into the crannies of our cliff. There was nowhere to hide and nothing more to be done. With an infernal shindy as loud as that of the Flying Scotsman in full career, a block as big as a table crashed past us a few yards away. No more followed, but we were heartily grateful to be out of range in mid-glacier a few minutes later.

We now trudged on quietly for a while down the gently inclined glacier, hoping to be finished with falling stones. On our right a long rocky arm came down from the Cima Paganini to end in abrupt cliffs. Our line of descent wound round beneath its knuckly fist. Suddenly, as we approached, a cataclysm occurred. A vast wedge of the cliff fell away as though the whole crag were disintegrating. The falling masses were visible for an instant turning on one another. Then in a cloud of dust-smoke and snow-spray they dashed in a thousand skipping and whirling blocks down the glacier. We stood spell-bound barely a hundred yards from the track where the destruction passed. Such cataclysms are uncommon, thank goodness, and quite out of the ordinary run of Alpine dangers. We had a strong feeling that the Graians were not playing fairly with us to let loose two such bombardments in one day on ground that would normally be considered safe and healthy. I have since gathered enough stories of similar occurrences in the Cogne district to think that in places it deserves a bad reputation for instability.

The choice before us now was not an easy one. Our natural route lay straight across the path of the rock-avalanche. One might suppose that after one outburst of this order quiet might be expected—long enough at least for a party to cross in safety. But the cliff was still groaning and creaking in an ominous manner. A constant trickle of small fragments was following the major masses down. It is true they were caught safely in the schrund at its foot, but the uneasy whisper and rattle of their fall suggested that a second convulsion was likely. Our only alternative to crossing the danger zone was to make a long detour out of range down the middle of the glacier. Unfortunately this area was horribly seamed by intricate crevasses. It was almost certain that we should find our way there cut by uncrossable chasms. After some debate, we resolved to make the passage of the danger zone and trust to our utmost speed to carry us through in safety. More easily decided upon than done! We dashed down at full pace to find, to our horror, just where we must pass and in the middle of the track of danger, an immense open collapsed crevasse. Its floor was a jumbled heap of *débris* and an escape with safety up the other wall would be easy; but at our feet a slope of some seventy feet of very steep ice looked as though we should have to spend a miserable half-hour chopping down it. We had counted without Joseph. Not a second's hesitation before he unroped me from the middle of the rope and called on I. A. R. to slide down. After a moment of dangling I. A. R. landed on a boulder and unroped; I then dangled down in my turn. Joseph, calling on us to catch him, then performed the steepest ice-glissade that ever an Alpinist's wildest dreams could imagine. Crouched like a human tripod on his heels and his axe, rigid and shaking with the strain, he somehow whizzed down into our arms. How he managed not to topple forwards headlong I never shall know. But somehow he arrived on us undamaged and then, without pausing an instant, we all dashed unroped up the opposite slope and bolted off into safety.

The remainder of our return to Cogne is hidden in a dreamy haze. Part of the way we might have been sleep-walking. I. A. R. at one stage, just before we got off the glacier, discovered a path high up on the wall of cliffs. It took much persuasion from us others to convince him it was a mirage. We found ourselves, later in the forest, looking up jumpily for falling stones at each sudden sound.

Down in the meadows at last by the side of the smooth-flowing *bise*, our minds turned to ideas of supper and bed as we ambled on and watched Cogne grow larger. But, when we arrived, Cogne was at the height of its summer congestion. We glowered more sourly than ever at the amiable families taking their evening constitutional, and had to be content with a barn shared by a large number of other people as the scene of our slumbers.

Deep they were, though much broken in the morning by the joyous play of a fat infant bouncing a ball. The others in the barn had all vanished long before we woke up. At breakfast we found O'Malley, Newton and their party, vague and mysterious about their plans as prudent Alpinists often are. I naïvely divulged ours and was taken aback when O'Malley remarked, slyly:

'Oh! The North Ridge of the Grivola! I should have thought that would be rather dull!'

Dull! Words failed me, etc., and so on! Which seemed to make O'Malley well satisfied with his leg-pull.

We drove off on a *charrette* dragged by an excited mule. His driver whipped him every time we swerved near the precipice, as a stimulant. When we left the road I climbed up on his back to economize leg power for the morrow. It was my first and last mule-back ride in the Alps. The crazy creature pranced up a paved path as steep as a staircase, and the groans of his owner as he toiled behind seemed to grow ever more remote. We brushed through shoulder-high clumps of sweet-smelling wild raspberries, and Joseph and I. A. R. dashed frantically about collecting sprays laden with my favourite fruit. This is now my Imperial dream-picture of a 'hut-grind'. We washed the fruit down on arrival with bowls of foaming milk.

The cottage of the *garde-chasse* at Noumenon is a little, square, whitewashed stone building standing in the midst of a pile of huge boulders. Irrigation rivulets murmur about it; a marshy meadow stretches from its door to the edge of the screes at the foot of the northern precipices of the mountain. Standing at the door in the evening light, it is impossible to judge their height or inclination. They lean uncertainly in shadow, a cold grey band of cliff, crowned by a bulge of glacier. Above and beyond, foreshortened out of recognition, the rocky East Ridge and the pure white curve of the North Ridge slope to meet at the summit. A small glacier basin is enclosed between them. When this has been gained, the rest of the ascent is perfectly straightforward. One has only to follow that curving ivory edge, dividing the triangle of the mountain, which all who have seen the Grivola from the main range of the Valais will remember.

We were all three very tired, an aftermath of the non-existent Piantonetto Hut and the overcrowded barn at Cogne. The walk up had been excessively hot. Even the fine hospitality of the *garde-chasse*, a lonely man with much charm of manner, who had been there twenty-seven years, did not keep us up long, though the candle-lit cosiness of his abode and the soft roaring of the stove were a temptation to linger.

A big climb throws, as it were, a shadow or a silence before it. One does not think any more about the ascent. It has drawn near and that is enough, and speculations, rife before, grow quiet. Only a doubt whether after all we should not feel too weary for serious exertions in the morning haunted our minds. Even Joseph showed plainly an urgent need for rest. On him would fall the whole brunt of the toil, and we knew that it might be very heavy. That queer dishonest half-hope of broken weather which surely attacks even the most enthusiastic was not far off as we tried to seize our few hours chance of slumber!

Thick slaty clouds hung motionless, and there was no stir in the air as we set out. The *garde-chasse* came to show us, in the baffling blindness of the night, the place where a single plank spanned the irrigation canal. The lantern was a mere blur as we squelched across the marches, and it would be impossible to say, even when we were toiling up the screes, if a hope or a fear that the weather had not broken was predominant. But our spirits cleared at dawn and we rose above the cloud-sea. There it lay beneath us, innumerable waves spreading northwards and eastwards out of sight, whelming the whole Aosta Valley, and upon it floated in the still clarity of the upper air, the Combin, the consort of the Grivola, long and low, like a battleship, and to right and left all the fleet of the Alps.

The ascent of the precipices which support the glacier we made by a series of left to right traverses, on bands of shale, steeply sloping and uncomfortable, but without difficulty. It would be easy to lose much time here if a bad line were chosen. The edge of the boot bites into the soft, brittle substance; at times one is almost kicking steps in it, and though we met nothing to bring a pause, the steepness, the absence of any solid supports, the insecure litter of shifting *débris* across which one must pass, combine to give an unpleasant feeling to these grey, shadowy, ever-sunless cliffs. They are not a bad prepa- ration, perhaps, for the ridge above, when this is found without snow, since they force one early in the day to forget that such things as hand-holds exist; but otherwise an approach to the upper climb from the Col de Lauzon Cabane by way of a col in the East Ridge would be preferable.

Through and across some immense crevasses, we came into the glacier basin and into the sunlight with a fierce joy. As we halted to eat our main meal of the day—bread and bitter marmalade—and put on crampons, a hail came down from the East Ridge. A party near the summit on the ordinary route had seen us. It was queer to think that they would be home again long before we reached the place from which they yodelled. We packed up, Joseph handing over his sack so as to be freer in his movements, and embarked upon the serious part of the expedition.

The lower edge of a narrow crevasse led us easily up and out on to the crest of the miraculous ridge. Even at its foot the sense of space falling wide on all three sides is extraordinary. The narrowing, curving, smooth unbroken crest sweeps up unchanging; an abstract perfection of form unequalled in the Alps. For awhile it offers a deceitful promise of a slight easing of the angle. Its middle section, at the point where the queer scimitar-like curve is greatest, seems to vanish. Above, it evidently steepens and steepens again. In fact the look of the final section to a party well launched upon the ascent is enough to cause hesitation. And we had time enough to look and speculate. At first a thin layer of perfect snow, clinging to the very edge of the ridge, allowed a reasonable rate of progress. But soon, where the crest of the ridge took on about the size and curve of a football, it thinned out; only smooth white ice was left. Steps became essential and Joseph's labour began.

We settled down to routine. We two tied on close together, giving Joseph enough rope, as it proved, to cut twenty-five steps at each bout. Then, while he rested a moment, we would move up to stoke him with small, juicy pears, of which by good fortune, we had several kilos with us. Some of these would be handed over each time to the toiler. We would settle down again as comfortably as threatened cramps, first in one leg, then in the other, then in both, would allow. With toes well home in the admirable nicks his ice-axe had shaped,

we would begin anew our spell-bound contemplation of a performance which more and more came to have something most easily
described as beauty. We counted these stages. In all he took the
whole rope out forty times. We counted the strokes required for
each step; they varied from thirteen to twenty-nine, as the angle and
quality of the ice varied. No stroke from beginning to end was half-
hearted or experimental. Each had its definite purpose, and the force
required for that purpose. Each, as it fell, sprayed up a shower of
scintillating ice-fragments that glittered in the sun like a fountain,
that leapt into the air and rushed down to us, bounding and spinning,
to pass and vanish with a rustle and a hum. We learned to hold our
hands well up or behind our backs, for these chips cut if they struck
the skin. And in the midst of this pulse of shining spray, swayed the
figure of the artist, shadowy against the sunlight. As often as not he
would hold his axe in one hand, swinging it freely above his head,
poising himself upon toes alone or with his crooked knee thrust into
the nick already cut. As the hours wore on, his strength seemed to
increase. He explained that he had been feeling a little tired when
he began, but that had passed! He was evidently now in the Seventh
Heaven! And still the ridge curved upwards unchanging. We seemed
as far as ever from the last wall and the crowning rocks. Would I
ever get the kink out of my neck again?

About half-way up we sat together in three bucket-like steps and
ate. Life seemed to have ceased, to have passed into a state of starry
contemplation. We discussed casually the impossibility of descent,
but refrained from raising the topic of the number of hours of cutting
still required. Then we went on peacefully with our slow ascent.

The ridge was steadily growing steeper and a moment came when
the final wall looked as steep and long as the whole arête. The question of time was becoming serious. If steps had to be cut all the way,
we should barely reach the summit with night. Joseph, alone, had
no doubts. As the angle rose, a fresh energy seemed to come to him.
After six hours continuous hewing, he seemed only now to find his
full powers. We, who had watched him with wondering admiration

all day and knew well from past experience of what order his reserves are, were astonished by the transformation. His usual smile gave place to an exultant grin. His teeth showed, and a Berserker's frenzy began to glitter in his eyes. The chips leaped higher and higher, but the steps were as good, or better, than before.

All day the cloud-sea below lapped against the ranges of the Alps, but we were in glittering sunshine. Towards late afternoon the great slow-flowing waves were broken by dark chasms, the under-earth showed through; then they lifted in detached masses, turned into the periwigs of invisible giants and lounged off.

Suddenly we found a streak of snow, less than an inch thick but sound. The demon in Joseph now roused was not to be denied. He fled up it, not at a walk, but at a run, and we had perforce to follow. Some more ice, then another very steep snow-streak treated as before. The wine of victory was going to Joseph's head. We scampered up the last 200 feet of the ridge as though we now had wings to fall back upon if need be, and it was really so steep that the possibility of falling backwards seemed not remote! A few minutes among the rubbish heaps which make up the Grivola rocks and we were at the summit.

The descent was the dangerous part of the expedition. We followed the ordinary route—there is almost a little path, so many feet have trampled it—along the crest of a ridge. It is one of several which stand up in low relief upon the great tilting side of the mountain between wide, shallow gullies, floored with worn slabs of rock and broken with zigzagging scree-littered shelves. We ought to have been safe on our ridge, but we were not. Twice we were almost wiped out by falling stones.

I. A. R. luckily caught sight of them coming and sang out. There was nothing to be heard and we gazed upwards wonderingly. Suddenly, high up under the upper crags that lean forward a little over the lower ridges, tiny puffs of cloud here, there, and everywhere, flashed out one after another. They look like smoke but are really dust flung up as the missiles strike against the cliff. With that we were all three scurrying like rabbits into the nearest holes. I. A. R. had the furthest to go to find one, and his rope caught round a spike of rock and had to be disengaged gently before he could follow us into partial shelter. Just in time. The whole mountain-side seemed to have wakened into whirring life and—*Crash!*—came a rock the size of a man just where we had been standing. Clicking and spinning, ricochetting across all the ridges, leaping and leaping again as though in a mad frenzy, they danced down to splash into the glacier snows. A sympathetic eye might find them a gay spectacle. But we were wondering when the next lot would be coming! We scuttled down, getting neckache from head-turning and wishing we had that third eye on top.

It was good to get away from the mountain, as ugly on the south-east as it is beautiful on the north, to cross the glacier, drop down the scree and wander with the cows across the meadows to the Col de Lauzon Cabane, well kept by admirable people. Dusk was falling as we went in to their friendly welcome.

The ex-hunting lodge was still deserted when I awoke on a perfect high-Alpine morning, to wander across its grassy court, chat with the women who were hanging out the washing, and feed my eyes on the Eastern Ranges. Joseph strolled up looking not the least bit tired. It was near lunch-time and he had news of a chicken in the kitchen. Perhaps one North Ridge called to Another. Somehow it slipped out that he had heard two climbers at the Vittorio Emmanuele Hut saying that the North Ridge of the Dent Blanche had not yet been climbed. Joseph gives nothing away unless he wishes to, and I did my best to imitate him at this. It was enough to give I. A. R. and me something to think about all the way to Aosta. There we made up our minds, discarded a handful of lively projects on Mont Blanc and told Joseph our ideas after dinner. It was fun to see him in an instant ablaze with enthusiasm. So we went across the square to toast the Witch in what turned out to be very bad champagne.

The revived Dent Blanche plan meant getting back to the foot of the peak as quickly as possible. We lunched at the hospice on the

Grand St Bernard, where it was raining, and were introduced by Joseph to his friends among the monks. They showed us their library and the collections with which various members of the fraternity have beguiled the leisure hours of their seclusion. The beetles, the geologic specimens, the shells, the antiquarian flotsam and jetsam— brooches, coins, pins dropped by travellers of other ages, lay there in their cases troubling the passer-by with their reminder of man's need to distract himself. Afterwards, in an 18th century room, the monks entertained us at a table with a wine whose soundness compared with that of the furniture, and followed it up with a bottle of Marsala brûlé. They struck us as men of a fine unexalted humanity, worthy of the place they have so long held in Europe's imagination. Their dogs nowadays are separately housed in kennels, a great improvement for those with sensitive nostrils. We finished by looking over the chapel, as bleak in effect as the mountains outside, and contributing to the box in which travellers may place what donations they please towards the charitable toils of the monks.

As we swept up the road once again from Sion on our way to Haudères, clouds were gathering ominously all along the flanks of the Rhône Valley. The Dent Blanche, when we arrived, was out of sight in a white haze of cloud!

It remained so while for three days, hoping against hope, we kicked our heels at the Hôtel de la Poste. There, like a fairy tale, the familiar scene unrolls itself. Yellow post-cars, far too large, squeeze their way furiously through the narrow alleys between dark over-hanging chalets. With churning of engines and clarion trills from their horns they come to rest in a crowded yard that has the functions of a village square without its space. There by the post-office the pack-trains are being loaded up for Arolla and Ferpècle. Piles of merchandise, packing-cases, pails of jam and sacks of letters lie about in heaps. Among them, a sight almost too much for any mule to bear, are the ever so sophisticated wardrobe-trunks of non-Alpine visitors. The pedestrian threads his way through them with a wary eye upon the heels of the mules that are hitched to every fence and door-post. The village women swing their long homespun skirts over the deep mud and stand about in their sabots for hours gossiping in the rain. They look pretty enough, but somehow unsuitable in their little black velvet boleros, their beribboned Dolly Varden hats perched inconveniently on piles of coiled hair. But in this finery they have toiled for generations in a fashion which might easily exhaust any strong Alpinist!

We came to know the scene almost too well as we fretted the time away restlessly, unable to settle down to anything like normal beings, as is the way of Alpinists on wet days. Time seems to be slipping away so swiftly yet so dully. Our only distractions were unwanted and uninteresting meals, that are mainly pauses between courses, in the company of silent Swiss families who consider the dangers of Alpinism grossly immoral. Gradually hope failed. It was clear to the most optimistic eye that the North Arête was off for the season.

We fled from all this to Arolla. Here all the real climbers were attempting to possess their souls in patience, not look out of the window too often, and keep warm round tepid electric radiators. The snow sifted down through the trees and clotted on the panes of the glass verandah which is the Mont Collon's main sitting-room. Detective novels, stocking-mending and bridge confused the dreariness of the outlook. The first fine day we rushed off to wade over the Mont Brûlé, a neglected peak with fine snow scenery. It was nine days since we had done anything, and Joseph, desperate at the poor yield of our time together, insisted on our going over the mountain, 'Nous avons toujours traversé!' he argued as we shivered in the wind on the summit. The rock-ridge down to the Col de Mont Brûlé was cloaked with powdery snow and I pulled a loose rock hold from under it which jerked my axe-head into my mouth. For a moment I was under the horrible illusion that I had knocked out all my front teeth. However, a split lip was the worst of the damage and we were soon able to continue our descent.

On the plateau under the Évêque our way home was broken by a strange reminder from the Alpine past. Almost simultaneously we glimpsed some flapping black object on a hummock of ice ahead. Joseph, with his habitual quickness and delicacy of feeling, pulled up. 'I think something may have happened,' he said, 'will you come or shall I look first?' We went on together to discover a fold of black silk waving in the breeze from what had been the rib of a large umbrella. Beneath it the ice showed the broken bones of a skeleton. A belt, an old square-toed shoe, a heavy silk cravat, an empty leather purse and the wooden stock of a gun soon appeared. The gun seemed to show that the lost traveller had been out hunting. He had been successful, for we discovered among the relics the skull and horns of a young chamois. What was strangest of all was a toothbrush! Down in Arolla we made wide enquiries and heard that a guide had seen the skeleton before us. He had some gold coins to show from the purse, Italian pieces of about 1780. The silk cravat and umbrella, the shoe and, most of all, the toothbrush showed that he could have been no local peasant; though what any gentleman could have been doing on the Col de Collon before 1800 is a matter for curious speculation. Perhaps he was a negotiant of the days before the glaciers became awkward, when there was a trade in cattle over the pass; or perhaps he was a local noble from the Aosta Valley who had strayed for sport into the upper regions and been overwhelmed in a *tourmente* or fallen into a crevasse. With this unsolved mystery our guided days closed for the year.

Joseph was inconsolable at our small bag of peaks. Actually it was his perseverance and quickness in seizing every opportunity which had given us the climbs of our one good week in the Graians. But with more new snow falling every day our dream of the Dent Blanche North Ridge was definitely smothered for the season. Joseph, coming down from taking a party up the Roussette—about the only expedition possible, several strong parties turning back from the Petite Dent—would have to be cheered up with stories of fox-hunting and racing, and accounts of wireless wonders and agricultural conditions in England—Joseph's interest in the world being varied and insatiable. In return he would tell us about marmot-hunting—a forbidden sport most of the year—which seizes the devotees like a madness. The victim will go up and spend a whole night digging. As towards dawn he gets nearer his prey's warm winter nest the animal himself will start tunnelling away in flight. So it becomes a race. There is always the chance that the marmot may make his way into some cranny of rock where the man cannot follow. But there are graver risks! Sometimes you must crawl nose first after your beasts, who at the last may face round with formidable teeth and claws for a death battle. Many are the bold hunters who have lost large parts of their noses! Joseph's animation at this stage in the story showed clearly that he had not been entirely innocent in his youth. Over the whole thing is the threat of the *gendarme*. There is a 1500-franc fine for winter marmot-hunting, no slight penalty to an Alpine peasant. Rightly, because the marmot, disturbed in his winter sleep, is sure to die even if he escapes his pursuer.

The Arolla *gendarme* was not a figure commanding very much respect that season. He told Joseph that there was little point in bothering to look for poachers as there were only two chamois left in the district. '*Mais si c'est comme ça*,' returned Joseph, '*maintenant il n'y en a plus, parce que justement on vient d'en tuer deux ces derniers jours!*'

On how guides get clients, Joseph was also enlightening. He said it was like fishing. A certain guide has a reputation, extraordinary in view of his record, because of '*un monsieur bavard qui lui fait de la réclame!*' This was apropos of a strange and foolish woman who stopped me on the stairs to ask, 'Are you a great mountaineer?'

But the moment came for leaving. Perhaps there would be better weather in the Eastern Alps to finish up our season, guideless. Joseph came to see us '*Un bout*' along the path to Haudères, and actually took my heavy sack down the whole way for me. On the way he pointed out his chalet on a sunny knoll at La Forclaz where he lives with his mother and sisters, and told us of the winter gloom under the day-long shadow of the Veisivi at Haudères. It was only the 22nd of August but already winter seemed to have begun.

We joined friends in the Italian Lakes and walked over from Lugano to Como by Monte Generoso—absurdly troubled by failing to remember whether it is from Monte Mottarone or Monte Generoso that Meredith 'surveys the Lombard plain' on the first page of *Vittoria*. The Lombard plain, however, was there all right as we looked out on a clear night after a day of thick heat haze. Like constellations in a nether sky the lights of its towns stretched out beneath us till they mingled with real stars.

We steamed, with regret for the central beauties of Como, to hideous Colico and walked from Chiavenna up the Val Bondasca, overjoyed to be returned to mountains again. How satisfying was the sense of the past in the narrow flagged Roman track winding up through the forest; though, being built for sandals or bare feet, it was difficult to walk on in nailed boots. How peaceful the deep-set, wide, stone windows in Vicosoprano and the three-century-old Gasthaus Krone, and how exciting the sharp spires of the granite Bregaglia! But the weather, which had seemed absolutely settled below, went on tricking us in the mountains and all the cliffs had a frosty sheen. We went up the Forno Glacier from Maloja and worked over the Passo de Casnile to the Albigna Hut in thick cloud. We expected to find it open, but it was too near the Italian frontier for such freedoms. The key was down the valley many thousands of feet below. It looked as though we would have to pass the night shivering in the little open porch where the wood was stored. The prospect, which hadn't seemed bad at first, grew worse as it came nearer! We had settled down to watch the rain driving by in the dusk and were planning log mattresses and log *duvets* when we heard footsteps. An unexpected relief arrived. A party had come up in spite of the bad weather and they unlocked the door. No one had been up for four days so we counted ourselves lucky. We had, of course, satisfied ourselves long before that burglary would have needed dynamite.

Next morning we found our way over the Passo de Zocca, still
in wet, cold cloud, and woke up the *gardien* of the Allievi Cabane.
He had been alone for days in his lofty box and was making up for
a summer of broken nights by a species of hibernation. He was
kind to us and fed us well. But there was no use in stopping and
waiting for weather with the roof of the hut deep in snow. On we
went, still chasing sunshine, down to the Bagni de Masino, a high
establishment with galleries crossing rivers, cell-like bedrooms and
subterranean baths. A heavenly place in which to linger in bad
weather. We did try the Punto Milano and got up to the Badile
Hut, but each time storms drove us down. Impatient again, we fled
eastwards to Bormio and the Ortler. Soon, at this rate, we should
reach Asia.

On the Stelvio we passed a pathetic party of plutocrats. They
were walking up it in enormous sables carrying heavy jewel and
dressing-cases in their hands. The hair-pin bends of the road had
been too much for their nerves and they dared not trust their
valuables to the conveyance of a hired car. At Trafoi we got a secret
glimpse of an Austrian map behind closed doors and shuttered
windows—the Italians made the possession of adequate mountain
maps a punishable offence in those days—and gained a clear idea
of the form of the Ortler. This, in a raging gale, was our last climb
of the season. A party with Austrian guides met us near the summit.
They had seen that I was leading, and when we crossed they
exclaimed, 'Ah, we knew you couldn't possibly be Italian!' Rancour,
due to the occupation, mixed with contempt for Italian mountaineering in their voices.

At night the telegraph lines through the village were rows of
black-and-white bobbins. The swallows were resting on their southward migration. Autumn had come. It was time to follow their
example and return to our own winter haunts.

CHAPTER XIV

WANDER YEARS

(1925–27)

Mürren and the High Tatra— Mountain comparisons—The lakes of the Canadian Rockies—Bears and porcupines—A gopher farm—A future climbing-ground—Forest fires—Glacier National Park, U.S.A.—Indian trails—Mount Baker—Fuji—Kanchanjanga— Knocked out—Leeches—Deluge.

Before my next bout of mountaineering in the Alps was to come a visit to Mürren at Christmas, a dash at Easter to the High Tatra and a two-year tour of the world. At Mürren, under the more than avuncular discipline of Arnold Lunn, I spent despairing hours on the practice slopes. I would like to say 'on ski'; alas, I seemed more often to be under them! Not often enough, though, I fear, to please my mentor. Did he not call me a funk— for not falling forwards on my nose—seventeen times in the first five minutes?

In the Tatra I tried to turn these lessons to account and found the Czechs and Austrians at Stary Smokovec much softer-hearted. Their conceptions of ski-ing were not so superlative. Rysy (8212 ft), easy enough in summer, seemed a challenging summit. Twenty volunteered to come up with me and six arrived to look, over the dwindling foothills, away to the Polish plains.

But all this and my Canadian, American and Himalayan adventures would fill another book. Here are only a few random recollections that come back at times insistently on the Alpine slopes. In other ranges you are always drawing comparisons with the Alps. Everybody in fact asks you about them. And in return you carry with you in the Alps a background of other mountain scenes. Mountains differ much more than those who are not specially interested in them imagine—being in this like sheep, I suppose! They vary from occasion to occasion and from one to another very much as one's friends do. You may like one person for reasons the very opposite of those for which you like another, and so the mountaineer feels towards the objects of his pursuit. You build up out of your experiences something very like a personality for each group and peak. A distinctive sentiment grows and you begin to feel toward each one of them as you don't feel toward any other. You stress this or that aspect; you expect them to behave in certain ways. And it may be as hard as with one's friends to say just what these aspects and ways are, much less explain them. This may be an illusion, but I think that if a magic carpet were to set me down unwarned in any of these mountain regions—from the Sussex Downs to the Himalayas—even in a corner I had never seen, I should know at once from this sentiment whereabouts I was. Something in the fall of the slopes, or the grasp of the vegetation, the tint of the rocks, the tension of the summit-lines, would tell me—though what exactly it was might beat all efforts at analysis. Can a lover explain just what is different from all others in his beloved?

Characteristic features for the Canadian Rockies, however, are easily recapturable. I entered that world through the best of introductions, the Canadian Alpine Club Camp. In 1925 it was at Lake O'Hara. There, at once, by the camp-fire, amid the shadowy fragrant balsams that crowd down to the water's edge, the indelible impression was made and the tie formed which was to pull at my heart and lead me back many times in later years. The blaze toasts your face and flickers up the cliffs, as you listen to the classical competition in bear stories. Beasts and waters, and forests with limestone curtains stained saffron, indigo and ochre above them, these are the memories that come back, but most of all the jade or malachite sheen of a still lakelet in its ring of solemn hemlock.

With bears I was soon to make contact. We had reached camp late, after a long day over Opabin, Wenchemna and Wastash passes. Paradise Valley, its meadows strewn with Indian paint-brush as with confetti, had lived up to its name and now we sat by the creek hungrily eating supper. Afterwards, by the camp-fire, yarns more fantastic than any fisherman's were told. Had the dinosaur appeared or the oranges and tropic vegetation, said just then to have been discovered in the frozen North, we should have accepted the situation with composure.

It was in such a mood that we turned in and were soon lying on half our blankets with the other half for covering. Above, the moon was so bright that the canvas of the tent shone with an unearthly glow. Inside, each of us prepared for sleep, conscious of the various small wanderers of the night who were now preparing boldly to approach us. Almost at the gate of sleep one felt the place filling with life and activity, busy little feet scampering, and once some creature, as it scurried along, brushed my hair.

All seemed very quiet at the moment I lost consciousness. I do not know how long afterwards it was that the bear visited us. He was a black bear, wandering in the starlight among the larch trees, smelling food. Gaining boldness he ambled closer, while we five girls slept peacefully on. But presently the sound of his heavy moving body, as he crushed through the bushes, woke us one by one.

We sat up, startled.

'What's that?' came a whisper.

We listened. The sounds had ceased.

'Nothing,' replied a would-be reassuring voice.

Just at that minute we all saw it together! A great dark silhouette on the moonlit canvas. It *certainly* was a bear, and a large one too.

For a moment we were paralysed. With admirable presence of mind, the most courageous member of the party picked up a boot. Taking careful aim, she hurled it with force at the head of the bear.

It found its mark. The animal, more surprised and alarmed than even we were, ran quickly away into the trees. For a long time there was silence. Then, with one voice, we all started talking. Finally, after some amused but anxious consultations, we decided to take it in turn to sit up with a lighted candle and an ice-axe to keep the marauder at bay. We others lay down listening to the myriad sounds of the silvery mountain night.

Another time I was returning alone down an empty valley in the Yoho after dusk when, there on the trail ahead, through the dimness, I caught a glimpse of a shadowy moving body. It looked very bulky. I pulled up short with my heart pounding. I had almost stepped on it! Luckily not, for as I stood straining my eyes and ears for its movement I heard a dry clicking. It was no more than an enormous porcupine. I had to laugh aloud, for it had looked as large as a bear. Porcupines are indeed a horrid nuisance. They creep into the tent at night and will eat your boots, unless you are wise enough to hang them, with anything else that is leathery, up on the tent-pole out of reach. I once had my camera-case half eaten under my pillow while I slept! But you can detect their presence easily by an unsavoury smell. There is an unwritten law that these pests are not to be killed; for they are among the few animals that a prospector or trapper can kill without a weapon if he runs out of food in the wilds.

More appealing are the chipmunks, neatly striped little squirrel-like creatures who grow so tame they will climb on your knee to be fed, stuffing their cheek-pouches almost to bursting-point before they scamper off to hide the treasure. You make nearer acquaintance, too, with whistlers (marmots), that are only seen and heard at a distance in the Alps. They will lie snarling at you only just out of reach in a rock-cleft. Much more shy are the coneys; but on sunny, rain-sheltered shelves in autumn you can find their strewings of cut hay that they have spread out to dry before carrying it down for their winter nest. Cosy, provident little beings!

Surprised by so much, I was an easy prey to jokes.

'Do you know a gopher?' asked somebody, taking my education in hand.

'There are millions about,' declared someone else.

'What are they like?' I asked innocently.

'Oh, similar to grizzly bear, only much bigger and fiercer!' an honest-faced person explained to me, dismayed. The gopher is a timid little beast, smaller than a rabbit and as ruinous to the land.

Remembering this, it is easier for me to credit that touching story of the proud English father who read to Lord Strathcona a letter from his ne'er-do-well 'remittance man' son in Canada containing this paragraph: 'I am getting on much better, but I need more capital. I have more than 600 head (gophers) on my ranch just now—all thriving.'

But the climber will ask, 'What about the peaks?' Useless to tell him that I went up everything about Lake O'Hara. Even the most single-souled rock climber will not want a list of the pitches on Odaray, Schaffer or Wiwaxy, or to hear that great Hungabee is rather like the Matterhorn, superb but decaying fast. Later I climbed nearly all the mountains that are accessible without pack-trains from the Canadian Pacific Railway centres; some, like Victoria—where a really Alpine hut confirms the impression—which might, but for the distant views, be among the snow ridges of the Oberland; others like Marpole, with its piles of unmortared limestone masonry, bringing in problems of loose rocks on a scale not often met with in the frequented Alps.

In this respect the Selkirks—another day in the train onward to the Pacific—are clear from blame. Here, with the heavier rainfall, the Douglas fir begins and the majesty of the forest is doubled. The summits that thrust up—no longer as gaudy limestone walls, but with the slenderer grace of steel-grey granite—are more thickly clad with snows. Mount Sir Donald, I felt, had as a climb little to lose by comparison with even the Rothorn, and in the Bugaboo chain to the south there were aiguilles that for daring and difficulty matched the Requin or the Géant. I was to climb some of these in

1933. There, in an almost empty unmapped country, is the future climbing-ground of the American continent. Some day, I suppose, there will be trails through it and huts to climb from, but now you have to go in with a pack train and an outfit—or hew your way in through deadfalls with 40 lbs on your back, if you have the summer to spare for exploration.

Over the Rockies and the Selkirks as the summer draws on hangs the smoke of the forest fires. After heavy rain the sky-line may be clear for a few days. Then the full scale of these ranges comes home to you, and you linger, till the last minute you dare, on your summit to absorb it. Dark and shadowy to the north, glittering with ice to the south, those hundreds of successive, serrated ridges reach out, drawing the imagination through the weeks of travel which would do no more than take you through one of their thousand recesses. But the smoke comes back as the fires take heart again. First as a yellowish opalescent local smear, than as brown mirk in the sky and a blue haze filling the forested valleys, it thickens until even the neighbour mountain becomes a mere ghost—an underprinted image of itself. And ever and again you pass through burnt-out areas; in endless files, black or silvery skeletons of trees lean crazily about the slopes; underfoot the ash kicks up in choking dust between the magenta spikes of the fire-weed, first of living things to return into the desolation.

After a winter further west, in the mining country of Slokan Lake, I went south for 1926 to the American Rockies of Glacier National Park. Here, with rather less snow on them, were the limestone ramparts again. The Great Northern Railway was hoping to open up more of it with trails, and some of my best days were experiments to test the attractions of ways over the Divide, from creek to creek, unvisited since the vanished days of the trappers. By old Indian trails, if we could find them; if not, by game trails, or up the river edges we would force our way, coming out at last above the forest to the relief of open park-land where you can see the peaks again. Rents in the turf would show where the bears had been rooting. But there

ahead was the rim of cliffs over which we had to climb—usually in
a hurry about sunset—to find our way down the other slope to the
timber line and a camp-fire bivouac. Climbing technique took a new
place and value then, became a means of more general travel.
Limestone is not easy ground to triumph over at sight! I recall times
when we failed to hit a practicable route and lay all night, as near
the blaze as we could, wondering what luck would be ours on the
morrow. Such crossings—over from Avalanche Basin or through the
Hidden Lake country, regions whose only earlier visitors were
legendary—had a glamour which not even ascents of Going-to-
the-Sun or Nothing-but-a-Dog Mountains, or three score others with
names as tempting, could equal.

These names are Indian, and the feel of the past in the American
Rockies is particularly strong. The stronger perhaps because the
Indians are so nearly no more. The bones of the buffaloes they slew
have been shipped off by rail as manure! The cliffs over which they
drove them in cloud-like, crashing herds are still shown, but these
old hunting trails are almost lost—grown over and choked by
spillikin heaps of windfall timber. To have puzzled them out a little
feels like a link with the Blackfeet. One evening, after a hard bout
of 'bush-wacking' with never a trail to help, a sentimental Scot
struck a cow-boy attitude by my tent's mouth to exclaim dramatically, 'Ah luve every trree in the wulderrness!' I had spent most of
the day clambering over fallen tree-trunks ten feet deep and could
not share his rapture. I felt vengeful, and when I heard that the
remnant of the Blackfeet, in making him into a Chief, had nearly
cooked him permanently in their sweat-bath, they went up again
in my estimation.

The Rockies, and even the Selkirks, are well known. Less familiar,
as yet, is the Coast Range. Two ascents there stand out for me:
Mount Baker by the North-east face, which felt like Mont Blanc
in the scale of its glacier scenery; and Shuksan, by a new route
which let us in for two foodless nights out high up on the way
home. Why this happened is another story. The enormous snowfall

in the Coast Range makes the glaciers curiously simple. There are plenty of crevasses but they are clean-cut and endearingly guileless. So free from Alpine treacheries that Marathon races up and down Mount Baker's easier side have been—'staged' is, I think, the word— with safety. The view from Mount Baker's summit reminded me deeply of the Hebrides. We were sheltering by the snow-muffled little crater, warming our feet, burning our boots and sniffing sulphur fumes, when a thin cloud which had been hanging about lifted to show us Puget Sound under the sinking sun. There, far before us, swam, high in the clear golden heavens, the incredible argosy of the islands. Innumerable they seemed, and illimitably remote, yet each as clear and distinct as a diamond's edge, the channels between them luminous like threads of molten gold. From these slopes at sunset the north-west coast is indeed a fabulous vision, more delectable than any dream of the Hesperides. In the midst, seventy miles away, is Vancouver. A day or two later, walking there amid the gay flower-beds that bloom unexpectedly twenty storeys up on the roof of the Vancouver Hotel, I became aware of a dim presence hanging, insubstantially, in the sky. Mount Baker was seemingly saying farewell.

—

Volcano signals to volcano round the rim of the Pacific. I was up early, as we steamed in towards Yokohama, hoping for such another view of Fuji Yama, and there it was—an immense white wisp, cloud-like but with a form no cloud possesses. It was winter and I had to wait some years before trying, once in rain, once in sunshine, what Fuji's 12,000 feet straight up from the sea-level are like. And of the Western Hills near Peking—those final waves of the Himalayan, central Asian system, over which that endless snake, the Great Wall, meanders—I had only a tantalizing taste this visit. I was to wander in them, in the Japanese Alps and in the Diamond Mountains of Korea to my heart's content later. The summer of

1927 was to bring the Himalayas. My Doctor sister Vi, then a radiologist in Delhi, along with I. A. R. and I, with a few porters, had a wander vacation among them.

It may or may not be true, as Confucius has it, that 'He who has gazed on the ocean finds lesser waters inconsiderable'. The parallel is not in the least true of mountains, but the first sight of Kanchanjanga does for a while make one wonder what will happen to one's conception of heights.

There are two ways towards the mountain from Darjeeling. One, a narrow, 12,000-ft ridge you follow for days together, was to bring us back; the other, which switchbacks up and down through the 2000 to 10,000 ft levels, took us in. On one of our breathless upward crawls in the heat that heralds the monsoon, the sun got me. Its late level rays must have done their work under the brim of my topee. At any rate the world for me went black and swam sickly, the path tilted up and then sank nowhere, and my two companions had hastily to improvise some sort of shade and find water. A sympathetic monk appeared from somewhere. Water came from a not distant pigsty, and with rest the world seemed to become more normal again. But the evil remained and it was pineapple and ginger only for me—nothing else would stay down—until I was back in civilization some three weeks later.

On the next march I learnt about leeches. More than enough! The drenched undergrowth was alive with them. Local opinion seemed to think they were then at their worst. I hope so. I have never seen anything more loathsome. On the extremities of the bushes fringing the path, queer little black twigs stood out at odd angles; as you passed they swayed hungrily towards you. If you stood still for a moment and watched, the leaf-drift for yards round could be seen stirring with a stealthy movement. A twig would twitch for no reason or a decayed skeleton leaf quiver. To a closer eye minute thread-like forms appeared, writhing like microscopic, detached elephant-trunks towards you. Looping themselves, head to tail, like the familiar caterpillars of our English gardens, they approached from every direction. To feel oneself the centre of so much striving was disquieting. The crannies of our boots soon came to harbour them by scores, the interstices between the laces tempting them to accumulate in intricate congeries difficult to dislodge. Less misguided specimens were constantly climbing up over boot-tops and puttees, and our axes (which, alas! never got their proper use on this expedition) proved invaluable as scrapers. The leech tenacity was amazing. The official method of destruction is to press small bags of salt against them. The salt steals their moisture and the leech at once becomes helpless. Our porters kept cigarettes going continuously for a similar purpose. The bite when they do find flesh is imperceptible. As they gorge themselves they expand and a greenish glutinous object is what you discover. It is astonishing how these small creatures, when abundant, absorb one's attention.

Out above the leech zone, giant rhododendrons flamed thirty feet high in hues from primrose to crimson. We camped not far from a forest of them. At dusk immense heavily upholstered yaks browsed about the tent and stumbled among the boulders. The dark outline of the near hillside—as it might be a shoulder above Bel Alp—cut sharply into the bleak precipices of Kanchanjanga's satellites. A chill breeze set the frail tent billowing and flapping, and to the south over Bengal formidable cloud masses leapt with lightning.

The goal of our dreams had been a spur of Kanchanjanga called Pandim. But the sun had knocked that plan on the head too! And though fate gave us clear mornings and evenings, the monsoon was breaking and the midday and midnight rain-storms were spreading out. Before they quite joined up, we had a clear ten minutes on the Guicha La (16,300 ft), when the cloud-veil thinned away and the whole height of the south face of Kanchanjanga was shown. Somewhere Blake makes a list of things which are 'portions of eternity, too great for the eye of man'. Another of them was before us. As the glance sweeps unrealizingly across these icy spaces, the imagination lags hopelessly behind. But the misty fingers from the south crept up, linked hands across miles of empty air, and the mountain was hidden again. What I saw was enough to give me the creeps now, whenever I think of the Bavarian party's doings on those ridges.[9]

Then the deluge began. It turned our retreat into something of a rout. One march ended in a yak-herd's bamboo shelter. The floor was aslush with yak-dung, but it was snowing by now and all our tents were out of action, through the hurricane of the night before. Shaggy monsters barged in from time to time through the night. A gigantic, barbaric woman who seemed to rule the place came out of a recess at dawn to clean up after them—clawing up fistfuls of muck in her many-ringed fingers and throwing it out through the doorway. She jangled with turquoise and silver.

At the first dak-bungalow, Phalut, I took to my bed for weeks. One evening just before I left, the weather lifted for an hour and there, above the tangled country we had come through, was Kanchanjanga again and his retainers; to the south was Darjeeling and the plains, and to the north-west, over a wall of cloud, Everest and the gaunter bulk of Makalu. For hundreds of miles, the frontier giants were guarding the Sacred Land of Tibet.

---

9   It is with a glow of awe and wonder that I think of the triumph—in May 1955—of Charles Evans' expedition: among the happiest and most successful ventures in the history of mountaineering.

CHAPTER XV

ALPINE RETURN

(*1927*)

The restoring scene—Perroc-Za Ridge and the North-east Mont Collon—Lötschental rain-watching—Snow-storm on the Petersgrat—Oeschinen-See again and forty concertinas.

Venice is a good port to land in from the East. Oh, the cool of the Mediterranean after the Red Sea! And from Venice the Alps seem very near. Though it was already September, we telegraphed to Joseph at Arolla and met him in the old familiar ramshackle hotel at Haudères. It was like a homecoming to see Arolla and Joseph again. The green of the meadows was startling after the parched East. How often one had imagined this scene! How soothing the familiarity of every unchanged corner of the path as we strolled up in the evening with Joseph to Arolla. The years between collapsed. It might have been a lifetime ago or yesterday that I was there. The same shoulders of the hills loomed against a cloudy sky. The same mules jangled past us over the white waste of the river-bed flats, and when we reached Arolla there too everything was unchanged. Joseph himself was as unchanged as anything else. The same eagerness to hear all about the world. The same longing to travel himself—later, in 1932, to be realized in his triumphant ascents, with the *Mission Scientifique Belge*, of the Ruwenzori peaks, the Mountains of the Moon, from the Belgian Congo side. The same shrewd natural comments and quick understanding of essentials. The same queer grin under his upturned nose.

The same delight in the prospect of any expedition out of the ordinary. Again it was clear that Joseph would have been the keenest of amateurs if his lot had not fallen in La Forclaz.

The sense of continuity was extraordinarily restful. Most Alpine travellers find themselves drawn to the mountains by a twofold pull—the impulse to go over new country and to revisit familiar scenes. And, after all the breaking of links which a long spell of travel imposes, the new scenes and new contacts and the strain of incessant novelty, to come back as it were to the best of one's past and fit into it again gives one a feeling of perpetuity. Every traveller must have felt how the eyes seem fresher, the senses keener, the whole personality more ready to receive the impact of all impressions. One is 'all there', as the saying is, since a large part of oneself is past experiences, and the aptitudes in perceiving that have formed. We were completely happy.

We wondered if we would be able to do anything after the prostration of India in hot weather. Joseph had only a few odd days free for us, being engaged for the Bietschhorn the following week. Actually we managed two climbs: the traverse of the Perroc to the Bertol Hut and the Northeast Ridge of the Collon. We tried to get slightly into training by scrambling over the Roussette. The Perroc Ridge proved a long business. We had been defeated on it in 1924, guideless and starting from the Col de Zarmine, and the pleasure of the expedition was not a little increased by a sense of revenge. But the way up to the Perroc is very long and toilsome, all straight uphill over moraine with only a sketch of a path. What an easement a hut up here for the less visited ridges of the Pointe de Genevois, Dent de Zallion and the face of the Za, two and a half hours above Arolla, would be! And why not a hut on the Plan de Bertol, surrounded as it is with rarely visited rock-climbs that are among the most attractive in the Alps, the Douves Blanches Arête, the opposite wall of the Bertol Glacier, the Bouquetins traverse and the Evêque? Lazy people's desiderata, these, perhaps, inspired by the luxuries of the Austrian Tyrol. Even those who would be the first to use and enjoy such huts may exclaim at me for 'Spoiling the Alps'!

The last rocks of the Perroc are good climbing—worth a long grind, or so one thinks when the grind is over; and the ridge along to the Pointe des Genevois besides being interesting going gives a memorable view across to the Matterhorn and the Dent Blanche. I don't doubt that our eyes strayed often to the North Ridge of the last, I know mine did, but there was a ban on talk about it—after we had once grinned sardonically at one another over the time we had wasted on it in Haudères in 1924. Joseph too seemed to have resigned himself to leaving it alone. But how beautiful the mountain looked, the Witch of the Eastern Heavens, and what a shame it would be if her most magnificent side should remain untouched!

We were tired before we came to the Za. The ridge took on that famous endlessness that afflicts the first week in the Alps. When at last we turned off to follow the glacier track to the Bertol, we were clear that we should need a thorough rest-day. We took it, mostly in our bunks, in the hut and so were ready to tackle the very little visited north-east flank of the Mont Collon next day. From Arolla this route looks like a straightforward ridge-climb of a tempting angle, with perhaps a short crisis at its summit where the bulge of the mountain's cap of ice may, in some years, prevent further progress. Seen from the Bertol the ridge disappears and is replaced by a series of broken buttresses not well connected with one another and divided by uninviting stone-swept gullies.

We knew it would be a long day and started early, making a short cut by passing through between the Pointes Sud de Bertol. We began well away to the south and found a series of connections—impossible to describe—from one steep cluster of cliffs to another—working over until, quite near to the summit, we rounded a flange of rock and found ourselves looking down the complicated North face of the Collon. Below, the Hôtel Mont Collon appeared like a grey box, shrivelled like something seen through the wrong end of a telescope. Nowhere did we find ourselves in any of the gullies or in danger from stone-fall—a witness to Joseph's general-ship; but the climbing in several places was hard and sensational, with sometimes a section of rocks not above suspicion for their soundness. On the whole the expedition is a serious one, though, if it were more climbed, it would doubtless become much easier. The final ice-cap, that year, gave no trouble; we just stepped up off the last sharp spikes of rocks on to the summit plateau of the Collon. For how long had it intrigued us—that secluded little snow-plain so high and so hidden! It fascinates every visitor to Arolla, who gazes up at it and wonders which of its three snowy mounds is the highest. Actually the summit is at the south.

On the way down we discovered that we were weary! After all, the Tropics had left a mark on our corpuscles. The late afternoon sun was scorching the rocks from under a pall of heavy thunder-cloud. The rocks are easy but we found them hard; they lead down, with several chimneys of the moderate English rock-climbing type, to the glacier basin. The way home makes a longish curve round the crevasse systems and the glacier ripples seemed to pass by very slowly. Evening was drawing in as we came up out of the wet snows to the shoulder where Jenkins' paint-box, now dry and tawny and fortunately empty, was waiting for us. We three seemed nearly to fill the tiny place. But we were snug there that night after our bowls of Maggi and tea, though the wind howled and snow fell and our hopes vanished either of traversing the Sengla—a peak across the Otemma Glacier that had haunted us for years—or of going over the Pigne and Mont Blanc de Seilon. Next morning latish during an *éclaircissement*, we had to have a photograph. But the little 'self-timer' was not to be found. However, Joseph produced a reel of cotton from somewhere and with all the enthusiasm of a school-boy for minor engineering, mounted the camera on a cairn and arranged ice-axes round which the thread ran over half the mountain, so that we could stand and sit together and take groups of ourselves. When they were developed we came out like an exhibit at Mme Tussaud's!

Next day was cloudless but Joseph was pledged to take the Père Capucin—that well-known Arolla figure—up the Douves Blanches Arête. We envied them as we went off on our own to traverse the Petite Dent de Veisivi. Then the weather broke yet again. Joseph's date for the Bietschhorn approached and it seemed best, as we had often planned to try the Bietschhorn ourselves, to go over there too. Fate was, however, against us. The Lötschental, when we reached it, was filled with driving rain. We sat in the hotel at Ried listening to it beating on the roof and feeling that there were familiar enough aspects of the Alps which were not so wildly attractive after all. Fortunately these fade in memory. And the coy Bietschhorn was to yield to us on our way back to the East in 1929.

In time the rain ceased and Joseph's Bietschhorn party had gone, disappointed, home. We resolved to disregard the weather and to wring one more climb, if we could, out of the end of the season. I. A. R. had had plans for the South-west Arête of the Gspaltenhorn or a *traversée intégrale* of the Blümlisalp peaks. Such things were palpably 'off', but we might perhaps be able to get up the Wilde Frau. So one doubtful morning we started for the Mutthorn Hut. The morning did not belie its promise. By the time we were launched on the snowy back of the Petersgrat, snow was falling in blinding clusters of flakes as though the contents of millions of celestial *duvets* were being shaken over us. The actuality was not as warm as the comparison, however. I recalled the summery day when I last went over the route and thought again how in the Alps circumstances alter everything, how even the easiest pass may become a place of terror. The Mutthorn Hut is curiously hidden as you come down to it from the Petersgrat. In such weather, with all tracks buried and nothing to be seen further ahead than your fingers, with a gale blowing you at times off your balance and coating your eyelashes and the edge of your *passe-montagne* with ice crystals, anyone might fail to find it. Joseph, however, proved to be unchanged in his capacity for miracles. As we stamped the snow off our legs and beat one another at the hut door, we felt it our fate to be snowbound there, remembering how it had gone with us four years before.

We were luckier this time. After snowing all night the morning cleared up early. We left, with the first sunshine, for the Blümlisalp Hut. But the elements were only playing with us. That evening the wind got up. Everything fluid in the hut froze solid. When we looked out in the morning the world was dim with a haze of flying ice-particles. Even the nearest peak looked filmy, remote and opalescent. The moment you put your nose out of shelter you were impelled to feel if it were still there. What clothes we had with us seemed hopelessly inadequate. Winter cold had come and the gale raving in the faint sunshine across the pass was as merciless and incessant as a Gobi draught. We did not hesitate long about giving up our peak and going down. We really had no choice. But it was with a sigh of regret that we hoisted our sacks and ran for the valley.

Down in the meadows, all was calm and sunny. 'Cheer up, Joseph! We shall have better luck next year,' we said prophetically, to ease the parting, as we walked along by the side of the Öschinen-See; but our hearts were heavy when we went out on the promontory to wave to him jogging down the path to Kandersteg and out of our sight. We spent the night at the lake wondering again at its unearthly glamour. How full the world was of unbelievably beautiful places! How reassuring to be back home again!

Inside the inn was a signed photograph of Sir Austen Chamberlain commemorating some interlude in the labours of the League of Nations. We felt indeed returned to Europe. By evening a Swiss caravan 180-strong arrived. Forty concertinas in full blast helped us away from our Elysium.

CHAPTER XVI

THE GREAT YEAR

(*1928*)

The Witch again—A glacier lets me down—Ah demain soir on chantera—Dawn on the Col de la Dent Blanche—The great slabs—Explorations at the climax—A springboard axe—Je chouques—Sunlight and triumph—An unextinguished candle—Heat-defence—An Alpine epic—The traverse of the Weisshorn—A close shave—An appalling glacier trap—Sudlenspitze-Nadelhorn—A blasting welcome—Simplon-St Bernard—Mont Dolent and a traitress—A hospitable frontier post—The Trélatête and heat—A ramoneur's bed—Facing the Sun—The Grandes Jorasses—A solitary climber—Head over heels down the cliff—A miraculous escape—The Tarentaise—Mushrooms and mass-suggestion—The Aiguille du Goûter and a rescue—Fatality.

A day came when we stood with the luggage in the car ready to drive down to Victoria, with tickets to Grenoble actually in our pockets. A telegraph-boy arrived with one minute to spare and a message from Joseph suggesting that as the season was so extraordinarily dry we might like to think again about the Dent Blanche! It took us until Victoria to write out our answer, and we were still feeling irrational when we found ourselves strolling with Joseph in the shadow of the Veisivi.

'All things considered,' as Théophile Ribot remarked, 'there is room to wonder whether there is not, in every *grande passion*, as much misery as joy.' There had been a marked absence of any mention of the Dent Blanche in our plans for some years. In fact we had officially quite given up the idea. In 1925, while I was in Canada, I. A. R. had spent more than half his climbing holiday at Haudères scowling dolefully with Joseph into the clouds which hung low about the Bricolla Alp. They built a stone house on the Col de la Dent Blanche (11,628 ft) in a snow-storm, probably just to show the mountain they were in earnest. When completed it seemed even chillier inside than out. The wind whistled so dismally through the chinks that long before it was finished each had privately renounced any intention of sleeping in it under any circumstances. Down came the sleeping-bags, spare ropes, stove, saucepan and all the other impedimenta again, and so ended that season.

Earlier that year a very strong Swiss party had camped on the Col for two days and declared the ascent hopeless. Later, in 1926, M. Kropf and the Zinal guides, Marcel Savioz and Jean Genoud, had made a descent, mainly by roping down, and had been benighted, in a far from enviable position, in the midst of the difficulties. We all seemed now convinced that enough had been sacrificed to folly. Anyhow, rather painstakingly, no one had mentioned it even obliquely when we came back from our world tour. Yet here we were plodding up through the sweet-smelling meadows, swaying with harebells and marguerites, towards it again!

To get into reasonable training from a distinctly minus condition within a week was our first task. This haste seemed necessary both because the long spell of extraordinarily fine, dry weather might break any day and because a rival party starting from the Mountet might, we feared, be on the mountain before long. There were other parties as to whose intentions we were more than a little suspicious and we were anxious to have at least the first try. So with an impatient eye on our distressingly unfit condition we toiled over the Pointe de Bricolla to the Moiry Hut and bustled over the little pinnacles of the Aiguille de l'Allée. Below the Moiry Hut the alp was carpeted with purple violas and sharp blue gentians so that it was hard to walk for fear of crushing them.

Next morning gave me an entirely new view of crevasses—an inside view, in fact. My first such exploration and, I hope, my last. At that time, with all respect for glacier traps, I would have agreed with Mr Finch, who says, in *The Making of a Mountaineer*, that 'in summer, except perhaps immediately after heavy falls of fresh snow, it should be possible for a party to avoid this danger altogether'—the danger, namely, of falling into a crevasse. On this occasion there had been no new snow. We were going tranquilly up a gentle, perfectly innocent-seeming slope when it happened. Our feet were sinking about an inch into good snow and I was treading in the impressions of Joseph's feet and enjoying the sparkle of the sunshine in the ice crystals of the surface. There is no way of describing the suddenness with which—as though some hidden hangman had pulled his lever—I dropped into darkness. I felt as though I were falling for hundreds of feet. Then the jerk came. A smothering cascade of ice and snow fragments was pouring over me and I was dangling helplessly in a noose on a rope that made me feel like a bar of cheese that is being divided. Luckily the walls of my crevasse, where I hung, bulged towards one another hour-glass fashion. With violent wriggles I was just able to touch one wall with my toes while working my shoulder against the other. Below me widened out a horrible blue-black gulf as vast as the inside of St Paul's, into whose invisible depths the fragments of the bridge which had collapsed with me vanished with a thudding uproar. Above me, the edges of the broken roof caught the sunshine. My rope—forward to Joseph, backwards to I. A. R.—had cut deeply through the eaves on each side.

Getting me out struck me as a long job, though they said it was not. We shall never agree on the time it took. Pity the poor judge who has such witnesses to listen to. Joseph had to make a detour round the crevasse while I. A. R. held me. Then with a joint effort they hauled me up. I was glad to see them and the daylight again. We looked hard but could see no sign of the crevasse except the gaping mouth of my pit. I walked for the rest of the day as though on a soap film.

From the summit of the Grand Cornier our Dent Blanche ridge looked at its best—gigantic, formidable and tantalizing in its still-concealed mysteries. What would happen at the overhang, we kept on wondering? It was quite evident where the main problem would be. We went down the Grand Cornier's East Ridge, a baking descent, and crossed to the Col de la Dent Blanche. The opposing faces of the Grand Cornier and the Dent Blanche—stripped of their snows, dry as they are in few years—were chanting and roaring to one another with falling *débris*. As we trudged wearily up the snows towards the Col a peculiar formation of slabs on the Cornier discharged a heavy stonefall by ricochet an incredibly long way across the glacier. The newly bared rock-faces seemed nearly every-where ready to slip away and bombard the slopes below. We resolved again to give up the climb if we could not keep strictly to the ridge.

We took two days' complete rest at Bricolla. Antoine, Joseph's brother, joined us, for we had decided to climb on two ropes for speed, linking up for the glacier and the difficult sections. Two on a rope go faster than three or four, as anyone who thinks of a loop caterpillar will understand. Antoine had missed his military service through a temporary physical defect and so cannot ever have his guide's certificate. But he is as sound a man on a mountain as could be wished, with an enchanting sense of humour and a serene belief in his brother's genius. His tranquil cheerfulness through the more exciting passages of the climb was an immense support to the party. Our first evening at Bricolla was enlivened by the appearance of a caravan which for no reason at all we took for our rivals. The second day needed some enlivenment. Our nerves were taut as before the start of a great race or an examination. We lay in bed as long as we could, we went out and lay on the grass, we lay in the shade, in the sun. But wherever we were, a peculiar restlessness seemed to assail us. Theoretically we were sleeping, or at least resting. Actually we were fretting ourselves sick. We could almost catch one another's glances sweeping round magnetically to that overhanging corner of the ridge. Antoine voiced the trouble perfectly as he glanced smilingly round our three serious faces: '*Ah, demain soir on chantera!*' We burst into laughter at being so easily caught.

We got away at one o'clock by lantern-light on July 20th, with every reason to expect a perfect day. Joseph, usually gently sociable in the early hours, this morning seemed aloof and austere. We had seen something like it before when setting out for unusual expeditions. The aloofness marks the concentration of his powers; he gains a mental poise as remarkable as his physical balance. Unlike many brilliant performers, he is never impulsive when at grips with the difficulties. His excitement takes the form of a severe self-control.

Dawn found us on the Col de la Dent Blanche, a rocky rib between two systems of glaciers. It was a freezingly cold, clear morning, and the Zermatt giants—Weisshorn, Rothorn, Gabelhorn—stood up in stark majesty between us and the growing light. We had breakfast (5.45 to 6.15 A.M.) and then split into two ropes. A two-hour scramble over miscellaneous rocks went quickly. Looking back now it seems to have passed like two minutes. Then came the only passage of poor rock on the climb, loose, fissile stuff which breaks away if handled unwarily. It was soon passed and we came to the great slabs.

These slabs trend at a very high angle over to the west, solid bare rocks steeper than a house-roof, sprinkled with grit and spattered even in a dry season with a thin, transparent, treacherous film of *verglas*. Anchorage is lacking, and their lower edge, which we skirted, overhangs. As we crept along it, the pebbles we swept aside to get clearer footing for our rubber shoes would hop a few feet and then vanish. Up from the depths would come a faint wail as they sang through thousands of feet of air. Larger pieces screamed savagely. The void below was hidden, but these eerie sounds reminded us of it. We turned upwards near the western limit of this eave and found two awkward and holdless chimneys to take us to a broken ledge which winds along immediately beneath the fearsome impending crags of the North Ridge.

There the flank of the upper half of the ridge literally overhangs

the slabs. It is cut by a number of clefts which from below may
have tempted the imaginations of many climbers. At closer quarters,
their gigantic scale and fierce angle are more apparent. A detached
pinnacle clinging to the edge of the slabs at this point was tipped
with sunlight. It forms the notch which shows up so well both
from the Bertol and the Mountet. All the rest of this face of the
mountain was still in deep, cold shadow. We scrambled out to the
pinnacle to survey the terrain, for now our projects and hopes were
to be put to the test. And desperate their chances seemed.

Anything less encouraging than the arête as seen from this point
would be hard to imagine. To begin with, the actual blade of the
narrow ridge above overhangs perceptibly at several points. To the
left a deep crack in its side seems to offer better chances of ascent,
only to end in a much worse overhang some 100 feet higher. Above
this, there flapped in the cold wind evidence of the Swiss party's
descent, a frayed loop of the rope they had left behind them, flung
back by the gales and hitched up among the crags. On the right is
the smooth, exceedingly steep wall of the vast couloir furrowing
the cliff down to the Glacier de la Dent Blanche. At one time we
had talked of crossing this couloir and returning, at a higher level,
to the ridge. But one glance into its bruised and stone-swept depths
was now enough. There was, however, something like a remotely
possible crack in its smooth wall, a crack which passed at its critical
point out of sight into the unknown.

In the searching breeze we clung to the bitterly cold rocks of
the pinnacle, and gazed at these crags black against the now
sun-filled blaze of the sky. We were just inside their shadow, a golden
touch or two showed where the angle of the ridge above eased off.
Our difficulties would be over when we reached that warm and
welcoming glow 150 feet above us, but for the moment they seemed
overwhelming. Whatever estimate subsequent parties may make of
this passage, there is no doubt that as a daunting spectacle it will
always hold high rank.

Joseph now began a series of explorations which seemed to us to touch the limiting mark of cragsmanship. He started by exploring the wall of the great couloir round the corner to the right—an anxious moment for us, since he was soon out of sight and we could easily tell by the inch by inch movement of the rope that the ground was exceedingly severe. We could do little to safeguard him as he slowly gained height. But Antoine's calm reflective confidence in his brother's skill, his quiet assumption that everything was normal, was a great reinforcement to our trust in Joseph's judgment. In such situations the amateur has a responsibility which can easily become agonizing. It was with a mixture of disappointment and relief that we began to take the rope in again, 90 feet of it, and soon we were welcoming Joseph among us once more. He had been within a few feet of success but those few feet had proved insuperable.

After a pause for chilled hands to regain their strength, the second possibility was reconnoitred. This was the crack on the left, which proved both extremely hard to get into and unluckily impossible to get out of at the top. With the greatest difficulty Joseph contrived to force nearly 100 feet of the crack. Then the problem of escaping from the overhangs which close this route came to a head. At one moment he seemed almost to be emulating a lizard on a ceiling. But human beings lack the necessary organs apparently, and we were forced to watch a series of descending movements extraordinarily reassuring in their witness to his climbing reserves. When he rejoined us on our belvedere, he told us that he had been within a few feet only of a series of holds that would have taken him up.

There remained the very nose of the ridge itself. It seemed a hopeless chance. A few sinuous, very shallow grooves wound up among its protuberant bosses, but they were mercilessly smooth and no square-cut hold showed as far as the eye could reach. There could be no rest or anchorage for the leader for at least 100 feet. And, to begin with, the base of the nose was undercut. Its very beginning seemed inaccessible. Once on the tip the leader would be on the steepest possible rock with a clear 3000-odd feet of space under the palms of his feet. Frankly it was almost with dismay that we saw Joseph, after a thoughtful survey, turn to it.

The first step was to mount the initial overhang. There happened to be a cleft in the rock under the eave into which an axe-shaft could be fixed, leaving the rest protruding like a spring-board over nothing. We made sure that it *was* fixed, but to gain its vibrating head without assisting holds was no easy matter. From this vantage point the overhang could be breasted. The next stretch turned, it seemed to us later, upon one rather rounded hold. Hand, knee and then foot it served, while the fingers found only pressure thrusts to direct the balance. Breathlessly we watched Joseph's smooth, seemingly effortless movements. He kept up a flow of *patois* remarks to Antoine as he worked across and upwards. Soon he was only a shapeless silhouette against the dazzle of the sky above. It seemed impossible that he should be able to stay at all in as steep and smooth a passage, much less that he should be able to continue. After a while, as the rope still ran out, his voice grew dim with distance and we lost sight of him in the glare. Suddenly came a sharp exclamation: it sounded like '*Je chouques!*' Antoine, calm as ever, translated, '*Il est là.*' The tension was over; or, rather, changed its direction altogether. Now it was our turn!

Most of the passage had to be done by the oddest series of counterpoised pressures I have ever had to manage. All on a surface too steep to allow any of the usual margin of balance. An occasional pinch-hold was a luxury. The friction of a rubber sole or the palm of the hand on some small awkwardly sloping surface had to be enough. It was with a very queer sense of unreality—as though a dream had got out of place—that I came at last to a rapturous Joseph perched on little or nothing and tied to the cliff with a network of rope by which he had supplied me with a spare hand-line.

The landing-place, on which I joined I. A. R., was a nook the size of a dinner-plate, with one handhold! It needs some experience for two people to stow themselves in such a place with comfort. The contortions of the human body are, fortunately, easier to perform than to describe. For a time we were busy with the problem of how to stay there together and keep the sacks, which had been hauled up on an independent rope, from departing. There was no room to put them on again as yet. But there is an old climbing maxim about halting-places, 'Where there is room for one there is room for two', which applies to cliff-faces though not to chimneys. The second man can at least stand on the first man's foot!

Joseph meanwhile was occupied with Antoine, to whom fell the job of bringing up the last axe and thus doing without it as a springboard for the overhang. Since he elected to climb the pitch in boots it has always been a mystery to me how he did it. The overhang involved him in a voluntary leap into the void. We believed him when he said it gave him '*Une drôle de sensation*'. But in time he came up the last bulge as placidly as ever, with a broad smile and an '*Ah, les amoureux!*' as he spied us clinging together to our joint and solitary hold. After this, what remained of the wall was only steep, its holds seemed superb in comparison with the passage below. Joseph disappeared again, there was another pause while the sacks and axes went up; and then, suddenly, we topped a wall of rough yellow rock to a ledge and the sunshine.

We lay and basked and ate and relaxed. The ridge above promised nothing more than is normal to a great Alpine ridge. Its rough, golden rocks stood up in bold, very practicable masses, enchanting to our eye by contrast to the shadowy, frowning walls below. The plaster of ice and snow patches that decorated them would this year give no trouble. Time now was our only opponent. It was 1.30 and we had a long way still to go, so for comfort and speed we roped in twos again. From time to time, down in the recesses of the mountain below us on the right, rocks would be thawed out by the sun, slip away, slide down a snow-patch, hop, whir and vanish into the great couloir, but we were in complete safety as we clambered on our ridge. Under the clear sky the Alps basked in a heat-haze. Less than a pin's head in size, the Bricolla Chalet, our starting-point, shone among its meadows.

Triumph gave us wings, and the rocks were really exhilarating, like the most sporting parts of the usual South Ridge of the mountain. Still, they were long, the day was far advanced (we had taken three hours and twenty minutes over the crucial two hundred feet) and it was five o'clock before we reached the summit. We did not pause for long, nor did we linger on the descent. In fact we raced down the southward rocks, for the sun sank with that peculiar suddenness it shows when you are sinking also. The valleys were filling with gloom as we turned down over the damp snows of the glacier. We were in no further hurry. We had only to walk, at leisure, home to bed. Only then did fatigue descend upon me—like a black bonnet, so that I stumbled on the granulated re-frozen ice of the dry glacier, and among the tangled moraines through which the track winds its way down to Bricolla. But a current of sleepy beatitude flowed through one's veins. Not even my right foot seemed heavy, on which by accident I had been wearing one of I. A. R.'s spare boots throughout the day! A spell had been exorcized, a dream replaced by a reality which transcended it. In all the literal force of the word we were content. Once again, as I turned into bed, the candle went unextinguished and guttered itself out unheeded, so suddenly did blissful sleep descend.

—

After the Dent Blanche a coma fell upon us. Everything else seemed somewhat of an anti-climax. But the perfect weather mysteriously continued, energy welled up again and the traverse of the Weisshorn began to exert an attraction. So we went over the Col d'Hérens to Zermatt. Fearful heat struck us on the pass, reviving for me all the complications left behind by my Himalayan sunstroke. In vain I wore a long silk scarf, wound puggaree-style round a double felt *terai* and floating down my back in a ridiculous fashion. The swelter of the

snowy hollows below the pass on the Zermatt side seemed to take
all strength away. I had not yet hit on the useful plan of filling the
inside of my hat with snow, which later on was to prove a partial
solution of an awkward problem. An uncomfortable solution
certainly, since it leads to my finding a hot day on the peaks nearly
as wetting as a rain-storm. The snow-water trickles agonizingly down
your neck, making you more than ever determined to run no risks
of possible nights out! But this drastic remedy does lift the paralysis
of the heat and makes expeditions possible which otherwise would
have to be renounced or undertaken only in cloudy weather. In my
tropic headgear friends accustomed to see me looking like a gipsy
with a bright-coloured handkerchief tied round my hair, hardly recognized me. On the path below the Schönbühl, in fact, H. M. Kelly
and his party on their way up to do the Zmutt Arête did their best
to cut me. It took them some moments to make out who I was. Kelly
asked what we had been doing. Feeling elated, but anxious not to
seem too pleased with ourselves, we mentioned the North Arête as
casually as possible. 'Oh, have you?' said Kelly, 'and where are you
off to now? We are going up the Zmutt Arête.' This was salutary to
one's vanity and henceforth I vowed to be more modest. This led to
more trouble later. All through the next winter indignant climbers
would come up with a pained air and say, 'I do think you might have
told us about your climb, instead of being such a dark horse and
letting us read in *The Times* about it!'

The Weisshorn Hut seemed a very long way up from Randa,
though the path is full of delightful turns where the view opens out
into the valley and under the shade of solitary pines one can breathe
for a moment a cooler air. It was extremely hot and we were glad to
reach the hut. In its recesses was a party sleeping after the day's climb.
When they woke up they proved to be Armand Charlet, a porter,
and a client down from the Schalligrat. Armand Charlet is the
most brilliant of the Chamonix guides, handsome, debonair,
dashing, famous all over the Alps for the speed and enterprise of his
expeditions.

Later in the season he was to lead the final search party in that long-drawn-out tragedy on the Petit Dru (August 14th—17th) which is one of the most heroic as it is among the most dreadful stories in the Alpine record. Four French climbers were ascending on two ropes when, 300 feet below the summit, the leader of the second party fell and was gravely injured. As he could not be moved one companion stayed with him while two went down to seek assistance. This was on the 14th. At the Charpoua Hut were three Swiss and two Italian climbers, who, on the morning of the 15th, fearing for the safety of the stranded party, set out to give them what help they could. At 4 P.M. they reached them, left with them all their food as well as all their underclothing, and turned to the descent. Soon afterwards a thunderstorm broke, with torrents of hail developing into heavy snow. The Italian party bivouacked on a partly sheltered ledge and came down next day in safety. The Swiss struggled on down through the night but had to wait for the dawn on the great ledge leading to the Charpoua Glacier exposed to all the fury of the weather with only their outer clothes and without food. A party of guides who had arrived at the hut brought them in frost-bitten and completely exhausted. One of them, aged twenty, died while being carried across.

Up on the Petit Dru the night was fearful. The wounded man lingered on till 1 P.M. on the 16th. His companion had seen, through a gap in the clouds, the guides start on their rescue of the Swiss party. When no help came he almost despaired. Meanwhile the two French climbers had reached Chamonix, returning with several volunteers to the Charpoua by the morning of the 16th. Here they found the cliffs plastered with snow and ice, and the guides there present unable to tackle the climb. None the less one of the original party, with another experienced amateur, resolved to go up. At 18.00, after great difficulty, they reached the survivor and descended with him to a better ledge lower down, to sit with him through his third night of terrible exposure. In the night Armand Charlet arrived at the Charpoua, coming from another expedition. Then and there he flung himself at the peak, followed by three of the strongest Chamonix guides. Just at dawn the waiting men saw him coming alone, at desperate speed, up the glazed, snow-powdered slabs. He had taken two hours forty minutes from the hut. The other guides arrived, worn out by the speed, and he dashed on to recover the corpse. In his haste he slipped, fell a hundred feet, was held by his second, but fractured his skull! When the others, who were descending, returned to the scene of this third accident he recovered consciousness. Bound up, he managed, with almost incredible resolution, to take the lead again, but on the glacier he collapsed and had to be carried down unconscious. The story, one of the saddest in Alpine history, is still one of the most noble, with its examples of self-sacrificing devotion and invincible courage. It is good to be able to add that Armand Charlet has so far recovered from his injury that recent chronicles of the French Alpine Club are filled annually with notes of his First Ascents and other exploits.

Joseph and Armand Charlet eyed each other curiously. We had had some suspicions that he might have had designs on our North Ridge. After some amusing exchanges he and his party set off down to Randa.

We lingered outside the hut watching a curious trio of amateurs crawling up towards us. When we learnt that they had come all the way from Prague without stopping, we understood why they seemed a little weary! The leader was not reticent about their programme. Their vast sacks contained complete bivouac equipment and provisions for ten days. They were to start in the morning up the Weisshorn, descend the Schalligrat, sleep somewhere between it and the Rothorn, continue over the Gabelhorn-Arbengrat-Viereselgrat, Tête de Valpelline, Dent d'Hérens—all without coming down—and wind up with the Matterhorn. We never heard anything more of this expedition, more's the pity, though I tried hard later on to find out.

Our own traverse of the Weisshorn gave us a shock. We found the climb most impressive in its grandeur and scale. It was hard later to imagine the endurance and resolution which took Geoffrey Young with his one leg so nearly to its summit. The last snow-slope, whose bad condition defeated him so unfairly, was in moderately good order for us and we went off down the Schalligrat with high hopes of an enjoyable rock-climb. The first section on the ridge was aerial and entrancing, but when we turned off to go down a rib to the Schalli-gletscher all the attractions seemed to come to an end. A huge loose block slid away at a touch—it had been resting on ice and was thawed out by the fierce heat of that extraordinary season—and frightened us by nearly taking hold of our rope as it fell. The day seemed full of narrow chances; stones threatened us as we dealt with the very awkward schrund. We were glad to be down on the glacier again. But here suddenly we came nearer than we had ever come to disaster.

We were going diagonally down a moderately steep slope covered with a two-foot layer of softish snow. Across it ran a large, open, innocent-looking crevasse, or rather a vast clear chasm with white perpendicular walls and no visible bottom. There were no over-hanging eaves, no treacherous lips to cause uncertainty, and Joseph led down to the point where the walls evidently closed in together. He gave it a prudent margin for safety, crossed and began to follow it at a distance of some six feet from its lower wall. I was at the crossing point and I. A. R. up above it on the fairly steep slope, where he could see exactly what happened. It was the unpredictable and inexplicable character of the incident, as with an earthquake or a lightning stroke from a clear sky, that made it so terrifying. I. A. R. could see Joseph wading almost knee-deep yards away from the edge of the chasm. Suddenly with a deep *Hrumph* the whole vertical snow and ice wall slid away and Joseph's legs appeared clear. The split had occurred just along the line of his footsteps. For a moment he hung in the balance as his foothold slipped away from under him; then he toppled over on to his axe and staggered into the snow below us, while with a hollow roar the mass of ice poured down into the darkness of the gulf. If he had gone with it, we should have all three disappeared within five seconds and for ever. Our fate would then have become one of the minor mysteries of mountaineering. So large a mass fell that Joseph would have dropped at least thirty feet before the pull came on me. I should have followed. I was already at the very brink, and the combined jerk would have plucked I. A. R. from his slope without his having a chance of holding. Down we should have gone like the tail of a kite into a bottomless chasm. That we did not was merely a matter of Joseph's being on his right foot rather than his left at the instant of the split. And no sagacity could have foretold that anything of the kind could occur and no precautions could have forestalled or met it.

The moment was the most dismaying of our joint Alpine career. It was too much for words and with one accord we forgathered on an evidently solid piece of the glacier and sat down together in silence—merely looking at one another with expressive eyes. We sat there for some time. For myself I was feeling horribly sick and the others looked rather green. That the whole glacier was in a very bad state had been obvious to us for some time, but no one could have expected such tricks as this! We had decided earlier not to cross it by the route that leads down an ice-ridge back towards the hut, but to get off its right bank as soon as we could and go straight down to Randa by the lower path. It was an extraordinarily cautious and tentative party that now tackled the remaining difficulties. In the end we climbed some way up the Schallihorn slopes and traversed off them to snow. All this had taken time, and dusk caught us before we got down to the faint beginning of the path. Usually when you gain a path you suppose that your troubles are over. But this proved in the night to be no ordinary path. It constantly ended in nothing at the edge of black overhanging walls of gorges filled with the tumult of invisible waterfalls. Then we would stumble by lantern-light over broken ground in, it seemed, irrational directions and pick it up again (or another path exactly like it) and repeat the process. How we thanked our stars that Joseph once, years before, had been up that way. At each crisis he seemed to carry the direction of the route in his head as though he had come up that morning. In the end, after 5000 feet, the bed of a rivulet let us down into the marshes of the valley floor. Another irrational circuit revealed a bridge and then, with infrequent lights showing on the side of the valley, we struck the railway track and wearily marched, it seemed for miles, along the ballast. About midnight we were knocking up the Railway Hotel and drinking delicious quarts of milk and soda-water. Whether this time we succeeded in blowing the candles out before sleep caught us, I do not remember!

But the perfect weather went on burning a hole in our consciences. It was too good to waste. Rest-days in Zermatt seemed almost sinful! We compromised by choosing more moderate expeditions. Geoffrey Young was in Zermatt, I remember, getting ready for his astounding ascent of the Matterhorn. He was charming about the Dent Blanche and seemed to know so much about it that we got the impression, rightly or wrongly, that he must once have been very attracted by it himself.

We crossed over the Adler-joch to Saas Fee and went over the Südlenspitze and Nadelhorn, a graceful piece of ridge wandering from one of the most conveniently situated huts in the Alps. Oh the pleasure of climbing along a well-cleaned arête with no *débris* to worry about, a sharp crest that winds and turns with knife edges of snow and keen, firm pinnacles of rock and that takes you down in the end to within a short walk, on honest glacier, of your hut again!

The joys of climbing from a high hut without the extra toil of some 5000 feet up from valley and down again, led us to go up to the little Weissmies Inn. As we approached it in the dusk the perils of a Swiss National Holiday were brought home to us. A festive company were letting off charges of blasting powder among the rocks near the path. Not till we were right among them did wild cries of '*Attention*' bring us to a halt. We attended then all right! And we arrived at the hut safely amid a shower of flying flinders.

We intended to do several peaks, but I. A. R. was out of sorts and went down again to the Rhône Valley, while I went with Joseph over the Fletschorn to the Simplon. So after all I did not escape a toilsome descent! The way up was amusing and easy, a simple glacier and a scramble among red rocks on to the ridge. As we reached the summit the wind rose to a fierce gale and we had a hurried scamper down the long rib of rocks to the glacier. We ran hard to escape the storm but the rain caught us on the alp, where a woman knee-deep in mud was making cheese. Children, caked in slime, were crawling about among the goats. We needed warm food and she gave us tepid milk out of a dirty bowl. But her friendliness made up for the dirt. I wondered how she could live in such filth. Obviously she did not notice it, yet the wallow here was every bit as bad as in the yak shelters of Sikkim and the smell was identical!

We had miles of road to walk up to the Simplon, and I looked pathetically at every car that passed. But there were no soft hearts in those cars. If you wanted to climb, then climb, they seemed to shout. In the end, as usual, half a mile below the summit, a derelict, puffing, home-made car stopped, and panted up with me to the Hospitz, poor Joseph having to finish on foot. I hoped to get on somehow down to Brigue, but though it was early afternoon no transport was available. Joseph rescued me from the hotel, and having special acquaintanceship with the monks (who are an offshoot from the St Bernard), arranged for me to stay—contrary to custom—at the Hospitz. We were lavishly entertained with wines and liqueurs, a pleasant incident repeated next day at the St Bernard after we had picked up I. A. R. at Martigny. And so to Courmayeur.

Mont Dolent was our first goal here. When we got to the little inn high up the Val Ferret we were disconcerted to find it apparently closed. Dusk was creeping up and we had no wish to go down again. A window was unfastened, so we lifted the sash and crept inside. Hardly had we done so than we saw two figures, man and woman, rushing like furies across the slopes towards us. Joseph, who has a deep distrust of the Italian temperament, seemed to think we should be in for a bad quarter of an hour. We gripped our axes and did our best to look both respectable and formidable. The unpleasantness soon passed; its acute period was fortunately brief and by supper-time cordiality reigned.

A thick fog shrouded the mountains in the early morning and for a while it was doubtful if we should find the way. But the sun came out as we went up the last stretch of the Mont Dolent and the famous view was all the better for the surprise. The Grandes Jorasses looked their most challenging, especially that Tronchey Arête which was one of the last conquests of the legendary Gugliermina brothers. They used to make the Alpine world marvel at the scale and pertinacity of their expeditions, taking up sleeping kit and spending whole half-weeks on their ascents of the Italian faces of Mont Blanc and Monte Rosa and the Aiguille Verte by its north-west slopes. In this they were pioneers in technique and the modern enthusiast with his Zdarsky sack thinks nothing of bivouacking in fair weather at any height. Mr Smythe's magnificent climbs on the Brenva Mont Blanc, for example, were made possible by these tactics.

When we got back to the inn, we found a Frenchman there who had come over the Col du Grand Ferret and proposed to go on down into Italy. A simple matter this, of course, but quite contrary to the strict regulations of Italian Government, for the Col du Grand Ferret is not one of the open passes. We felt strongly inclined to recommend him to go on by night to Courmayeur, since a *poste* of soldiers, reinforced by Fascisti, was due up at the inn early each morning. To any mountaineer who is willing to walk for a few hours by night the official Italian 'closing of the frontier' is necessarily a farce. It can only keep in or out an unadventurous and presumably not very dangerous type of traveller. Possibly it is designed primarily to give the army something to do in a healthy environment. Technically it is impossible to close a high mountain frontier against a mountaineer who is really determined to go through. On the other hand, as a well-disciplined German once said to me when I proposed to slip over the Pfitscher Joch from Austria into Italy, 'But you are not allowed to go that way'. This settled the question for him!

Our Frenchman was too tired to go on, however, without a good night's rest, and so provided us with a little drama in the morning. The inn stands a short way back from the tip of a sharp promontory that divides the valley. Lying on its crest you can watch the approach of a party of soldiers for hours before they disappear under the lee of your cliff. Then if you wish to evade them you have only to stroll down one side of the knoll as they walk up the other. You will then have an ample twenty minutes to make your get-away into the forests before they can possibly see you. Our Frenchman was up to none of this strategy. Unfortunately for him, he relied upon the good faith of the *patronne*, our little Fury of the previous evening. The Fury proved a Delilah or a Judith to him. He believed her when she advised him to stay in his bedroom during the visit of the *poste*. And then she gave him away to the soldiers the moment they arrived! Down he had to go to Turin on charge, with a prospect of life in purely official circles for the rest of his holiday. The traitress meanwhile was not above taking me secretly into a back room to propose manœuvres with a false bill in order to avoid the Government stamp-tax, which she considered unnecessary red-tape!

Our adventures with the Frontier Guard continued when we went up to the Col de la Seigne for the Trélatête. The Combal Lake was vociferous with frogs and we passed two soldiers going down with large clusters of frogs' legs dangling from their hands. They stopped us in an unpleasant style which changed instantly when they discovered our nationality. They had taken us for French—on whom they seemed resolved to waste no civilities.

When we reached the upper chalets, where we hoped to find hay-beds, everything was shut up tight though there were plenty of signs of recent military occupation. After a long wait and much deliberation we concluded that the *poste* had gone down for the night and decided, as the chill of evening increased, to break into a promising-looking barn. Fortunately it resisted our attempts, for we soon spied a party of two, accompanied by a huge dog, making rapidly up the slopes towards us. Hoping they would not detect any traces of our attempted burglarious entry, we sat down to wait for them in some trepidation. Joseph's expression—he had been the most energetic of the burglars—reminded us of the cat in whose mouth butter would not melt. But the soldiers when they arrived were cordiality itself. They invited us in, lit an extra large fire, routed out a spare sheepskin covering for me, made up a special straw-bed, and generally were the perfect hosts—all in an Italian to which unluckily we could not reply. Sign language went a long way that night.

The Trélatête was one of my worst experiences of Alpine heat-stroke. The glaciers gave us a lot of trouble and the final rocks were already warm as we reached them. We had chosen the Trélatête partly to take a look across the Miage Valley at the great couloir that leads up to the Brouillard Arête of Mont Blanc. As we suspected, it seemed all ice that year; grey, furrowed and repellent; and our plans for an attempt upon it dissolved as we looked. The way down for me was only a long sick struggle. There were a few clouds passing slowly across the sky and each time the sunshine was cut off the wave of renewed power told me clearly what was happening. The cloud would pass; the sunshine pour in again; and I would find myself almost helpless. It was exactly as though some hand on the tap of my life were turning it on or off. In some of the bays of the crags the heat was truly fearful, but it seemed absurd to be so incapacitated by it. Will-power was of no avail. In mere fatigue it can galvanize the forces, but not so with this malady. I tried my best, but it was like a fainting fit. Those who have had real heat-stroke know that there is no fighting against it when the headache and giddiness overwhelm you.

As a result we were late in getting off the glaciers. On the ridge leading up to them the Italian A.C. have placed one of their amusing 'dog kennel' bivouac shelters. The little hutch has a board-floor and an arching semicircular roof only about four feet high. The last user of this one seemed to be Mr Haskett-Smith. I. A. R. and I were much tempted to stay there on our descent. It was the last day of Joseph's engagement with us, and he had to get back to Courmayeur that night. So we agreed that he should go ahead at speed to make sure of arriving before dark, while we followed at a more restful pace. After saying good-bye, and watching him disappear in little clouds of scree-dust down into the valley, we sat down by the dog-kennel to deliberate. The flaw in the plan of sleeping there was that we were foodless. All the places we had passed on the way up had failed us as provisioning sources. The meat we had expected to buy had been spotted with archipelagos of blue-bottle blowings and the bread had all been eaten by somebody else!

Our problem was: Would we be too hungry to sleep? We sat and considered how hungry we were already. The experiment seemed conclusive; it would be better to waste no more time but go on valleywards as fast as we could, while the light lasted. We reached La Visaille, eventually, to find it full of singing Italian soldiers. The *patron*, who by profession was a *ramoneur*, however, offered his own bed, in which he assured us we would be very comfortable. The bed satisfied all the expectations that his trade aroused, and furthermore abundantly lived up to one of the Oldest Traditions in Alpine literature. It would be incorrect, would it not, to write a book of Alpine memoirs without a single mention of a flea?

—

After this I had to play at a new and curious Alpine game: Facing the Sun. It became all-important to avoid slopes and ridges that gave Apollo a chance of discharging his shafts at my back. During his hours of strength my only chance of reasonable progress uphill was to advance upon him with an extra-large double-felt hat preceding me as a shield. On ordinary zigzags—those from Saas

Fee up to the Mischabel Hut for example—we even noticed that the zigs would take twice as long as zags of equal length. Such are some of the effects of a rashly incurred sun-stroke in the Tropics!

For these reasons, at the point where you gather wood for fuel at the upper fringes of the forest under the Grandes Jorasses, I. A. R. and I sat down to watch Joseph, Dorothy Thompson and a porter dwindle to dots on the upper slopes of moraine while we waited for the edge of the afternoon shadow to drop over us. When it arrived we followed. But we were left far behind and soon were forced into one of those evening, uphill scampers that are the usual Alpine penalty for sloth. Indeed darkness was not far off when we came to the foot of that astonishing little rock-climb that leads up to the hut. In the Lakes it would count as a very moderate course, but it is steep; the holds, though good, are far apart, and at its foot is a kind of schrund that gapes wide and deep. It is certainly harder *as rock-climbing* than anything else to be found on the ordinary route up the mountain. An Alpinist with a bulky sack can be pardoned for wondering half-way up it whether he is on the right route, especially as it is no place to fall off.

We were just starting when, suddenly, out of the gathering dusk, a gaunt and gigantic figure strode up and without warning began to harangue us on its difficulties in emphatic gestures and mixed languages. He proved to be a solitary German climber. On close inspection he exactly resembled the type, otherwise so hard to discover, that was so familiar to us all during the War through the cartoons of Raemaekers. He was bony, close-cropped, powerful and clumsy. He began at once to tell us about his recent exploits. A night out on the Aiguille Verte with a chance companion he had picked up at the Couvercle was the chief of them. His notion, we gathered, was to pick us up! Or else some stray companions at the hut. Perhaps some amiable party would include him? The scheme, for many reasons, left us cold. For one thing, the hut holds just eight people; and there were already up there, Dorothy Thompson, Joseph, a porter, two Italian girl-novices and the two last guides left in Courmayeur—which, with us, made nine and with him would make ten! We did our best to point out the objections firmly and kindly. But in vain did we attempt to persuade him to return to the valley. He was set upon ascending the mountain willy-nilly and soon was crying that he preferred to do so alone. With the glaciers in the open state prevailing this season the preference seemed to us almost to indicate derangement. We were therefore the less surprised when, after a look at the little climb ahead, he announced his intention of reaching the hut by another route—by the glacier on the right. We knew that there could be only one result of this—at the best we should all suffer a sleepless night in the hut. There would be interminable shoutings, endless conjectures and then about midnight the infuriated antics of a rescue party. He went on declaring his resolution to go up the mountain alone, and nothing would change it. So in the end we made the best of a bad business and borrowed his rope to bring him up the climb, a little aghast to discover that he was all at sea on it.

His welcome at the hut was a poor one. A circle of dismayed faces received this outsize, extra man, and watched the elaborate cooking he at once undertook. He covered the table with aluminium ware and stoves; his sack disgorged tins until the hut seemed to contain nothing else. With elephantine graciousness he kept offering the messes that resulted from his cooking to all who put their noses inside. No efforts were spared to establish amicable relations by these means. But in vain. We were all anxious to get to bed and very uncertain as to how we should ever manage it.

Meanwhile many secret confabulations were in progress outside. It is easy at this distance to wonder why none of us could be 'sporting' and add him to a rope to give him a grand day's climbing as one would do in the Lakes. But in the Alps the proposition is quite different; time and reserve forces allow no such margins. The two Italian girls were complete novices, with two of the feeblest guides it has ever been my misfortune to watch perform. Dorothy Thompson and Joseph Georges had invited the two of us to join ropes with them in view of the perfectly foul condition of the glaciers. The addition of this over-weight and singularly inept unknown to our rope on such a long climb was a responsibility we none of us cared to undertake. The dilemma he presented was abominable. We told him again that we could do nothing for him, to which he replied haughtily that he would need nothing—and the whole hut then set to work to sleep in an electric atmosphere. Our joint impression was that only the unknown slept—to judge from his *basso profundo* trumpetings.

Secretly we were all hoping that he would go on sleeping till too late to start the climb. But when we stole out of the hut at 2 o'clock he had already begun to cook himself a beef stew. The night was very black and full of noisy winds. Crossing vast crevasses on invisible bridges by lantern-light is never a cheerful occupation. It was no increase to our gaiety when I. A. R. reported that a lantern was following us behind! The Italian girls were already in difficulties with their steps and Joseph in fact was quite busy fielding them. Their guides were pecking miserably and most ineffectively at what were very steep bulges of ice between the yawning gulfs of crevasses. We all felt we had our hands quite full with what was happening ahead, when a guttural exclamation behind called us to notice that the candle had dropped out of his lantern into a crevasse! We passed a spare candle back to our Solitary. Illumination, when restored, revealed a very independent, not to say haughty, figure sternly refusing all advice and assistance. And indeed we had no rope whatsoever to spare after turning two short ropes into a rope for four. On we went.

At a particularly awkward step I. A. R. lingered to offer a steadying hand, which was firmly declined. When he turned to proceed he felt himself seized by the ankle. It was therefore no small relief to the party when in the early dawn we sidled off the first glacier on to the rocks. Here matters for a while seemed to go better, but alas, our Solitary developed a taste for independent routes. These variations tended to land him into helpless 'spread-eagles' and a helping hand then was accepted before our hero had time to think or to refuse. In spite of our fury, we could not withhold admiration for his pertinacity and abandon.

So the day wore on with more than a hint of storm in the upper sky. The snow on the higher glaciers was wretchedly soft. The route was complicated, the heat very oppressive; we were all glad to scramble up the final slope and take a brief survey of the Mer de Glace basin. But already the Aiguilles were hung with banners of storm clouds. The first storm of the season was coming on. The first of that series which was to produce the grim disaster on the Dru.

Down the easy upper rocks we trotted. They are seamed with shallow grooves in which patches of ice occasionally lingered. At the shoulder above the glacier we stopped for a hasty meal. As we stooped to the sacks there was a crackle of discharge about us, and we had a disagreeable impression as of a hot iron sweeping near our scalps.

Just as we were recovering from this, came the grand climax of the day. A startled shout from above and a large boulder came trundling down the cliff. Close after it, head over heels, followed the Solitary, who had lingered to enjoy the view from the summit. His cries were heart-rending as he bounded and spun down and past us towards the plunge of the cliff. Not one of us thought he had a chance. I shall never forget the sick qualm of horror and helplessness with which we watched him snatch at a boulder as he passed. It came away in his clasp. Suddenly the miracle happened. At the very edge of the great drop a sharp spike of rock pushed itself up beneath his coat and there he was, transfixed and arrested, not a moment too soon. Joseph was already unroped and flying across the cliff to his side. The Solitary must have bounded down at least two hundred feet; but by the time Joseph reached him he had extracted from his pocket a capacious brass case of surgical appliances. Joseph, whose skill in First Aid is considerable, found everything laid out before him. His injuries proved surprisingly slight though his appearance was horrifying, the blood which covered him came only from skin scratches. It was an unspeakable relief to find him in such good shape and able to continue normally with the four hours of descent which remained.

Down in the hut the sinister aspects of the adventure receded and the grotesquer features came forward. The Solitary's first act was to open the rest of his tins. The sight of him with half a dripping peach in one hand and a cube of bully beef in the other, rinsing the alternate mouthfuls down with cupfuls of coffee and draughts of *eau de vie*, was a fine barrier against that other too torturing picture of a helpless, falling human body. After this repast he became strange in his behaviour and made us suspect he may have suffered from concussion. I remember watching Joseph refusing with adamant politeness an offer of what looked like 500 francs for his First Aid services on the mountain. He preferred to be free to give *ce drôle de type* a piece of his mind.

The last act was a fitting close to this comico-horrible adventure. It took place down in Courmayeur the evening following; we had slept again at the hut on account of the bad weather. We were sitting in the beer garden watching the exquisitely turned-out Italian ladies taking their evening promenade. There came a little commotion among them, a flutter of admiration, and through the throng passed the truly arresting figure of our hero crowned with white bandages and liberally patched with plaster, still in his skewered and blood-stained coat. He too was taking his evening promenade—a mountain figure for all to marvel at. He seemed very satisfied with his ascent of the Grandes Jorasses and was leaving on the morrow fortified for a solitary attack on the Grand Paradis!

—

Our homeward course was a devious one. We made a rapid walking tour through the Tarentaise in late autumn to see its possibilities as a training centre for next year. At Entre deux Eaux we had a thrilling experience and a fine test of our power to resist mass suggestion. Running at dusk through the long grassy Vallon de la

Rocheure, I suddenly spied a superb cluster of mushrooms. Soon our hats were full of the luscious fungi, and when we came to Madame Richard's inn we naturally proposed, with her assistance, to make our supper of them. At this she was in consternation. They were poisonous. No hand of hers should touch them. The Juge d'Instruction, who would examine the case after we were dead, should not find her involved. She would keep well out of it. As for me, I could do as I pleased. I was a little dashed by all this. However, as I was certain I knew a good mushroom when I saw one, I persuaded her to let me have a saucepan and some milk, and in a little while we were seated before large bowls of mushroom stew. Just as we were beginning upon them a stir outside made us look up. There, plastered against the window, noses like snails on the panes, were all the faces of the hamlet! They were watching, with awestruck solemnity, the foreigners poisoning themselves! If mass-expectation could have affected us, I should not be alive now to write the tale. The stew was delicious. There were enough mushrooms for lunch to-morrow also, but should we still be there? We feasted in as care-free a spirit as we could manage. The excitement without meanwhile grew more and more intense. Our least movement or change of expression was seen as a preliminary symptom. I fear it was something of a disappointment to the public when we asked for our candles, said good-night and went normally up to bed.

I have since heard from an authority that the identical mushroom that in England is a healthful food in some districts can be deadly. If so, and if Entre deux Eaux is such a district, it is possible that we had a lucky escape!

We were leaving for England when, at Annecy, the glorious weather returned. Mont Blanc shouted at us 'Come back!' so we jumped out of our train and into another which went to St Gervais. We wanted to go up by the Aiguille du Goûter Route guideless as a finale to the season. The train takes you up all the hot, tiresome lower reaches and deposits you, in a crowd of tourists, at the Col de Voza. Thence up the path to the Tête Rousse Hut one is constantly overtaken by racing, panting walkers. The hut is near the foot of the rocky slope that leads up to the crest of the Aiguille de Goûter, on which stands a smaller hut with a reputation for being crowded. The slope is easy but not clear from danger of stone-falls on hot afternoons or when other parties are going up it ahead.

The weather seemed on the point of breaking again, so we decided to sleep at the lower hut and make up the extra two or three hours by an earlier start in the cool morning. The afternoon passed talking to a fantastic youth, in shorts and a shirt only, who proposed to take a boy of fourteen in the same kit up to the summit in the morning and down to Chamonix by the ordinary route, *ropeless*. He assured us that ordinary mountaineers were foolishly fussy and much encumbered by their apparatus of ice-axes, crampons and ropes. He said he went up every week-end at *grande vitesse*. Unfortunately his last fourteen-year-old victim had been stupidly sick 'from the altitude' before they reached the Vallot. He took it in very bad part when, like an Aunt Jane, I hinted there might be other reasons for the youth's absurd collapse.

When this amusement waned, there was the ice-tunnel, which protects St Gervais from further floodings, to be examined. In 1892 a torrent of mud burst out of this glacier, went down to St Gervais in thirty-two minutes and buried 175 people. Now a tunnel in the ice drains the water away. It was lined by two types of ice-crystal, of a feathery and a star-like pattern, equally elaborate and fairy-like. From its mouth you can look down to the crevassed snow-basin to which the Aiguille du Goûter rock-face falls. The full height of the cliff is over 2000 feet, so it was startling to be told that the week before a solitary Russian climber had succeeded in falling down it, to survive skinned but unbroken. He had gone up late and failed to hit the right route just as dusk fell. All the night long he had kept both huts awake with shouts from somewhere near the summit in a stone-swept couloir. At dawn, when a search party went up to look for him, the shouts stopped. He had been knocked off his perch by a stone-fall, rolled down the entire gully, jumped the schrund and landed on some snow between two crevasses. Here he was spotted, after some time, by the searchers far above. When they got to him he was dancing wildly and seeing skeletons hand-in-hand wheeling round him!

This story may have excited our imaginations, for when, at dusk, the hut porter came in to say there was a party stuck high up on the rocks, we found ourselves ready to expect anything. We stood and strained our eyes in the chill evening breeze while the porter pointed out the two figures sitting in the gully just in the line of the stone-falls. We saw something, but it seemed surprisingly immovable for climbers and very like two stones. On the other hand the dusk had just made one of its sudden leaps towards darkness, something might have been clear three minutes before which was doubtful now, and it was impossible to be certain that we were really looking where the porter was pointing. A party of two had gone up latish—looking weary and not over-competent—and there was no improbability in their being stuck. As to their sitting down in the gully, where stones were likeliest to come, well, some people will do anything on a mountain, and it might seem to them sheltered from the night airs.

The porter now began a series of strenuous howls, which certainly evoked not only echoes but replies from the cliff. By the time darkness had arrived he had managed to persuade us that a party was stranded up there. Now it was our turn to persuade him that something ought to be done about it. The night was looking decidedly like turning nasty. There were no other climbers in the hut; evidently if anything were done we should have to do it. So, in the feverish bad temper that attends setting out on search parties, we put our boots on, overcame the porter's reluctance and tramped off up the slopes.

How far we got that evening is hard to say. We got high enough to make the absence of any replies to our shouts most disheartening. In the end we had to admit that seeking people who wouldn't or couldn't reply, over ground like that, in the dark, was not a reasonable undertaking. There was nothing for it but to go down again and see what was to be seen in the morning.

In the night a blustering gale got up, driving showers of sleet that slashed against the windows. It was dismal lying in a snug bed and imagining the miseries of a crag-bound party. I. A. R.'s conscience didn't allow him a wink of sleep, though mine behaved shamefully better. We were up before dawn, a dawn of driving clouds that hid the cliff almost continuously. More howls from the porter, of an astonishingly piercing quality—and faintly but clearly, yes, unmistakably a reply! A gap in the mists swept across the crags and there was the porter, arm outstretched, transfixed, pointing again. We could see no one, as before; but mountain eyes are well known to be telescopic. There was nothing for it but to stuff our sacks with bottles of hot coffee and blankets and set off as quickly as we could up into the grey drizzle again.

This time we could make the porter come right up to the very spot where he had actually seen them. And there they were—a red rock and a brown rock comfortably settled on a ledge in the gully! It was hard to know whether relief or disappointment or annoyance was uppermost as we turned about and ran down to breakfast.

The season ended sadly. We were really due to leave for Geneva that evening and our start for Mont Blanc was baulked. We spent the day sauntering down in capricious weather, analysing the gaits of the walkers who were coming up to the Tête Rousse. In the midst of the stream of panting spasmodic pedestrians came a party of four experienced climbers, instantly noticeable for the even, tranquil, rhythmic union with which they were walking together up the moraine path. We stopped to talk with them. They were from Geneva, a strong responsible party full of an infectious enjoyment of the day and the expedition. They were eager that we should turn back and go up with them, and almost persuaded us to add an extra day to our holiday; but the weather was still doubtful for Mont Blanc and reluctantly we continued downwards. Next

morning, from Geneva, Mont Blanc was gleaming under a clear
sky and we thought often and enviously of them as we strolled in
its hot streets. The evening papers came out with news of an Alpine
accident. Coming down, at the point where all the difficulties were
over, at the well-known crossing by the Pierre à l'Échelle, an
avalanche of stones had swept down across the path and the leader,
with whom we had talked most, had been struck and instantly
killed. If we had gone with them? We might all have been ten
minutes later, and no accident would have happened. What a toss-
penny game at moments mountaineering seemed. Holding the
damp printed news-sheet in the Rue de Mont Blanc, it was impossible not to feel 'There, but for the Grace of God . . .' The best of
our Alpine seasons had come to an end.

North ridge of the Dent Blanche mounts (slanting in the picture slightly from
left to right) to a point a florin's breadth below and to the left of the apparent
summit. Thence the slabs trend across almost to the foot of the high right snow
funnel. The black bulge of the cliff which is outlined against the snow is the
great difficulty. Above it the route follows the crest to the summit.

Dorothea Pilley and Joseph Georges, Switzerland, c. 1926.

Dorothea, Ivor and Joseph, the Bertol Hut, Switzerland, in 1928.

INDEX